COSMO

The Yearbook of the Traditional Cosmology ~~~~~,

Volume 7

WOMEN AND SOVEREIGNTY

edited by
LOUISE OLGA FRADENBURG

General Editor of Cosmos: Emily Lyle

EDINBURGH UNIVERSITY PRESS

Advisory Board

Grants from St. Andrews University, University College Cork, and Dartmouth College are gratefully acknowledged.

© Edinburgh University Press 1992
22 George Square, Edinburgh

Set in Linotron Times Roman
by Photoprint Ltd, Torquay and
printed in Great Britain by
Page Bros Ltd, Norwich

A CIP record for this book is available
from the British Library

ISBN 0 7486 0320 4 (paper)

Contents

Preface

This volume is drawn primarily from papers presented at the Conference on Women and Sovereignty at St Andrews, Scotland, from August 30 to September 5, 1990. It does not reflect the full range of interests and approaches represented at the conference; rather, it is a record of only one part, that relating to the theory and practice of Western medieval and early modern queenship.

A few essays in this volume do, however, lie outside this limited scope: Charles Jedrej's essay on "Rain Makers, Women, and Sovereignty in the Sahel and East Africa" and Andrew Duff-Cooper's work on "Women and Sovereignty in Balinese Lombok and in Japan" suggest in especially powerful ways how some of the issues involved in the study of queenship may be of cross-cultural significance, and how approaching sovereignty as cultural practice might urge us to question how we define sovereignty in the first place; Emily Lyle's "A Line of Queens as the Pivot of a Cosmology" proposes a new reading of the importance of queens in early Indo-European culture and cosmology—one that offers a methodological alternative to current historicist practice by proposing that certain aspects of queenly power may have had a very long history indeed. Moreover, in keeping with the interdisciplinary interests that motivated the conference, the essays, despite their primary concern with medieval and early modern Europe, have been grouped in ways that try to foreground methodological and theoretical considerations.

Thanks are due to the Traditional Cosmology Society for its support of the conference, and especially to Emily Lyle and Rosemary Muir Wright, who inspired and organized us. The generosity of the American Council of Learned Societies permitted the attendance at the Conference of a number of US scholars. The Interdisciplinary Humanities Center of the University of California – Santa Barbara provided a grant for editorial assistance. The good counsel and hard work of Patricia Ingham and Rebecca Douglas were invaluable; the members of the Advisory Board, and in particular Carla Freccero, helped enormously in shaping the present form of *Women and Sovereignty*. Above all I am grateful to my contributors and to the participants in the St Andrews Conference.

I also owe thanks to the University of Wisconsin Press for allowing me to reprint in this volume portions of my book *City, Marriage, Tournament: Arts of Rule in Late Medieval Scotland*.

LOUISE FRADENBURG

IN MEMORIAM:
ANDREW DUFF-COOPER

LOUISE OLGA FRADENBURG

Introduction: Rethinking Queenship

In the last two decades, the study of women and power has constituted one of the most groundbreaking areas of cultural analysis inspired by feminist theory and historical scholarship. This volume aims to contribute to, and extend, this field of inquiry by outlining and pursuing several interrelated problems. Its essays share a conviction that historical and cultural approaches to sovereignty have been, and will remain, inadequate until they explore how forms of sovereignty produce and are produced by the cartographies of gender relevant to their cultural circumstances. Sovereignty, simply, does not exist apart from gender; sovereignty serves and pursues ends through the matrix of cultural constructions of gender, and it becomes a means of perpetuating and transforming those constructions. But these essays go further. They argue that the practice of sovereignty *depends* on the use of both the "masculine" and the "feminine," in fact that sovereignty is established not only through the elaboration of these constructs—whereby, for example, king and queen might be taken as "masculinity" and "femininity" in the register of the absolute or the ideal—but also through the dislocation and fluidity of these constructs. Sovereignty is a site of gender-transgression and crossover, although it does not necessarily follow that sovereignty has revolutionary designs on gender constructs; most often the ultimate effect of the plasticity of gender in the field of sovereignty is the celebratory confirmation of "difference".[1]

In consequence, these essays argue, the role of queenship in shaping relations of domination and subordination has been not only specific but central and critical. For example, though I will argue in my essay on "Sovereign Love: The Wedding of Margaret Tudor and James IV of Scotland" that Margaret's royal entry wishfully enacted her domestication through pageants of consent, her transformation thereby into Queen of Scotland enabled an ambitious and indeed dangerous new set of alliances, a real attempt (however multiple, sporadic, and unforeseen its effects) to remake both the domestic world of Scotland and its place within the larger world. And Elizabeth Zelensky's essay on "The Function of Religious Imagery during the Regency of Sofiia Alekseevna of Muscovy" will explore how the study of queenship might refigure certain aspects of Max Weber's work on charisma; queenship, she proposes, may have provided "the emotional basis of support for the early modern monarchy, and ultimately for the State itself."

The importance of ideas, images, and activities associated with queenship is explored in Dean Miller's "Byzantine Sovereignty and Feminine Potencies" through a consideration of Dumézil's analysis of tripartite Indo-European social functions. Miller contends that this analysis, if applied to Byzantine sovereignty, must be re-mapped according to gender-boundaries and their transgression. The Byzantine Emperor stakes his claim to imperial sovereignty, his claim to being and representing "all" things, by appropriating for himself potencies and imagery which in many other cultures are understood as proper to queen-consorts. Andrew Duff-Cooper argues that imperial sovereignty in Japan, in particular its intense articulation of the mystical-jural axis and its concomitant elaboration of the former as the field of its being and its history, must be understood in light of Japanese culture's collocation of the "feminine" with the "unseen" and the "hidden"; the Emperor's distance from worldly politics links him, through the gendering of cultural space and in many other ways, with the feminine.

Indeed, most of the sovereigns studied in *Women and Sovereignty*, whatever their biological sex, are neither exclusively "masculine" or "feminine." Nearly every essay in this volume explores or implies the plasticity of gender in the field of sovereignty—a plasticity which seems to be related to sovereignty's urge toward totality, inclusiveness, and exemplarity (its need to gain a purchase on both sexes and on all the cultural functions with which they are severally associated). Such plasticity seems also to be related to sovereignty's urge toward exclusivity—its need to mark its difference from the subject, which so often takes the form of an extraordinary body or sexuality such as permissible incest, special blood, the body politic and, at least in some of its counterparts, that body politic's promiscuous relations with fictive as well as real entities. The enactment of multiple, transgressive gender-positions, *and* the exemplification of perfectly ordered "masculinity" or "femininity" together become important means whereby sovereigns can negotiate those apparently contradictory functions designated by Bataille as "heterogeneity" (the sovereign's need to be different from his subjects, to be extraordinary, excessive, dangerous) and "homogeneity" (the sovereign's need to be the same as his subjects, to be ordinary, proper, law-abiding).[2]

Studies of gender and sovereignty like those of Miller and Duff-Cooper have important implications for the field of medieval and early modern sovereignty in part because they suggest the historical and cultural range of sovereignty's exploitation of gender paradoxes, and thus provide crucial potential counter-readings of the significance of female "princes," such as Queen Elizabeth I, around whom neo-Petrarchan Renaissance studies of queenship still obsessively constellate. Diana Henderson's "Elizabeth's Watchful Eye and George Peele's Gaze: Examining Female Power Beyond the Individual" analyzes that constellation through a reading of the treatment of flattery both in Peele's *Arraignment of Paris* and in recent Renaissance scholarship. Her analysis suggests that a critical preoccupation with the construction of Elizabeth's (and her male subjects') masculinity, or with her power to defeat all female rivals for the love and regard of men, ends merely by, once again, privileging the masculine and closing down the play of gender. Henderson argues that if we are to achieve a fuller understanding of the deployment of gender during Elizabeth's reign, we must also attend to representations of Elizabeth as exemplar of and participant in female community; and we must attend not only to discourses that solicit competition but also to those—like flattery—that solicit identification. The paradoxicality of that female prince Elizabeth might best be read not as the result of an altogether unique set of circumstances—the supposedly amazing accident of her succession—but rather as a particular deployment of the plasticity of gender in the field of sovereignty.

Because the essays in this volume are concerned to see gender and sovereignty in this way, they are as much concerned to understand consortship as they are to understand queenly regency and regnancy. If in fact sovereignty depends upon and exists through constructions of gender (and transgressions thereof), then kingly as well as queenly potencies must be re-read in terms of gender, and kingly and queenly potencies must be re-read as always mutually implicated. As Emily Lyle's study of archaic Indo-European queenship in terms of kinship and inheritance suggests, queens and kings alike practice a marital and familial politics. A significant part of all the politics they practice will be marital and familial—especially when, but not only when, dynastic and state power are closely involved. Thus Carla Freccero begins her essay on "Marguerite de Navarre and the Politics of Maternal Sovereignty" with a critique of the way both traditional and new historicisms have privatized marriage, arguing in contrast that marriage is "the political marketplace for state and family in sixteenth-century France." Her essay studies Marguerite de Navarre's interventions in her husband's and her brother's struggles over the marital future of Marguerite's daughter, Jeanne d'Albret, as well as accounts of Jeanne's own interventions; Marguerite's *Heptameron* illuminates the nature of a specifically "maternal authority"—its complexly mediated powers of negotiation, its interest in empowering daughters, but also its enlistment in the service of patriarchal political economies. My essay on Margaret Tudor's wedding is also concerned with the problematics of consent and loyalty in marital politics; it explores the pageantry of "sovereign love," the ways in which the rituals of royal marriage apotheosize, through the dramatization of courtship, consent and "choiceness"—by which I mean that kind of extraordinariness which results either from having been chosen by the powerful or from having the power to choose. The queen's consent to the courtship of the king models, for the city, the creation of a "loving" and therefore pacified community, one which experiences its bond with its sovereign as a fantastic effect of freedom rather than of coercion.[3]

Charles T. Wood's essay on Elizabeth Woodville and Elizabeth of York argues that the necessarily divided loyalties of medieval queens enjoin upon them a particularly challenging marital and familial politics; Wood explores some of the ways in which the divided loyalties of queens—which is to say their critical role in alliance-formation—present both opportunities and dangers to the practice of statecraft. While kings also must negotiate complex and even conflicting loyalties, and while the familial politics of kings must therefore be thought in terms of a network of interests rather than in terms of singular agency, these essays point to one of the most important ways in which gender constructs sovereignty in medieval and early modern Europe: for queens, the link between marriage and sovereignty was specially intense, since during this period it was usually by means of marriage that queens *became* queens—a transformation which seems so often to involve the domestication of a certain strangeness—whereas kings most often became kings through the funerals of their predecessors. When queens are "in-marriers" they both exemplify sovereignty and depend upon it; coming to an "inside" from an "outside," and bearing something of the outside with them, they are simultaneously inside and outside what Victor Turner, in *The Ritual Process*, calls

"hierarchy" or "structure," and are often linked with "communitarian" images and activities.[4]

In such circumstances, queens take on certain kinds of work for
sovereignty: they can effect and represent the unity achieved
through alliance, but they also can exploit and "personify"
rivalries, "old grievances."[5] When, on the basis of their foreignness,
their femaleness, the in-betweenness of their regencies, or the
ambiguous nature of their sovereignty, queens are constructed as
what, in Turner's terms, we might call "liminal" figures—marginal
to official institutions and practices of authority, though in various
ways embedded within them, or made "symbolic" of them—the
result is their particularly intense association with the concepts
both of division and of unity. The symbolic capital of queenship is
thus built upon the central role of queens in alliance-formation:
queens embody the unity of nation or people or land, or they
embody the forces that might tear that unity to pieces.

But the tension generated even in this brief discussion between
the issue of the queenly practice of alliance-formation, on the one
hand, and representations of queens as unifying or divisive, on the
other, might itself encourage us to consider more directly the
concept of liminality, which is open to the criticism that it
replicates rather than simply describes the marginalization of
powerful women. Though "liminality" has the advantage of
referring directly, as it were, to the results of marginalization, and
thus of calling to mind the mystifying effects of many cultural presentations of female authority, the term may inhibit consideration
of alliance-formation as a queenly practice—however decentered
or even occluded the agencies involved, as Freccero's and Abby
Zanger's essays suggest—and may obscure the extent to which
such a practice performs central and crucial work in the making of
history and the remaking of the world. Accordingly, while
liminality is still used here and elsewhere in *Women and
Sovereignty*, terms like "interstitiality" or "in-betweenness" are
sometimes used in order to suggest that the condition of many
forms of queenship may be found not so much in the glamorized,
special, suspended states associated with communitas as in the fact
of queens' being so often at the nodal points of cultural work, of
their working to enable the crossing-over of difference into
identity, the unfamiliar into the familiar. In this sense queenship is
profoundly adventurous, though this point should not be taken as
an invitation to pursue sentimentalizing biographical accounts that
would posit the existence of pioneering queenly intentions. The
implications of a replacement or complication of the concept of
liminality with that of interstitiality for our understanding of the

material conditions of queenship, moreover, are considerable: for example, the work of both Emily Lyle and Máire Herbert reminds us that sometimes it is the king who is the outsider—a conqueror, an in-marrier—and still the queen may perform important practical and mythic functions in establishing the sovereignty of such a man, however much the importance of those functions may at times be misrecognized.

In Charles Wood's essay, Elizabeth of York, whose claim to the throne of England was at least as good as (if not superior to) that of her husband, Henry VII, had, as it were, to be *made* strange; Wood charts the many ways in which Henry tried to signify the singularity of his sovereignty, the dependence of Elizabeth's queenship on his kingship, despite the very real dependence of the Tudor dynasty's claims on Elizabeth's blood, and despite the advantages to be gained from stressing the marriage of two houses. Melinda Zook's essay on "History's Mary" studies a similar problem: the union of William and Mary and the history of Mary's construction either as loving wife to the foreign man whose claim to the throne of England her blood legitimized, or as disloyal daughter to the Stuart father, James II, who fled his kingdom as a result of her husband's invasion of England. Zook shows how Mary's in-betweenness—which is to say her pivotal role in familial politics at a crucial historical juncture—produced in turn a kind of discursive crisis, in which contesting representations of Mary fought out both the implications of dynastic change effected in 1688/89, and the further implications of such change for the potency of sovereignty in post-Revolution England.

Liminality as a strategic instrument for the empowerment of queens is explored in Elizabeth Zelensky's "'Sophia the Wisdom of God': The Function of Religious Imagery during the Regency of Sofiia Alekseevna of Muscovy." Zelensky contends that, during the course of her regency, Sofiia Alekseevna deliberately and programmatically emphasized certain liminal images already present, but dormant, in the political discourse of Muscovy. By drawing an analogy between the theological position of "Sophia the Wisdom of God" in the Christian cosmos and her own actual role in the government of Muscovy, Sofiia Alekseevna created the imagic means by which both her legitimacy as a ruler and her liminality as an unmarried woman could be expressed. In contrast, Rosemary Muir Wright's "The Virgin in the Sun and in the Tree" suggest that set-apartness, at least in the case of the Virgin Mary, may have posed obstacles to, as well as assisted, the regularization and perpetuation of queenly power. The relation between Marian imagery and secular queenship is also explored in John Carmi

Parsons' essay on "Ritual and Symbol in the English Medieval Queenship". Muir Wright argues that Mary's sovereignty was presented as distinct from earthly queenship through artistic allusions not only to the Virgin's special, sacred genealogy (the Jesse tree) but also to the Woman Clothed with the Sun, the "Mulier Amicta Sole" of the Apocalypse. The association of the Virgin with "tense expectancy" and "great hope" could, however, find its way into the imagery of secular queenship.

As these essays indicate, one important historical form of secular queenship seems to be the particularly close association of queens with kinds of time marked as extraordinary: with regencies, minorities, absences, dynastic transition. The marking of queenly time as unusual has itself obscured how regularly and frequently queens have ruled. For example, many of the important histories of the ruling elites of fifteenth- and sixteenth-century Scotland still rely almost exclusively on the organizing principle of kings' reigns or kings' activities, when in fact this period is characterized by repeated and very lengthy minorities during which regents like Mary of Gueldres, Margaret Tudor or Mary of Guise struggled (however briefly in some cases) to rule and to make history.[6] Interstitiality produced both by the structural complexity of queenly loyalties and by the out-of-joint times in which queens most often "officially" ruled makes faction an important and highly visible form of the experience of queenly rule (a disorderliness and changefulness often simply projected onto the queen in question, as for example in the case of Margaret Tudor's treatment by many historians). Though we must keep in mind that very little is still known about the participation of queens in rule during "ordinary" times, queens (as was true in late medieval Scotland) often emerge with special force, both in recent scholarly writing and in earlier discourses and practices, at moments of crisis, of "passage," when rulers are marrying, dying or being born, coming into or losing their power; when aristocratic fortunes are made and unmade; at moments when change makes way for both ambition and failure, gain and loss.

Thus Máire Herbert's essay on "Goddess and King: The Sacred Marriage in Early Ireland" shows how the study of mythic representations of queenship might be refigured through attention to the very link between queenship and change; Herbert shows that myths have histories by exploring the link between the motif of sacred marriage, on the one hand, and cultural change on the other, particularly in the traumatic forms of foreign settlement and conquest. Susanna Åkerman's essay "On the Impossibility of Abdicating: Queen Christina of Sweden and the Spiritual Crown" focuses on a time when sovereignty itself began to be put in question, when rulers were being executed by their people, when Queen Christina of Sweden abdicated her throne and became the center of a storm of millenarian pamphleteering across Europe. Åkerman argues that Queen Christina's abdication—and the subsequent history of that cross-dressing "*mondo vagabonda*" (her aspiration to other crowns both temporal and spiritual, her scandalous exercise of the sovereign right of execution)—incited and shaped discourses on the nature of sovereignty: on whether, for example, sovereignty must be *placed* in a nation, or even in the person of a ruling monarch, in order to *be* sovereignty. The dislocations of sovereignty in seventeenth-century Europe, and the important involvement of women in those dislocations, are charted from a different direction by Sharon Arnoult, whose "Sovereignties of Body and Soul: Women's Political and Religious Actions in the English Civil War" studies radical Englishwomen's use of the concept of the sovereignty of the soul during their struggle for the right to function as political Subjects.[7] Arnoult's essay reminds us how certain cultural cartographies of gender and sovereignty idealize and masculinize the position of (Sovereign) Subject, thus problematizing woman's "equality of soul" along with her status as "political being," as Subject of history or community; her essay also documents the importance of discourses of sovereignty in the history of women's resistance movements.[8]

The liminalizing of political woman can make woman the bearer of some of Judaeo-Christian sovereignty's most arduous contradictions: its positing of absolute agency in the person of a Creator, whom all creatures serve and on whom all creatures depend; its positing also of the human being as a creature free to love, capable of consenting to its obedience. Both Creator and creature, Sovereign and subject, are ideally posited as freely, generously given, the one unto the other, in a way that lovingly exceeds the inequities that bind the creature to the Creator's law. Queenship often becomes paradigmatic of the difficult alchemy whereby the subject, hence at times the nation, is made to act as sovereign, as capable of the consensual activity that will, paradoxically, bind subject and nation to the king.[9]

It is perhaps in part for this reason that queens have played important roles in the distribution of patronage, that is, in the politics and economics of petition: queenly power, as John Carmi Parsons' essay suggests, is frequently presented as intercessory; rituals of queenship often focus on petitionary or intercessory moments, celebrating and thereby insisting on the special periodicity of queenship and its consequently circumscribed access to resources, celebrating and insisting also on the complexities, opportunities and dangers involved in the doubling of woman and sovereignty. Parsons argues that the polyvalence of the symbols deployed in medieval queenship rituals expresses the paradoxicality of female rule by both acknowledging, and asserting the limits of, queenly power; at once apotropaic and reverential, such rituals wishfully inscribe the queen's "unofficial" power as well as her "isolation from her husband's public authority."

Among the most important rituals that enact and shape expectations of queenship are ceremonies associated with marriage, explored in my essay and in Abby Zanger's "Fashioning the Body Politic: Imagining the Queen in the Marriage of Louis XIV." Zanger's study of the representational strategies involved in such ceremonials focuses on the domestication of the foreign queen through sartorial transfiguration: the "reclothing" of Marie-Thérèse of Austria during the festivities for her wedding marks her transformation from princess to queen, "from one culture or symbolic system . . . to another," as well as her bodily resistance to such transformation. In this process, Zanger argues, the political is shifted "onto the material of fashion," in the hope that international tensions might be played out on the comparatively safe location of a young girl's body.

The displacement of "affairs of state" by "affairs of style" charted by Zanger thus points to the queen's body as site of crossover between subjection and sovereignty, between cultures, between different spheres and practices of power: public and private, official and unofficial. The ritual importance to queenship of the motif of entry itself, hence of the power to open gates and gateways, repeats in occluded form the labor of interstitiality. The study of queenship appears, in fact, to demand broad reconsideration of distinctions between public and private, official and unofficial—as well as of the methods, places, forms, and agents that historical writing has traditionally associated with sovereignty. Charles Jedrej's essay on women rainmakers in Africa powerfully instantiates how the study of women and sovereignty marks the need to reconsider the very nature of rule: in exploring how rainmaking *is* a form of authority often organized around marriage and practiced by wives as well as by husbands, Jedrej's work suggests that our preconceptions of where power is enacted and by whom may blind us to the ordinariness or regularity of women's exercise of power, and to cultural dependence upon that work.

Like Abby Zanger's essay, Jocelyn Wogan-Browne's "Queens, Virgins and Mothers: Hagiographic Representations of the Abbess and her Powers in Twelfth- and Thirteenth-Century Britain" studies techniques of the body and of bodily representation, in this case those that qualify the abbess for the complex of subjection and sovereignty that constituted her position. Wogan-Browne's essay focuses a number of issues of great importance to the study of women and sovereignty: for example, the question of "resources," of the abbess's power to provide. Wogan-Browne's work suggests the possibility that the privatizing or liminalizing of women's power might secure for a given culture—say, Duff-Cooper's Japan, or Freccero's early modern France—an inadequately compensated and therefore frequently destabilized labour of rule and regulation, particularly within the bounds of the "occluded territory" of female communities. Wogan-Browne's term "occluded territory" emphasizes the crucial matter of place, of the literal cartography of gender and sovereignty: will women practice the work of sovereignty in "sub-cultures, . . . on conceded and partially occluded territory" or within borders that can be defended? The abbess' wielding of "institutional power as experimenter rather than as its fully official inheritor" prompts us to ask: do strategies that render queenship "unofficial" in fact seek to prevent the development of protocols and histories for queenship? The essays in *Women and Sovereignty* cannot hope to answer these questions definitively, but they provide new ways of framing them, and new ways of understanding the significance to cultural analysis of the workings of gender in relations of domination and subordination.

NOTES

1 Discourses and practices of sovereignty frequently present gender constructs as "essential," as part of a divine or natural order of things, which it is the duty of sovereigns not only to uphold in their subjects but to express through the very form of their being. But even in such productions of sovereignty's gendered "essence" or identity, gender must be "plastic"—that is, as the *Oxford English Dictionary* puts it, "capable of being moulded, fashioned, modified, or impressed; impressionable, pliable; susceptible to influence; pliant, supple, flexible." Gender is provisional and practicable, that is. open to changing practices. Susanna Åkerman has pointed me to Unger's definition (following Roberts 1967) of "plasticity" as "practical opportunism and flexible work relations . . . attained by particular institutions and ideas" (Unger 1987:2), involving "stratagems of imagination and activity" (12–13); the marital politics of queens and kings, discussed below, would be a case in point.

2 See Bataille (1985) on sovereignty as a coordination of the "homogeneous" (commensurability; productive, useful society) and the "heterogeneous" ("elements that are impossible to assimilate"): "since the king is the object in which homogeneous society has found its reason for being, maintaining this relationship demands that he conduct himself in such a way that the *homogeneous* society can exist *for him*"; but the king must also constitute himself as "a single *heterogeneous* object" (147).

3 See Bourdieu (1985 [1977]: 171) on techniques of transmutation, "by the sincere fiction of a disinterested exchange," of "the inevitable, and inevitably interested relations imposed by kinship, neighborhood or work, into elective relations of reciprocity."

4 Turner (1977 [1969]:106–7) compares and contrasts two different, but nonetheless (in Turner's argument) complementary, ways of experiencing and organizing social experience: "communitas," on the one hand, and "hierarchy" or "structure" on the other. "Communitas" privileges totality, homogeneity, equality, unity, identity; "hierarchy" privileges differences of rank, heterogeneity, inequality, difference. Turner's theoretical analysis is problematic insofar as it proposes a totalization of culture within which his distinction between communitarian and stratified experience is folded; that is, he provides no account of the problem of "resistance," or of the related problem of how change takes place in cultures whose disruptive and egalitarian energies are so completely absorbed by ritual as his analysis would suggest. But his work does have the advantage of suggesting some ways in which elites might gain (as they must if they are to survive) access to certain kinds of resources, particularly those with which sovereignty cannot easily identify itself in direct ways.

5 Stafford (1983:29, 46) argues that the ideal of dynastic unity, and of the queen's role in creating that unity, is one whose potency derives in part from the "reality of family tension": "As intruders who are suspect, wielding power within the tensions and crosscurrents of the family but denied the expression of legitimate aggression, wives and queens are accused of domestic crimes, of encompassing their ends by covert means, by plots, poison and witchcraft."

6 For example, the table of contents in Ranald Nicholson (1974) mentions not a single queen, presenting instead chapter titles like "The Minority of James II and the Little Schism," "The Minority of James III and the Acquisition of Orkney and Shetland." Norman Macdougall's books are biographies of kings (*James III* [1982] and *James IV* [1989]). Gordon Donaldson's *Scottish Kings* (1977 [1967])

pays some attention to the minorities—for example, on the minority of James III, he notes that "Once more, as after the death of James I, the resolution of the Queen Mother to meet the challenge and continue her husband's policy may well have helped to shape the situation" (96)—but fails to appreciate their considerable significance for the character of rule (which, again, proved often enough to be the character of queenly rule) in later medieval Scotland. I discuss this issue at greater length in the chapter on "Sovereign Love" in my book *City, Marriage, Tournament* (1991).

7 The term "Subject" is used here in its psychoanalytic and philosophical sense, i.e. as "the self or ego," in contradistinction to "Object," rather than in the sense of "one who is under the dominion of a monarch or reigning prince" (*OED*). Here I use the upper-case "S" to indicate the former meaning, lower-case "s" to indicate the latter; but often both meanings are involved at once, and then I use lower-case "s." See my essay on "Sovereign Love," pp. 78ff; the contradictory meanings of the term *subject* bring out the interchangeability of freedoms and constraints with which that essay is concerned.

8 For the term "political being" see Glass (1989:1), whose study of the politics of psychosis, community, and selfhood argues that the construction of the "self" must be theorized in terms of the self's experience of the "polis."

9 Thus in Julia Kristeva's analysis of the Song of Songs, "the Sublime, regal one turns into God having an amorous dialogue with his beloved, the nation of Israel"; the Shulammite in turn submits, but as Subject, made "equal" through her love to the other's sovereignty. An entire "nation" can thereby imagine itself as the Shulammite chosen by God (1987: 95–100).

REFERENCES

Bataille, Georges (1985). "The Psychological Structure of Fascism," in *Visions of Excess: Selected Writings, 1927–1939*, ed. Allan Stoekl, trans. Allan Stoekl, with Carl R. Lovitt and Donald M. Leslie, Jr. Minneapolis: University of Minnesota Press.

Bourdieu, Pierre (1985 [1977]). *Outline of a Theory of Practice*, trans. Richard Nice. Cambridge: Cambridge University Press.

Donaldson, Gordon (1977 [1967]). *Scottish Kings*. London: B. T. Batsford.

Fradenburg, Louise Olga (1991). *City, Marriage, Tournament: Arts of Rule in Late Medieval Scotland*. Madison, WI: University of Wisconsin Press.

Glass, James M. (1989). *Private Terror/Public Life: Psychosis and the Politics of Community*. Ithaca, NY: Cornell University Press.

Kristeva, Julia (1987). *Tales of Love*, trans. Leon S. Roudiez. New York: Columbia University Press.

Macdougall, Norman T. (1982). *James III: A Political Study*. Edinburgh: John Donald.

—— (1989). *James IV*. Edinburgh: John Donald.

Nicholson, Ranald (1978 [1974]). *Scotland: The Later Middle Ages*. Edinburgh: Oliver and Boyd.

Roberts, Michael (1967). "Gustav Adolph and the Art of War." In *Essays on Swedish History*. Minneapolis: University of Minnesota Press.

Stafford, Pauline (1983). *Queens, Concubines, and Dowagers: The King's Wife in the Early Middle Ages*. Athens, GA: University of Georgia Press.

Turner, Victor (1977 [1969]). *The Ritual Process: Structure and Anti-Structure*. Ithaca: Cornell University Press.

Unger, Roberto Mangabeira (1987). *Plasticity into Power: Comparative-Historical Studies on the Institutional Conditions of Economic and Military Success*. Cambridge: Cambridge University Press.

Queens, Virgins and Mothers: Hagiographic Representations
of the Abbess and her Powers in Twelfth- and Thirteenth-
Century Britain

One position from which medieval women exercised sovereignty
of a kind is that of abbess. As Gold argues of medieval female
monastic experience in general, the position of abbess involved
contradictions between the opportunity of gaining "educational,
spiritual and administrative experience . . . and the limitations on
that opportunity imposed by an ideology proclaiming feminine
weakness" (1985: 77). Medieval abbesses might have seigneurial
and domanial powers over their estates, but in canon law were
forbidden to preach or read the gospel in public, to veil
consecrated virgins, hear confession, or give liturgical blessing
(Shahar 1983: 37–8; Metz 1985: 98–103). Over the daily lives of
their convents abbesses had powers of administration and super-
vision, but these are held "à l'exclusion toutefois . . . de toute
juridiction spirituelle proprement dite, de tout pouvoir des clefs ou
pouvoir d'ordre" (Baucher 1935: col. 69). In many ways, abbesses,
women of royal and noble birth with significant administrative and
territorial responsibilities, offer a version of rank and rule in the
religious life which can be compared with secular queens.

In comparison with abbots, though not in comparison with
women generally, there is relatively little direct access to abbesses'
own formulations of their experience. Something is known of the
history of medieval nunneries, something of the correspondence of
abbesses and prioresses survives, and a few exceptional abbesses
(Heloise and Hildegarde for instance) have written at greater
length on their views of their responsibilities.[1] The hagiography of
abbess saints, however, forms a significant post-Conquest corpus,
greatly enlarged in the fifteenth and sixteenth centuries by the
inclusion of native abbess Lives in nationalist and historicizing
British legendaries.[2] Although the figures for abbesses are very
small in relation to the number of Lives of male saints, they are
significant as a proportion of female saints,[3] and the question of

how this major source for the representation of abbesses' careers images their sovereignty is worth exploring. In the space available here, I want to concentrate on late twelfth to fourteenth-century representations of British abbesses in the vernacular Lives which are a major source of women and laymen's images of sanctity. The later medieval Lives form a still larger group and deserve separate study.[4]

Important vernacular abbess Lives of the earlier period are the Anglo-Norman Lives of Osith of Chich (Baker 1911), Modwenna of Burton-on-Trent (Baker and Bell 1947) and Audrey [Etheldreda] of Ely (Södergård 1955), and the Middle English Lives of the early South English Legendary (Bridget of Ireland, Edburga of Winchester, Etheldreda of Ely, Frideswide of Oxford, Mildred of Thanet, Winifred of Flintshire).[5] Only the Anglo-Norman *Vie sainte Audrée* (Södergård 1955) is certainly by a woman, though other anonymous Lives, especially in Anglo-Norman, cannot be ruled out as not by women. A proportion of Anglo-Norman hagiography was patronized by or dedicated to queens, abbessess and nuns, while three Lives (including *Audrée*) are certainly by nuns.[6] Hagiographic portrayals nonetheless seem likely to inform us principally about perceptions of abbesses on the part of the male clerical authors of saints' Lives. As part of the dominant culture within which women exist, however, such portrayals contribute to female self-images, and for all the authorial dominance of one gender, do not necessarily cease entirely to encode self-perceptions and historical experience for the other.

Post-Conquest interest in cult patronage and revenues and in the Normanization of British history promoted vigorous re-development of the traditions of Anglo-Latin hagiography. Eleventh and twelfth-century historians and hagiographers reformulated Anglo-Saxon sanctity, transmitting and developing the cults it was so much more often in Norman interests to promote than to crush (Ridyard 1988). An important hagiographic patterning of female sanctity is updated and further articulated in the re-working of earlier monastic sources for particular religious houses. Recent studies of Latin hagiographers such as Goscelin [of St. Bertin and Canterbury] and Osbert of Clare have revealed how much their narrative morphology for the abbess/patroness saint overlaps in the selection and ordering of themes. A sequence of motifs—of lineage, vocation, humility and ascesis, saintly illnesses and deaths, and miracles of protection, vengeance and healing—forms the abbesses' biographical trajectory (Millinger 1984: 115–28; Ridyard 1988: ch. 4; Braswell 1971: 300–302). This pattern (and in some cases the particular *vitae* by Goscelin and Osbert) endures in the

abbess *vitae* of the great fourteenth and fifteenth-century Latin
and English collections of British saints. I want to comment
(necessarily briefly and selectively) on some of these motifs, the
powers they encode, and their development in vernacular hagiography of the twelfth and thirteenth centuries.

ROYALTY AND VOCATION

In England as on the continent, pre-Conquest abbess saints were
usually of royal birth, and royalty or at least upper nobility
continued to be a primary asset in an abbess' ability to secure
social and financial support for her house (Meyer 1981; Ridyard
1988 ch. 3; Stafford 1983: ch. 7). In Anglo-Norman England, royal
Anglo-Saxon nunneries were once more closely associated with
the court and Anglo-Norman kings appointed their female
relatives as abbesses in the major houses.[7] Royalty and sanctity
are closely identified in the writings of Goscelin, late eleventh-
and early twelfth-century biographer of tenth-century royal
English abbesses (Millinger 1984; Colker 1965). His images of the
nunnery as royal court and the abbess as queen reflect the
originary and continuing significance of royal patronage in
ensuring institutional stability for the great Anglo-Saxon nunneries
in both their pre- and post-Conquest existence. So, for instance,
Goscelin's portrait of an abbey and its abbess/patroness saint in
the day of judgement promises that

> then, your Wilton (he is writing for Eve, a recluse professed
> AD 1065 at Wilton) will be a large and spacious city . . .
> whence the daughters of Syon will see all their England . . .
> your powerful queen Edith [potens regina tua, Eadgytha] will
> arrive, leading her beloved spouse with all his angels and
> archangels, apostles and martyrs, kings and fathers of Rome
> and England, with her father Edgar and her brother Edward,
> with Thecla, Agnes, Cecilia, Argive, Catherine, a great crowd
> of virgins with all the family of Wilton (Talbot 1955: 115).[8]

Here the image of the abbess Edith as a queen in the heavenly
court with which her monastery becomes assimilated encodes
powerful capacities for patronage on earth, while also imaging
transcendent spiritual status. The abbess is an earthly leader, a
queen of heaven and a bride of Christ, and her spiritual powers
both confirm and transcend her royalty. The symbolic mapping of
social and spiritual onto each other is also pervasively used in the
vernacular hagiography of female saints and in treatises for women
in religious lives. The court of heaven is a topos by which professionally chaste women and in particular consecrated virgins are
encouraged to view themselves as queens and brides of Christ.[9]

High birth encodes the exemplary female saint's access to grace in a form apparently deemed particularly encouraging to the female religious or devout laywoman, and female saints remain aristocratic, rich and beautiful in insular Lives. The royalty of an abbess can thus, according to context, signify historical and/or actual socio-economic powers from which her house can benefit, or (particularly in vernacular hagiography where the abbess' Life may circulate independent of her original house and cult centre) a view of the kind of social aspiration liable to make religious lives attractive and sustainable for other women, or both. That the figure of the queen can be thus multiplied and made open to imaginative identification and aspiration by those not of royal birth suggests a notional element in the power of secular queens and a gender-asymmetry in heaven (readers of male saints' Lives are not encouraged to view themselves as kings of heaven, since the rank of king is real and unique, in comparison to the derivative status of queens).

Consignment to a nunnery might be a matter of individual choice or of relegation. It might signal the renunciation of, or failure in, child-bearing in the case of younger queens and the preferred or enforced retirement of queen mothers in later life. Young girls might prefer the life of the convent to dynastic marital exchange or might be enclosed there for lack of suitable marriage arrangements (Schulenberg 1988; Stafford 1990). Nunneries functioned both as aristocratic *gynacea* and as potential theatres of action for women, and remain ambivalent locations (Schulenberg 1988; Stafford 1983: ch. 7). They are places of refuge and disposal, places women want to retreat to and to get out of, places women can be found in but to which they may not be entirely confined. Ambivalent literary stereotyping of the female community registers these ambiguities: while the abbess may be queen of a community that pre-figures and becomes assimilated into the court of heaven, the convent can also be seen as a bordello, the nun as concubine and the abbess as procuress: the female community may be both ideal allegorical model and satiric topos (Power 1922: ch. 13).

VIRGINITY AND MATERNITY

Virginity

In choosing heavenly rather than earthly sovereignty, the royal women who reject the world for the convent are also choosing virginity, or at least, professional chastity. For their Latin biographers this is one of the most important characterizing features of holy women and it continues to be so in the vernacular

Lives. In practice churchmen preferred to appoint as abbesses experienced women rather than life-long professed virgins with little experience of the outside world. Abelard, indeed, calls the appointment of "virgins . . . rather than women who have known men" a "pernicious practice" (Radice 1974: 200; McLaughlin 1956: 252), and canon law itself declares that, providing the absence of virginity is not publicly embarrassing, a widow and biological mother may be elected to this position (Baucher 1935: col. 64). Nonetheless, virginity is an important component of the abbess's authority in hagiographical representation, and even where biological motherhood makes praise of virginity impossible, the saint is portrayed as a reluctant performer of minimum marital duties before embarking on her preferred life of chastity (Ridyard 1988: 89–92). The virgin saint, especially the virgin martyr, is a favoured female hagiographic type,[10] but is particularly developed and focussed on in the twelfth century. Hagiographic accounts of chaste literal marriage as well as of the spiritual marriage of the bride of Christ abound. Hagiographic virginity and the figure of the virgin spouse or martyr are important focuses for the high medieval contestation of secular and ecclesiastical marriage models and practices (Durling 1986–7). The female saint is constructed as far as possible in the virgin martyr mold. If she does not suffer a *passio* she will be, at least, a martyr to asceticism: if she is married, she will be a virgin spouse: if she has children, she will be a chaste spouse as soon as possible. If she has daughters they will preferably enter the religious life, so that biological motherhood can be seen as productive of spiritual lineage.

If the saint is an abbess, her struggle to maintain her virginity against enforced betrothal will often be a major part of her qualifications and experience for attaining abbesshood. In Latin and vernacular biographies of abbesses for whom no developed pre-Conquest Lives existed, rejection of an ardent and angry suitor, against whom virginity and fidelity to a Christian career are to be defended, becomes virtually *de rigueur*. Frideswide of Oxford, Winifred of Flintshire, Eanswyth of Folkestone, Cyneburga of Gloucester, among others, are represented as founding their houses after rejecting and evading insistent sexual pursuit, and the contemporary life of the prioress Christina of Markyate shows her married against her will but successfully contriving to maintain her virginity until released to her religious career.[11]

The increasing influence of the virgin martyr model can be seen diachronically in the pre- and post-Conquest Lives of Etheldreda, the abbess-saint most frequently represented in narrative. Etheldreda's principal attribute is her virginity, maintained through two marriages before she becomes foundress and abbess of Ely. In Bede and Ælfric's Lives, her first husband quickly dies and her second, Ecgfrid, is a reluctant, but untroublesome chaste spouse who eventually lets Etheldreda go to his aunt's monastery at Coldingham (Colgrave and Mynors 1969: 390–6; Ælfric XX: lines 34–5). The post-Conquest Anglo-Norman Life, following its Latin source, develops Etheldreda's resistance and Ecgfrid's villainy: he comes back to try to throw her out of Coldingham, and then pursues her as she flees to Ely, so that a miracle putting the sea between them at St. Ebb's head is needed before Etheldreda can escape to her religious career (Södergård 1955: 90–3: lines 1273–1381).[12] Bede, while claiming Etheldreda as the type of virginity, does not develop her resistance in this way. And where, for Ælfric (who follows Bede and also portrays Ecgfrid as reluctant but unaggressive), Etheldreda's life is an example to all laymen ("woruld-menn", line 120), in Marie of Chatteris' thirteenth-century Anglo-Norman Life as in the [Middle English] South English Legendary, she is an example of and to virtuous women.[13]

Virginity's gender-marking as primarily female is thus heightened along with the re-writing of the virgin saint into a romantic career of resistance to seduction and loyalty as a *sponsa Christi*. Though this emphasizes the future abbess's will-power and determination, it also makes her the heroine of a spiritual romance, read in terms of her gender and [withheld] sexuality. Male saints, though represented as chaste husbands by such influential twelfth and thirteenth-century figures as St. Alexis, are not so represented as a preliminary to becoming an abbot. It is also striking that the virgin martyr is the favoured model, and that the Virgin Mary herself is not used as a legitimating model for the religious woman who has been married and may be a biological mother. The Virgin's status remains that of a rule-proving exception.

Maternity

Even if many historical abbesses had not been older experienced women with adult children by the time of their appointment, the abbess-saint's ability to engender, govern and propagate a community makes her a symbolic mother. The rule of abbesses is imaged as maternal, as that of abbots is paternal.[14] In Goscelin's *Vita Mildrethae*, contrasted English and French abbesses are used in confirmation of England's reputation as an island of saints (Rollason 1982: 126). In the Middle English Life of St. Mildred which uses Goscelin's text as its source,[15] the two territories become the locations of psychologically good and bad mother-abbesses and the possibilities they enshrine for the virgin-heroine.

Mildred's [good, biological] mother, abbess Domn Eafe, sends her daughter to be educated at Chelles, in Northern France, where the young princess resists the wicked and bribable French abbess's plans to marry her to a royal suitor. The furious abbess attempts one of the few virgin martyrdoms represented as carried out by a woman: she locks Mildred in an oven—"as me bakeþ a cake" (Vernon f. 42r: col.a)—for three hours. Like the three youths in the fiery furnace (often invoked as precedents of faith-under-trial in virgin martyr lives and mentioned in Goscelin's *vita* at this point, Rollason 1982: Appendix C: 125), Mildred's dedication to virginity survives this attempt to ignite her in mortal fires. She sits happily in the oven singing psalm 16 ("þorwh fuir þou woundest me/Ac þat nis in me ifounde. nouȝt þat uuel be", Vernon f. 42r: col. a) and proving that so "clene a þing is maidhed. þat no fuir ne may brenne/hose wuste hit al hire lyf. and wiþ hire beere hit henne" (Vernon f. 42r: col.a). The abbess, her plans for Mildred's sexual socialization having thus failed both literally and symbolically, can only, on opening the oven, beat and trample Mildred and tear off her tresses. Mildred sends these to her mother with "lettres of alle hire wo" (Vernon f. 42r: col. b), and, rescued and returned across the Channel to Domn Eafe's home foundation of Minster-in-Thanet, succeeds her mother as abbess.

The abbess-mother figure in the vernacular text displays the complexities of choosing and maintaining career virginity. The alien mother-abbess encourages biological propagation: the good mother, though having experienced literal motherhood, converts her production of daughters to a spiritual lineage. Mildred's experience with the bad mother-abbess thus provides a monitory account of the dangers of sexual desire (its flames cognate with those of hell) and the dangers of internalizing its social reinforcement and approbation. As Mildred herself reflects (in a line for which there is occasion but no equivalent in Goscelin's text), not only does safety demand that she flee the wicked abbess and her advocacy of the suitor-prince, but "þe kynde of my ȝong blod unstable is. i dred" (Vernon f. 42r: col. b). As an exemplary account of the psychological and biological factors to be dealt with in the choice of career virginity, this vernacular abbess Life is both concise and precise. Its account of the abbess-mother, however, displays the paradoxes of maternity as an image of rule, maternity being both essential (to the production of virgins) and regrettable (as the counter to virginity). Even within a female subculture virginity cannot be unequivocally nourished: in respect to abbess virgins and mothers, spiritual maternity is both founded on and in tension with its biological referent. As Caroline Bynum has argued, twelfth- and thirteenth-century elaboration of maternal imagery may have been more empowering for abbots than abbesses. The use of maternal imagery as a gender-permeable metaphor adds dimensions of nurture and affectivity to the authority of the abbot, while for abbesses, such imagery reasserts female gender and its paradoxes without further adding to their authority (1982: 141–54, 250–2).

FEMALE COMMUNITY AND THE BODY: ASCESIS AND PENANCE

Once the future abbess has abandoned the public political world, she rules a parallel but subordinate female court or community in which her spiritual and in some cases biological dynasty will be propagated, but contained. A female lineage which incorporates and transcends biological ties is thus created: in the very nature of its ties to royal and noble patronage, it is not without links and influence in male lines of power, but it is parallel, separate and enclosed, not the locus of actual transmission of power. In the vernacular Life of St. Mildred, the paradoxical inheritance of a member of this high-status female sub-culture is displayed, but the production of a spiritual dynasty is approved. When Domn Eafe (who founds Minster-in-Thanet) encourages her three daughters (Milburga, Mildred and Miltrudis) to become (non-biological) foundresses (and abbess-mothers in their turn), her productivity is applauded in the *South English Legendary's* Life: "me þynkeþ þat was a good barn tem. þeih þat weore to vewe/Ac beter beoþ a vewe goode. þen a hep of schrewe" (Vernon f. 42r: col a). Similarly in the treatment of the abbess as royal and her convent as a part of the heavenly court, actual royalty and the social prestige of a high-class *gynaceum* combine to present serious but containable socio-economic influence in an image which seems to have been felt as quite pleasing by clerical writers.[16]

Containment is the *sine qua non* of a female convent. Strict active enclosure prevailed for nuns in the high middle ages, and defining and maintaining the boundaries of female communities is an abiding preoccupation of the medieval church (Schulenberg 1984), intimately related to the preoccupation with sealing up and containing the female body, its humeral flows, numerous orifices and purgations (Robertson 1989). Concern with sealing in the female community is reiterated in the homologous concern with the body of its leader. Even more spectacularly than her nuns, an abbess must exercise control over the body she has withdrawn from sexual currency. The humility and asceticism of royal Anglo-

Saxon abbesses (manifested in, for example, service of their sister nuns, patient submission to disease, absence of baths, etc.) develops in the twelfth and thirteenth centuries towards mortification, penance and even mutilation. This seems to reflect contemporary development of penitential theory and practice and the focussing of penance on the female body. Male solitaries and ascetics are represented as performing feats of endurance and deprivation, but there is a particular intensity and necessity ascribed to control of the female body (Bynum 1987; Robertson 1989). Clerical stories recommending female internalization of violent feelings, such as those in which truly virtuous nuns are declared to have cut off their own noses rather than be raped, are well documented (Schulenberg 1986). One of several striking examples of mutilation as a precondition of entry to a successful career as abbess is found in a *South English Legendary* version of the life of Brigid of Kildare. The saint prays for help in repelling the heart of the duke to whom she has been forcibly betrothed: she is rewarded by God's removal of one of her eyes which is miraculously restored once her father and suitor permit her to take the veil (d'Evelyn and Mill 1956 vol. I: 45–6, lines 221–31, 241–9).

The Brigid Life is shaped in accordance with the virgin martyr conventions by which female sexuality, when withheld, is both punished (by literal pagan suitors) and rewarded (by the Christ bridegroom); but even in a Life which presents martyrdom as the daily ascesis of conventional life, savage images of physical punishment are intimate to the licensing of female religous careers. In *La vie sainte Modwenne*, Modwenna's follower Orbilla is miraculously aged in an instant by the saint as a solution to her spiritual daughter's anxiety about her fitness to undertake rule of one of Modwenna's foundations (Baker and Bell 1947: lines 572–80). Another of Modwenna's spiritual daughters, Brigne, is blinded through the saint's intervention, the better to fit her for the turning away from the world involved in the rule of a female community (5517–28 and 5541–46). The abbess' ability to rule or negate her own body and those of her followers figures her rule of the community, and it is a rule expressed with some savagery in the post-Conquest Lives. Something of the psychological cost and intensity with which the female community is contained is symbolically expressed here, in a manner not necessarily incompatible with the more pleasing vision of the convent as aristocratic *gynaceum*. Nevertheless, the bodily self-denial which qualifies the abbess for rule is complemented and compensated by the acquisition of powers of provision and control, registered in hagiographic miracles (cf. Bynum 1987).

MIRACLES

The administrative and managerial powers of abbess-saints and the extent and strength of their cults are encoded in the miracles asociated with them (Ward 1982; McNamara 1985; Ridyard 1988: ch. 4). The thematic value of miracles for accounts of abbesses is early signalled in Bede's account of Ethelburga of Barking, "upright of life and constantly planning for the needs of her community, as many miracles attest" (Colgrave and Mynors 1969: 356; Sherley-Price 1955: 218). Goscelin and Osbert's use of miracles to express the power of patronage wielded by foundress- and abbess-saints has recently been shown to be systematic and significant (Ridyard 1988: ch. 8; Millinger 1984). Within vernacular hagiography, miracles constitute both an intertextual system of conventions and a contextually rich source of thematic meaning.

The most extensive post-Conquest vernacular life of an abbess is one in which the saint is viewed not only posthumously but throughout as a miracle-worker. Although (even because) St. Modwenna is a legendary composite of several Irish figures from different centuries, the careful twelfth-century promotion of her cult by the abbot of Burton-on-Trent and the lengthy and elaborate vernacular version of his reworked *vita* provide useful evidence for contemporary perceptions of the successful foundress-abbess (Price 1988: 173–5). That miracles can encode the powers and concerns of a thirteenth-century abbess emerges in considering Modwenna's miracles together with the life of a thirteenth-century abbey, Lacock, in Wiltshire, and its foundress and first abbess Ela.[17]

Modwenna's provision miracles include changing rock to rock salt (1559–60), changing water to wine (2841–44), filling a cistern for a convent suffering drought (3053–6), providing robes for one impoverished convent (3621–32) and food for another (5062–4). Among her posthumous provisions for her daughter-houses are timber for renovation (7553–7558), and ale for a visiting bishop from the waters of a spring in which she had ascetically taken cold baths in life (7633–36, 7673–76). She also creates new hot springs when preparing a bath for a spiritually-disturbed hermit (1449–56), and she keeps a calf carried off by wolves miraculously unharmed for two disconsolate herdsmen (1649–52). Modwenna resurrects both a pig (for an inappropriately generous swineherd, 789-92) and a calf (for an impoverished nobleman who has sacrificed his last animal to feed her, 4113–16) and she provides a miraculous feast with which the same straitened nobleman can feed his visiting overlord and king (4224–48). Among her miracles

of protection, she converts a wolf into a cattle dog (289–96) and
two cattle-thieves into penitents (357–432), induces narcolepsy in a
marauding band of robbers (969–78) and converts its leader (1049–
90). She also reforms an angry swineherd who feels his pigs'
pasture rights are threatened by the sisters' exiguous diet and their
potential competition for roots and raw herbs in the forest (677–88).

These accounts of conventual provision and of relations with the
community (throughout its class range) beyond the convent look
less like Celtic whimsy than the actions of a foundress, patroness
and administrator. Set against the concerns of a thirteenth-century
foundation with extensive estates such as Lacock, they are not
unlike the range of matters with which an abbess was concerned.
For running the abbey's domain, the Lacock cartularies record a
reeve, a hayward, ploughmen, shepherds, cowherds, wagoners, a
goatherd, a swineherd, a fisherman, a forester (VCH *Wilts* III:
309–11). Lacock was largely fed from its own lands and questions
of pasture-rights and enclosure arose from time to time for its
abbess (VCH 307, 312). Though the abbess had a clerical staff,
and stewards and bailiffs dealt with the daily management of the
abbey's estates, she was ultimately responsible. For Modwenna,
flotation miracles are a means of carrying out her administrative
responsibilities "les maisuns ordiner/Ke jo ai a guverner"
(3735–6): they speed communications and increase administrative
efficiency within her *parochia* (Price 1988: 181). The abbess of
Lacock could send robbers taken on her land to the Abbot of
Cirencester's prison, but the resultant fines were collected for her
use (VCH 307): Modwenna personally and miraculously defends
her convent against robbers (969–78, 1049–90). Modwenna creates
hot springs miraculously (1405–12): Lacock diverted local streams
and built an aqueduct for its own use, not without contention from
neighboring landowners (VCH 304).

In addition to the powers and concerns expressed in miracles,
other points in Modwenna's Life have potential resonance for
contemporary thirteenth-century rulers of female religious. Lacock's
foundress, Ela, countess of Salisbury and wife of William
Longsword, spent much of her long widowhood from AD 1226–61
as the first abbess of her new convent, and vigorously used her
royal and noble connections in establishing and supporting it
(VCH 304–5, 308). Modwenna, semi-legendary Irish princess and
abbess of Killevy, Streneshalch, Lunfortin and Burton, uses her
royal and ecclesiastical connections to found all over Britain, and
her fund-raising among kings and princes differs only in scale
from Ela's. Both abbesses recruit from their own family and class
connections: royal and noble relatives send their daughters to

them. Late in her career Modwenna takes a reclusive sabbatical on an island in the Trent (5769–5828): Ela resigned as abbess and had four quiet years before her death (VCH 304). Modwenna makes provision for young children (221–28), while the abbess of Lacock had wardship of both male and female minors (VCH 306–7). Modwenna has personal and professional friendships with bishops, hermits and other holy men as well as kings and princes (eg. St. Columba, line 4596; St. Kevin, line 1021; Prince Auvré, line 1896): Ela was friendly with Edmund Rich (later Archbishop of Canterbury and eventually canonized), who may have inspired the foundation of Lacock (Lawrence 1960: 58 n.1, 53, 55, 102).

In addition to the more usual supervisory posthumous appearances to her spiritual daughters, Modwenna's Life includes, in scenes from the routine of administration and leadership during her lifetime, many speeches and homilies given to her nuns in discipline or exhortation. Long experience of rule in a community is suggested in her insights (for instance, when her convent cannot cross a miraculously-risen river, Modwenna knows that one nun is secretly carrying more food than she should, lines 3413–544). Modwenna also displays protective concern for individual nuns, most strikingly in the miraculous resurrection of the maiden Osith, drowned as she brings a book to Modwenna from the abbess Edith of Polesworth (lines 2585–720; Bethell 84–5, 104–6). An angelic voice warns Modwenna that all is not well (2653–660), the two distressed abbesses encounter each other by the river and, in response to Modwenna's prayers to the God "ki Lazarun resuscita" (2689), Osith is revived after three days in the river. Miraculous powers here are heightened concerns, perceptions and abilities such as might be shared by a thirteenth-century noblewoman occupied in what Modwenna describes to one of her spiritual daughters as "[our] difficult occupation" ("dur mester," 3717).

Lacock was a French-speaking abbey and owned several French manuscripts.[18] There is no evidence that *La vie sainte Modwenne* circulated in Wiltshire, but my argument is not that Ela did or could have read this Life, but that *Modwenne*'s lavish display of female abbatial powers need not be seen, either in its own terms or alongside the life of a thirteenth-century foundress-abbess and administrator of large agrarian estates, as self-evidently fantastic. If unusually mobile and wide-ranging in her founding and managerial activities, Modwenna is a role-model idealized in degree rather than kind.

Parallels with a legendary and highly successful saint are readily apparent in the case of a rich abbey like Lacock, but less nobly-endowed religious careers may still have found Modwenna's achievements inspiring. England's other contemporary thirteenth-century candidate for female sanctity (like Ela, not in the event canonized) was Blessed Margaret Rich, prioress of the Cistercian house of Catesby in Northamptonshire. As a prioress she is a more typical figure for thirteenth-century nunneries than Ela, since very few post-Conquest foundations for women were of sufficient size and rank to be run by an abbess.[19] Of more modest family than Ela, Margaret's name survives principally because she was the sister of Edmund Rich, Archbishop of Canterbury, who as a male cleric had opportunities for meritocratic advancement beyond his family origins (Lawrence 1960: 106–12). When his mother died, Edmund sought a small convent for his sisters Margaret and Alice (his Latin *vitae* claim that this was out of a pious revulsion from simoniac dowry requirements, though Lawrence suggests (107) that Edmund's sisters were unacceptably unaristocratic for larger nunneries). Margaret became prioress of Catesby, and she and Alice (in a modest echo of the patronage exercised by Anglo-Saxon princess saints) eventually brought revenue to this house when their brother left them his cloak and triptych, relics which made Catesby a cult centre of St. Edmund (VCH *Northants* II: 122). Margaret was also probably influential in getting a grant from the king in 1247 of a weekly Monday market in Catesby and in 1249 a fair beginning on the eve of St. Edmund's translation (ibid.). The Middle English life of Edmund mentions Margaret as being buried at Catesby, with her sister, "bi-fore þe heiȝe weuede" (Horstmann 1887: 436, line 163) in a chapel built to the memory of her brother, and claims that "for heom hauez setþe ore louerd i-do: miracles mani on" (line 162). There are no further details in the case of Margaret's unspectacular religious sovereignty, and the Anglo-Norman life of Edmund ascribes the miracles to the relics rather than the sisters' intercession: Edmund's "mantel" and "tablette" are "medecine . . . plus ke triacle" (Baker 1929: 372, lines 1585–94).

Many of the developments in post-Conquest imagery both suggest relative diminution of abbesses' powers, and, insofar as they contribute to gender-based stereotyping, themselves contribute to the relative invisibility of women as rulers within the religious life, or rather to the occluded visibility of the enclosed female community, at once separated from and contained within male monastic and ecclesiastical institutions. The career of Margaret Rich, recorded in the margins of her brother's career and lived in much poorer institutions than those which received him, seems the typical post-Conquest profile. Nevertheless, there are some resonances between hagiographical conventions and the lives of medieval women religious which suggest that these Lives could express (as well as enclose and co-opt for patriarchy) the historical experience of British foundresses and abbesses. Read carefully from a plurality of perspectives, the lives of British abbesses reveal the polysemous ability of hagiographic conventions to encode stereotype, expectation, historical experience, contemporary receptions, and re-encodings of these varied materials and interests, in a range of authorial and audience investments.

These representations of the abbess' rule present a complex and ambivalent account of female sovereignty. As represented in hagiographic miracles, abbesses wield real power in ruling their community, in contributing to its maintenance and traditions, in their ecclesiastical network of associated institutions and connections, and in the economy of their local community. Yet, as suggested in the gender-based images of abbesses—as mothers, virgins, female bodies, personally-ascetic providers of sustenance —even the highest ranking, longest-established and economically most secure communities ruled over by abbesses remain essentially sub-cultures, contained within male monasticism, on conceded and partially occluded territory. In Anglo-Norman England a number of powerful and prestigious women engaged in female religious rule. Their experience of and access to power and to representation is undeniable, yet in both the practices and the symbolism of institutional monasticism, this female experience of rule remains contained and, as the proportions of abbess Lives to accounts of virgin martyrs suggest, liminal. Determining whether or not this is always true of female religious rule would require extended comparison with the Continent and with later medieval insular sources.[20] In post-Conquest Britain, however, though the abbess is given hagiographic representation, the actual experience of abbesses seems either less important than, or containable within, gender-based stereotypes. Like secular queens, the level of socio-economic resource available to and represented by the abbess is qualified by her gender, with the result that each abbess is both everywoman and an individual who must wield institutional power as an experimenter rather than as its fully official inheritor. Equally, the abbess' literary representations both express and re-contain her female rule.

NOTES

I am grateful to the Traditional Cosmology Society and to Prof. Louise Fradenburg for the invitation to give this paper and to Louise Fradenburg for much helpful editorial comment.

1 On English and continental nunneries see Eckenstein
  1896; on post-Conquest nunneries, Thompson 1984 and
  Elkins 1988; on later medieval English nunneries, Power
  1922. For Heloise, see Muckle 1955: 240–281 and Radice
  1974: 159–79; Hildegard's *Explanatio Regulae S. Benedicti*
  is in PL 197. 1053–66. Thompson 1991 was published
  while this article was in press.

2 There are three Anglo-Norman abbess Lives in the
  twelfth and thirteenth centuries (OSITH, MODWENNA,
  AUDREE: Meyer 1906: 328–458; Legge 1950), seven
  English Lives in the *South English Legendary's* recensions
  in the thirteenth and fourteenth centuries (BRIDGET
  [two versions], EDBURGA, ETHELDREDA, FRIDES-
  WIDE, MILDRED, WINIFRED: d'Evelyn 1967: 561–635)
  and eight English Lives in the fourteenth and fifteenth centuries (BRIDGET [1438 *Gilte Legend*], BRIDGET OF
  SWEDEN, CLARE OF ASSISI, EDITH OF WILTON
  and ETHELDREDA [quatrains in MS Cotton Faustina
  B III], FRIDESWIDE [*Gilte Legend*], KATHERINE OF
  SWEDEN, WENEFRIDE [Caxton 1483 *Golden Legend*
  and separate Life, 1485]; see d'Evelyn 1967: 561–635).
  The text containing the greatest number of abbess Lives is
  John of Tynmouth's *Sanctilogium Anglie* (156 Latin
  biographies and associated texts including 28 female saints
  of whom 24 are presented as abbesses), with its fifteenth-
  century rearrangement by Capgrave as *Nova Legenda
  Anglie* (Horstmann 1901) and English epitome (Pynson
  1516). On other abbess Lives (such as RADEGUND and
  WERBURGA) printed by Caxton, Pynson and others,
  see Gerould 1916, ch. VII; White 1963; d'Evelyn 1967:
  561–645. The boundaries of the abbess corpus remain
  necessarily flexible: I am primarily concerned with canonized women now known, or by medieval writers believed,
  to have held the position of abbess, but the biographies of
  some foundress and patroness saints are virtually identical
  in motifs and themes with those of abbesses (for example,
  Edburga of Winchester: see Braswell 1971; Ridyard 1988:
  ch. 4), while some Lives of women who were certainly
  abbesses are assimiliated to the narrative patterns of other
  saintly types.

3 For example, the most comprehensive manuscript of the
  South English Legendary (the fifteenth-century MS Bodley
  779) includes in its 135 items 21 Lives of women, of whom
  6 are British abbesses (Horstmann 1887: xxii-xxiii).

4 See note 2 above for references. It is also worth noting
  that in addition to their circulation and re-writing in male
  religious houses, Latin Lives of abbesses are not entirely
  absent from post-Conquest nunneries: for example, British

Library MS Lansdowne 436 (fourteenth-century) belonged to the nunnery of Romsey (Ker 1964: 164) and contains among its 47 items, 12 Lives of women, all abbess-saints.

5 For the shorter and longer Middle English Bridget Lives respectively, see Horstmann 1887: 192–3 and d'Evelyn and Mill 1956 vol. I: 37–46; for Edburga, Braswell 1971; for Etheldreda, Frideswide, Mildred and Winifred, Horstmann 1889: 312–23. Since this latter edition has proven difficult to obtain, I have used MS Egerton 1993, microfilm of MS Bodley 779, the Vernon facsimile (Doyle 1987), and information about SEL collation (Görlach 1974: 141–3, 175, 196–7).

6 See further Legge 1963 [1978]: 369 *et passim*; Wogan-Browne forthcoming.

7 Twelfth-century abbesses of Barking, for example, included Henry I's first queen, Maud/Matilda, Stephen's queen Maud and (from c. 1175?) the natural daughter of Henry II (VCH *Essex* II: 119).

8 See also Talbot 1955: 113. Edith was probably never abbess of Wilton (VCH *Wilts* III: 231–2, 241–2), but was early believed to have been (her *Vita brevior* is entitled "De sancta Editha virgine et abbatissa": Wilmart 1938: 13 and 15–16).

9 A full and explicit example can be found in the *Letter on Virginity for the Encouragement of Virgins* (Millett and Wogan-Browne 1990: 2–43).

10 Among the 27 Ælfrician Lives, the 8 Lives of women include 6 virgin martyrs, one transvestite female abbot and one British abbess (Ælfric); twelfth and thirteenth-century Anglo-Norman Lives include 8 virgin martyrs, 3 repentant harlots, 3 virgin abbesses and (at the end of the thirteenth century) one housewife (Martha) and one ascetic wife and mother (Elizabeth of Hungary); virgin martyrs predominate in the manuscripts of the *South English Legendary* (Görlach 1974: "Contents of Major SEL Manuscripts," Diagram for pp. 306–9); in the most comprehensive manuscript (MS Bodley 779), the 21 female saints lives (counting the "elleue þousend uirginis" as one item) include 11 virgin martyrs, 2 repentant harlots, 6 British abbesses, one housewife (Martha) and the Virgin Mary's mother, Anne (Horstmann 1887: xxii-iii).

11 For brief accounts and bibliography see Farmer 1982. Cyneburga's legend(s) are confused, both between the supposed abbess and virgin of Gloucester and the abbess of Castor (see Grosjean 1961: 168). For Eanswyth, see Horstmann 1901: 296–300, esp. 297–8; for Frideswide *A.SS.*, Oct. VIII, 533–90 (p. 536, S11, 20); for Winifred

A.SS., Nov. I (1987), 691–759 (pp. 711–13). For Christina, see Talbot 1959.

12 For the Latin source of this passage see Blake 1962: 27–8. In the late fourteenth-century Life in British Library MS Cotton Faustina B. III, Egfrid becomes "good" once more and there is no St. Ebb's Head miracle: see Horstmann 1881: 288, lines 245–56.

13 The *South English Legendary* Life makes Etheldreda (Ældri) an example specifically for women ("So fareþ all oþur wyues nouþe", Vernon f. 33r, col. b; "Also fareþ þis wyues ȝut", f. 33v, col. a); *La vie sainte Audrée* was initially written for a convent of Anglo-Norman nuns (Legge 1963 [1978]: 264) and its extant manuscript belonged to the convent of Campsey where it was used for meal-time readings (Legge 1950: 112). The remaining vernacular version of Etheldreda's Life prior to the sixteenth century was probably written for the nuns of Wilton (Horstmann 1881: 282).

14 Baucher 1935: col. 66, IV; Metz 1985: 99. The thirteenth-century Winteney rule explicitly makes this point, adding the abbess (as mother) to the standard derivation of "abbot" from "abba": "on þan we clypiod aba, þat is fæder, abbodesse, þat is modor ȝenemned" (Schroer 1888: 15). The address "mother of virgins" is a standard salutation to abbesses in letters (see eg. Williamson 1929: 153, Letter 42).

15 For the unpublished Middle English text I have used MS Egerton 1993, ff. 176r–178r and the facsimile of Ms Vernon ff. 41v–42r (Doyle 1987). For convenience, references in the text are to the Vernon facsimile. On the Latin tradition and texts concerning Mildred, see Rollason 1982: ch. 2 and App. A; on Mildred's mother, ibid. 9–11.

16 See, in addition to Goscelin's elaboration of the topos, Osbert of Clare (Williamson 1929: 139–40, Letter 40). Compare here the *Pearl*-poet's presentation of the father-narrator's naive but relieved contemplation of his daughter as one of a "cumly . . . pakke of joly juele" perhaps quite well-accommodated in the dormitories of the heavenly Jerusalem (*Pearl* ed. Gordon 1953: lines 929ff.).

17 Ela, Countess of Salisbury, wife of William Longespée (natural son of Henry II and Fair Rosamund) and her foundation of Lacock are documented in the cartularies and annals of Lacock and in a more detailed history of its foundress, the "Book of Lacock" (B. L. MS Cotton Vitellius A. VIII, ff. 113, now largely illegible; see Rogers 1978: 2). A detailed account is available in VCH *Wilts* III: 303–16. Ela was widowed in AD 1226 after William returned from the crusades, and lived on until AD 1261.

She built the Carthusian priory at Hinton, Somerset, and a nunnery of Augustinian canonesses at Lacock, where the first nuns were veiled in AD 1232. After herself taking the habit at Lacock in AD 1237 or 1238, Ela became its abbess, taking over in AD 1239 or 1240 from her temporary prioress Wymarca.

18 VCH *Wilts* III: 309. On MS Welbeck ICI, owned by Campsey abbey and containing Lives of Modwenna, Osith and Edmund Rich, see Baker and Bell 1947: xi-xii. Legge's suggestion (1950: 96) that Edmund wrote the Anglo-Norman *Mirour de Seinte Eglyse* for Ela is tempting, but neither the recent edition of the Latin or the Anglo-Norman text has turned up any evidence linking extant manuscripts with Lacock, and it is now proposed that the text was written in 1213–4 at Merton, Surrey (see Forshaw 1973 and Wilshere 1986: xix).

19 See Thompson 1984; Elkins 1988: 1–2. While one nunnery's thirteenth-century translation of the Benedictine rule still refers to the head of the house as "abbodissa," later versions assume that she will have only the rank of prioress (Eckenstein 1896: 204–6; Schroer 1888: 15 *et passim*; Böddeker 1979:64–7, lines 336–534).

20 For an account based on Continental French evidence, see Johnson 1991. This study valuably charts shifts over time in the medieval status of religious women, though the argument that only "dogged feminism" would see such women as part of a female sub-culture (265) does not take account of the under-representation of women's viewpoints in the available records.

REFERENCES

Ælfric (1966 [1881–90]). *Ælfric's Lives of Saints*, ed. W. W. Skeat. EETS OS 76, 82, 94, 114. London. Rpt. as one vol. Oxford: Oxford UP.

Baker, A. T. (1911). An Anglo-French Life of St Osith. *MLR* 6: 476–502.

—— (1929). La vie de saint Edmond, Archevêque de Cantorbéry. *Romania* 55: 332–81.

—— and Alexander Bell, eds. (1947). *St. Modwenna*. ANTS 7. Oxford: Blackwell.

Baucher, J. (1935). Abbesse. *Dictionnaire de droit canonique*. Ed. R. Naz et. al. 1935–1965. Paris: Letouzey et Ane. Vol 1: cols. 67–79.

Bethell, D. (1970). The Lives of St. Osyth of Essex and St. Osyth of Aylesbury. *Anal. Boll.* 88: 75–127.

Blake, E. O., ed. (1962). *Liber Eliensis*. Camden Society 3rd ser. XCII. London: Royal Historical Society.

Böddeker, K. (1979). Versifizierte Benediktinerregel im "northern dialect." *Englische Studien* 2: 64–7.

Bodleian Library, Oxford MS Bodley 779 (microfilm).

Braswell, Laurel (1971). Saint Edburga of Winchester: a Study of her Cult A.D. 950–1500, with an Edition of the Fourteenth-century Middle English and Latin Lives. *Med. Studs.* 33: 292–333.

British Library Egerton Ms 1993, f. 176r–178r.

Bynum, Caroline Walker (1982). *Jesus as Mother: Studies in the Spirituality of the High Middle Ages*. Berkeley and Los Angeles: University of California Press.

—— (1987). *Holy Feast and Holy Fast: the Religious Significance of Food to Medieval Women*. Cambridge: Cambridge UP.

Colgrave, B. and R. A. B. Mynors, eds. (1969). *Bede's Ecclesiastical History of the English People*. Oxford: Clarendon Press.

Colker, Marvin (1965). Texts of Jocelyn of Canterbury which Relate to the History of Barking Abbey. *Studia Monastica* 7: 383–460.

Doyle, A.I., ed. (1987). *The Vernon Manuscript: A Facsimile of Bodleian Library Oxford, MS Eng. Poet. a.1*. Woodbridge: Boydell and Brewer.

Durling, Nancy Vine (1986–7). Hagiography and Lineage: the Example of the Old French *Vie de saint Alexis*. *Rom. Phil.* 40: 451–469.

Eckenstein, Lina (1896). *Woman Under Monasticism: Chapters on Saint Lore and Convent Life AD 500–1500*. Cambridge: Cambridge UP.

Elkins, Sharon (1988). *Holy Women of Twelfth Century England*. Chapel Hill and London: North Carolina UP.

d'Evelyn, Charlotte (1967). Saints' Legends: Bibliography. *Manual of the Writings in Middle English 1050–1500*. Vol. 2. Ed. Albert E. Hartung. Connecticut Academy of Arts and Sciences. New Haven, 561–635.

d'Evelyn, Charlotte and Anna J. Mill, eds. (1956). *The South English Legendary*. 2 vols. EETS OS 235, 236. London: Oxford UP.

Farmer, D. H. (1982). *The Oxford Dictionary of Saints*. Oxford: Oxford UP.

Forshaw, Helen, ed. (1973). *Edmund of Abingdon, Speculum Religiosorum and Speculum Ecclesie*. Auctores Britannici Medii Aevi III. London: Oxford UP for the British Academy.

Gerould, G. H. (1916). *Saints Legends*. Boston and New York: Houghton Mifflin.

Gold, Penny Schine (1985). *The Lady and the Virgin: Image, Attitude and Experience in Twelfth-Century France*. Chicago: University of Chicago Press.

Gordon, E. V. (1953). *Pearl*. Oxford: Clarendon Press.

Görlach, Manfred (1974). *The Textual Tradition of the South English Legendary*. Leeds Texts and Monographs, N.S. 6, Leeds: Univ. Leeds, School of English.

Grosjean, P. (1961). Saints Anglo-Saxons des Marches Gauloises. *Anal. Boll.* 79: 161–9.

Horstmann, C., ed. (1881). *Altenglische Legenden*. Neue Folge. Heilbronn.

—— (1887). *The Early South English Legendary*. EETS OS 87. London: Trubner.

—— (1899). Des MS Bodl. 779 jüngere Zusatzlegenden zur südlichen Legendensammlung. *Archiv* 82: 312–23.

—— (1901). *Nova Legenda Anglie*. 2 vols. Oxford: Clarendon Press.

Johnson, Penelope D. (1991). *Equal in Monastic Profession: Religious Women in Medieval France*. Chicago and London: University of Chicago Press.

Ker, N. R. (1964). *Medieval Libraries of Great Britain*. London: Royal Historical Society.

Lawrence, C. H. (1960). *St. Edmund of Abingdon: A Study in Hagiography and History*. Oxford: Clarendon Press.

Legge, M. Dominica. (1950). *Anglo-Norman in the Cloisters*. Edinburgh: Edinburgh UP.

—— (1963 [1978]). *Anglo-Norman Literature and its Background*. Oxford: Clarendon Press. Rpt.

McLaughlin, T. P. (1956). Abelard's Rule for Religious Women. *Med. Studs*. 18: 241–92.

MacNamara, Jo Ann (1985). A Legacy of Miracles: Hagiography and Nunneries in Merovingian Gaul. *Women of the Medieval World: Essays in Honor of John H. Mundy*, ed. Julius Kirschner and Suzanne Wemple. Oxford: Blackwell, 36–53.

Metz, René (1985). Le statut de la femme en droit canonique médiéval. *Recueils de la Societé Jean Bodin* 12. Bruxelles, 1962, 99–103. Rpt. in *La femme et l'enfant dans le droit canonique médiéval*. London: Variorum Reprints, Art. 4.

Meyer, Marc A. (1981). Patronage of the West Saxon Royal Nunneries in late Anglo-Saxon England. *Rev. Ben.* 91: 332–58.

Meyer, Paul (1906). Légendes en vers. *Histoire Littéraire de la France*, XXXIII. Académie des Inscriptions et Belles Lettres. Paris: Imprimerie nationale, 328–458.

Millett, Bella and Jocelyn Wogan-Browne, ed. and trans. (1990). *Letter on Virginity for the Encouragement of Virgins*. In *Medieval English Prose for Women*. Oxford: Oxford UP.

Millinger, Susan (1984). Humility and Power: Anglo-Saxon Nuns in Anglo-Norman Hagiography. In Nichols and Shank, 5–28.

Muckle, J. T. (1955). The Letter of Heloise on Religious Life and Abelard's First Reply. *Medieval Studies* 17: 240–81.

Nichols, John A. and Lillian T. Shank, eds. (1984). *Distant Echoes*. Medieval Religious Women 1. Cistercian Studies Series no. 71. Kalamazoo.

Power, E. (1922). *Medieval English Nunneries*. Cambridge Studies in Medieval Life and Thought. Cambridge: Cambridge UP.

Price, J. (1988). *"La vie sainte Modwenne"*: A Neglected Anglo-Norman Hagiographic Text. *Medium Aevum*: 47 172–189.

Pynson, R. (1516). The *Kalendre or Newe Legende of Englande*. London: British Library.

Radice, Betty, tr. (1974). *The Letters of Abelard and Heloise*. Harmondsworth: Penguin.

Ridyard, Susan (1988). *The Royal Saints of Anglo-Saxon England*. Cambridge: Cambridge UP.

Robertson, Elizabeth (1989). The Rule of the Body: the Feminine Spirituality of the *Ancrene Wisse*. *Seeking the Woman in Late Medieval and Renaissance Writings: Essays in Feminist Contextual Criticism*, ed. S. Fisher and J. E. Halley, Knoxville: Tennessee UP, 109–34.

Rogers, Kenneth H. (1978). *Lacock Abbey Charters*. Wiltshire Record Society, XXXIV. Devizes.

Rollason, D. W. (1982). *The Mildrith Legend: A Study in Early Medieval Hagiography*. Leicester: Leicester UP.

Schroer, M. M. Arnold (1888). *Die Winteney Version der Regula S. Benedicti*. Halle.

Schulenberg, J. T. (1984). Strict Active Enclosure and its Effects on the Female Monastic Experience (ca. 500–1100). In Nichols and Shank, 51–86.

—— (1986). The Heroics of Virginity: Brides of Christ and Sacrificial Mutilation (ca. 500–1000). *Women in the Middle Age and the Renaissance: Literary and Historical Perspectives*, ed. Mary Beth Rose, Syracuse, N.Y.: Syracuse UP, 29–72.

—— (1988). Female Sanctity: Public and Private Rôles, ca. 500–1000. *Women and Power in the Middle Ages*, ed. Mary Erler and Maryanne Kowaleski. Athens and London: Georgia UP.

Shahar, Shulamith. (1983). *The Fourth Estate: A History of Women in the Middle Ages*. London and New York: Methuen.

Sherley-Price, L., tr. (1955). *Bede. History of the English Church and People*. Harmondsworth: Penguin.

Södergård, Osten, ed. (1955). *La vie sainte Audrée, poème anglo-normand du XIIIe siècle*. Uppsala.

Stafford, Pauline (1983). *Queens, Concubines and Dowagers:*

the King's Wife in the Early Middle Ages. London: Batsford.

—— (1990). The King's Wife in Wessex, 800–1066. *New Readings on Women in Old English Literature*, ed. Helen Damico and Alexandra Hennessey Olsen. Bloomington and Indianapolis: Indiana UP, 56–78.

Talbot, C. H., ed. (1955). *The Liber confortatorius* of Goscelin of Saint Bertin. *Analecta Monastica* ser. 3, Studia Anselmiana, t. 37.

—— ed. and tr. (1959 [1987]). *The Life of Christina of Markyate. A Twelfth Century Recluse.* Oxford: Clarendon Press. Rpt.

Thompson, Sally (1984). Why English Nunneries Had No History: A Study of the Problems of the English Nunneries Founded after the Conquest. In Nichols and Shank, 131–149.

—— (1991). *Medieval Women Religious: The Founding of English Nunneries after the Norman Conquest.* Oxford: Oxford UP.

VCH *Northants* II (1906). *The Victoria History of the County of Northampton.* Vol. 2. Ed. R. M. Serjeantson and W. Ryland D. Adkins. London: Constable.

VCH *Wilts* III (1956). *A History of Wiltshire.* Vol. 3. Ed. R. B. Pugh and Elizabeth Crittall. *The Victoria History of the Counties of England.* London: Oxford UP for the Institute of Historical Research.

Vernon manuscript: see above under Doyle.

Ward, Benedicta (1982 [1987]). *Miracles and the Medieval Mind: Theory, Record and Event, 1000–1215.* London: Scholar Press. Rpt. Aldershot: Wildwood House.

Wilmart, A. (1938). La légende de sainte Edithe en prose et vers par le moine Goscelin. *Anal. Boll.* 56: 5–106.

Williamson, E., ed. (1929). *The Letters of Osbert of Clare Prior of Westminster.* London: Oxford UP.

White, Helen (1963). Early Renaissance Saints' Lives. *Ann. Med.* 4: 93–123.

Wilshere, A. D., ed. (1986). *Miroure de Seinte Eglyse.* ANTS 40. London: ANTS.

Wogan-Browne, Jocelyn (forthcoming). Women and Anglo-Norman Hagiography. In *Women and Literature in Britain 1100–1500*, ed. Carol Meale. Cambridge: Cambridge UP.

ROSEMARY MUIR WRIGHT

The Virgin in the Sun and in the Tree

The Coronation of the Virgin is an artistic theme forged in theological controversy and subjected to a complex network of visual traditions despite its almost canonical definition by the middle of the thirteenth century on the sculptured doorways of French cathedrals. It has been held that the theme and its visual equivalents had their origin on French soil in the ambience of Abelard and Suger of St. Denis (Verdier 1976: 233).[1] However, this definitive formula, focussing as it does on the expression of Mary's royal status through the coronation ceremonial, belies a more wide reaching heritage which sets the visual forms of her royalty apart from those of secular queens.

This paper will focus on the way in which this heritage ensured that the growing secularisation of imagery in the thirteenth century did not disguise the very real separateness of the queenship of the Virgin. Such parallels as there were, belonged to the honour due to Mary in reverence and worship. Although her sovereignty was unique, she could be approached and apprehended through the practices of earthly obeisance. The ceremonial aspects of Mary's crowning functioned not only as a means of approach, however, but also as a channel for the emotional aspects of her devotion, encouraging the belief that there was a real connection between secular queenship and that of Mary.

But if we were to concentrate on the traditions out of which the idea of Mary's queenship grew, we might hesitate to draw such parallels. Even when the imagery of the coronation seems closest to that of secular crownings, the artist is careful to enlarge the representation to draw attention to the theological aspects of Mary as Queen. Such expansions include the allusion to Jesse Tree symbolism, the linking of the crowning with the Assumption, the absence of any human presence at the moment of Mary's Triumph and the visual references to the Virgin as Ecclesia. The authority of the coronation symbolism is rooted in the patristic concept of Mary as a collective symbol which effectively severs the connection with secular queenship. The process by which Mary becomes visualized as sovereign depends on the way in which early symbols of cosmic queenship fused in the imagery of the coronation because of an affinity of formal relationships. At least as far as the early stages of that process were concerned, the Church was concerned to emphasise the collective aspect of Mary in assuming the role of Ecclesia and that dual identity meant that she was not to be considered like other women however royal, but as a singular exemption from the laws governing her feminine state. It meant that churchmen could venerate her without compromise even in terms more appropriate to earthly adoration, as it was taken for granted that such terms were addressed to a concept of Divine Motherhood and not to an ideal of womankind. The artistic process of necessity reflected the conceptual.[2]

Thus the Coronation of the Virgin cannot be seen exclusively as the manifestation of an emotional and humanistic impulse, arising out of the groundswell of popular devotion, nor as the result of political and social strategies which set her apart as a role model for other queens by according to her all the trappings of royal status. Mary Warner's assertion that "The honour paid to Mary as Queen redounded to the honour of Queens, to the exclusion of other women . . ." (Warner 1976: 104), may be the accidental consequence of a suitable symbol being ready to hand when the rights of aristocratic women needed visual expression.

The crucial factor for my own argument is the manner in which artists made clear that the royalty of the Virgin was like no other queenship[3] (Gold 1985: 70, 73). Every effort was made to establish how unlike other coronations this ceremony was. I want to explore two of the artistic traditions which set the Virgin's sovereignty apart from the historical forces which shaped the idea. There is a corpus of textual sources in liturgical, apocryphal and literary texts to support the visual transformation of the veneration of the Virgin into the cult image of the thirteenth century (Verdier 1980: 81–112). But it is the visual codes as distinct from the verbal that are the concern of this paper. The visual traditions crucial to reinforcing the claims of the Virgin to sovereign power deal with her ancestry and her cosmic role. These traditions show how that sacred genealogy is given focus in the symbolism of the Tree of Jesse and how her cosmic significance is evoked through the visual references to the imagery of the Woman Clothed with the Sun, the "Mulier Amicta Sole" of the Apocalypse.

THE SOURCES OF THE JESSE TREE

The foliate coils of lush vegetation in the archivolts of Coronation tympana, often peopled with the figures of the ancestors of Christ in the open lobes of the stone fretwork, refer to the great prophecy of Isaiah: "Et egredietur virga de radice Iesse, et flos de radice eius ascendet" (Isaiah 9: 1–3). The well-known conflation of virga with virgo created the ambivalence by which the Virgin became the blossom of the flowering branch which emerged from the sleeping prophet's side in the developed imagery of the Jesse Tree (Watson 1934: 4).[4] The branch, "virga de radice," soon became a tree, which housed other ancestors of Christ, as the artists sought to give visual expression to the meaning of the ascending sequence of radix, virga, flos, spiritus of the Latin text. The coiling branches evoked the idea of organic and irresistible growth in the genealogical stem leading to the Virgin and to her Son. This sacred genealogy of Old Testament prophecy identified the legitimate sources from David and Solomon by which the sovereignty of the Virgin was vindicated. The idea emerged in the visual arts earlier than the middle of the twelfth century, despite the tendency to attribute this imagery also to Suger of St. Denis.[5] The regality of this genealogy is emphasised not only by figures like David and Solomon, but also by the inclusion of prophets like Daniel whose works testified to the cosmic nature of Mary's inheritance. The words of Daniel, well known through the Pseudo-Augustinian Sermon and in contemporary Prophet Dramas in versified form, appear in certain illustrations of the Jesse Tree. For example, the words "Cum venerit Sanctus sanctorum, cessabit unctio" pointed forward to the coming of Christ (Watson 1934: 165).[6] In a similar way Daniel's account of the dream visions of Nebuchadnezzar predicted the restoration of Jerusalem: "When the most Holy shall have come, anointing shall cease." Another prophetic figure often associated with the Virgin's ancestry is the legendary Sibyl, whose poetic words as recorded in Virgil's Fourth Eclogue were interpreted as relating to the Virgin.

> "Iam redit et Virgo, redeunt Saturnia regna
> Iam nova progenies caelo demittur alto."

> [Now returns the Virgin also, and the rule of Saturn.
> Now a new progeny is sent down from the highest.]
> (Warner 1976: 386)

This too, had its visual equivalent in manuscript illumination, for in the so-called Ingeborg Psalter (Musée Condé, Chantilly, MS. 91695), produced in the years before 1210, the crowned figure of the Sibyl shares with the biblical Prophets the attribute of the dove of inspiration. These prophecies point to the manner in which the Virgin's royal status supersedes or eclipses all other types of female sovereignty. Mary's genealogy is one of destiny rather than blood.

Figure 1

Now what is interesting is how the artistic image of a
genealogical tree arose, assuming that the development of a full
branched stem was not simply the visual enlargement of the happy
accident by which the rod of Jesse burgeoned into a Virgin
blossom. The expanded imagery of the flowering rod as the dream
tree growing from Jesse's side must have been stimulated by other
tree symbolism available to the artist. Of the various tree formulas
current in the Middle Ages, one singular example seems to be
worth looking at in more detail as a potential source for the
imagery of the full grown tree from the side of the sleeping man. In
this example, the tree is also the centre of a vision, namely that of
Nebuchadnezzar, who in the second dream recounted by Daniel
saw a great tree, hewn at the roots by an Angel Guardian (Figure
1). This image is on folio 232 verso of the Liber Floridus, of
Lambert of St. Omer (Ghent University Library, MS. 92). This
encyclopaedia, completed by 1120, was composed within a broadly
unified scheme in which present times and future prophecy were
carefully interwoven.[7] Penelope Mayo has suggested the motif
forces behind the compilation of the text and called attention to
the highly original quality of the imagery, including that of
Nebuchadnezzar's Dream on folio 232 (Mayo 1973: 31–67). It is
the visual combination of royalty and tree which must invite
attention, especially when combined with the inscriptions referring
to the ages of man and the Apocalyptic Last Days.

The dream tree was of course described in the biblical account,
but its visual thrust would have been more forceful for the
manuscript's users because the dream tree visually recalls the
previous image of the tree of Virtues on folio 231 verso, by
repeating the various leaf patterns of the latter tree (subtitled
"The Church of the Faithful"). The fruits of the Tree of Virtue
blossom as medallions, in one of whose kernels is set the image of
a female figure, who is labelled Fides. She bears a crown similar to
that worn by Ecclesia on folio 253 recto. As if to enforce the
symbiosis of these types, Lambert has written a commentary on
the Tree symbol:

> The Arbor Bona, which is the Queen to the right of God,
> drawn about with variety, is the Church of the Faithful made
> up of diverse virtues.

It would seem that the author himself saw a connection between
the saving grace of the faithful Church and the proof of the
sovereignty of God as revealed in the story of Nebuchadnezzar.
On folio 232 verso, the slumbering king lies on a rich gold
embroidered bolster in the sleeping pose familiar from classical
sources, with his head resting on his bent arm. The bedclothes

barely hide the recumbent body below the drapery. As the King of Babylon, Nebuchadnezzar is distinguished from the figure of the Guardian by his diadem type crown, which recalls imperial symbolism. The Watcher or Guardian is also robed like a king, with his mantle knotted on his shoulder, but he stands entranced like a mighty monolith, his axe laid to the foot of the tree. The inscriptions show a clear specificity of time and place.[8] They refer to the Fall of Babylon as set firmly in historical time, being so many years into Nebuchadnezzar's reign.

Where did Lambert find the model for his illustration and why should it be particularly relevant to the Marian imagery related to the prophecy of Isaiah? We know that he may have had access to illustrated Spanish books where the theme of Nebuchadnezzar's dream is familiar, and we know that stylistically the design may even hark back to an Anglo-Saxon source (Swarzenski 1973: 25).

> It is a style reminiscent of the tremulous technique of metal engraving and still betraying beneath its hardened forms, Anglo-Saxon inspiration.

Gerhart Ladner has pointed out a link between the ancient near East and Judaeo-Christian traditions of tree symbolism, citing the example in the British Museum of the Assyrian sculpture of Ashur-Nasir-Pal and the Sacred Tree (Ladner 1979: 223–256). He noted how Lambert's Tree of Life is similarly fused with the symbolism of cosmic kingship for the second dream of Nebuchadnezzar is associated with just rulership. As Daniel prophesied, the opportunity was left for grace, though it appears to be an open question in that account as to how this grace was to be earned. One way may have been through travail and tribulation. Lambert redirects to the listeners of his own time the message that the sovereignty of God is the absolute authority. As in the days of Nebuchadnezzar, Jerusalem had again fallen to the Infidels, only to be restored to Christianity in 1099 by the First Crusade. Lambert's text clearly links the Crusade with the Apocalypse and the ultimate restoration of Jerusalem, for in another illustration, folio 253 recto, he represents the reconciliation of the Church and the Synagogue as taking place in the environment of Jerusalem and in association with the Second Advent. Is there a place here in Lambert's scheme for the Virgin which might encourage the association of the Tree with the imagery of Mary? According to Mayo, the figure of the Guardian as the Crusader King on folio 232v

> . . . stands on the brink of an uncertain future. He has to be successful in battle for Antichrist is abroad and only Christ or his Church can effect his triumph over the adversary.

> (Mayo 1973: 67)

Figure 2

No mention here of the Virgin. Yet an astonishing image of the Virgin probably did preface the Apocalypse picture cycle in the original manuscript of the Liber Floridus. This lost image is reflected in the illustration in the Wölfenbüttel copy, MS. Gud. Lat. 2.1 4305 which carries, on folio 14 verso, the image of an annunciate angel addressing a seated Madonna and child to accompany the text of a Hymn which begins "Fons Misericordia." Mary is visually associated with the reconciliation of Christian and Jew in the New Jerusalem by the presence on folio 253 verso of the Baptismal font set behind the figure of Ecclesia (Figure 2). The lost image may have been intended to invoke the mediation of the Virgin in the apocalyptic tribulations to come (Swarzenski 1973: 73). Once again, the link is made between the promise of God to his Church in the vision of the New Jerusalem and the figure of the Virgin.

It needed only the intrusion of the Virgin as the means of Grace rather than the trials of the Book of Daniel, first to transform the Old Testament tree of Nebuchadnezzar into the triumphal foliage of the Tree of Jesse and then to associate it with the life-giving Tree of the Book of Revelations in Chapter 22.

> In the midst of the street of it, and on either side of the river, was there a tree of life, which bare twelve manner of fruits.
> (Revelations 22:2)

Although none of the earliest examples of the Jesse Tree as cited by Watson really come close to the image of the Liber Floridus, it does not seem impossible that the dream of Nebuchadnezzar was the formative image in the shaping of the later Jesse Tree iconography. Nine illustrated copies of Lambert's book from the twelfth to the sixteenth centuries have survived, so we may assume that it circulated not just as a compendium of secular and theological thought, but as an artist's reference manual. According to Swarzenski, there is a distinction to be made between the rough draft quality of Lambert's text and the finished look of the illustrations, which suggests that their details were carefully transcribed and even recombined by Lambert himself:[9] "The illustrations in Lambert's autograph are copied with iconographically almost pedantic accuracy" (Swarzenski 1973: 22). This deliberation over the imagery of his text must have ensured the accurate recording of imagery central to the author's understanding of the signs of his own time, one of which was certainly the true image of the Virgin as Mother of God.

A SOURCE FOR THE ARA COELI

As we have observed, the figure of Daniel could be paired in the Jesse Tree inhabitants with the figure of the classical Sibyl, who pointed out to Augustus a heavenly vision of a woman enthroned with her child as heralding the arrival of one greater even than the

Emperor of Rome. This sibylline prophecy offers a further demonstration of the exclusive quality of the sovereignty of the Virgin. To find an example of this theme contemporary with Lambert's text we would do well to look at evidence from England. It has been suggested that in the miniature cycle of the Winchester Psalter (British Library MS Cotton Nero. C.4), produced for St. Swithins Abbey, Winchester, we have a corpus of the available imagery of the Virgin current in twelfth-century England (Crown 1976: 182),[10] including an image of the developed Jesse Tree type on folio 9.

Just as the figure of the Virgin had been included in the pictorial references of the Liber Floridus with the Dream Tree and Ecclesia, so we might find similar inclusions in this Winchester cycle. There the Jesse Tree image on folio 9 is linked to the image of Maria, Regina Angelorum, on folio 30. Although it has been accepted that this latter image functioned as an icon, the inclusion of such a powerful eastern reference may have invited the memory of Jerusalem and the tradition of the Church from early Christian times. The reminder of the heritage of Ecclesia is given concrete shape in the Marian cycle. In harking back as it does to an early Christian source and exhibiting such awareness of antique proto-types, the Winchester Psalter shares certain features with the Liber Floridus, especially in their representation of the history of salvation as a struggle between the forces of good and evil.

More pertinent to this argument is the fact that the Winchester Psalter contains an image which encouraged the fusion of themes which would support the developing iconography of the Virgin's sovereignty. On folio 8 recto, the domestic scene depicting the birth of the Virgin, though derived from the legends of the Virgin's infancy, has no known precedent (Figure 3). "Anna lies in a bed above which curtains and lamps are suspended. A servant sits to the right holding the Virgin" (Haney 1986: 92). Professor Wormald identified the woman bearing the child at the right as the midwife who responded to Anna's enquiry about her child (Wormald 1973: 17).[11] However, this explanation seems unsatisfactory. The seated woman with the child bears a much closer resemblance to the Hodegetria, the icon of the Virgin enthroned with the child on her left knee. In the Psalter picture, Anna appears wide-eyed, her gaze fixed on a distant focus—like the Angel Guardian in the Dream of Nebuchadnezzar in Lambert's illustration—while the group under the right-hand arch seems to be floating on a bank of clouds. Is not this a vision of her daughter's role? Anna points upwards as if to indicate the source of her vision. However, the figure of the "midwife" does not

Figure 3a

appear to be haloed, while the child is nimbed. Could it be that the artist, faced with a dream vision, distinguished Mary at this point in the narrative from subsequent representations by omitting the halo, or was it an oversight? Or is this a case of a double image in which the artist deliberately manipulated the rendering of the midwife to suggest to the listening audience the nature of this child to be born, and thus prepared the Psalter's user for the significance to be attached to those scenes of the Virgin's infancy as in some way prefiguring that of Christ? Only in the Jesse Tree illustration is the Virgin crowned. The "dream" of Anna recalls that associated with the vision of the Sibyl as interpreted by St. Augustine:

Iudicci signum: tellus sudore madescet ex caelo Rex adveniet per saecla futurus scilicet in carne praesens ut iudicet orbem (*De Civitate Dei* 18, 23)

Influential in the dissemination of the theme was a fifth or sixth

Figure 3b

century sermon, "Contra Judaeos, Paganos et Arianos," which was regularly recited during the Christmas office and which finally developed into a lectio in the period under discussion (Cuttler 1965: 24). Jocelyn Wogan-Browne has generously offered me evidence of interest in the Sibyl's legend in Anglo-Norman England, where the early account given by Orosius has been translated into Anglo-Saxon (Wogan-Browne forthcoming). In the surviving texts of the lectio, the Sibyl is included with Vergil and Nebuchadnezzar as one of the seers of the pagan world who foretold the coming of Christ. The Winchester Psalter may offer evidence for the existence of the imagery of the "Ara Coeli," the vision of the Virgin enthroned with the child as shown to the Emperor Augustus by the Sibyl. Ara Coeli and Regina Angelorum are thus two titles implied by the imagery which strengthen the notion of the heritage of the Church's teaching which is so pronounced in the Psalter. If the manuscript were used for the spiritual direction of others, it might also reflect something of the controversies over the nature of the Virgin. The years of the Psalter's production were spangled with controversy over the Immaculate Conception, despite the inclusion of the Feast of the Conception as part of the Liturgy by the Council of London in 1129.[12] The Anglo-Saxon tradition of English Marian imagery had created a reservoir of pictorial solution which could have been particularly responsive to new iconographies.

As the classical myth of the Sibylline vision was used to support the distinctive role of the Virgin both in and through time, this image was itself reinforced by another which I will offer as the second formative element in the process whereby Mary becomes sovereign. This is the imagery of the "Mulier Amicta Sole" of the Book of Revelation. This image is decisive in the ascendency of Mary in visual terms. The Apocalyptic Woman, like her counterpart in the Ara Coeli, is also a visionary apparition; she too appears to owe her formal representation to Eastern sources, and she too may have had her Western origins in Lambert's treatise.

The crucial cycle of sixteen full-page Apocalypse illustrations is missing from the Ghent manuscript and we have to guess at them from the images in the Wolfenbuttel copy MS. Gud. Lat 2.1 (4305) dating from the last quarter of the twelfth century, which is a direct reflection of the original (Figure 4). In the copy, the woman is seated astride the inverted curve of the rainbow, while fiery rings radiate out from behind her body. She wears a wimple and an elaborately embroidered tunic and she is crowned, as it were, by a huge dish-plate aureole inset with stars. Now such a rapprochment between the female figures in the Book of Revelation could have allowed the entry of the Virgin into the traditional formulae of the Apocalypse which illustrate the role of the Church in the distribution of grace. Already as early as about 1140, Ecclesia had been shown enthroned with Christ as the Sponsa described in the Book of Revelation on the typanum of Quenington parish church in Gloucestershire. "Let us be glad and rejoice, and give honour to him: for the marriage of the Lamb is come, and his wife hath made herself ready" (Revelation 19: 7). Once the Bride is identified with the Virgin through the use of the nuptial imagery of Psalm 44, the figure of Ecclesia enthroned with her bridegroom is superseded by that of the Virgin enthroned in the heavenly Paradise with the Father or the Son. In the Liber Floridus, Christ crowns Ecclesia on the site of the restored Jerusalem of the new Zion (Figure 2). The Baptismal font set behind ecclesia is explained by the artist in the inscription written along the contour of Christ's crowning arm:

Figure 4

Fons patens ecclesie
omnibus; in ablutionem
peccatorum omnum.

Just as the Church had been the means of grace through its power
of absolution, so this role of mediatrix gradually came to be seen
as the special agency of the Virgin. The transfer of authority had
been signalled by Lambert's unusual image of the Virgin,
addressed by the angel presumably in terms evoked by the hymn
on the accompanying text which hails her as the Fountain of
Mercy. The equivalence of the verbal and the visual text may have
ensured the transposition of the Virgin to the place formerly
assigned to the female figure of the Church.

From the first half of the twelfth century we can trace a further
development in the way in which this Mary/Ecclesia image was
embellished. This ensured the royal attributes of Mary—not
simply as Queen of the Angels with her Angel Body Guard and
the trappings of imperial state, but as the Shulammite Bride of the
Song of Songs. The interpretation of the Biblical love poem
slipped from an ecclesiological to a Marian interpretation, largely
as a result of the writings of St. Bernard. This last change was to be
a determining factor in the imagery of the coronation of the
Virgin, for it accorded to her all the splendour and physical
adornment of a royal bride. More significant for the exploitation
of this imagery was the sensual and metaphorical language of the
description. In at least one French version of the poem, the author
infuses the commentary with terms of courtly romance, effectively
bringing this difficult poem into the experience and conceptual
systems of his listening audience (Pickford 1974: 34).[13] Moreover,
the cosmic nature of that ceremonial triumph is also implied in the
poetry of the Song of Songs by the metaphors of gold, of sun-light,
radiance, and sweet odours. This cosmic aspect may have been
enlarged as a result of the revived interest in the imagery of the
Apocalypse, stimulated by the crusading fervour. The Church
may have seized on the propaganda potential of the one
comparable image of divine splendour, namely the "Great
Wonder," the Apocalyptic Woman as a device which could
function like a battle standard. Both the idea of regality and
generation are contained in this single image, for the woman is
crowned with stars and swollen with child.

THE WOMAN CLOTHED IN THE SUN

Western writers had proposed various solutions for the interpretation
of the twelfth chapter of the Book of Revelation. The Woman had
been variously identified as the Christian Church, or else the

ancient Church of both the Old and the New Testaments or the Virgin. In recent exegesis, she was described as "either a collective with double import or a collective and individual" (Le Frois 1954: 61). The unique quality of this visionary image lies in the fact that the Woman is wearing the sun as her garment. The Jewish hagiographer of the Book of Revelation made clear that it was the sun itself that clothed her, thus investing her with divinity. She was literally "clothed with God." She brought forth a child who was to be Lord of the World and divine. As she had the moon beneath her feet, so she was to be considered as being above the changeable, imperfect world which she had conquered. The author's use of the word "footstool" further marks the Woman as sovereign and conqueress, a cosmic authority which is designated by her crown being not of gold but of stars. Thus the crown is neither simply a victory garland nor a sign of royal rank, but a symbol of celestial governance. The image of the Woman Clothed with the Sun was, however, ambivalent in its identification. Ecclesia or Mary? The Church was described as mother in the title, Mater Ecclesia, but Mary, because she was Theotokos, Mother of God, shared this idea while bearing yet another title as the acknowledged Queen of Heaven. By the end of the eleventh century, in the writings of Peter Damian for example, there is evidence of a shift of emphasis such that Mary became seen as Mother of the Church. In this fusion of motifs, Ecclesia and Mary, a new symbol was formed which may have supported the claims for secular queens as potential bearers of authority and as the guardians of legitimate descent in the person of the heir.

In this respect sovereignty is a very active political reality and the sovereignty of the Virgin also operated in the daily affairs of men and women. The decisive factor in this diffusion of influence is that of St. Bernard, through his great sermon "Dominica Infra Octavan Assumptionis Beata Virgine Maria," which effectively placed Mary above the Church as a two-way door to Salvation as well as a devotional focus (Bergamini 1985: 39–43).[14] Mary became seen as the vehicle by which grace could be conferred on the petitioner and as the mediatrix for the faithful with the Godhead. Thus the sovereignty of the Virgin is not autonomous but operates through a higher authority, recourse to which is continually available. Bernard's Apocalyptical Mary as an agent in salvation found a fertile home in England because of the rich tradition of Marian imagery to which we have already referred and because of the role of secular queens, which may have made England particularly receptive to this idea.

What was needed was a symbol by which the artist could make

visible this sovereignty over the world. The earliest picture cycles of the Apocalypse in the mid-thirteenth century seem to have taken as a possible model the Byzantine type of Madonna image in which the Virgin is represented with a medallion encircled on her body, on which a tiny image of the child is implanted. Mary as the vessel for the Incarnation is clearly formulated by the womblike enclosure of the child, whose power seems to break through the substance of the flesh and gleam like a sun-burst from his mother's form. The Beatus Apocalypse of the Iberian tradition betrays the Western adaptation of this idea, for in a twelfth- or thirteenth-century Spanish Apocalypse now in Paris (Bibl. Nat. MS 2290, folios 110v–111), the Woman is rendered twice, both as the celestial Church suspended in the firmament above the moon and also as the Earthly Church. In this latter case she is seated in the *orans* position recalling the Byzantine type of the Virgin as Regina Angelorum, enthroned without the child. The implicit distinction between the Church and the Virgin may have been preserved by artists during the twelfth century, for even in some thirteenth-century Anglo-Norman cycles an echo of this distinction is still present. The duality of Mary's royalty—both as Queen of heaven and as the human individual chosen to be the mother of Christ—presented difficulties for a composite image.

In the Douce Apocalypse (Oxford, Bodl. Lib. MS Douce 180) a subtle differentiation is made between the Woman Clothed with the Sun on folio 42 and the woman who gave birth to a male child and was pursued by the Dragon on folio 43 (Figure 5). The two women are dressed differently. The Woman Clothed with the Sun wears a red/orange overdress with split sleeves like a maternity robe, and she is veiled. The accompanying Commentary identifies her as the Church: "Hic mulier ecclesiam designat." The woman with the child has a blue mantle over a red robe which is edged with gold bands, and her head is covered with a wimple. In the Trinity Apocalypse (Cambridge, Trinity Coll. MS 950), which may have offered some models for Douce, again the two women are dressed differently on folio 13v. Again the Commentary marks out the Woman Clothed with the Sun as the Church: "Cette feme signifie seinte eglise." But the conjunction comes in the text supporting the picture of the woman nourished in the desert and tormented by the Dragon:

Nus poum entendr la benuree
Marie par ceste femme en cest lieu.

However, the pressure mounted to identify them as one and the same. In many images of the Anglo-Norman cycles, the Woman with the child is represented in the pose of the Virgin of the

Nativity as she reclines with the Infant, though in this case protected from the Dragon by the encircling ring of fire. In the Apocalypse narrative, the woman then offers the child to Heaven's angelic messenger in such a way as to recall the imagery of the Presentation in the Temple. Then the Woman is given wings to escape the wiles of the dragon to a place of safety in the wilderness, where she is fed by angels. The source of this imagery may have been borrowed from the Eastern tradition, in which the Virgin is fed by angels in the Temple as described in Eastern apocryphal writings (Nelson 1985: Plates 12, 18). Thus it is at least possible that the formative sources for the figure of the Woman clothed with the Sun encouraged the identification of that redemptive queen with the Ara Coeli, an iconic image which was also visionary and signalled sovereignty over the peoples of the world. This fusion of the idea of the Virgin with that of the Woman of the Apocalypse seems to have been encouraged in the mid-thirteenth-century during the years of expectancy around the promised date of the Final Times in 1260, as predicted by the extreme wing of the Franciscan order and fanned by the fears of the spread of the Mongol conquests in Eastern Europe. It does seem that the image of the Virgin is responsive to crisis within the Church by reaffirming the theological basis of her sovereignty.

> Endowed with all the power of the cosmic attributes, she sits enthroned or stands, a transcendent, celestial figure. Her identity with contemporary representations of the Queen of Heaven is striking. (Bergamini 1985: 142–143)

But even if the influential image of the Virgin in the Sun had effectively overwhelmed the older image of Ecclesia, there was a further implication for the development of the Virgin's royal status which was created by her association with the text of the Apocalypse. This was the identification of the Virgin with the Bride of the Lamb who was called to the marriage feast in the final reunion of Christ with his Church. It is in this development that the singularity of the coronation of the Virgin lies, for because of these traditions of Apocalyptic exegesis, Mary is at once the Mother of Christ and his Bride. How was this complexity to be revealed? Just as the Jesse tree formula was concerned with the genealogy of Christ through his human mother, so interest in the Virgin as an individual reawakened in the speculation concerning her death and assumption.

The impetus for the new image of the Virgin as the Woman clothed with the Sun may have come from the East in the form of icons and model sheets and transportable pilgrim objects. It is in Byzantium, perhaps in the region of Constantinople itself, that the theme of Maria Regina or Mary as Queen of the Angels developed (Andaloro 1986: 103).[15] To Syriac images of the Ascension, we owe the source of the standing Virgin of the Assumption. The Eastern icon of the Virgin with the Child encased within the contours of her body and the Imperial trappings of this royal Queen and her attendant angel bodyguard—all this could have been transmitted to the West in the two great waves of Byzantine influence in the twelfth century following the First Crusade (Weitzmann 1982: 55–69). The imagery of the Coronation may owe something to the development in the East of the Feast of the Coronatio Mariae, which was identical with the Feast of the Assumption of Maria. This latter feast had been instituted by the Patriarch of Jerusalem for the day of the heliacic disappearance of Spica, the main star of Virgo (Zarnecki 1950: 11, note 2).

More intriguing is the myth of the ascent into Heaven of the Goddess Istar-In-Ni-Na, for Ishtar or Ashtaroth was worshipped in Syria and Palestine and formed part of Hebrew mythology by her love for the shepherd Tammuz. This earth Goddess had temples in Palestine. The Central panel, for example, of a large wall painting from the Palace of Zimrilim at Mari shows the King before the Goddess Ishtar, in the presence of other Deities (Stronmenger 1964: plate 165). An interesting image from the same source shows the great palm tree with an interceding Goddess, and recalls in a strange way the tree of Nebuchadnezzar and the Guardian of the Liber Floridus. A statuette of a seated couple, from the Temple of Ishtar at Mari, also echoes the seated figures of the synthronos. The Eastern origin of this imagery, possibly brought back to the West by the Crusades, is still reflected in Eastern Roman funerary relief art where the Goddess Ishtar has been adapted from the Hellenistic Tyche (Figure 5).[16] It is most likely that knowledge of Eastern icons was transmitted to the West in the pages of model books and may have influenced literature. In the Life of Christina of Markyate, the author tells how she had a vision of the Virgin arrayed like an Empress; that Life also contained a newly translated poem from the Byzantine world (Baker 1978: 201). It is like an Empress that the Virgin is portrayed in the early Jesse Tree of the Salzburg Antiphonium (St. Peter's Abbey, MS.a. 12, fol. 7) and in the early Beatus Apocalypses of Spain, where this imperial figure is also identified as the Woman Clothed with the Sun. It is like an Empress that Ecclesia is crowned on the Mount of Olives in Lambert's illustration of Christ between the Church and the Synagogue.

Given the tense expectancy of the climate in which the first Apocalypse picture cycles were produced and the eschatological

r ſignum magnum appa
ruit in celo mulier amicta
ſole er luna ſub pedibʒ eius. er in
capite eius corona ſtellarum du
odecim. er in utero habens clama
bat in doloribʒ; er cruciabatur ut
parerer.

Figure 5

mood of the First Crusade which coloured the Liber Floridus, it is possible that an Eastern image of a royal figure, crowned in the heavens, could be associated with the "Great Wonder" of the Woman of the Apocalypse who stood in the sun with stars upon her head. This image of the Virgin as crowned above the heavens became associated with the veneration of Mary as an individual, but one who was exempt through a unique dispensation from the penalty of death. It is but a short step to envisage Mary's reception into Heaven to be united with her Son as the moment when she receives her heavenly crown; thus the iconic image of the Virgin in the Sun gave way to the dramatic narrative of her coronation. The language of the Apocalypse equated her with the radiance of the morning star and with the gold of the sun and with the jewelled brilliance of the New Jerusalem, visual attributes which encouraged further embellishment from those texts which extolled the properties of light (such as were used by Suger of St. Denis).

But this radiance which seemed more appropriate to a mystical concept of the Virgin's sovereignty was rendered less remote as the imagery of the Song of Songs slipped into the anthems and liturgy of the Assumption, for she could be visualised as an earthly queen or royal bride graciously called by her bridegroom to adorn his throne as she herself was adorned with gold.

> Who is she that looketh forth as the morning,
> fair as the moon, clear as the sun . . .
> (Song of Songs 6:10)

Moreover, the language of the Song of Songs was couched in terms of deep human passion, which opened up a channel of worship hitherto denied by the inaccessibility of the Virgin's royal status. It seems likely that when artists came to design images involving secular queenship, they constructed their picture on the basis of the recognizable formula of the Virgin's sovereignty. Perhaps because of the source on which such representations were based, the images of secular queenship carry no overtones of aggression or the abuse of power. It is difficult to give an example of the tyrant queen as being in any way derived from the Marian iconography; instead such an image of the abuse of royal power would have to be adapted from the iconography of male rule. So optimistic and unthreatening was the image of the Virgin's royalty that secular queenship may have found the perfect propaganda model in the developing imagery of the coronation of the Virgin from the early twelfth century.

On the basis of the visual traditions and the developing concepts of the Virgin's role in salvation, the evidence does not suggest a real connection between Mary's queenship and that of secular queens; however, the visual relationship was mediated by attempts to suggest parallels. From the beginning, the accent had always been on the visual sign which set the Virgin apart, both through her cosmic role and through her human assumption. The Virgin in the Tree and the Virgin in the Sun were shadowy presences even when the imagery appeared to suggest the experience of secular ceremonial. These ghosts within the imagery ensured the link between the Virgin and the New Jerusalem as described by John in the Book of Revelation. The poetic imagery of the Virgin sustained the reassuring certainty of John's description of the Holy City:

> Having the glory of God and her light was like unto a stone most precious, even like a jasper stone, clear as crystal.
> (Revelation 21:11)

Like John's record of God's promise to mankind, the imagery of Mary, crowned in the splendour of the heavenly ceremonial, held out a great hope.

NOTES

1 Emile Mâle's thesis that Suger was the creator of the subject has been challenged by Verdier (1976) who puts forward the name of Peter Abelard on the basis of his homily on the Assumption. The scenario of the reception into the Heavenly Jerusalem evokes the imagery of those descriptive passages in Psalm 45 which were applied to the Virgin's triumph in the homilies on the Feast of the Dormition by Andrew of Crete and John of Damascene (Warner 1976: 115 and Verdier 1980: 103–105). This rendered her a cosmic force existing outside time and therefore an agent in God's plan for salvation.

2 All this material is collected and carefully analysed in Verdier (1980), and divided into four categories: literary, liturgical, doctrinal, and exegetical.

3 See Schine Gold (1985: 73): "The artistic and theological images of the Virgin were, like the images of women in secular literature, the creations of men, and can be understood as fulfilling the emotional needs of the monks and clerics who created them."

4 The textual basis of this conflation of ideas is discussed in Watson (1934: 4). By the thirteenth century, Alan de Lisle stressed the similarity of the sound between the two words, which could be interchanged by the exchange of a single letter: "Haec eleganter dicitur virga, ratione nominis . . . quoniam mutatione A in O, de virga fit virgo." Patr. lat. 210. 246.

5 In Chapter 7, pp. 77–78, Watson (1934) urges a closer look at what might be rudimentary forms of the Jesse Tree representation to discount the idea of Suger's authorship.

6 Watson (1934) noted that the Sibyl was associated with Nebuchadnezzar and Vergil as one of the pagan seers. Cuttler (1965) recorded that an image of the Erythrean prophetess was once in the Church of the Holy Sepulchre at Jerusalem.

7 See the summary of Harry Bober's account in the Colloquium Papers edited by Derolez (1973: 18): "As the specific and special occasion for the composition of the Liber Floridus, the author proposed that its main accent and focus was upon the First Crusade and the place of Flanders and St. Omer in history."

8 See the persuasive analysis of the relation between text and image in Mayo (1973).

9 Aspects of the iconography have been discussed in an unpublished M.A. thesis by Kirsty Beck, St. Andrews, 1991.

10 See Carol Uhlig Crown's thesis (1976) where she examines the theme of the Virgin's role in the Divine Plan for the redemption of man.

11 The questioning of the midwife as it occurs in the Protevangelium reads as follows: "And her months were fulfilled, and in the nine month Anna brought forth. And she said unto the midwife, what have I brought forth? And she said, a female. And Anna said: My soul is magnified this day . . ."

12 Anglo-Saxon precedent for the idea of the Virgin's coronation had been contained in embryo in the Benedictional of St. Aethelwold of 980. There, at the scene of the dormition, the hand of God descends from the clouds holding a crown above the figure on the bier to signal the Virgin's triumph over death.

13 See the edition of MS. 173 of the Bibliothèque Municipale of Le Mans (Pickford 1974: 34–35): "We are in the presence not of another more or less traditional commentary on the Song of Songs, but of a romance which is also at the same time an exegesis of the Song of Songs" (34).

14 Bergamini (1985: 56) gives the text and translation of Sermon 63: "Hoc itaque modo et ex Maria ordoiisse videtur Eclesia."

15 Andaloro (1986) discusses the significance of the wall mosaics in the church of the amphitheatre at Durazzo discovered in 1967, plate 36 and page 111.

16 Colledge (1976: 135) notes how the Hellenistic influence, by the middle or late 1st century reliefs, resulted in the awkward turning of the frontal figure's legs to accommodate

the older profile thrones: "Ishtar has borrowed the
swimming figure at her feet from the early iconography of
the influential early Hellenistic statue of the Tyche of
Antioch." See plate 38.

REFERENCES

Andalaro, Maria (1986). I Mosaici Parietali di Durazzo o
   dell' Origine Constantinopitana del Thema Iconografico.
   *Studien zur Spätantiken und Byzantinischen Kunst.
   Friedrich Wilhelm Deichmann Gewidmet*. Teil 3. Bonn:
   Dr. Rudolph Habelt G.M.B.H.
Bergamini, Laurie Jones (1985). From Narrative to Icon: The
   Virgin Mary and the Woman of the Apocalypse in 13th-
   century English Art and Literature. Ph.D. Thesis: Univer-
   sity of Connecticut. Ann Arbor: University Microfilms
   International.
Colledge, Malcolm (1976). *The Art of Palmyra*. London:
   Thames and Hudson.
Crown, Carol Uhligh (1976). The Winchester Psalter: Icono-
   graphic Sources and Themes of the Virgin Mary,
   Kingship and Law. Ph.D. Thesis. Washington University.
   Ann Arbor: University Microfilms International.
Cuttler, Anthony (1965). Octavian and the Sibyl in Christian
   Hands. *Vergilius* 11: 22–32.
Dérolez, Albert (1967). Un Colloque sur le Liber Floridus.
   Scriptorium 21: 307–312.
—— (1973). *Liber Floridus Colloquium*. Ghent: Storia et
   Scientia. P.V.B.A.
Gold, Penny Schine (1985). *The Lady and the Virgin: Image,
   Attitude and Experience in 12th-century France*. Chicago:
   University of Chicago Press.
Haney, Kristine Edmondson (1986). *The Winchester Psalter:
   An Iconographic Study*. Leicester: University of Leicester
   Press.
Kantorowicz, Ernst (1947). The Quinity of Winchester. *Art
   Bulletin* 29: 73–85.
Ladner, Gerhart (1979). Medieval and Modern Understanding
   of Symbolism: A Comparison. *Speculum* 54: 223–256.
Le Frois, Bernard (1954). *The Woman Clothed With the Sun:
   Individual or Collective?* Rome: Orbis Catholicus.
Mayo, Penelope (1973). The Crusaders Under the Palm.
   Dumbarton Oaks Papers 27: 31–67.
Mentré, Mireille (1984). *Création et Apocalypse: Histoire
   d'un Regard Humain sur le Divin*. Paris.
Muir Wright, Rosemary (1986). The Iconography of the
   Coronation of the Virgin. *Kingship*, ed. Emily Lyle
   Cosmos 2: 52–82.
Pickford, Cedric (1974). *The Song of Songs: A 12th-century*

French Version. London: Oxford University Press for the University of Hull.

Rademacher, Franz (1972). *Die Regina Angelorum in der Kunst des Frühen Mittelalters*. Dusseldorf: Schwann.

Stronmenger, Eva (1964). *The Art of Mesopotamia*. London: Thames and Hudson.

Swarzenski, Hans (1973). Comments on the Figural Decoration. *Liber Floridus Colloquium*, in Dérolez 1973.

Verdier, Philippe (1976). Suger a-t-il été en France le Créateur du Thème Iconographique du Couronnement de la Vierge? *Gesta* 15: 227–235.

—— (1980). *Le Couronnement de la Vierge: Les Origines et les Premiers Développements d'un Thème Iconographique*. Montréal: Publications de l'Institut d'Etudes Médiévales Albert-le-Grand.

Warner, Marina (1976). *Alone of All Her Sex: The Myth and Cult of the Virgin Mary*. London: Pan Books.

Watson, Arthur (1934). *The Early Iconography of the Tree of Jesse*. London: Oxford University Press.

Weitzmann, Kurt (1982). *Art in the Medieval West and its Contacts With Byzantium*. London: Variorum Reprints.

Wogan-Browne, Jocelyn (forthcoming). Reading the World: The Hereford Mappa Mundi. *Parergon*.

Zarnecki, George (1950). The Coronation of the Virgin in a Capital from Reading Abbey. *Journal of the Warburg and Courtauld Institutes* 13: 1–12.

JOHN CARMI PARSONS

Ritual and Symbol in the English Medieval Queenship to 1500

The majority of recent studies on queenship in the Christian
Middle Ages have had as their focus the nature of a queen's
position, the means whereby she reached it, the resources it
offered her and the use she made of them to sustain and protect
herself. Such studies have greatly expanded understanding of
medieval queenship, not least by demonstrating that despite a
secondary official role, queens effectively exerted "unofficial"
power, and in common with most women in patriarchal societies
they actively sought to maximize that power. But in such societies
women's power is associated with their physical nature and with
the social roles to which they are assigned by reason of that nature.
Seen as intuitive, emotional and irrational, a danger to forces that
ensure social order, women's power is subordinated and controlled,
largely by confining them to the domestic arena to which their
physical nature appears to relegate them. A king's wife, however,
challenged the male social order with the paradox of a woman
established in an intimate relationship to the public authority of
the husband who embodied the forces of social order: as his
bedfellow and ideally mother of the future king, she could wield
manipulative influence to great effect.[1]

By examining the ritual context of English medieval queenship,
this essay will explore some of the ways in which society addressed
the paradox the queen represented, and the ways in which queens
sought to maximize their power. Current inquiry has greatly
facilitated the investigation of ritual by broadening its definition
and it is accordingly approached here as repetitive, socially
standardized behavior, secular or religious, that takes place at
locations and times that have symbolic meaning.[2] Rituals of
queenship thus embrace not only coronation, but as well entry
pageantry, marriage, childbearing, the receiving of petitions, and
funerals. My argument is that though the queen's power was

acknowledged in some rituals, and while she communicated impressions of that power to the realm through other ritualized acts, the multivocality and ambiguity of the symbols through which these rituals were expressed allowed participants to perceive them as enacting limitations on her power (Kertzer 1988: 11; cf. Turner 1969: 14–15, 42–3, 100–5).

A convenient example will be the moment of first encounter as a new royal wife was welcomed into the kingdom, the obvious moment for the community to convey some idea of what they expected of her. We know little of these occasions for earlier centuries save that they were sumptuous, as for example Eleanor of Castile's entry to London in 1255.[3] The extant details connect this occasion intimately with Henry III's obsessive cult of Edward the Confessor. A year earlier, Henry was disappointed in his hopes that Eleanor's wedding to his son Edward would coincide with the feast of the Confessor's translation (13 October); in 1255, he intended that her entry should take place on that day, but her arrival at Dover in rather shabby array forced the king to postpone the event for four days. When she reached Westminster, Eleanor was provided with a rich clasp for her first oblation at the shrine of English kingship's patron saint.[4] She was very likely also given a copy of Matthew Paris' life of St Edward, to impart knowledge of the dynastic saint and to initiate her into the cult as a means to "naturalize" her,[5] a critical consideration for England as royal brides were usually sought outside the kingdom and their foreignness intensified feelings of distrust.[6] Martin Kaufmann (1990) has recently pointed out, moreover, that Matthew's version of St Edward's life expands upon its prototype, Ailred's Latin *vita*, to convey expectations of good kingship, so perhaps Eleanor was meant to learn from the example of St Edward's wife Edith, rather inaccurately portrayed by Matthew as a modest and virtuous queen.[7] A life of the dynastic saint at best conveyed privileged knowledge for a limited audience, but communities perhaps evolved such gift-giving into the rich pageantry of the later medieval period, as a more public, visual means to communicate expectations of good rulership.[8] I shall at any rate examine other rituals of queenship with the idea that they too embodied instruction and limitation.

The queen's arrival in England was usually followed in short order by marriage and coronation, and as the most important ritual of queenship, the investiture naturally claims much of our attention. Coronation recognized the queen as "a person of dignity and excellence" (Ehrlich 1921: 207), but the rite's purpose was less to confirm her as a ruler than to designate her as the king's legitimate wife and the mother of his lawful heir. The close relationship between her marriage and coronation is evident in the ceremony's prayers derived from *benedictiones super sponsas*, and wedding imagery was furthered by the queen's appearance at the rite with her hair let down on her shoulders as though a virgin.[9] Other prayers sought to ensure the birth of heirs, acknowledging that the queen was raised by God to share the royal couch, but at the same time exhorting her that her behavior within marriage should merit the palm next to virginity, so that with the five prudent virgins she might be worthy of the Celestial Bridegroom.[10] These utterances conceded the physical reality of her relationship to the king and the significance of her reproductive role, and testified that marriage and motherhood gave her a claim to influence and power. But fictional virginity and admonitions to chaste demeanor suggest apprehension for the links between the queen's power and her female roles as wife and mother.

Other coronation practices more explicitly emphasized that the queen's position was subordinate to the king's. An eleventh-century variant of the Second Recension of the English coronation order saluted the king's wife as a partner in the royal dignity, but so explicit an association of woman and power disappeared from twelfth-century recensions: the medieval period attributed charisma to women more willingly than it acknowledged their power.[11] Unlike the king, his wife was required to pause as she entered the coronation church, while a prayer remarked the frailty of woman and cited the example of Judith to stress that only with divine aid could she overcome such disabilities. As the queen took no oath, she was not established in a defined relationship to the realm, nor was the kingdom obligated to her by oaths of homage. She was anointed with holy oil, not with chrism, before she received a ring for integrity of faith and a crown of majesty for honor and dignity, and her first act after investiture was to bow to the king, "adoring the royal majesty as is fitting" (Legg 1901: lvii, 85, 100–1).

Until the composition in the 1380s of the earliest rubricated order for the English coronation (the Westminster *Liber regalis*), moreover, the English orders do not mention the queen's sceptre, the item among the regalia that symbolizes royal power. Earlier omission of the sceptres does not prove they were lacking, for Matilda of Flanders (*d.* 1087) and Eleanor of Castile (*d.* 1290) possessed scepters (Musset 1967, no. 16; Byerly 1977, no. 2011), and from 1118 at the latest the queens were shown with scepters on their seals, the official image that represented them to the world.[12] Eleanor of Provence walked to her 1236 coronation under a canopy carried by barons of the Cinque Ports, a practice not recorded in coronation orders before the *Liber regalis*, and during the rite Eleanor likely received the scepter and virge with which she appears on her seal.[13] That the queen was given a scepter at investitures before the 1380s is made all but certain by a 1359 inventory of regalia in Westminster Abbey, which records a silver-gilt scepter "for the queen"; to have merited that description it must have been so used at least for Philippa's coronation in 1330 (Robinson 1909: 19, 71; Legg 1901: 54–56, 79–80, 242–44).

There is, then, every likelihood that in England the queen received a scepter and perhaps a virge by 1330, probably earlier. But here a distinction must be observed between "received" and "was invested with," for the *Liber regalis* provides that the celebrant merely handed the queen scepter and virge without formalities: unlike her crown and ring, her scepters were not blessed, she received them without an "accipe" formula, and there was no subsequent prayer addressing their significance (Legg 1901: 21–22, 37–39, 100–1, 108–12; Ullman 1961: 96–107). (French practice by *ca* 1230 saw the celebrant present the queen with scepter and virge, an act performed "without prayers" in the later thirteenth century but given an appropriate "accipe" formula probably in 1364, shortly before the *Liber regalis* first remarked the English queen's scepter (Chevalier 1900: 225; cf. Jackson 1984: 26, 222; Martène 1736–37, col. 633, cf. Jackson *loc. cit.*; Dewick 1899, col. 47). Additional insights can be distilled from the single, non-liturgical glimpse we have of a thirteenth-century queen's investiture, an illumination of Edith's coronation in the only extant MS of Matthew Paris' life of Edward the Confessor.[14] The illumination shows the celebrant crowning Edith as a kneeling lay dignitary puts a scepter into her hand, and though we cannot be certain that this is an accurate depiction of thirteenth-century practice, an explanation for the layman's role as portrayed is offered by the same volume's depictions of the coronations of the Confessor and of the usurper Harold II. The former shows the celebrant bestowing both crown and scepter, but in a scene clearly meant to convey the illegitimate nature of Harold's power he is shown crowning himself as a layman brings the scepter.[15] That Edith's scepter is delivered by a layman thus signifies that while like Harold she has power of some kind, hers is not the authority vested in the consecrated king. And this surely explains the less formal manner in which later English queens were given their scepters.

It was natural for the ceremony that confirmed the queen's eminence and suggested some limits to her power to indicate as well the proper ways in which her influence should be used. The

Liber regalis provides that after her investiture the queen was enthroned to her husband's left, on a seat lower than his, an arrangement that appears to represent long earlier tradition.[16] French practice again offers some points for comparison; the French queen too took a lower throne at her coronation, (Chevalier 1900:225; Dewick 1899, col. 10; Sherman 1977: 270) but probably by 1318, on occasions other than the coronation, she was seated to the king's right as enjoined by scripture (*III Reg.* 2: 19; *Ps.* 44:10). This custom was rationalized with the assertion that potential queens-regent were thereby associated with the power symbolized by the king's scepter.[17] The merest glance at English history shows that no queen after 1066 exercised full sovereign powers as regent in her son's minority; and as we are already coming to see, the tendency in English ritual was to dissociate the king's wife from his authority. That the English queen's seat to the king's left signified her isolation from the authority symbolized by his scepter, and *vice versa* her association with qualities embodied in the virge of justice and equity held in his left hand during the coronation,[18] is implied by an aspect of English coronation practice that appears to have passed unnoticed.

On the day of her coronation in January 1236, Eleanor of Provence secured from Henry III a pardon for a man imprisoned for trespass of the forest. The twelve-year-old girl had been in England only two weeks and can have had scant understanding of the transgression for which she secured the pardon; we are probably right in seeing the event as a carefully arranged performance, if not as an act the new queen was expected to perform. Similar pardons or acts of grace were obtained by Joan of Navarre in February 1403 and by Katherine of Valois in February 1421, and Anne of Bohemia may have been intended to do so in January 1382,[19] so unrecorded custom may well have called for an act of intercession at the queen's investiture although we have no evidence as to exactly how or when it was performed. Certainly there were some customs, associated with the coronation but not part of the religious service, that can only be limpingly documented; one obscure usage briefly glimpsed in the thirteenth century gave the queen "by ancient and approved custom. . . . by reason of her new creation" the right to present a new nun in every convent in the realm.[20] French queens, in contrast, were specifically granted the power to pardon criminals as part of their coronation honors, a privilege originally claimed by French kings and extended to their wives to associate them with the dignity of the Crown (McCartney; Jackson 1984: 94–114). In England no such grants were made, and the queen's intercession with the king remained necessary.

What is known of the appearance of the royal scepters can perhaps shed a little more light on the matter. Before the *Liber regalis* we have only sigillographic and artistic evidence, but apart from Henry I's wives (who both used the same seal matrix) these sources always show the queens with floriated scepters, riotously so as in the illumination of Edith's coronation or, as on seals, with a stylised fleur-de-lis.[21] This artistic convention preserved its vigor long after the queens were invested with the avian regalia of the *Liber regalis*; Anne Neville, for example, appears with a floriated scepter in the illuminated history of her family known as the Rous Roll (Sutton and Hammond 1983: plate 9). The scepter's persistent floriation in art and on the queen's seals strongly recalls the flowering rods of Aaron and Jesse, Biblical images commonly seen as figures of the Virgin Mary (de Saxonia 1975: 196, 236, 263, 352–71; St Laurence 1890–99: 193, 468). In particular, Richard of St Laurence's interpretation of the flowering rod has significant overtones for a queen's intercessory role: the Virgin, as the rod, mediates between her human origins, the roots of the rod, and her Son, symbolized by the flower (St Laurence 1890–99: 790; cf. Owst 1961: 20). For an era keenly aware of symbolic meanings, then, the floriated scepter with which the queens were commonly represented would have had strong Marian connotations closely related to the intercessory role. Thus, in the context of a ritual that did not establish the queen in a defined relationship to the realm, her coronation intercession realized a role suggested by the order's reference to Esther, invited by the queen's proximity to the king's virge of justice and equity, and symbolized by the scepter with which she was portrayed to the world.

The combination of symbol and action relating coronation and intercession for the English queen has obvious links with the Heavenly Coronation, which offered a visual demonstration of the Virgin's presence at her Son's side and her capacity to intercede with Him. The Virgin became the merciful intercessor between sinful man and a judging God as the Church in the eleventh and twelfth centuries extended its government and expanded its presence in all aspects of Christian life (Turner 1978: 140, 171, 198–99). In much the same way and at the same period, burgeoning administration in England widened the gap between ruler and ruled, a situation in which recourse to intercessors is common among those held remote from power and in which the rituals of rulership are likely to be aggressively developed (Leach

1969: 85–122; Kertzer 1988: 52–54). The king's wife emerged as a popular intercessory figure, and as I have shown elsewhere queens exploited the intercessory role to nourish impressions of their influence, making it in effect a ritual of queenship whose Marian associations subtly impressed themselves upon rich and poor, lay and religious alike. Townspeople at St Albans in 1275 borrowed language from popular Marian devotions when enlisting Eleanor of Castile's intercession with Edward I, assuring her that they placed all their hope in her just as they trusted in the mercy and pity of the Queen of Heaven. Bishop Grosseteste in 1243, and an anonymous St Albans chronicler in 1308, drew on established Marian sermon imagery in likening the effects of a queen's mercy on the realm to the light of dawn that scatters the shadows of error and discord.[22] As Marian imagery both exalted and limited medieval women (Turner 1978: 154; Miles 1985: 75–89; Gold 1985: 70–75; Bedos-Rezak 1988: 75–76; Bedos-Rezak 1990: 7 and n. 67), moreover, a queen's role as intercessor allowed different social groups to negotiate their relationship to her. The poor projected onto the king's wife their hopes for mercy and invested her with the clement and gracious image of the Virgin Mother; for the nobility, the submissive, interceding Queen of Heaven implied the queen's subjection to her husband and legitimized a role in which her power and influence were exercised for the benefit of the realm and its inhabitants. (It is worth pointing out here that the image of the triumphant Virgin, with scepter, did not long outlast the twelfth century but was quickly superseded by the submissive, interceding Virgin who receives from her Son a crown—but no scepter [Gold 1985: 51–65; Muir Wright 1986].)

Associations between intercession by an earthly queen and her Heavenly counterpart were to be more explicitly elaborated in later medieval pageantry, which welcomed new queens with tableaux depicting intercession by the Queen of Heaven in direct juxtaposition with that by an earthly queen.[23] Rather than pile up examples from those pageants, however, I will deal here with rituals that marked significant moments as the queen fulfilled her role in the life of the realm. Hopes for royal issue were linked to the Virgin's favor at least from the ninth century (Kantorowicz 1965: 88–89; Rawcliffe 1987: 237–38), and the births of royal children were occasions for rituals rich in Marian imagery, affording Christological allusions for future kings as queens' coronation intercessions presumably did for their husbands. The coronation order related a queen's childbearing to that of women of the Davidic house: Sarah, Rebecca, Leah, and Rachel, ending with the birth of Christ from the womb of the Virgin—a liturgical counterpoise to the Trees of Jesse that linked the Queen of Heaven to males of the Davidic lineage.[24] Royal procreation and the Marian image could be linked subtly, as when Margaret of Anjou entered London in 1445 to discover Noah's Ark bearing the legend "Ingredimini, et replete terram," an obvious allusion to the lack of royal heirs in the 1440s, but nobody could have overlooked affiliations between the Old Testament Arks and the Virgin Mother.[25] The court was more explicit: the coronation's Davidic-dynastic overtones give unmistakable meaning to Henry III's order that a Tree of Jesse be painted in his wife's chamber at Windsor in the year after their marriage (Borenius 1943: 49). The order for the queen's churching in the *Liber regie capelle*, composed between 1445 and 1449, prescribed that she process to the chapel as the choir chanted "Nunc dimittis" and "Lumen ad relevacionem gentium," antiphons explicitly identified "as for the purification of the blessed Mary," and as the queen knelt at the chapel door "some other antiphon of the blessed Virgin" was to be sung (Ullman 1961: 72–73; Staniland 1987). The Marian symbolism discussed above also related to the queen's reproductive function: the fleur-de-lis of her scepter touched the Virgin's queenship and fertility as well as the Tree of Jesse, evoking dynastic motherhood and echoing the juxtaposition of the queen's childbearing and the Davidic line.[26] The scepter thus implied a link between royal childbirth and intercession that was also ritually enacted, for the births of her children were moments for petitioners to approach the queen, as happened at least twice to the helpfully prolific Eleanor of Castile; her gift to St Paul's Cathedral of two baudekyns showing the Virgin in childbirth thus develops some startling resonances indeed (*CPR 1266–1272*: 226; *CCIR 1279–1288*: 263; Parsons 1984: 245–65; Lehmann-Brockhaus 1955–60, no. 2930).

The association of dynastic motherhood and the queen's intercessory role also calls attention to the environment in which she received petitioners. A letter from a lady petitioner to Eleanor of Castile refers to their meeting "at Macclesfield before your bed." This immediately recalls the king's state bed in the Painted Chamber at Westminster as a symbol of majesty and the focal point of meetings there,[27] but the queen's bed commandingly focused attention on the fact that the king visited her chamber for conjugal relations and her children were born there.[28] The queen's choice of her bedchambers to receive those who sought her help thus confronted petitioners with powerful allusions to these two bases of her power, echoed by the use of her elaborate *lit de parade* as the starting-point for the procession to her churching. We may well agree with Georges Duby that this was the queen's "real throne," and manipulation of its symbolic meanings was a natural way for her to emphasize the influence manifest in her intercessory role and to link herself with her Heavenly counterpart.[29]

The ritual of the fifteenth-century chapel royal in fact associated the king's wife with the Marian cult on a daily basis,[30] suggesting that the court was deliberately exploiting links with the Queen of Heaven to enhance the image of the queen of England. Lest it be thought that such links were restricted to the court we may consider the ceremony for the reception of the king and queen at an episcopal town, as found in a late fourteenth-century Exeter pontifical. The bishop met them with processional cross and incense, and escorted them to the cathedral where the king made his devotions while the choir chanted "Summe trinitate," an antiphon whose text speaks of the majesty of the Trinity and the subjection of the world to the law of God. The queen was then received with an antiphon whose text stresses a woman's compliant dissociation from power and her devotion to the Heavenly King: "Regnum mundi et totum ornatum seculi contempsi propter amorem domini mei Iesu Christi. . . . Eructavit cor meum verbum bonum; dico opera mea regi, quem vidi, quem amavi, in quem credisti, quem dilexi" (Barnes 1847: 280; Maskell 1847: 330; Hesbert 1963–79, no. 7524). The response ("Eructavit cor meum") is from Vulgate *Ps.* 44, the opulent coronation imagery of which was a handy resource for chroniclers describing royal investitures. But for greeting and instructing a queen the greater significance lies in the psalm's prominence in the liturgy for the Assumption of the Virgin, a context that gave *Ps.* 44 its impact on the iconography of the Heavenly Coronation.[31] The psalm text's resonance with the Assumption liturgy could hardly have been missed and so, even as she was received with honor and incense, the king's wife was subtly faced once again with the Marian image of a submissive queen.

At the end of her life too, the queen became the focus of ritual and so served the interests of kingship. In the first instance of an English royal funeral deliberately exploited to enhance the monarchy, Eleanor of Castile was given a regalian burial in 1290.[32] The resplendent anniversary service Edward I endowed for Eleanor at Westminster Abbey had direct and lasting effects upon the foundation of chantries throughout England, and the Eleanor crosses with their statues heraldically identified as the late queen, exported to the provinces a sort of authorized version of her gracious image—complete with scepter (Cook 1963: 8; cf. Geertz 1985: 19–20). Such precedents were followed in later reigns, for though no queen of England was ever memorialized like Eleanor, even one of such dubious reputation as Isabella went to the grave shrouded in the mantle she wore at her wedding to Edward II, a surprising choice in her case if less so for her successor Philippa who followed suit: a last reminder that the queen's "dignity and excellence" originated with her marriage to the king (Blackley 1980: 23–47; Hope 1907: 544; Cannadine 1983: 150–51).

The funerary use of the queens' wedding mantles links the beginning and end of queenship and of the rituals that surrounded the king's wife, their central concerns neatly summed up in John Capgrave's meditations upon Margaret of Anjou's wedding in 1445: though the royal marriage should honour God in its chastity like that of Tobias and Sara, the queen should be as a fertile vine and the English should obtain peace from her marriage as the Jews did from Esther's.[33] Capgrave's positive view of Margaret's wifely and maternal roles finds its opposite in the criticism launched against queens who were believed to dominate husbands or sons.[34] Both, of course, throw into relief a single ideal of queenly behavior, a model reinforced by the rituals and symbols that pointed to an unofficial sphere for the proper exercise of the queen's power and influence. The queen's prescribed isolation from her husband's public authority touches, too, on the tendency prevalent in male medieval writing to place in opposition not only male and female but the qualities associated with them. For a king's wife, this set up a complementarity of powers: he the intelligence, she the heart, or the king as law and the queen as mercy, and the power of such male-female constructs in defining queens' roles is evident in male writers' use of masculinizing formulae to praise queens while stressing feminine weakness and deviousness when criticizing them. But queens rarely if ever recognized a need to imitate male behavior. Even as they insisted that the queen was subject to her husband, rituals of queenship acknowledged that she enjoyed power, however informal or unofficial. And the queen could find ample opportunity to seek her goals through manipulation of the same rituals and symbols by which the community emphasized her modesty and submissiveness.

NOTES

1 Stafford 1983; cf. Taylor 1979. In Rosaldo and Lamphere 1974, see Collier 1974: 89–96; the terms authority, power and influence are used here as defined by Rosaldo 1974: 21 and Lamphere 1974: 99–100.

2 Kertzer 1988: 2–5, 8–9. The approach taken here is similar to that described in Nelson 1977.

3 *Cal. Liberate Rolls* iv: 234, 241, 244, 247, 271; *Cal. Close*

Rolls 1254–1256: 128, 144–45, 225; Stapleton 1846: 22; Stubbs 1882–83 i: 48.

4 Beretta 1984: 99; *Cal. Close Rolls 1254–1256*: 136, 145; *Cal. Liberate Rolls* iv: 243.

5 Vaughan 1958: 168–81; Binski 1990: 339–40. Her copy was repaired, 1288 (Byerly 1986, no. 3217).

6 Especially as regarded her influence over her son (Stubbs 1882–83: 57, 59).

7 Cutler 1973: 225–26, 228; but cf. Barlow 1963: 51–52, and Barlow 1970: 25, 93, 115–16, 124, 177–78, 189–90, 192–93 and Binski 1990: 343–44.

8 I am grateful to Professor Gordon Kipling for allowing me to consult a draft of his forthcoming book on medieval royal entries, in which these pageants are examined in detail.

9 Ward 1939: 161 n. 1, and Bouman 1957: 151. Basic to any study of the English service is Brückmann 1964. The loose hair is first noted in the *Liber regalis* (L. Legg 1901: 100, 108), but C. R. Sherman shows that in France the custom was centuries older than the first reference to it in 1364 (1977:271–72).

10 L. Legg 1901: 37, 38–39, 109–110, 111 (added from the *Ordo romanus* in the twelfth century). Cf. Kantorowicz 1965: 86–88; Nelson 1977: 50–71, esp. 63, 71; Jackson 1984: 30–31.

11 Richardson 1960: 122; J. W. Legg 1902: 62–63, 171-72 (note the anthem at 62: "Hodie nobis dei prouidentia caeli stillauerunt karismata").

12 Birch 1887–1900 i: 98–101. English queens sealed during their marriages, but the earliest French queens known to have sealed did so only as widows (Bedos-Rezak 1988:61–82, esp. 63–64 and pl. 2 at 64). Scepters figure on the tombs of Eleanor of Castile and Philippa of Hainaut (*d*. 1369), and on the crosses raised to Eleanor's memory (Colvin, Brown and Taylor 1963: 479–85; Alexander and Binski 1987, nos. 368–79).

13 Hall 1896 ii: 755–60; Birch 1887–1900 i: 98–99. Two scepters borne before Henry III in 1236 were carried by knights because the privilege "belonged to no one by right," but from 1189 at the latest the king's scepters were borne by earls or dukes (Brückmann 1964: 543; L. Legg 1901: 48, 100, 108, 165, 180, 195–96; Sutton and Hammond 1983: 276). The 1236 scepters were thus apparently for the queen.

14 Cambridge, University Library, Ee. iii. 59. Prepared *ca* 1255 in a London or Westminster shop close to the court, this volume was perhaps owned by Henry III's wife (Alexander and Binski 1987, no. 39; but the MS could be

that given Eleanor of Castile in 1255 and repaired in 1288 [above, note 5]).

15 Plates of the illuminations in L. Legg 1901: between pp. 108–9, 90–91 and 96–97. I am indebted to Dr. Janet Nelson for consultation on this point.

16 L. Legg 1901: 101, 112, 228; Sutton and Hammond 1983: 218, 279; Hall 1970: Henry VIII, folio 3v, and Thomas and Thornbury 1983: 340–41. Cf. Stevenson 1959: 10–14 and notes; Barlow 1962: 42 (Pauline Stafford and I have not yet reached accord on the significance of these texts).

17 I owe this information to Elizabeth McCartney.

18 The king's scepter was cruciform, his virge topped by a dove; the former symbolized the power to command and chastise (L. Legg 1901: 97–98; Ayloffe 1786: 376–431, esp. 384). Note too the relationship developed by medieval commentators between "virgo" and "virga" and the consequent stress on Esther touching Ahasuerus' golden "virga" (*Esther* 4: 11) as a type of Marian intercession (Albertus Magnus 1890–99: 389; St Laurence 1890–99: 797).

19 *Cal. Close Rolls 1234–1237*: 229; *Cal. Patent Rolls 1401–1405*: 199, 207, 209; Strickland 1851 ii: 134–35 (but cf. Stowe 1615: 384–85). General pardons for trespasses in the Peasants' Revolt, granted at Anne of Bohemia's request before she crossed the Channel, were perhaps meant to have been conceded at her coronation (*Cal. Close Rolls 1381–1385*: 105, 109).

20 *Cal. Patent Rolls 1232–1247*: 155; P.R.O., S. C. 1/30/49 (s.d.), orders the sheriff of Beds. to distrain nuns at Chicksands who refused to admit a nun presented by the queen "ex antiqua et approbata consuetudine. . . . racione sue noue creacionis."

21 Birch 1887–1900 i: 98–99. The gilt scepter and ivory virge prescribed for the queen in the *Liber regalis* were surmounted by doves (L. Legg 1901: 274–75); cf. Smith 1935: 15, 17; Sutton and Hammond 1983: 276 n. 95.

22 The St Albans letter is P.R.O., S.C. 1/11/90, undated; cf. Riley 1867–69: 411–12; Luard 1861: 310–11; Riley 1865: 49–50. See also Huneycutt (forthcoming) and Parsons (forthcoming). Deshman 1988: 204–40 attributes to tenth-century emergence of a Christ-centered monastic piety the shift from Carolingian Davidic-theocentric kingship to Ottonian Christ-centered kingship.

23 I again express my gratitude to Gordon Kipling for generously allowing me to consult in typescript his forthcoming work on medieval royal entries.

24 L. Legg 1901: 37, 101, 109 (a prayer added to the Third Recension from the *Ordo Romanus*); Watson 1934.

25 Stow 1615: 384–85 (based on *Gen.* 9:7). Cf. de Saxonia

1975, 167–68, 535–36; St Laurence 1890–99 36: 447–55; Albertus Magnus, *Biblia Mariana*, in *Opera omnia*, 37: 366–67.

26 Bedos-Rezak 1988: 75–76, and 1990: 7–8; the Tree of Jesse is linked to the fleur-de-lis by Johnson 1961: 1–22.

27 Binski 1986: 36–38. The letter to Eleanor, from Lucy de Grey, is P.R.O., S.C. 1/30/97 (undated), reading in part: "Duce dame remembrez vous ke vus me comandastes a mayclesfeud deuant vostre lyt, ke Je vous dusse amentiuer de ce ke vous me promistes vostre mercy. . . ."

28 That the king visited the queen's chamber is implicit in the incident in Byerly 1986, no. 980, also recorded in 1278 (P.R.O., C 47/4/1 folio 27v) and 1290 (C 47/4/5 folio 45v). Cf. Byerly, nos. 947–49; Luard 1890 ii: 228; Paris 1872–84 iii: 497–98.

29 Ullman 1961: 72–73; Duby 1983: 234. On women's manipulation of symbols, see Taylor 1979: 13; Rosaldo 1974: 37.

30 Ullman 1961: 59–60. The queen's daily presence at certain rituals recalls ancient queens' cultic duties: Bleeker 1959: 266–68; Gurney 1958: 108–9, 120–21.

31 Gold 1985: 55–56; Duby 1981: 124–25, 158–60; cf. Muir Wright 1986: 58–59. The critical verse is *Ps*. 44: 10, "Astitit regina a dextriis tuis" (*Ps*. 45: 9 [AV] in Gold 1985: 56 n. 33).

32 Ullman 1961: 115, provides that the queen be buried in like manner to the king; for Eleanor of Castile, see Luard 1890 iii: 171–72.

33 Hingeston 1858: 135–37, based on *Ps*. 128:3, *Tobit* 8: 4–10, and *Esther*.

34 E.g., Eleanor of Provence (Paris 1872–84 iii: 388; iv: 259, 487, 510; Stubbs 1882–83 i: 57, 59). She was accused, like Eleanor of Aquitaine, of stirring up discord between husband and son (Luard 1864–69 iii: 215).

35 Taylor 1979: 11–12; Bynum 1987: 282–83. For examples, Riley 1865: 49; Luard 1890 ii: 500; iii: 72. Cf. Stafford 1983: 30, and Bandel 1955: 113–18.

REFERENCES

Albertus Magnus (1890–99). *Biblia Mariana*. In Borgnet and Borgnet 1890–99, vol. 37, pp. 365–445.

Alexander, J. and P. Binski (1987). *Age of Chivalry: Art in Plantagenet England, 1200–1400*. London: Royal Academy.

Ayloffe, J. (1786). An Account of the Body of King Edward the First, as it appeared on opening his tomb in the Year 1774. *Archaeologia* 3, 376–431.

Bandel, B. (1955). The English Chronicler's Attitude toward Women. *Journal of the History of Ideas* 16, 113–18.

Barlow, F., ed. (1962). *Vita Edwardi Regis qui apud West-monasterium requiescit.* London: Nelson.
—— (1963). *The English Church, 1000–1066.* London: Longmans.
—— (1970). *Edward the Confessor.* London: Eyre and Spottiswoode.
Barnes, R., ed. (1847). *Liber Pontificalis of Edmund Lacy, Bishop of Exeter: a Manuscript of the Fourteenth Century.* Exeter: W. Roberts.
Bedos-Rezak, B. (1988). Women, Seals and Power in Medieval France, 1150–1350. In *Women and Power in Medieval France*, eds. M. Erler, M. Kowaleski. Athens, GA: University of Georgia Press.
—— (1990). Medieval Women in French Sigillographic Sources. In *Medieval Women and the Sources of Medieval History*, ed. J. Rosenthal, Athens, GA: University of Georgia Press.
Beretta, A. Ballesteros (1984 [1963]). *Alfonso X el Sabio.* Barcelona: El Albir.
Binski, Paul (1986). *The Painted Chamber at Westminster.* London.
—— (1990). Reflections on *La Estoire de Saint Aedward le rei*: hagiography and kingship in thirteenth century England. *Journal of Medieval History* 16, 333–50.
Birch, W. de Gray (1887–1900). *Catalogue of Seals in the Department of Manuscripts in the British Museum.* 6 vols. London: The British Museum.
Blackley, F. D. (1980). Isabella of France, Queen of England (1308–1358), and the late medieval cult of the dead. *Canadian Journal of History* 15, 23–47.
Bleeker, C. J. (1959). The Position of the Queen in Ancient Egypt. In *The Sacral Kingship: Contributions to the Central Theme of the VIIIth International Congress for the History of Religions (Rome, April 1955)*, 261–68. Leiden: Brill.
Borenius, T. (1943). The Cycle of Images in the Palaces and Castles of Henry III. *Journal of the Warburg and Courtauld Institutes* 6, 40–50.
Borgnet, A. and E. Borgnet, eds. (1890–99). *D. Alberti Magni . . . Opera Omnia.* 38 vols. Paris: Louis Vivès.
Bouman, C. A. (1957). *Sacring and Crowning: The Develop-ment of the Latin Ritual for the Anointing of Kings and the Coronation of an Emperor before the Eleventh Century.* Groningen: J. B. Wolters.
Brückmann, J. J. (1964). *English Coronations 1216–1308: The Edition of Coronation Ordines.* Diss., University of Toronto.
Byerly, B. and C. R. (1977). *Records of the Wardrobe and Household, 1285–1286.* London: HMSO.

—— (1986). *Records of the Wardrobe and Household, 1286–1290*. London: HMSO.

Bynum, C. W. (1987). *Holy Feast and Holy Fast: The Religious Significance of Food to Medieval Women*. Berkeley: University of California Press.

Cal. Close Rolls 1234–1237 (1909). London: HMSO.

Cal. Close Rolls 1254–1256 (1931). London: HMSO.

Cal. Close Rolls 1381–1385 (1920). London: HMSO.

Cal. Liberate Rolls, IV (1960). London: HMSO.

Cal. Patent Rolls 1232–1247 (1906). London: HMSO.

Cannadine, D. (1981). The Context, Performance and Meaning of Ritual: The British Monarchy and the "Invention of Tradition," in *The Invention of Tradition*, eds. E. Hobsbawm, T. Ranger, 101–64. Cambridge: CUP.

Chevalier, C. U. (1900). *Martyrologe, Calendrier, Ordinaires et Prosaires de la Métropole de Reims (viiie-xiiie siècles)*. Paris.

Collier, J. F. (1974). Women in Politics. In Rosaldo and Lamphere, pp. 89–96.

Colvin, H. M., R. A. Brown and A. J. Taylor (1963). *The History of the King's Works, I: The Middle Ages*. 2 vols. London: HMSO.

Cook, G. H. (1963). *Medieval Chantries and Chantry Chapels*. 2nd ed. London: Phoenix House.

Cutler, K. E. (1973). Edith, Queen of England, 1045–1066. *Mediaeval Studies* 25, 222–31.

De Saxonia, Conradus O.F.M. (1975). *Speculum seu Salutatio Beatae Mariae Virginis ac Sermones Mariani*, ed. P. de Alcantara Martinez O.F.M. Bibliotheca Franciscana Ascetica Medii Aevi, 11. Grottaferrata: Collegium S. Bonaventurae.

Deshman, R. (1988). *Benedictus Monarcha et Monachus: Early Medieval Ruler Theology and the Anglo-Saxon Reform*. *Frühmittelalterliche Studien* 22, 204–40.

Dewick, E. S. (1899). *The Coronation Book of Charles V, King of France (Cottonian MS Tiberius B VIII)*. Henry Bradshaw Society 16. London.

Duby, Georges (1981). *The Age of the Cathedrals*, trans. E. Levieux, B. Thompson. Chicago: University of Chicago Press.

—— (1983). *The Knight, the Lady and the Priest: The Making of Modern Marriage in Medieval France*, trans. Barbara Bray. New York: Pantheon Books.

Ehrlich, L. (1921). *Proceedings against the Crown, 1216–1377*. Oxford: Clarendon Press.

Geertz, C. (1985). Centers, Kings and Charisma: Reflections on the Symbolics of Power. In *Rites of Power: Symbolism, Ritual and Politics Since the Middle Ages*, ed. S. Wilentz, 13–38. Philadelphia: University of Pennsylvania Press.

Gold, Penny Schine (1985). *The Lady and the Virgin: Image, Attitude and Experience in Twelfth-Century France.* Chicago: University of Chicago Press.

Gurney, O. R. (1958). Hittite Kingship. In *Myth, Ritual and Kingship: Essays on the Theory and Practice of Kingship in the Ancient Near East and in Israel,* ed. S. H. Hooke, pp. 105–21. Oxford: Clarendon Press.

Hall, E. (1970 [1550]). *The Union of the two Noble Families of Lancaster and York.* Menston: Scolar Press.

Hall, H. (1896). *Red Book of the Exchequer.* 3 vols. Rolls series 99. London.

Hesbert, R.-J., ed. (1963–70). *Corpus Antiphonalium Officii.* 6 vols. Rome: Herder.

Hingeston, F. C., ed. (1858). *Johannis Capgrave Liber de Illustribus Henricis.* Rolls series 7. London.

Hope, W. H. St. John (1907). On the Funeral Effigies of the Kings and Queens of England, with specific reference to those in the Abbey Church of Westminster. *Archaeologia* 60.ii, 517–70.

Huneycutt, L. (forthcoming). Intercession and the High-Medieval Queen: The *Esther* Topos. In papers from "Power of the Weak?"; see under Parsons.

Jackson, R. (1984). *Vive le Roi! A History of the French Coronation from Charles V to Charles X.* Chapel Hill: University of North Carolina Press.

Johnson, J. R. (1961). The Tree of Jesse Window of Chartres: *Laudes Regiae. Speculum* 36, 1–22.

Kantorowicz, Ernst H. (1965). The Carolingian King in the Bible of San Paolo fuori le Mura. In *Selected Studies by Ernst H. Kantorowicz,* eds. M. Cherniavsky, R. Giesey, pp. 82–94. Locust Valley, NJ: J. J. Augustin.

Kaufmann, Martin (n.d.). Pictorial Hagiography and the Politics of Kingship. Paper presented at Twenty-Fifth International Congress on Medieval Studies, Kalamazoo, 12 May 1990.

Kertzer, D. I. (1988). *Ritual, Politics and Power.* New Haven: Yale University Press.

Lamphere, L. (1974). Strategies, Cooperation and Conflict among Women in Domestic Groups. In Rosaldo and Lamphere, pp. 97–112.

Leach, E. (1969). *Genesis as Myth and Other Essays.* London: Cape.

Legg, J. W. (1902). *Three Coronation Orders.* Henry Bradshaw Society 19.

Legg, L. G. W. (1901). *English Coronation Records.* Westminster: A. Constable.

Lehmann-Brockhaus, O. (1955–60). *Lateinische Schriftquellen zur Kunst in England, Wales und Schottland.* 5 vols. Munich: Prestel.

Luard, H., ed. (1861). *Roberti Grosseteste Epistolae*. Rolls series 25. London

——, ed. (1864–69). *Annales Prioratus de Dunstaplia*. In *Annales Monastici*, iii. 5 vols. Rolls series 36. London.

——, ed. (1890). *Flores historiarum*. 3 vols. Rolls series 95. London.

Martène, E. (1736–37). *De Antiquis Ecclesiae Ritibus Libri*. 2nd ed., 4 vols. Antwerp: J.-B. de la Bry.

Maskell, W., ed. (1847). *Monumenta ritualia ecclesiae Anglicanae, or occasional offices of the Church of England according to the ancient use of Salisbury*. 3 vols. Oxford: Clarendon Press.

Miles, M. (1985). *Image as Insight: Visual Understanding in Western Christianity and Secular Culture*. Boston: Beacon.

Musset, L. (1967). *Les actes de Guillaume le Conquérant et de la reine Mathilde pour les abbayes Caennaises*. Caen.

Nelson, J. L. (1977). Inauguration Rituals. In *Early Medieval Kingship*, eds. P. H. Sawyer, I. N. Wood, pp. 50–71. Leeds: Leeds University Press.

Owst, G. R. (1961). *Literature and Pulpit in Medieval England: A Neglected Chapter in the History of English Letters and of the English People*. Cambridge: CUP.

Paris, Matthew (1872–84). *Chronica Majora*, ed. H. Luard. 7 vols. Rolls series 57. London.

Parsons, J. C. (forthcoming). Esther's Eclipse? The Queen's Intercession in Thirteenth-Century England. In papers from "Power of the Weak? The Authority and Influence of Medieval Women," Annual Conference at the Centre for Medieval Studies, University of Toronto, February 1990.

—— (1984). The Year of Eleanor of Castile's Birth, and her Children by Edward I. *Mediaeval Studies* 46, 245–65.

Rawcliffe, C. (1987). Richard, Duke of York, the King's "obeisant liegeman": a new source for the Protectorates of 1454 and 1455. *Bulletin of the Institute of Historical Research* 60, 232–39.

Richardson, H. G. (1960). The Coronation in Medieval England: The Evolution of the Office and the Oath. *Traditio* 16, 111–202.

Riley, H. T., ed. (1865). *Opus chronicorum. In Johannis de Trokelowe et Henrici de Blaneford Chronica et Annales*. Rolls series 28.iii. London.

——, ed. (1867–69). *Gesta Abbatum Sancti Albani*. 2 vols. Rolls series 28. iv. London.

Robinson, J. A. (1909). *The History of Westminster Abbey by John Flete*. Cambridge: CUP.

Rosaldo, M. Z. (1974). Woman, Culture and Society: A Theoretical Overview. In Rosaldo and Lamphere, 17–42.

Rosaldo, M. Z. and L. Lamphere (1974). *Woman, Culture and Society*. Stanford: Stanford University Press.

St Laurence, Richard of (1890–99). *De Laudibus Beatae Mariae Virginis Libri XII*. In A. and E. Borgnet, vol. 36, pp. 1–841.

Sherman, C. R. (1977). The Queen in Charles V's "Coronation Book": Jeanne de Bourbon and the "Ordo ad Reginam Benedicendam." *Viator* 8, 255–98.

Smith, G. (1935). *The Coronation of Elizabeth Woodville, Queen Consort of Edward IV, on May 26th, 1465*. London: Ellis.

Stafford, Pauline (1983). *Queens, Concubines and Dowagers: The King's Wife in the Early Middle Ages*. Athens, GA: University of Georgia Press.

Staniland, K. (1987). Royal Entry into the World. In *England in the Fifteenth Century: Proceedings of the 1986 Harlaxton Symposium*, ed. D. Williams, pp. 297–313. Woodbridge, Suffolk: Boydell and Brewer.

Stapleton, T., ed. (1846). *Liber de Antiquis Legibus*. Camden Society, 34. London.

Stevenson, W. H. (1959 [1904]). *Asser's Life of King Alfred*. Oxford: Clarendon Press.

Stow, J. (1615). *Annales, or a Generall History of England*. London: Thomas Dawson.

Strickland, A. (1851). *Lives of the Queens of England*. 2nd ed. 8 vols. London: Hurst and Blackett.

Stubbs, W., ed. (1882–83). *Annales Londonienses*. In *Chronicles of the Reigns of Edward I and Edward II*. Rolls series 76. London.

Sutton, A. F. and P. W. Hammond, eds. (1983). *The Coronation of Richard III: The Extant Documents*. New York: St. Martin's Press.

Taylor, J. (1979). *Eva Perón: The Myths of a Woman*. Chicago.

Thomas, A. H. and I. D. Thornbury, eds. (1983 [1938]). *The Great Chronicle of London*. Gloucester: A. Sutton.

Turner, V. and E. (1978). *Image and Pilgrimage in Christian Culture: Anthropological Perspectives*. Oxford: Blackwell.

Ullman, W., ed. (1961). *Liber regie capelle: A Manuscript in the Biblioteca Publica, Evora*. Henry Bradshaw Society 92. London.

Vaughan, R. (1958). *Matthew Paris*. Cambridge: CUP.

Ward, P. L. (1939). The Coronation Ceremony in Medieval England. *Speculum* 14, 160–78.

Watson, A. (1934). *The Early Iconography of the Tree of Jesse*. Oxford: OUP.

Wright, Rosemary Muir (1986). The Iconography of the Coronation of the Virgin. In *Kingship*, ed. Emily Lyle (*Cosmos* 2, 53–82).

LOUISE OLGA FRADENBURG

Sovereign Love: The Wedding of Margaret Tudor and James IV of Scotland

Sovereigns are characterized by a special richness both of bodily experience and of theatricality, and hence by a capacity for metaphor which allows movement between embodiment and disembodiment in a way forbidden to the subject. Because the sovereign "is" all things, the sovereign becomes the privileged site of surplus, of Being, of "superreality." Though sovereigns must stand for boundaries, justice, and reason, the power of predication I have just described can also turn the sovereign into a threat to boundaries, person and number. This relation to excess vivifies, but also imperils, purity, because if there is not enough ordinariness or "homogeneity" in the sovereign—if his or her link to the everyday and the merely real is cut altogether—the sovereign will seem to be excessive, too much, too "heterogeneous," not like us at all, and therefore foreign.[1]

Sovereigns thus must compose themselves as different from their subjects, but their subjects must nonetheless be able to identify with them. And the creation of bonds of reverence and of identification will be interdependent with the vibrancy and certainty of bodily experience. As Kristeva writes in her commentary on the Song of Songs (1987: 90):

> Supreme authority, be it royal or divine, can be loved as flesh while remaining essentially inaccessible; the intensity of love comes precisely from that combination of received jouissance and taboo, from a basic separation that nevertheless unites.

"Basic separation," distance, absence, the disembodied quality of our objects of belief—in short, lack—is not necessarily given, nor is it a liability for a sovereign: the sovereign is created as distant, and the distance allows him or her to be desired in a particular way, as Ideal, as Extraordinary. And yet the distance of the ideal nonetheless requires "corporealization," "sensualization," if the Extraordinary is to have fully at his or her disposal a power of conviction, a reality so beyond question that it becomes superreality. This experience I will call "sovereign love." Sovereign love is a means of creating, and shaping the creativity of, desire or aspiration; but sovereign love can thereby shape desire so that its creativity, its economically and socially productive power, may be laid open to interference, even forestalled. The sovereign's mixing of lack and fullness—whereby the sovereign may be desired as inaccessible ideal, *and* loved as flesh—enables the subject to feel simultaneously at one with, and free of, power. The mutuality of lack and fulfillment that characterizes sovereign love thus assists the experiential transformation of what Pierre Bourdieu calls "coerced relations" into elective and reciprocal ones (1977: 171).

In the Song of Songs, the king's special entitlement to the body of the world—which is to say, materially speaking, his wealth—is prepared for through an eroticization of the world's body. As in later pastoral, an affective expansionism is put into place; the body of the world is ensouled with the soul of a lover, the lover's soul embodied with the body of the world.[2] And the king is posited as one who loves: the body of the world is borrowed to substantiate the king's love for his people, his free choice of them, their election, absurd because beyond merit, beyond exchange.[3] Just so in St. Bernard's commentary on the Song of Songs, the love of the Shulammite for Solomon cannot be economized: "this is what a bride is, whoever she is; the possessions and hope of a bride are a single love."[4]

Aspiration, inequities of distribution, differences of power and wealth, disappear into the infinite lack of mirrored yearning; the Shulammite may work in the vineyards or among the flocks, but the king, too, "is" a shepherd. Aspiration is managed by images of fulfillment, and the limits set to aspiration are idealized and re-represented as freedom. The sovereign risks exposure in order to achieve an appearance of intimacy, of reciprocity—what Bourdieu calls the "*symbolic* violence" of deceptively elective relations (1977: 237 n. 47). Thus the involuntary elements of the subject's surrender to the monarch's "power of alteration" (Scarry 1985) can, through an apparent exchange of confidences, be re-fashioned as free, as willed, in short as love.

We might usefully consider sovereignty's simultaneous accessibility and inaccessibility with regard to Victor Turner's opposition between "communitas" and "hierarchy": "hierarchy," or "structure," privileges difference of rank, heterogeneity, inequality; "communitas" privileges totality, homogeneity, equality, identity.[5] The sovereign must represent not only the apex of "structure"; he must also represent the "total community," its "territory" and its "resources" (Turner 1977: 98). Communitarian ritual creates and expresses affective and conceptual unities—like nation, people— that seem larger, more inclusive, than structural specifications like monarchy, estates, dynasty, lineage. "Liminal" groups—that is, groups (women, for example) largely excluded from official structures of power and wealth—may threaten, in fact or in fantasy, the interior unity of families, lineages, classes. But they can serve also to embody principles of wholeness and unity, because the very "outsideness" of the liminal to particularized hierarchical interests can make the liminal seem "above" or "beyond" such interests (1977: 99–100, 114, 166–68). Communitarian experience—understood here not as natural or inevitable to social existence, but as an artificed set of strategic opportunities—becomes a means whereby the resources that have been excluded or "liminalized" by particular structures, resources of risk, change, danger, newness, unthinkability, may be tapped. It thereby obscures constraint, and seems to restore the "elective" quality of coerced relations. Communitas is one of the means by which power makes love: it is the (ritual) refashioning of captivation as an experience of freedom, a remaking of the subject to enable identification with, and idealization of, an authority experienced as liberating and unifying rather than repressive and divisive; and it is a suspending of statuses or ranks to which the subject might aspire, of futures into which the subject might project his or her designs.[6] As just such a redemption of the *difference* between sovereign and subject, communitas is essential to sovereign love: it captures productive desire *for* hierarchy.

The power of marriage to create lasting bonds, and thereby new configurations of personhood—to create unities where before there were differences—is a power much admired by sovereigns. Because of their shared concern with the creation of unities and of distinctions, sovereignty and marriage can articulate for each other the concept of a relation of enduring obligation, enduring and obligatory *because* based on choice: on consensual love. For queens, the link between marriage and sovereignty is specially intense, since it is usually by means of the former that they achieve the latter—a transformation which, as for the Shulammite in the Song of Songs, seems always to involve the domestication of a certain strangeness.[7] As I suggest in the "Introduction," queens often seem to present communitarian solutions to problems of sovereignty.[8] For, in contrast to kings, queens usually both exemplify sovereignty *and* are subject to it; queens are simultaneously inside and outside "structure." Their differenced identity works in one further way: most queens come to an "inside" from an "outside," and bear something of the outside with them. As such, they represent a distance—real and symbolic—that has, ideally, been traversed. The queen's power to alter identity can serve purposes like unification; this is one reason why wedding pageantry often stresses communitarian themes. Queens can, as Pauline Stafford has argued, come to represent the unity achieved through alliance, and at the same time may "personify" rivalries, "old grievances."[9] The "liminality" or interstitiality of queens— their foreignness and their femaleness—is the source of their particularly intense association with the concepts both of division and of unity ("Introduction": 5). Thus queens can moreover enable the distance, disembodiment, transcendence of kingship— and thereby its difference from its subjects, its heterogeneity—by taking on the risks, bearing the burdens, but also reaping the particular rewards of presence, immediacy, accessibility. Queenship may make accessible the body of sovereignty, so that sovereignty may be "loved in the flesh," while its circulation is limited and its extraordinary character preserved. In turn, the affective fusion of "woman" with "nation" or "land" or "people" made possible by the figure of the queen enables the eroticization, and hence containment, of the subject's ambitions regarding nation, land, people.

Through marriage the queen is anointed, set apart from other women, at once made and recognized as extraordinary; it is also through marriage that she becomes part of the "people" she will rule, and which in many cases she will come to symbolize, again partly *because* of the aura of strangeness that never completely leaves her. She thus becomes the paradigm of the subject's impossible identification with the sovereign. For woman, subject, nation, should not exclusively be imagined as "the Other" to the sovereign: woman, subject, nation, must in relation to the king be theorized both as sovereign Subject *and* object, both capable of choice *and* bound, made captive, by consent; and it follows that the kind of bond sought by sovereigns with their subjects will not necessarily be experienced as the kind of bond enjoyed by the owner of a possession, that is, by someone fixed "securely," at least in his mind, in the position of sovereign Subject, capable of enjoying the object of his possession. Rather, it is the kind of bond that involves, and risks, a mixture of difference and sameness, equality and inequality; it is the kind of bond that seeks love, that must have an answer, and hence must take place between beings capable of answering, hence capable of sovereignty, hence distinguishable from each other, though only for those moments when questions and answers are ritually articulated. Hence, again, though the safety of the sovereign's right of possession in woman, subject, nation, is what is finally at stake, sovereignty stands to lose but also to gain most if this relation is experienced subjectively, in the form of fidelity; that is, if an often brutal relation of social and economic "necessity" is refigured as volitional.

As a version of the sensuous ideality of sovereign love, marriage is, in Kristeva's terms, "legalized passion" (1987: 90, 227). Marriage is a site of crossover, between change and fixity, identity and difference, freedom and constraint, pleasure and sacrifice. Marriage impels the crossing of thresholds, movement from the familiar to the strange, union with new worlds: the refiguration and extension of bonds and loyalties; even, as in sovereignty, the renumbering of personhood (the husband's multiplies, the wife's "sinks").[10] Precisely because of the adventurousness, even at times the imperial expansiveness, of marriage—particularly of what Bourdieu calls "extraordinary" political marriage—marriage has the potential to threaten with change the stability of the very social and political structures it works to extend.[11] The identificatory power of marriage—its capacity to undo distinctions, to equal the unequal—is bound up with the function of marriage as a site of pleasure and law, sexual desire and procreative labor, adventure and security.

In 1502, the Peace of Glasgow—the first treaty of "perpetual" peace between Scotland and England since 1328—was concluded with the treaty of marriage between Margaret Tudor and James IV. The Peace was sealed—and indeed lasted until Henry VII's death in 1509—by the spectacular ceremonies of the coronation and wedding in 1503. These events inaugurated a period of roughly a quarter century during which brother and sister Tudors ruled both England and Scotland. "From 1509 until 1516," writes Ranald Nicholson, "James's queen [Margaret] was Henry [VIII's] heir presumptive," a fact which she seems to have celebrated by giving "her second son, Arthur (born in 1509 only to die in 1510) the name once borne by Henry VIII's elder brother, a name that was 'British' rather than Scottish or English" (1974: 595). It was in fact to be Margaret's son James who would carry on the Stewart dynasty, and whose grandson, James VI of Scotland, would later become James I of England.

Yet despite these interesting consequences, historians have not always granted the Peace of Glasgow, and the marriage which crowned it, very much significance; given that conflict between Scotland and England continued drearily and sometimes violently throughout the rest of the sixteenth century, it has been tempting to some to regard the alliance as superficial or short-lived in its effects and to discount the possibility that the imaginative work performed by it may have refigured the future despite, or perhaps even because of, unintended or scattered effects.[12] Though it is clear that both hindsight and contemporary politics were at work in the weight given to the marriage of James IV and Margaret Tudor by a number of later commentators, it is at least worth remembering that, according to Bishop Leslie, Henry VII reassured those counselors opposed to the marriage alliance because they feared it might someday put a Scottish king on the throne of England by arguing that, if Margaret succeeded to the throne, England would profit rather than lose by it: for "the les cumis to the incres of the mair, Scotland wil cum till Jngland, and nocht Jngland to Scotland."[13]

Leslie supported the succession of Mary Stewart to the throne of England, so perhaps his story should be regarded as too interested to be clarifying; given, too, that James IV's father, James III, had long pursued rapprochement with England, the alliance might also seem less surprising an idea than it might otherwise have done. But James III's failure to make a pro-English policy acceptable to his nobility was one of the chief disasters of his reign; and it is worthy of note that his son, who joined the rebellion against him, eventually adopted rather than rejected the policy of peace with England that must have seemed, at the time at any rate, to have helped cost his father his throne.[14] It might in fact be said that the practical difficulties of honouring the alliance and the history of "Anglophobia" preceding it are exactly what made the alliance an extraordinary and adventurous one. However self-evidently beneficial an alliance between England and Scotland might, moreover, have seemed to politically judicious counselors like Bishop Elphinstone, it cannot have failed to present the appearance of enormous risk: a risk symbolized by the very fact that Margaret's chief escort, the Earl of Surrey, would later be responsible for the destruction of the Scottish forces at Flodden; a risk for which James IV's well-documented encouragement of a self-conscious Scottish nationalism might even be read as talismanic.[15] A thoroughgoing transformation of Scotland's relationship to the outside world must have seemed to have been at stake, for the alliance suspended ties of loyalty to France that were, at least in the language of diplomacy, immemorial, however uneven in practice; and it promised to link two kingdoms whose enmity was as longstanding and well-guarded, even as well-loved, as it is possible for an enmity to be.

Bourdieu has argued that extraordinary marriage—the kind of marriage that makes, and therefore risks, prestige—is an effect of distance; and the distances that had to be crossed in order to bring about the Peace of Glasgow were considerable. That the marriage was "extraordinary" indeed was probably not lost on contemporaries. Henry VII's sense of his daughter's potential destiny may explain why Margaret's baptism was celebrated on St. Andrew's day (November 30), and why her christening took place in the church near Westminster Abbey dedicated to St. Margaret, Queen of Scotland (Mackie 1958: 105; Strickland 1859: 2–3). Henry VII's elaborate preparations for the wedding may also have included a gift of the Book of Hours in which St. Margaret—who, as Buchanan points out, "had also been reared as an English princess"—figures prominently.[16] The identification of Margaret Tudor with her extraordinary predecessor may, moreover, have had some lasting power for Margaret's, and Scotland's, understanding of her role; St. Margaret, for centuries a potent icon in the myth-making of Scotland, received important attention in the late fifteenth and early sixteenth centuries, a development for which Margaret Tudor may have been partly responsible.[17]

The wedding preparations ongoing in Scotland in 1502 included not only arrangements for Margaret's reception in the south and for the tourneying that was to play an important part in the wedding festivities, but also the wardrobing of the entire court, hangings for Margaret's bed of state, the making of her crown, the refurbishing of royal residences, and the building of an entirely new palace in Edinburgh—Holyrood—for the occasion (Mackie 1958: 102–3; *LHTA* 2: liii–lxxiii). "Even the prodigal king," writes Mackie, "became alarmed at the costliness of the preparations for the marriage. He resolved to rectify his financial position, not by cutting down his expenditure, but by discovering the philosopher's stone" (Mackie 1958: 103). It was indeed at this time that James IV's extensive patronage of alchemical research began; the pages of the Treasurer's Accounts are littered with disbursements to "quinta essencia" (*LHTA* 2: lxxiii–lxxix; see also Fradenburg 1991: 308 n. 21). According to Macfarlane, moreover, the Accounts suggest that the wedding, which by Scottish standards was outrageously expensive, inaugurated a new financial expansionism which was to continue throughout the rest of James's reign (Macfarlane 1985: 419; cf. Macdougall 1989: 147, 155).

One of the purposes of the court festival is to represent the economic power of the prince as a form of supernatural intervention, indeed a kind of alchemy, a "power of alteration"; and James's new interest in alchemy, his new embrace of expensive display, suggest that a powerful sense of change, of new vigor, had come upon the monarch of Scotland. The festivities for his wedding were likely considered innovative, since nothing really like them had been seen in Scotland before.[18] They exploited extraordinary marriage as a means of articulating the ambitions of sovereignty and as a means of giving sovereignty its purchase on ambition: on newness, vitality, movement. On the occasion of Margaret's wedding, Tudor and Stewart ambitions with respect to European politics, and anxieties with respect to domestic unity, worked in concert to produce an apotheosis of union as the source of communal honor. But what is most distinctive about these festivities is not their intense exaltation of acts of union *per se*, but rather their exaltation of the changefulness, the transformative power, of acts of union.

It is easy enough to point out the real and apparent obstacles to the triumph of union at this time. For Henry, the threat of fragmentation took the form of Ireland, and of his own northern magnates; Buchanan notes that Margaret's bridal tour of the north of England was particularly intensive, and the north was the part of the country "where there had been most disaffection for the new monarchy" (Buchanan 1985: 18). For James IV the threat of fragmentation took the form of Gaelic Scotland and the Lordship of the Isles, and of the powerful southern magnates who formed his chief political base and were most in a position to do him harm. Lordship in the north of England and in the south of Scotland had depended for centuries on repeated, mimetic acts of border violence; a lasting peace might thus pacify lordship in more ways than one, but might, of course, as had happened with James III, enrage it. What would become of retaliation, of that apparently remunerative allegiance of the plunderer to the past? What futuristic economy, both of honor and of wealth, would succeed it? Would union in fact produce enough honor for "all"? Or would "all" so refigure difference that, as in Henry VII's formulation to his council and as in marital law, "the les [would come] to the incres of the mair"? Would Scotland end, in effect, by becoming the bride, not the husband, of England?

The treaty of 1502 thus linked two kings aware of the vulnerability of borderlines both within their kingdoms and without, who were willing to risk focus on those very borderlines in order to uphold for their kingdoms a powerful image of union, an image of the power of sovereignty to effect an extraordinary uniting of differences, an image, in fact, of sovereignty as constituted through its power so to alter. They strove to achieve at once, in a fashion and to a degree extraordinary in the history of relations between the two countries, the two goals to which, according to Bourdieu, marriage addresses itself: integration (security, sameness, the cohesion of the social order at any given time and throughout time) and alliance (adventure, difference, the expansion and transformation of the social order at any given time and throughout time). Henry and James strove, in fact, to make these two often contradictory goals coincide, so that the one would seem to depend completely on the other. It is not easy to make daring and safety, or aspiration and contentment, into simultaneous experiences, particularly when the enemy with whom one is risking one's safety, or perhaps even more importantly the enemy with respect to whom one is apparently giving up one's power to take risks, is in fact the old enemy. But since Henry and James were asking their borders to give up a centuries-old economy of honor based on hazard, it makes sense that they would seek to affirm the honor of risking identity through union and taking a chance on security.[19]

The quality of "exploit," of "prowess," which Bourdieu attributes to extraordinary marriage is expressed not only in the tourneying with which the marriage celebrations were punctuated throughout—a reminder that marriage and war function as two aspects of the sovereign power of alteration, however often they might be represented as opposites—but also in the statement that begins John Younge, Somerset Herald's description of Margaret's departure from England in the *Fyancells*.[20]

Younge writes:

> To the Exaltation of Noblesse shal be rehersed in thys littyl Treatys the Honor of the right noble Departinge owte of the Realme of Inglaund, of the right high and mighty, and the right excellent Princesse Margaret, by the Grace of God, Quene of Scotland. Also to th'Entent to comfort the Herts of Age for to here it, and to gyffe Coraige to the Yong to do thereafter in such Case to come: For sens the Hour of the said Departing, to the End of her Voyage, shal be written the Names of the Noblesse, after thyr Dignityz, Astats, and Degrees, that in this conveying were ordeined. The Gentylls after thyr Byrth, and the Meaner after thyr Place, and so of the others that shal be, to th' Entent that Ichon in his Right may be worshiped: For such valiant Spyrits desire after ther Deservyng, to have thereof Law[d]e, since all ther Thoughts have ben to doe Things to the Pleasure of the King, and to the Honor of her Majesty. Wherfor of ther Geftys and Maners during the sayd Voyage, togeder with those of them that apon the Marchers of the Lordschips shal be founden, as well

Spritualls and Temporalls, thorough the said Realme of
Inglaund, till the Comyng of the Intryng of the Realme of
Scotland, and since after, of the Nobles Dyds that to the sayd
Realme shal be doon, and of the Mettyngs in suche Forme ye
shall knowe, unto the extreame Conclusion of the vary noble
Mariage betwix the King of the Scotts and the sayd Quene. In
hop that the same be concluded, made, and solempnized, to
the Lawde of God, and of the two Realmes, and bee to the
Pleasur of all Christyns. (265)

Margaret's departure, says Younge, itself has "Honor": through a
grandeur of movement, through expansive narrative reach ("unto
the extreame Conclusion") and inclusiveness ("The Gentylls after
thyr Byrth, and the Meaner after thyr Place"), Margaret's
"Departinge" expresses that extraordinariness, that absolute
heterogeneity which is the sovereign form of honor. Through its
expansiveness, moreover, the "Departinge" infuses structure ("after
thyr Byrth," "after thyr Place") with communitas; the "Noblesse"
of Margaret's movements is brought out by the vastness and
variety of her entourage—those who accompany her, those who
greet her at the borders, "Spritualls" as well as "Temporalls."
The exemplary function of the "Departinge" must be located here:
in its melding together of hierarchy and communitas, of heterogeneity and homogeneity, so that the "excellent"—the very best—
can come to seem representative, inclusive. By its very unusualness,
this marriage will conjoin "all"; all have a part to play, the honor
of all is at stake, all shall participate in the "Lawde" of "the two
Realmes," of God; the *Fyancells* itself shall "bee to the Pleasur
of all Christyns," and will inspirit the future—the "Yong"—with
the "Coraige . . . to do thereafter in such Case to come." Political
marriages, as Bourdieu notes, cannot be repeated, because the
alliance is devalued if it is common; but Younge's description of
Margaret's departure imagines a capacity for self-transformation
which—*because* it is the "Departinge" of such an excellent
princess—extends, in turn, not only to her people, but also to the
people "to come." The *Fyancells* asserts that the daring of
Margaret's journey—of her consent, her choice, her adventure—
is, and will be, everyone's daring.

   That daring is recapitulated by the narrative reach of the
Fyancells, achieved not so much through the actual length of the
work—it is not a very long work—but through its continuous
elaboration of beginnings and endings, meetings and greetings,
departures and farewells, whereby the "distance symbolic of
prestige" is given amplitude, play. Thus, for example, Dorset,
Derby and Essex convey Margaret from Colieweston "by the

Space of one Mylle, and after they toke Licence in kissing her"
(266); and then they returned to Colieweston. Movement is
temporalized, time is made into movement; timing and gesture are
the essence of such pageants because through them loyalties are
shifted, bonds loosened and tied, differences confronted and
conjoined, distances crossed. Borders are intensely articulated: at
important points, such as the crossing into Scotland, Margaret is
conveyed not on her horse but on her litter, the means and
gestures of conveyance themselves richly elaborated and decorated;
the crossing into Scotland is given a detailed and lengthy
description—it is specially important to know who greets Margaret
there (the Archbishop of Glasgow), and who leaves her there (the
Earl of Northumberland).[21] The *Fyancells* always notes how far
citizens have emerged from their places of residence in order to
greet Margaret: distance is calibrated with respect to boundaries,
placement and displacement (268–69). The movements of the
inhabitants of the places visited by Margaret embody greeting's
habit, in welcoming, of first reaching out, displacing itself.
Margaret's mobility thus seeks union through the acquisition of
knowledge: parts of the country seem to emerge from anonymity
to join for a time in the awareness of the entourage that represents
and is crossing through the whole, before returning, transformed,
to homes now more securely in synecdochal relation to the
community of the realm (269).

In extraordinary marriage as in the tournament and the
aristocratic funeral, the heralds preside over the dangerous
crossings, the confrontations, that create honor: with the Earl of
Northumberland, for example, is "Northumberland Harault,"
"arayed of his said Liveray of Velvet, berring hys Cotte, sens the
mettyng tyll to hys Departyng, thorough all the Entryng and Yssye
of good Townes and Citez" (272); and of course there is Somerset
Herald himself, author of the *Fyancells*. In the *Fyancells*,
transition is ritualized to a degree as extraordinary as are the risks
involved; the *Fyancells* dedicates itself to the celebration of
rupture, discontinuity, change, without which honor could not
enact itself—even as it dedicates itself to the celebration of the
continuity and identity wherein honor, once tested, argues that it
has always resided. Younge's narrative moves between vulnerability and invulnerability, risk and protection. Controlling the
ceaseless ebb and flow of particular persons and places in the
Fyancells is rhythm itself: in different places, the same kinds of
places (bridges, gates), the same kinds of gestures (kissing the
cross), the same responses ("it was a fayr Sight for to se") are
repeated, just as Margaret's voice seems entirely scripted. The

multitudes themselves appear regularly, in each place, in "so grett Nombre." To come out, to come forward, to greet, is to consent to be bonded. But to come out, to come forward, to greet, is also to risk the limelight; the commons are articulated and, like lordship, given borderlines to cross and confront, only joining in greeting rather than in combat. To be named, to emerge from the communitarian multitudinousness of many places, "many Lordes," "So grett nombre," has in the *Fyancells* something of the same force as the emergence of the warrior from the anonymous chaos of battle into single combat, as the emergence of the bride—a movement anticipated repeatedly, insistently, throughout the royal progress—from obscurity into brilliant splendor, "cronned with a varey ryche Cronne of Gold garnished with Pierrery and Perles" (292): the epiphanic emergence of warrior and bride are made to coincide in the consensual poetics of the *Fyancells*.

At Colieweston, then, Henry VII made Margaret "to bee convayed vary nobelly out of his sayd Realme; as more playnly shal be here folowing remembred, toward the right high and mighty and right excellent Prince Jamys, by the Grace of God, Kyng of Scotys, in following the good Luffe, fraternall Dilleccion, and Intelligence of Maryage betwix hym and the saide Quene" (255–56). As in the Song of Songs, love is posited as the force that issues in movement in the *Fyancells*; the "Departinge" is an impressive instance of the placements and displacements, embodyings and disembodyings, of sovereign love. Roy Strong remarks that the royal entry was "the most public" of all forms of spectacle (Strong 1973: 23); and this publicity—this unusual accessibility of sovereign, on the one hand, and massed populace on the other—is enhanced when royal entry is associated with royal marriage. But while Margaret's progress is accordingly inclusive and ritualized, its purpose is the delectation of parting and change—of breaking with the past, of entering a new life, a new world, and, for James as well as for Margaret, the onset of a newly potent "maturity," i.e. an official sexuality and fertility.

That, in Scotland, marriage marked a change not just in the life of a king but in his power to practice rule is suggested by the experience of James IV's own father, James III, when, during his minority, he took the occasion of his marriage to free himself from the control of the powerful Boyd family.[22] James IV had achieved adulthood and was in full possession of his powers at the time of his marriage, but the transformation wrought by the marriage in his habits of expenditure and display seems, as we have noted, to indicate a new reach, a new expansiveness, for the crown. This new expansiveness is also displayed in the marriage celebrations themselves, the ritual of holding state immediately after the wedding, and James's belting of forty-one knights and creation of three new earls (Arran, Montrose and Glencairn) in the queen's honor. Moreover, James's many and notorious promiscuities appear to have caused and perhaps made him vulnerable to domestic political conflict and intrigue; what was needed was "distant," glorious marriage—not the infighting of the endogamous impulse—and the legitimate heirs produced thereby. James did not, as did Henry VII, have before him the task of certifying a new dynasty; he nonetheless had "to set his own [dynastic] house in order," though he never renounced his unofficial lovers.[23]

And while the marriage of James and Margaret made transition extraordinarily public, in doing so it made public intimacy itself; James and Margaret emerge as newly, extraordinarily, visible, but one aspect of this emergence is precisely their entitlement to a dramatized obscurity and privacy.

Thus, not surprisingly, the moment when James and Margaret actually make love is, in the *Fyancells*, unrepresentable, but Younge draws attention both to it and to its unrepresentability. He writes of the wedding night that "the Kinge had the Qwene aparte, and they went togeder. God by his grace will hold them in long Prosperitye. At Even grett Numbre of Fyers wer maid thorough the Towne of Edenbowrgh" (296). It is obvious enough that what is at stake here is the protection of the paradoxicality through which sovereignty tries to construct itself, in this case for the gaze of the spectator whose voyeurism is solicited: sovereignty must be at once divinized, but also fully human; it is disembodied at one of its moments of greatest embodiment. But the patterning of publicity with intimacy runs throughout the *Fyancells*, and one of its chief artists in this regard was, Younge would have us believe, the king himself.

At the first meeting of Margaret and James, which took place in Dalkeith during a four-day lull preparatory to the entry into Edinburgh, the king and queen "maid grett Reverences the one to the tother, his Hed being bare, and they kyssed togeder, and in lykwys kyssed the Ladyes, and others also. And he in especiall welcomed the Erl of Surrey varey hertly" (283). But this spectacle of generalized greeting is immediately succeeded by a moment of apparent privacy, a moment that appears to be chosen, unscripted, unregulated, which therefore has as one of its purposes the singling out of the chosen ones: "Then the Quene and he went asyd and commoned togeder by long Space" (283). They are, of course, being watched; it is a theatricalization of set-apartness. But while Younge will tell us how they looked and what seemed to be going on ("She held good Manere, and he bare heded during the Tym, and many Courteysyes passed"), he will not, apparently because he cannot, give us details. At this moment when they first appear together before us, they seem to disappear, and they are meant to arouse our voyeuristic curiosity.

On the next day, the king makes what Buchanan describes as a "surprise visit": the Queen had lost her horses in a stable fire the night before, and a retinue including the Archbishops of York and Glasgow, the Bishop of Durham, the Earl of Surrey and the Earl of Bothwell set out "Att foure of the Clok, after Dynner," to meet the king, who was coming to comfort the queen (283). But

> The Kynge flyinge as the Bird that syks hyr Pray, tuke other Waye, and cam prively to the said Castell, and entred within the Chammer with a small Company, wher he founde the Qwene playinge at the Cardes. At the Entrynge, the Qwene avaunced hyr toward hym in receyvinge hym varey gladly, and of Good Wyll kyssing hym, and after he gaffe Salut to the Ladyes and Company presente." (284)

Orchestrated and unspontaneous though this flight of the sovereign's desire may have been—weighed down by the conventionality, the repetition, of courtly love—the point of the king's gesture, and of the simile that accompanies it, is partly to surprise, to leaven the expected with the unexpected, however expected, in turn, his so doing. Through such gestures—gestures which at once transgress and celebrate the expected—the king must try to authenticate his desire, and authenticate himself as sovereign lover (cf. Buchanan 1985: 36). The very movements of James's body as described in the *Fyancells* remind us, too, that James was a notoriously restless, energetic, peripatetic king: after he leaves the queen, he "went to hys Horse, on whom he did lepe, without puttynge the Fowt within the Sterrop" (a feat which he will perform more than once during the course of the celebrations); "And the sayd Horse was a right fayr Courser, and incontynent the King sported, follow who myght" (284). We are supposed to feel the urgency, rapidity, unpredictability of his movements, his headlong love; we are to feel the vibrancy of his comings and goings, the vitality of his capacity to appear and disappear, hence, paradoxically, the certainty of his passionate being through its very uncertainty. Were it not so, he could not seem to love in a supremely honorable way; he could not prove himself as supreme in "Coraige," as sovereign lover.

The progress into Edinburgh thus has as one of its chief purposes the provision of a space and time for courtship. James must court Margaret because consent—which includes the possibility

that the beloved may not choose to love in return—provides for
marriage one of the elements of chance on which honor depends.
The rituals of royal courtship thus resemble the tournament in this
respect too: chance, art, timing, effort, risk, adventure must be
inscribed within them, the more so as the outcome is secure,
predetermined. That this is so is, once again, indicated by the
importance of tourneying within the marriage celebrations themselves, in particular by the tournament which interrupts the
progress on its way to Edinburgh—in which a knight "by Avantur"
robs another knight of his lady, and James intervenes, in the role
played by Theseus in *The Knight's Tale*, to settle their differences
(280).[24] Significantly, the issue of their conflict, at least as the
wronged knight presents it, is the power of "Owtrage" to break
secure bonds:

> they did well ther Devor, tyll that the Kynge cam hymselfe,
> the Qwene behynd hym, crying Paix, and caused them for to
> be departed. After this the King called them before hym, and
> demaunded them the Cause of ther Difference. The Caller
> sayd, Syre, he hath taken from me my Lady Paramour,
> whereof I was insurte of hyr by Faith. The Defender
> answered, Syre, I schall defend me ageynst hym apon this
> Cas: Then sayd the Kynge to the sayd Defender, brynge
> youre Frends, and ye schall be appoynted a Day for to agre
> you.

"[W]herof I was insurte of hyr by Faith": the point of this pageant
is, in part, to reintroduce—in a preordained way—the vulnerability
of faith, the effort needed to sustain and create it. The pageant is a
reminder of the createdness of the very bonds which sovereign
marriage must at the same time portray as destined, inevitable,
absolute. It reminds us that in love as in war it is not always easy to
distinguish oneself in a way so clear as to take on the form of
absolute certainty or extraordinariness; and it is meant to remind
us of the way in which that power of alteration—in this case, that
power of distinction—which is violence, can seem to dwell within
that power of alteration known as courtship: the king's persuasions
have brutal counterparts. The use of violence to distinguish the
lover is reworked in this pageant, as it is in Chaucer's *Knight's Tale*
and *Parliament of Fowls*, and in Dunbar's *The Thrissill and the
Rois*; in James's wedding tournament the sovereign emerges as he
who is supremely entitled to his bride, and therefore as he who
can exert the power of distinction over other aristocratic lovers.
But just before leaving that "wild" space in which, we are to
believe, anything could happen—in which courtship might fail, or
bonds be broken—for the paradise into which Edinburgh has been

transformed, Discord, and its power to unmake superreality, has been recalled. It has been recalled because sovereign love, as one of the works of honor, loves to be embattled. Through such means, a displaced activity is found for aspiration: that is, the activity of honor—the reward being, not chunks of territory or plundered livestock, but the love and faith of woman.

Finally, then, in the *Fyancells*, courtship and courtliness provide for a complex play of communitas and structure, in which the king's refusals to take precedence over Margaret put structure (distinction, heterogeneity) at risk, seeming, like his other courtship gestures, to depart from precedent, but at the same time displaying his power to effect union, thereby to overcome the difference not only of his subjects but even of his enemies. By such means are inequalities experientially, affectively transformed into equalities, and the "lesser"—so hopefully identified as Margaret—ritually merged with the great. Thus after the royal entry, the king and queen go to the abbey of Holyrood; the Archbishop of St. Andrews gives the king a relic to kiss, but he insists that Margaret kiss it first. The king refuses to kneel down first, "bot both togeder"; afterwards, "the King transported himself to the Pallais, thorough the Clostre, holdynge allwayes the Qwene by the Body, . . . tyll he had brought hyr within her Chammer" (290). At the banquet after the wedding, the king desires the heralds first to cry the largesse of the queen; "And because there was noe more then three Cotts of Armes of Inglaund, the Kyng wold not suffer more thenne thre of his awne"; and finally, the king refuses altogether to have his largesse cried, "saying, that it souffysed to cry hers" (295). Moreover, the very fact that James had Margaret crowned at the time of her entry may itself be evidence of the risks he was willing to take in celebrating the strength of royal ambition and choice.[25] By such means we are told that the powerful love of the Scottish king for the English queen has overcome the differences between them: "Wear me as a seal upon your heart, / as a seal upon your arm; / for love is strong as death."

At stake, however, is the domestication of England by Scotland: Margaret's differences—her Englishness, her femaleness—are represented as re-formed, through the identificatory power of love, for the power of Scotland's identity. The queen's consent to the courtship of the king models for the city of Edinburgh and for the nation of Scotland the creation of a "loving" and therefore pacified community, one which experiences its bond with its sovereign as a fantastic effect of freedom rather than of coercion. In the wedding of James and Margaret, queenship becomes paradigmatic of the difficult alchemy whereby the subject and the nation are made to act as sovereign—as capable of the consensual activity that will, paradoxically, bind subject and nation to the king.[26] But the pageantry of consent is not simply a celebration of unchanging monarchical order; it marks the presence of risk and change. When an English princess enters Scotland and becomes its Queen, the world is newer, and the "kingdoms old" are cast "Into another mold."[27]

NOTES

1 See Bataille 1985 on sovereignty as a coordination of the "homogeneous" (commensurability; productive, useful society) and the "heterogeneous" ("elements that are impossible to assimilate"): "since the king is the object in which homogeneous society has found its reason for being, maintaining this relationship demands that he conduct himself in such a way that the *homogeneous* society can exist *for him*"; but the king must also constitute himself as "a single *heterogeneous* object" (147).

2 On Elizabeth I's use of pastoral genres and motifs to turn "public relations of power into intimate relationships of love" see Montrose 1980: 155, 157, 158.

3 Kristeva's reading of the Song of Songs stresses "the immediate love of God for his people, a love that demands neither merit nor justification but is based on preference and choice" (1987: 84).

4 'Sponsae hic est, quia haec sponsa est, quaecumque est; sponsae res et spes unus est amor.' See Kelly 1975: 307, citing *Sermones super Cantica canticorum* 83.5.

5 Turner 1977: 106–7; see "Introduction": 4–5 and n. 4 for further discussion of Turner.

6 Cf. Kristeva's remarks, in her study of Celine, on the "attempt to substitute *another Law* . . . that would be absolute, full, and reassuring . . . for the constraining and frustrating symbolic one," for the deprivations and in-equities that complicate identifications with authority in stratified societies (1982: 178).

7 According to John Younge, Somerset Herald's account of Margaret Tudor's progress and wedding—an account commonly known as the *Fyancells*—Margaret Tudor was anointed during the celebration of her bridal Mass, "After wich the Kynge gaffe hyr the Septre in hyr Haund" (1770: 294). *Fyancells* is a somewhat misleading short title, since it refers only to one part of Younge's account of the rituals and festivities of Margaret's wedding, but since it is familiar to scholars of late medieval Scottish literature I have used it here. I thank Gordon Kipling for drawing my attention to the difficulties of Leland's text

and the College of Arms MS of Younge's narrative (College of Arms MS 1st M.13); see Kipling's "Textual Introduction" in Kipling 1990.

8 Pauline Stafford's important work on early medieval queenship is relevant here: she suggests that by managing patronage, early medieval queens preserved "the essential distance and impartiality of royalty" and thus "provided for the charisma of royalty itself" (1983: 99, 101, 107–9).

9 Stafford 1983: 191 suggests that "sympathetic identification and the exclusion of women from direct rivalry in the roles of men may create strong bonds between royal women and their sons or brothers the kings, and allow queens to become regents or chief counsellors in situations where kings have reason to fear other men." She also argues that the ideal of dynastic unity, and of the queen's role in creating that unity, is one whose potency derives in part from the "reality of family tension": "As intruders who are suspect, wielding power within the tensions and crosscurrents of the family but denied the expression of legitimate aggression, wives and queens are accused of domestic crimes, of encompassing their ends by covert means, by plots, poison and witchcraft" (1983: 29, 46).

10 G. Campbell Paton, writing on the *ius mariti* as it is developed in the medieval Scottish law code *Regiam Majestatem*, explains that "on marriage the husband acquired power over the person of his wife, who was considered to have no legal *persona*. As ruler of the house he had the control of her person and conduct" (1958: 99). In legal theory, the "sinking of [the wife's] . . . person in the husband" (101) is the obverse of the extension of the sovereign's person.

11 Lynda Boose has written about the "exogamous impulse" encoded in marriage ritual in "The Father and the Bride in Shakespeare" (1982: 340). Bourdieu contrasts the two values "all marriages seek to 'maximize' ": "the integration of the minimal unit and its security" versus "alliance and prestige, that is, opening up to the outside world, towards strangers. The choice between fission and fusion, the inside and the outside, security and adventure, is posed anew with each marriage" (1977: 57).

12 Nicholson emphasizes the peacefulness of James's reign but sees the effects of the alliance as dashed by the disastrous battle of Flodden, in which James lost his life (1974: 556, 595, 606; for a similar view see Mackie 1958: 269). Ferguson describes the period after Flodden as one of "slow, uncertain and spasmodic rapprochement between England and Scotland" (1977: 41). Norman Macdougall, in his important study *James IV*, is very skeptical about

the success of the Peace of Glasgow, and stresses the brittleness of the alliance and the atmosphere of suspicion and "mistrust" that still prevailed from 1502 onward. It is true that, as Macdougall writes, "it cannot be said that the treaty of 1502 was occasioned by any spontaneous outburst of Anglo-Scottish amity" (1989: 249), but I do not find the recent historical literature arguing that position so naively.

13 Cody and Murison 1890: Bk. 8. 117–18. Ferguson discusses the speech and uses it as evidence for the seriousness of Henry VII's intentions for peace (1977: 40).

14 See Ferguson 1977: 39–40; Macdougall 1989: 149. If, as Macdougall argues, the alliance of 1474 "may be regarded as the forerunner of the much more famous treaty of perpetual peace of 1502" and signaled "an important shift of emphasis in Scottish foreign policy," then 1502 may still be assumed to mark a shift of importance given the failure of the 1474 alliance (1977: 109–10).

15 Nicholson argues for the "nationalist aim" of many of the cultural and technological activities of James IV and his contemporaries (1974: 592). On Elphinstone, see Macfarlane 1985: 426.

16 See Buchanan 1985: 16. Macfarlane's discussion of the Book of Hours discusses the question of whether the book was a gift from Henry or from James IV (1961: 6–7).

17 Macfarlane notes that Bishop Elphinstone's *Aberdeen Breviary* deliberately highlighted "the importance of national saints like Andrew, Ninian, Columba and Queen Margaret" (1985: 244). James Foullis wrote a Sapphic ode in praise of St. Margaret; in their edition, IJsewijn and Thomson note that "when Foullis was writing it, another Margaret (Tudor) was queen of Scotland" (1975: 144). According to Buchanan, Margaret, worried about her fertility, acquired the *sark* (shirt) of St. Margaret, "an important relic" whose "timely discovery" was considered an excellent omen for the sixteenth-century queen" (1985: 57). James V was born not long afterward.

18 See Strong 1973: 76, on the "court festival" and its "assertion" of "man's ability to . . . harness the natural resources of the universe." On the question of the innovativeness of the Edinburgh pageants, see Withington 1918: 81. Neither the wedding of James II in 1449 to Mary of Gueldres nor of James III to Margaret of Denmark seem to have involved elaborate pageantry. Gordon Kipling's forthcoming book on medieval royal entries documents the rich history and shared conventions of such celebrations; but while the Edinburgh pageants of 1503 are clearly part of a tradition, there is also an ambitious-

ness to them that requires analysis. I thank Professor Kipling for providing me with a copy of his fifth chapter "Assumpt Aboue the Heuenly Ierarchie."

19 See Macdougall 1989: 256 on "the perennial difficulty of keeping the peace on the borders, where violent infringements of the treaty were part of life, and part also of the normal give-and-take of Anglo-Scottish diplomacy." He notes also the symbolism of James's leading, in August and early September 1504, a large host to the West March to join Lord Dacre, the English warden, in a "punitive raid on Eskdale" (251).

20 For the possibility that James IV may have jousted himself after his wedding, see the entries in *LHTA* 2: 206–7 for "harnessing/is for the King," "ane armyng sword," "ane lang riding suord," "ane gilt dagar deliverit to the King," and so forth.

21 Tufte notes the importance of the car or chariot to the epithalamium (1970: 28).

22 See Macfarlane 1985: 155 and Nicholson 1974: 418. James II had also taken the occasion of his marriage to Mary of Gueldres to free himself from the control of the Livingstons.

23 See Mackie 1958: 94. Mackie has stressed in his account of the wedding the difficulties posed by James's sexual adventurism: an earlier mistress poisoned, a "brood of illegitimate children," another mistress "secluded at Darnaway" (100, 94; see also Buchanan 1985: 37–38). James's promiscuity is also referred to in Dunbar's *The Thrissill and the Rois*, a poem probably written for the occasion of the wedding; and Pedro de Ayala, Spanish Ambassador to James's court, mentions the king's "love intrigues" (Brown 1891: 311).

24 It is not clear from the *Fyancells* whether the conclusion of this pageant was to become the subject of one of the later jousts in Edinburgh. The two knights involved were Patrick Hamilton and Patrick Sinclair, and they are mentioned as among those who jousted after the wedding (Younge 1770: 298), but the plot of their initial encounter is not mentioned again.

25 Apparently it was not unusual for princes to delay coronation of spouses until well after their entries, often until first pregnancy, particularly if the marriage were a dangerous one (Gordon Kipling, personal communication). In Scotland, however, there were precedents for the early coronation of royal brides: Nicholson notes that Mary of Gueldres, married to James II in 1449 in Holyrood abbey, "was crowned shortly afterwards" (1974: 348).

26 Thus in Julia Kristeva's analysis of the Song of Songs, "the Sublime, regal one turns into God having an amorous

dialogue with his beloved, the nation of Israel"; the Shulammite in turn submits, but as Subject, made "equal" through her love to the other's sovereignty. An entire "nation" can thereby imagine itself as the Shulammite chosen by God (1987: 95–100).

27 Marvell's "Horatian Ode," 11. 35–36.

REFERENCES

Bataille, Georges (1985). The Psychological Structure of Fascism, in *Visions of Excess*: Selected Writings, 1927–1939, ed. Allan Stoekl, trans. Allan Stoekl, with Carl R. Lovitt and Donald M. Leslie, Jr. Minneapolis: University of Minnesota Press.

Boose, Lynda (1982). The Father and the Bride in Shakespeare. *PMLA* 97: 340.

Bourdieu, Pierre (1977). *Outline of A Theory of Practice*, trans. Richard Nice. Cambridge: Cambridge University Press.

Brown, P. Hume (1891). *Early Travellers in Scotland*. Edinburgh: D. Douglas.

Buchanan, Patricia Hill (1985). *Margaret Tudor, Queen of Scots*. Edinburgh: Scottish Academic Press, 1985.

Cody, E. G. and William Murison, eds. (1890). *The Historie of Scotland Wrytten first in Latin by the Most Reuerend and Worthy Jhone Leslie Bishop of Rosse and Translated in Scottish by Father James Dalrymple*. Edinburgh: William Blackwood and Sons.

Cooper, Rt. Hon. Lord, ed. and trans. (1947). *Regiam Majestatem . . . Quoniam Attachiamenta*. Edinburgh: J. Skinner and Co.

Ferguson, William (1977). *Scotland's Relations with England: A Survey to 1707*. Edinburgh: John Donald.

Fradenburg, Louise O. (1991). *City, Marriage, Tournament: Arts of Rule in Late Medieval Scotland*. Madison: University of Wisconsin Press.

IJsewijn, J. and D. F. S. Thomson (1975). The Latin Poems of Jacobus Follisius or James Foullis of Edinburgh. *Humanistica Lovaniensia* 24.

Kelly, Henry Ansgar (1975). *Love and Marriage in the Age of Chaucer*. Ithaca: Cornell University Press.

Kipling, Gordon, ed. (1990). *The Receyt of the Ladie Kateryne,* EETS o.s. no. 296. London: Oxford University Press.

Kristeva, Julia (1987). *Tales of Love*, trans. Leon S. Roudiez. New York: Columbia University Press.

—— (1982). *Powers of Horror: An Essay on Abjection*, trans. Leon S. Roudiez. New York: Columbia University Press.

LHTA (1877–1916). *Compota thesaurariorum regum Scotorum, Accounts of the Lord High Treasurer of Scotland*, 12 vols. Edinburgh: H. M. General Register House.

Macdougall, Norman T. (1989). *James IV*. Edinburgh: John Donald.

—— (1977). Foreign relations: England and France, in Jennifer M. Brown [Wormald], ed. *Scottish Society in the Fifteenth Century*. New York: St. Martin's Press.

Macfarlane, Leslie J. (1985). *William Elphinstone and the Kingdom of Scotland, 1431–1514: The Struggle for Order*. Aberdeen: Aberdeen University Press.

—— (1961). The Book of Hours of James IV and Margaret Tudor. *Innes Review* 11: 3–21.

MacGregor, Duncan, ed. and trans. (1905). *The Rathen Manual*. Aberdeen: Aberdeen Ecclesiological Society.

Mackie, R. L. (1958). *King James IV of Scotland: A Brief Survey of His Life and Times*. Edinburgh: Oliver and Boyd.

Montrose, Louis Adrian (1980). "Eliza, Queen of shepheardes" and the Pastoral of Power. *English Literary Renaissance* 10: 153–82.

Nicholson, Ranald (1974). *Scotland: The Later Middle Ages*. Edinburgh: Oliver and Boyd.

Paton, G. Campbell H. (1958). Husband and Wife: Property Rights and Relationships, in *An Introduction to Scottish Legal History*, 99–115. Edinburgh: Robert Cunningham and Sons.

Scarry, Elaine (1985). *The Body in Pain: The Making and Unmaking of the World*. New York: Oxford University Press.

Stafford, Pauline (1983). *Queens, Concubines, and Dowagers: The King's Wife in the Early Middle Ages*. Athens: University of Georgia Press.

Strickland, Agnes (1859). *Lives of the Queens of Scotland and English Princesses Connected with the Regal Succession of Great Britain*. New York: Harper.

Strong, Roy (1973). *Splendour at Court: Renaissance Spectacle and the Theater of Power*. Boston: Houghton Mifflin, 1973.

Turner, Victor (1977 [1969]). *The Ritual Process: Structure and Anti-Structure*. Aldine; rpt. Ithaca: Cornell University Press.

Withington, R. (1918). *English Pageantry: An Historical Outline*. Vol. 1. Cambridge, MA: Harvard University Press.

Younge, John, Somerset Herald (1770). *The Fyancells of Margaret, eldest Daughter of King Henry VIIth to James*

King of Scotland: Together with her Departure from England, Journey into Scotland, her Reception and Marriage there, and the great Feasts held on that Account; Written by John Younge, Somerset Herald, who attended the said Princess on her Journey, in John Leland, *De Rebus Britannicis Collectanea*. Tomus Tertius. London: Gvl. et. Jo. Richardson.

ABBY ZANGER

Fashioning the Body Politic:
Imagining the Queen in the Marriage of Louis XIV

> . . . je n'espère pas, veu la contrariété de ces deux nations,
> que quelque paix qui se fasse jamais, nous nous puissions
> rencontrer habillez de la mesme façon.
> (Mazarin, August 10, 1659)[1]

On December 10, 1987, the lower right hand side of the front page
of the *New York Times* contained a picture of Nancy Reagan and
Raisa Gorbachev under the heading "Frost in the White House for
2 First Ladies." The story accompanying the picture concerned
tension between the wives of the two superpower leaders and
relayed the following very snide evaluation of the Soviet first lady
. . . or rather of her clothing:

> "A bit cocktailish don't you think?" said one White House
> aide about Mrs. Gorbachev's outfit: a black crepe dress with
> satin collar and cummerbund and rhinestone buckle, black
> suede stiletto shoes and clutch bag and rhinestone appliqué on
> her baggy hose.

The context of this anecdote was the reporting of an international
political negotiation, the first Reagan-Gorbachev summit held on
American soil. But, as the newspaper displaced the coverage from
front center to lower right, it also shifted its attention from affairs
of state, dealings between world leaders, to affairs of style, social
relations between the wives of leaders. This refocusing of
international tension from the arena of the negotiating table to
that of the wardrobe was not simply the reporting of an anecdote,
however. For even in an era of political détente, it had to be made
clear to the public that the foreign interlocutor was still a political
enemy: since it would not have been appropriate to directly
criticize or denigrate the Soviet Prime Minister, the angst
associated with his country's evil potential was, first, voiced by an
insignificant figure, an aide, and, second, displaced onto the

person of the wife, or more precisely onto her clothing, a safe sphere to critique since apparently far removed from the serious realm of politics. Reporting on Raisa's clothing, therefore, allowed the *New York Times*, and by extension the state apparatus, to safely assert American hegemony over Soviet technology and taste. Democracy was thus able to triumph in December 1987 while détente could also progress unhindered.

If a discussion of clothing in the marriage of Louis XIV begins by reading from the December 1987 *New York Times*, it is because the function of Raisa Gorbachev's clothing in that story illustrates how, as Mary Douglas has shown in *Purity and Danger*, "The body is a model which can stand for any bounded system." For Douglas, the body's

> boundaries can represent any boundaries which are threatened or precarious. The body is a complex structure. The function of its different parts and their relation afford a source of symbols for other complex structures. We cannot possibly interpret rituals concerning excreta, breast milk, saliva and the rest unless we are prepared to see in the body a symbol of society, and to see the powers and dangers credited to the social structure reproduced in small on the human body. (1988: 115)

That relation between body and social structure seen in the Nancy-Raisa anecdote is the focus of this essay. For the analysis which follows concerns another example of the shifting of the political onto the material of fashion (and the body) within the context of international negotiation: the *Traité des Pyrenées*/Treaty of the Pyrenees. Occurring in 1660, this agreement between France and Spain was meant to adjudicate territorial disputes and thereby resolve generations of Bourbon-Hapsbourg "cold-war" tensions. The sphere of displacement for French enmity in this accord was the Spanish infanta, María Teresa of Austria, whose marriage to Louis XIV was a cornerstone of the treaty. The discussion which follows focuses on comments about the infanta and the way she was dressed, comments made at the moment of her arrival in France. The goal in analyzing these remarks is to illustrate how the infanta's clothing, and by extension her body, may not have been such a safe sphere on which to play out political relations. In so doing, I am proposing that the infanta's clothing had import not only for her own image, but also for that of the "Roi Machine"/ Sun King who, in 1660, eight months before his accession to the throne (upon the death of his minister Mazarin), was not yet the stable political figure or symbol we so often take for granted in our equation of absolutist symbolics with sovereignty.

The first comments about the infanta I shall focus on were printed in an occasional pamphlet, an irregularly published 10 to 12 page news gazette, one of many such texts produced to report the details of the royal treaty-wedding occurring far from the urban centers of population, on the border between France and Spain. This particular pamphlet, *La Pompe et Magnificence faite au mariage du Roy et de L'Infante D'Espagne. Ensemble les entretiens qui ont esté faits entre les deux Roys, & les deux Reynes, dans l'Isle de la Conference. Et Relation de ce qui s'est passé mesmes apres la Consommation* [*The Pomp and Magnificence created for the marriage of the King and the Infanta of Spain. The entirety of the discussion which took place between the two Kings, and the Queens, on the Island of the Conference. And the Relation of what occurred even after the Consummation*], was published in Toulouse in 1660 by the Imprimeurs ordinaires du Roy, and then in Paris by an equally reputable publisher, Jean Promé (i.e. it was officially sanctioned by the King).[2] The popularity of this text's content is evidenced by its multiple editions.

Structurally, *La Pompe . . .* is divided into two parts. Section one, dated June 8, begins by describing a meeting held two days earlier in which the king was first formally introduced to his new bride on an island in a river between the two countries (this was also the meeting in which the treaty was signed). That same section continues on to recount the June 7 encounter in which the infanta was actually handed over to the French. Section two, dated June 11, details the infanta's first days in France, the French marriage mass, and the activities around that ceremony, including allusions to the consummation. In sum, this text treats the most highly charged and formalized moments of the marriage-treaty: the signing of the accord and the transfer (and consumption) of the goods. What is described, then, should be seen as a liminal or transitional moment in which the two courts, former adversaries, are face-to-face, on the threshold, literally and figuratively, of a new political and familial co-existence or order. No figure better encapsulates that flux and changeability than the infanta: married to Louis XIV by procuration in Spain before being handed over as was traditional in such alliances, the infanta, in the moments described, is no longer Spanish, and not yet truly French.[3]

One might say, therefore, that what we read in the pamphlet reporting the marriage is the story of a princess's transformation from *Infanta* María Teresa, to *Reine* Marie-Thérèse, from one culture or symbolic system (Spanish) to another (French).[4] Given that context, what better way to mark the change than by her clothing . . . more precisely her reclothing? This fact is illustrated early in the text when the narrator recounts a conversation which took place between Louis XIV and his mother prior to their departure for the island where they would finally take custody of the infanta:

> Sa Majesté partant pour y aller, dit qu'il pretendoit dès ce soir là consommer le Mariage, qu'il croyoit d'ailleurs bien achevé, & témoigna ardeur pour cela: Mais la Reyne mere qui vouloit auparavant habiller la Reyne à la Françoise, & la rendre encore plus aymable, dit au Roy qu'il restoit quelque ceremonie de l'Eglise, qui ne se pouvoit faire qu'aujourd'huy.(7)

> His Majesty, leaving to go there, said that he intended that very night to consummate the marriage that he believed to be otherwise well accomplished, and he showed much ardor for this: But the Queen mother who wished to dress the Queen in the French style beforehand, and make her even more pleasing/desirable, said to the King that there remained some Church ceremony that could be done only today.

Note here that in the queen mother's estimation, in order for Louis XIV to consummate his marriage, it was necessary to make the infanta look French, fit the French notion of desirability. It is as if, dressed in her native garb, she could not speak the language of Bourbon taste; she was true to the etymology of her title, *infans*, without language. She would be desirable or attractive, be "aymable," only if she were able to communicate within her new cultural context. That communication, however, was to be largely passive; the queen mother's goal was simply to make the infanta readable as object of desire, that is wearer of the clothing or signs of the French court.[5]

One must ask at this point exactly what message those signs and that clothing were meant to transmit? What language must the infanta be made to speak to and for her husband? It was, I would argue, the language of the Bourbon triumph over the Spanish Hapsbourgs. The act of reclothing was, quite literally, a territorialization of the Hapsbourg body by the Bourbon family. Such an appropriation or colonization had in fact already been figured in the iconography of the war which led to the treaty in question. Consider, for example, a 1658 engraving celebrating the French conquest of Spanish-occupied Flanders, the victory which ultimately led to the larger Spanish defeat (Figure 1). In the image, Flanders is having her Spanish garments removed and is being reclothed in French fashion by the allegorical female figure of France; the top center medallion contains a description "LA

Figure 1. *La Flandre Despouillée des habits d'Espagne* (Bibliothèque Nationale, Paris)

FLANDRE Despouillée des habits d'Espagne et revestue à la Française" [FLANDERS being stripped of her Spanish clothing and reclothed in the French style] which clarifies any doubt as to what is occurring in the tableau. The French garb that Flanders is to put on is clearly identified by its fleurs-de-lys motif and it figures prominently in the center of the picture, held high by one of the soldiers; a cape, also covered with fleurs-de-lys, is held by a second allegorical female figure located behind and to the right of France. Note as well that this is not a private event: the audience is large and includes (1) soldiers with their swords drawn (is this a rape?); (2) figures viewing from below, glimpsed in the spaces between the central characters' lower bodies; (3) the king carried by cupids, in a medallion above; and (4) the reader/viewer for whom the act is staged, or more precisely framed by the miniatures of the various cities conquered by Louis XIV (these cities being summarized by the figure of Flanders). In sum, this engraving offered a scenario depicting the triumph of the French Bourbons over the Spanish Hapsbourgs being reenacted on the body via the reclothing of the allegorical princess Flanders.

It would seem likely that the infanta María Teresa as described in the pamphlet was meant to occupy the same position in the scenario of her marriage that Flanders occupied in the engraving considered above. That would have been the program of the machinery of royal symbolism. I would suggest, however, that the infanta was not so easily placed into that symbolic matrix. For she was not just an allegorical symbol, but had a material reality which was capable, even in officially sanctioned literature, of placing that symbolic scenario in question.

Not surprisingly, the infanta's problematic materiality confronted the French within or via the sphere of fashion. For even if one thinks of clothing as only a cultural signifier, something abstract or symbolic, it is immediately apparent in reading the pamphlet description that what the infanta wore caused very concrete problems for the French. Consider, for example, the description of the mechanics of the infanta's definitive departure for France:

> On la mit en suite dans son beau carosse, dont Elle occupa tout le devant, à cause de son gard'Infant qu'elle ne voulut pas oster. Le Roy & la Reyne Mere estoient au fonds . . .(8)

> She was then put in her beautiful carriage where she took up the whole front because of her farthingale (*gard'Infant*) that she did not wish to take off. The King and Queen Mother were in back . . .

In taking possession of their new queen, the French were obliged to give her the entire front of the carriage because of an item of clothing, her *gard'Infant*, that she *chose* not to remove ("qu'elle ne voulut pas oster"/that she did not want to take off). One surmises from the explanation that something was amiss in the positions within the carriage. The deviation here, however, was not that the infanta was in front and the king and queen mother in the back; the king's traditional position in the coach was indeed "au fonds/ in back."[6] Rather, what was abnormal was that the infanta was not next to her husband, but alone in what might have been her mother-in-law's place; what had apparently occurred was that the expected shift in position between the former queen, now a queen mother, and the former infanta, now a queen, had not taken place. The Oedipal implications of this triangulation should be evident; indeed there are hints in this text and in others of the queen mother's resistance to stepping aside for another woman. What should be underlined for this discussion, however, is the fact that the deviation in the infanta's placement was portrayed both as the infanta's choice and as linked to her *gard'Infant*, to something about her dress.

To understand why this item of wearing apparel—in English the farthingale, in seventeenth-century French the *gard-infant*, *vertugadin*, or *vertugale*—was so imposing for the French that it caused them (or allowed them) to displace the infanta from her rightful place (and lay the blame for that displacement on the princess' choice), one must look beyond the journalistic accounts to other contemporary references to the item in question. The memoirs of Madame de Motteville are a particularly helpful source since, as an aide to Anne of Austria, Motteville's comments about the Spanish women she saw during the marriage ceremonies can be seen to stand in for or repeat the sentiments of the queen mother. What is immediately noticeable is Motteville's disdain of Spanish fashion in general and of the *gard-infant* in particular:

> l'Habit et la Coiffure des Femmes d'Espagne me fit de la peine à voir . . . leur Gard-Infante étoit une machine à demi ronde & monstrueuse; car, il sembloit que c'étoient plusieurs cercles de Tonneau cousus en dedans de leurs Juppes, hormis que les Cercles sont ronds, et que leur Gard-Infante étoit aplati un peu par devant et par derrière & s'élargissoit par les côtez. Quand elles marchoient, cette Machine se haussoit et baissoit, et faisoit enfin une fort laide figure. (1723: 87–8)

> the clothing and coiffure of the Spanish women pained me to see . . . their farthingale was a machine half round and monstrous, because it seemed to be several wooden hoops sewn under their skirts, except that hoops are round and their farthingale was flattened a bit in the front and the back, and swelled out on the sides. When they walked, this machine moved up and down, and made for a very ugly appearance.

Not mincing words, Motteville refers to Spanish women's skirts as monstrous, invoking a traditional link between women and monstrosity, as well as a more contemporary attitude toward the outmoded or baroque. For, the farthingale, a style popular across France, Spain, and Italy in the late sixteenth and early seventeenth centuries had ceded to a more natural cut in France by 1660, the shift in style being coherent with the larger aesthetic shift from baroque to classical; the former, connected with ostentation, would characterize the exaggerated Spanish skirt while the latter, less excessive and more discreet, would function in accordance with the classical exigencies of hidden art.[7] The skirt, furthermore, may have also seemed monstrous to Motteville not only because it highlighted the Spanish body as outmoded (baroque), but because its very difference made that body more notable and thus more visible than the French body classical.[8] Indeed, the *Gard-Infante*, as Motteville called the item, by its very size, dwarfed the French body, male and female.[9]

Another excellent source for understanding the seventeenth-century attitude toward the farthingale is a contemporary dictionary, the *Dictionnaire Universel*, written by the academician and satirist Antoine Furetière. Furetière offered two definitions for the item, one under the entry *garde-infant* and the other under the complimentary term I mentioned earlier, *vertugadin*:

Grand vertugadin que portent les femmes Espagnoles sur les reins, & qu'on portoit il y a quelque temps en France, qui sert à empêcher qu'elles ne soient incommodées dans la presse: c'est une espece de ceinture rembourrée ou soutenuë par de gros fils de fer, qui est fort utile aux femmes grosses.

C'étoit une piece de l'habillement des femmes, qu'elles mettoient à leur ceinture pour relever leurs juppes de quatre ou cinq pouces. Il étoit fait de grosse toile tenduë sur de gros fil de fer. Il les garentissoit de la presse, & étoit fort favorable aux filles qui s'étoient laissé gâter la taille.

A large farthingale/vertugadin that the Spanish women wear just above their hips, and that was worn some time ago in France, which serves to stop them from being jostled in a crowd: it is a kind of belt, stuffed, or held up by thick wire, which is very useful to pregnant women.

It was an item of women's clothing, that they used to put on their belt to raise up their skirts four or five inches. It was made of heavy cloth stretched over thick wires. It protected them from crowds and was quite favorable to girls who had let their figures be spoiled.

Note that while the dictionary writer Furetière, like Motteville, characterized the *garde-infant* or *vertugadin* as an unwieldy, uncomfortable, and outmoded fashion, he also pointed out certain advantages of the skirt. It could function to protect women from being crushed in a crowd just as it "protected" the infanta from being crowded in the carriage. It could as well conceal bodily defects, figures spoiled, even by pregnancy. What I think should be obvious about the *garde-infant* from both Furetière and Motteville is that this object functioned on two levels: its very size and construction actually protected the woman from a crowd, even if it hindered her movement, but at the expense of reconceptualizing or refashioning her body-line, making her appear monstrous. The impact of this item, as much real as imaginary, was to separate and distinguish the infanta concretely and symbolically from the space or scenario the French had constructed for her.[10]

Nowhere is the dual symbolic/concrete status of the *garde-infant* more evident than in the one aspect of it glossed over in citing Furetière and Motteville: the item was "fort utile aux femmes grosses/very useful to pregnant women" because it concealed their misshapen (pregnant) bodies and thus allowed them to continue appearing in public. That is why it was called a *garde-infant* in the pamphlet, accurately translating the Spanish term *guardainfante*, guard of the *infante*, child or fetus in Spanish and *infant*, Spanish prince in French.[11] Interestingly, however, Madame de Motteville calls the apparatus a *Gard-Infante*, subtly suggesting the truth about the item that it actually protects the woman or *infanta* by concealing her unborn child (or bodily secret); it doesn't protect the child or prince at all, but more likely threatens it, given the apparatus' weight and construction. I should note, however, that Motteville did not invent this analogy or slippage between the fate of the woman and that of the fetus. One anecdote about the farthingale's origin is that it was conceived by queen Juana of Portugal to hide a pregnancy that was obviously not the progeny of her invalid husband. And, in Webster's 1623 play *The Duchess of Malfi*, one finds the same association when Bosolo, spying on the Duchess for her brothers, suspects she is concealing pregnancy, and bemoans the fact that her clothing impedes his view:

> A whirlwind strike off these bawd farthingales,
> For, but for that, and the loose-bodied gown,
> I should have discover'd apparently
> The young springal cutting a caper in her belly.[12]

Motteville thus plays on an established perception that subtly shifts the protected position from fetus to woman, eliding the two identities since in fact the *gard(e)-infant(e)* protected the woman by making her childlike, *infans* or silent, in its covering or concealing the "pregnant" or adult female body; this silencing allowed her to participate in court events by providing a social or symbolic contour at a moment when her own shape would have been considered decidedly unappealing or transgressive, even disruptive, of the categories of socialility or desirability. Thus what might appear to be a linguistic slip on the part of Madame de Motteville is actually not a faux-pas at all, but a subtle pun made by a woman who, as the daughter of a Spanish mother and French father, was fully bilingual and bicultural.[13] Madame de Motteville thus had a unique perspective on the boundaries of clothing and body as well as on the experience of crossing cultures, a perspective she would have gained from contact with her mother and her queen. As an aide to the queen, a rather insignificant status, Motteville may also have been uniquely positioned to point out that which might be troubling or anxiety-provoking within this political scenario of the treaty-marriage: the possibility of a concealed disruption.[14] For, is it not possible that under the machinery of the *gard(e)-infant(e)*, the infanta might not be so pure or innocent and that she might indeed be filled with bad seed, a sort of Trojan horse, and therefore unavailable for conquest, not the blank screen on which the French could play out/write their scenario (the hanger for their clothing), but rather an obstruction?

All this is not to say that the infanta actually arrived in France pregnant, but rather that the image of her clothing as a monstrous machine (concealing something) offered apt material for the French anxiety about the princess's availability for their political agenda, for their mise-en-scène of triumphant conquest. For any new queen would have to contain the seeds for producing a male heir, and that was certainly the goal of this particular match which ultimately allowed the French to usurp the Hapsbourg throne in the early eighteenth century by virtue of bloodline as well as "diplomacy."[15] Such virtual fecundity had to be suggested in presenting the new queen to her country, even if it threatened the image of her virginity, the purity necessary for theological and political (i.e. symbolic) reasons. The dilemma facing the Bourbon imagination in this case, therefore, was how to suggest the infanta's virginity—that she was a blank screen upon which the French could play out/write their scenario of conquest—without negating her fecundity—something necessary, but potentially menacing because virtual (being in essence or effect, but not in fact). Interestingly, that very aspect of virtuality is suggested by one of the French terms for the *guardainfante, vertugadin*. Although the term would seem to imply it is an item which guards virtue, the word's etymology actually points to a more subtle issue: *vertugadin* comes from the Middle French and Old Spanish for verdant, green, and/or the young shoot of a tree.[16] Thus, the skirt is actually not guarding virtue, but suggesting a presence which is incipient (and unpredictable) because not yet ripe or mature.

The *guardainfante* thus encircles the *infante* (or that which is

childlike or embryonic) in the *infanta* and, as such, points out that
she may be unavailable for Louis XIV's sexual conquest, something
the queen mother had suggested in the conversation cited from
the pamphlet. Whatever is virtual must thus be unmasked in order
for the Spanish princess to become a French queen; the *infante* or
embryonic must be brought out by the French who must
demonstrate to the whole world that the body of the *infante* in the
infanta is their own, that she is available for their political
appropriation or encoding (maturation). It is not surprising, then,
that the infanta had to be transformed or reclothed before the
consummation. Anything her clothing concealed, revealed, or
suggested had to be quickly eliminated or clarified, which was
precisely what occurred when, as we learn from *La Pompe* . . .,
the next day, the infanta appeared at Mass, "en habit Espagnol, &
coiffée moitié à la Françoise/in Spanish dress, and coiffed half in
the French style . . ." which, I should underline, made her "plus
belle & plus aimable qu'elle n'avoit encore paru/more beautiful
and more desirable than she had ever seemed"(9). And not
unexpectedly, the day after that, the pamphlet goes on to inform
its reader, the infanta appeared at the French wedding mass:

> vestuë à la Françoise d'un habit de brocard blanc, coiffée
> encore un peu à l'Espagnole, la Couronne sur la teste enrichie
> de beaucoup de pierreries, & . . . le Manteau de la Reyne qui
> estoit de velours bleu semé de fleurs de lis d'or & doublé-
> d'hermine . . .(12)

> clothed in the French fashion in a dress of white brocade, still
> coiffed a little bit in the Spanish manner, the Crown on her
> head enriched by many gems and . . . wearing the Cape of the
> Queen which was of blue velour strewn with gold fleurs-de-lys
> and lined with ermine . . .

Covered in fleurs-de-lys like her allegorical sister Flanders, and
without her Spanish skirt, although with just a pleasing and safely
positioned hint of that which had been erased or consumed since
she was "coiffée encore un peu à l'Espagnole," Marie-Thérèse was
ultimately cleared of any suspicious clothing and made into the
perfect symbol of queenship for the French ceremonial. Like
Flanders, the infanta seemed to have fallen to the French sword.

"Seemed" is the operative word here, however. For, unlike the
case of the engraved Flanders, the real infanta still carried within
her the (concealed) threat/seed of interfering with or interrupting
the scenario written for her, as becomes evident in a curious detail
related about the events which followed the mass:

> . . . on arriva chez la Reine mere environ les 3 heures &

demie: La Reyne estoit toute en eau à cause du poids de ses habits, de ses pierreries & de son gran manteau, on l'a des-habilla & on la mit au lict, où Elle disna seule . . .(15)

. . . the royal party arrived at the Queen mother's at around 3:30: The Queen was all in water (sweating) because of the weight of her clothing, of her gems and of her large cape, she was undressed and put to bed where she dined alone . . .

Evidently, wrapping an infanta in ermine in June in the Pyrenees did not produce a French queen. It produced a sweaty infanta! More precisely, it produced a body which reacted in a manner not so easily absorbed into, and perhaps even disruptive of, the ceremonial, that is symbolic, scene. For, the French act of vestmental appropriation only served to accentuate what was concealed, not to control it. As such the sweat or "eau" must be seen to indicate effort, in this case the effort of the infanta's body to conform once the clothing which provided her Spanish identity or contour was removed.[17] The sweat shows the difficulty of the transformation and disrupts the ceremonial scene quite concretely. For in seventeenth-century France, sweat did not soil the body, but rather the clothing. As the research of Georges Vigarello has shown, hygiene in the period did not lead to bathing the body, but required the cleansing or changing of clothing.[18]

Thus, in a society which defined status and position by style and which was in the process of redefining the notion of bodily cleanliness, such interrupting detail may have served to denigrate the infanta, but it must also be understood as having allowed her some resistance to the French symbolic matrix . . . or at least to its clothing: the removal of the infanta's French garb did not reveal her purity (or lack thereof) as much as it occasioned a bodily rebellion which reminded everyone that there was an uncontrollable body present under the signs of Frenchness imposed on it. As such, the sweat served to separate the infanta from her new family ("on la mit au lict/she was put to bed") and their clothing ("on l'a des-habilla/she was undressed"), occasioning her removal from the larger public sphere of the court activities following the Mass. One might say, therefore, that the detail about the sweat interrupted the more formal and formulaic language of royal ceremonial, underlining the dissonance between the idealized image of the queen and the reality of the infanta and disturbing the symbolic display of power by drawing attention to the material side of the events more directly than the "ugly" Spanish clothing had ever done. In sum, what becomes apparent in reading this popular pamphlet is that the real monstrous machine mentioned by

Madame de Motteville was not the infanta's skirt or the apparatus which held it up, but rather the internal mechanisms of the princess's body, dynamics which could not be contained, even by the potent symbols of French monarchy.

This essay began by suggesting that political agendas are at times transposed onto the body, which then becomes a model or microcosm of society. Seen as such, however, the body seems to be a rather static model, a passive receptor or mirror of another scenario. From reading the pamphlets about Marie-Thérèse in which issues of Bourbon hegemony are indeed replayed on the body of the Hapsbourg princess at the moment of her passage into France, it becomes apparent that the process may not be so one-sided, since the body itself seems to participate in the dynamic, speaking for or producing a new queen, albeit in a somewhat unexpected way, via the process of abjection, sweat, which disrupts the categories imposed upon it.[19] One might characterize this bodily process as a kind of abject habitus, a practice which corrupts the rules or boundaries of the French symbolic system from within, more precisely from the dampened space between the Spanish body and the French fashion system. This transgressive refashioning of the body politic within the highly choreographed and ritualized atmosphere of the court society supersedes Douglas' idea of the body as a model, with which I began this essay. A better metaphor to describe the representation of the infanta's body would be one of fluid mechanics, proposed in the opening lines of Luce Irigaray's playful essay on that subject. For Irigaray, the feminine is the fluid and her force is comparable to the complex dynamics of that slippery matter:

> It is already getting around—at what rate? in what contexts? in spite of what resistances?—that women diffuse themselves according to the modalities scarcely compatible with the framework of the ruling symbolics. Which doesn't happen without causing some turbulence, we might even say some whirlwinds, that ought to be reconfined within solid walls of principle, to keep from spreading to infinity. Otherwise they might even go so far as to disturb that third agency designated as the real—a transgression and confusion of boundaries that it is important to restore to their proper order.[20]

Highlighting the connection between the potentially transgressive nature of (feminine) fluid mechanics and the similarly disruptive potential of the infanta's sweaty body, we can now extend Douglas' equation of the body with society to take into account a more dynamic notion of the body as energy or force; the infanta's body with its excreta would no longer be model or mirror of the prince (and his absolutist scenario), but energy or force affecting (or exerted upon) that sovereign body.

In concluding, nonetheless, it is important to underline that while comments about the infanta's monstrous clothing allow the French to subtly position themselves as victorious over the Spaniards, they also illustrate French anxiety about its victory, when these comments point to a body which may be actively highlighting their inability to figure or project their dominance of it. For, the discussion of clothing shows that it is possible for the French conquest to be bounded/limited/exceeded by the body of the infanta in so far as it may not have been so evident that this Spanish body could ever be made into a French queen, draped with French signs and fit into French categories of meaning and acceptability; the infanta-queen might always bear within herself the germs of a disruptive, negating body, pregnant or sweaty, that is Spanish and unacceptable, especially when the apparel masking it is removed. We should not, however, read this bodily response as a successful rebellion; the infanta's fluid mechanics may not have exerted force on the bodies around her, at least not in a manner significant for the absolutist symbolic system. For, at the moment of her marriage, the infanta, with or without her monstrous clothing, sweaty or clean (raw or cooked), was caught in a difficult position: she could either give up her own Spanish body and be translated into textual and iconographic symbol, or she could remain without a position, an uncomfortable, sweaty infanta with no status at all except as monster (negative and other). In the end, Marie-Thérèse opted for the former fate; she positioned herself on the margins of Louis XIV's court, an insignificant and invisible figure in the history of seventeenth-century France. Nonetheless, if she did ultimately fulfill her assigned role as simply political symbol, lapsing into anonymity behind the king and his mistresses, it was only after offering us a new perspective on absolutist sovereignty by leaving her mark, literally and figuratively, on the royal raiment.

NOTES

I wish to thank the members of the "Forgotten Women" reading group (Nadine Bérenguier, Sheila ffolliott, Nelly Furman, Elizabeth Goldsmith, Erica Harth, Susan Jackson, and Anne Menke, none of whom are forgotten women) at Harvard's Center for Literary and Cultural Studies for their insight and input into this material. I also wish to thank Alex Halasz, Cheryl Herr, and Jodi Billinkoff for their generous suggestions.

1 "I do not expect, given the differences between these two nations, that whatever agreement we may come to, we shall be able to meet each other dressed in the same manner" (Mazarin 1690: 46). This statement comes from a letter written to Le Tellier from Saint Jean de Luz. The comment follows a discussion about keeping the French and Spaniards apart during the treaty negotiations in order to avoid a replay of Spanish interactions dating back to Louis XI and Henry IV of Castille in which the difference in clothing was a subject of mockery. Mazarin asks Le Tellier not to read the letter in public since he thinks the topic will seem ridiculous and that will have "mauvais effets." (All translations of seventeenth-century texts cited are provided by the author of this essay as working copy to aid the reader who is not fluent in French.)

2 Though neither text prints a *privilège*, there was no litigation (as there had been in other cases) by the journalist François Colletet who held the permission ("privilège") to report the events, nor by his publisher Jean-Baptiste Loyson, to whom Colletet had ceded his rights. This was most likely because the text would have been the first printed report of the marriage, produced in installments as the events occurred, utilizing the nearest authorized printer and then forwarded quickly to Paris for wider distribution. I thank Roger Chartier for pointing this out upon comparing the two editions of the pamphlets. If this hypothesis is indeed accurate, then there would have been no need (or ability) to contest the legitimacy of this pamphlet. When Colletet's texts did begin appearing, furthermore, such publications would no longer have been necessary.

3 One might consider the marriage and its ceremonies as a "right of passage" in the sense that is utilized by the anthropologist Arnold Van Gennep in his study *The Rites of Passage*.

4 When I use the term symbolic here I am not just alluding to an aesthetic phenomenon, but am suggesting as well several different theoretical models which, I believe, converge on the example I am discussing. These models include: (1) Lacan's usage of the term symbolic insofar as the infanta can be said to occupy the imaginary sphere where she has not yet engaged with the world of Louis XIV's language, even if she did function in the symbolic sphere within the Spanish context, (2) Baudrillard's notion of the political economy of symbolic relations, and (3) Bourdieu's revision of Lévi-Strauss' and Mauss' work on exchange in which he emphasizes the dynamic nature of symbolic interaction in what he calls the habitus. For

the last notion of the symbolic I should point out that the historian Roger Chartier has fruitfully utilized the anthropological dimension of habitus in his essay "Social Figuration and Habitus, Reading Elias" in his translated collection of essays titled: *Cultural History: Between Practices and Representations* (1988: 71–94).

5 This is quite a delicate process since to assert that the infanta needs to be refashioned is a manner of criticizing her and her country and thus might potentially unsettle the delicate détente between France and Spain. That may explain why the idea of refashioning is placed in the mouth of the queen mother, herself a former infanta, in a move that the sociologist Pierre Bourdieu refers to as "cross-censorship," when a member of a social group guards and indeed enforces a code which he or she may not experience as totally positive. Bourdieu introduces this concept in the penultimate page of *Outline of a Theory of Practice*, when he discusses the "work of euphemization" and notes ". . . the *cross-censorship* to which each agent submits with impatience but which he imposes on all the others" (1977: 196). The idea is further developed in Bourdieu's *Distinction*.

6 It is difficult to find information about coaching etiquette. One source of information is Taar 1969. Nonetheless, that the infanta's position deviated from the usual may be surmised as well from a Spanish description of the event in which the princess' position closest to the horses is explained as being the best place in France: "Entraron en el coche, sentándose la novia a los caballos, que es en Francia el mayor lugar." That the pamphlet writer found it necessary to explain the infanta's placement in terms of French cultural practices suggests something is not correct, just as does the French pamphlet writer's offering the skirt as a reason for her placement. The Spanish citation comes from *Relación* 1959: 28. The original edition dated from 1660.

7 In fact, Madame de Motteville is using the adjective in much the same vein as a contemporary playwright, Pierre Corneille, used its nominative counterpart to describe his play *L'Illusion comique* as "un étrange monstre . . . invention bizarre et extravagante." Corneille described his 1646 play-within-a-play in this manner because it contained elements which would seem monstrous or overly complicated in a milieu rejecting the excess ostentation of the baroque for an aesthetic based on discretion or hidden art. The *Gard-Infante* would also have been seen as a baroque remnant within a newly coded aesthetic. See Corneille, ed. Couton 1971: 627. The

remarks are found in the Dedication to Mademoiselle M.F.D.R. written for the published edition of the play.

8 This puffed-out style of skirt revolutionized the line of dress when it came into fashion. A contemporary parallel that might help us understand the impact of this new fashion would be the mini-skirt which so radically transformed our notion of clothing and the body some twenty-five years ago. The popularity of the farthingale in seventeenth-century Spain is surprising given its excessive and exaggerated line and the rather strict sumptuary laws of that country.

For an excellent overview of the shifts in fashion in Europe during the early modern period see Boucher 1967. Boucher's study is particularly helpful for its attention to the larger economic, political, social, and artistic context of the shifts in fashion she describes.

9 That the infanta, in her skirt, was perceived as dwarfing her new French family can be seen in the painter Le Brun's depictions of the events of the marriage, part of a larger cycle he produced as designs for a series of tapestries portraying the king's history. The images are reproduced frequently in discussions of the marriage. See, for example, Ducéré 1903.

10 It is interesting that Motteville uses the term *machine*, something which enables or empowers its user; the word comes from the Latin and from the Greek for expedient or means. The "fort laide figure" of the Spanish woman as she walks and her machine-like skirt bobs up and down may well be more than simply ridiculous, it may do more than just mark the Spanish difference. For, the metal and wire infrastructure (which is actually the *garde-infant*, not the skirt), the very material of torture when taken within the Spanish context, can become that of liberation when moved to another milieu, one with a different order of symbolic relations and signs and one in which the Spanish woman plays a different role than she does on her home turf. Might not the movement of the large skirt which provides distance and cover, also suggest some sort of hidden threat to the French order as it suggests the operation and protection (the enablement of) some real and symbolic power which lies beneath?

For the etymology of machine see *Webster* 1977: 688. See also *American Heritage* 1985.

11 All the Spanish dictionaries consulted offered the same etymology. See, for example, *Diccionario* 1984: "*De guardar e infante*, por ser prenda con que podían ocultar su estado las mujeres embarazadas." I wish to thank Mary Berg, Research Associate in Residence at Harvard's Center

for Literary and Cultural Studies during 1989–1990, for drawing my attention to this fact.

12 These lines are from Act II, scene ii. See Webster 1986: 200. For the anecdote about Juana of Portual, see Boucher 1967: 205.

13 This double heritage made Madame de Motteville import-ant to Anne of Austria who was herself a former infanta, i.e. both French and Spanish. Anne of Austria was the sister of Philip IV, the monarch with whom the French were negotiating in 1660. That she was of Spanish origin was a liability throughout her reign, as she was often suspected of having sympathy for the Hapsbourgs. In descriptions of her reunion with her brother, she is said to have apologized for being too good a Frenchwoman over the years of the two nations warring.

14 I believe she does so quite explicitly later on in the same section of the memoirs treating the 1660 marriage when she notes that the "Infante-Reine" (as she calls her) "étoit aimable ainsi à demi déshabilée; car le Gard-Infante étoit une chose si monstrueuse, que quand les Femmes Espagnoles ne l'avoient point elles étoient beaucoup mieux" (106–7). Here she is expressing collective relief about the infanta's physical body; she is underlining that the monstrous clothing can indeed conceal, but that she has seen the infanta's body, as has the royal family, and it is indeed pure and desirable.

That Motteville should be the figure policing the infanta's body is not surprising. As mentioned in note 5, Bourdieu has suggested that it is often a member of a social group suffering from a code of behavior who guards and indeed enforces the governing ideology.

15 Indeed the current titular monarch of Spain is Juan Carlos de Borbón, the only current reigning heir of the Bourbon line.

16 One can see as well a possible connection between those slender, pliant shoots and the materials used to construct the hoop skirt. One final connection to note is that *vertugadin* was also a gardening term for which Furetière offered the following definition: "Terme de Jardinage; c'est un glacis de gazon en amphitheatre, dont les lignes circulaires, qui le renferment ne sont pas parallêles." This usage is no longer current, but one can see the linkage between the definition and the notion of fertility I suggest.

17 In the seventeenth century, as today, sweat signified effort. For example, Antione Furetière's *Dictionnaire Universelle* offers the following example: "Suer sang & *eau*; pour dire, Faire un effort, ou un travail extraordinaire pour parvenir à quelque chose" under the proverbial uses

of the term *eau*. It also signified agitation as can be seen in Molière's *L'Ecole des femmes,* when Arnolphe, disturbed to learn his intended bride has another suitor and frustrated by his foolish house staff, states: "Je suis en eau: prenons un peu d'haleine;/Il faut que je m'évente, et que je me promène." (II, ii, ll. 403–404).

18 See Vigarello 1985 for a discussion of the evolution of hygiene in the classical period. I thank Ron Tobin for pointing out this work to me as it has been an invaluable aid in this study.

19 I am thinking here of the Kristevan notion of abjection as that which is outside, and thus disruptive of categories: "It is thus not the lack of cleanliness or health that cause abjection but what disturbs identity, system, order. What does not respect borders, positions, rules. The in-between, the ambiguous, the composite." See Kristeva, *Pouvoirs de l'horreur, Essai sur l'abjection* 1980. This citation is taken from the English translation *The Powers of Horror* 1983: 4. It is interesting for the case of the infanta that even if the processes of abjection as theorized by Kristeva are capable of producing meaning, the abject is that which has no position within the system, or whose position is neither inside nor outside. That may well be the infanta's position as the meaningful center of attention who is also the positionless locus of the marriage ceremony.

20 See Irigaray 1985: 106; French original 1977.

REFERENCES

American Heritage (1985). *The American Heritage Dictionary of Indo-European Roots.* Boston: Houghton Mifflin.

Boucher, François (1967). *20,000 Years of Fashion: the History of Costume and Personal Adornment.* New York: H. N. Abrams.

Bourdieu, Pierre, trans. R. Nice (1977). *Outline of a Theory of Practice.* Cambridge: CUP.

—— trans. R. Nice (1984). *Distinction: a Social Critique of The Judgement of Taste.* Cambridge, MA: Harvard University Press.

Chartier, Roger, trans. Lydia G. Cocherane (1988). Social Figuration and Habitus, Reading Elias. In *Cultural History: Between Practices and Representations.* Ithaca: Cornell University Press.

Corneille, Pierre, ed. G. Couton (1971). *Théâtre Complet,* Tome I. Paris: Garnier Frères.

Diccionario (1984). *Diccionario de la Lengua española.* Madrid: Real Academia Española.

Douglas, Mary (1988). *Purity and Danger.* London: ARK.

Ducéré, E. (1903). *Le mariage de Louis XIV d'après les*

contemporains et des documents inédits. Bayonne: Imprimerie A. Lamaignère.

Furetière, Antoine (1690). *Dictionnaire Universel*. La Haye: Arnout and Renier Leers.

Irigaray, Luce (1977). *Ce sexe qui n'en est pas un*. Paris: Editions de Minuit.

—— trans. C. Porter (1985). The "Mechanics" of Fluids. In *This Sex Which Is Not One*. Ithaca: Cornell University Press.

Kristeva, Julia (1980). *Pouvoirs de l'horreur, Essai sur l'abjection*. Paris: Editions du Seuil.

—— trans. L. S. Roudiez (1983). *The Powers of Horror*. New York: Columbia University Press.

Mazarin, Jules (1690). *Lettres du Cardinal Mazarin où l'on voit le secret de la Négotiation de la Paix des Pirenées; & la Relation des conferences qu'il a eües pour ce sujet avec D. Louis de Haro, Ministre d'Espagne. Avec d'autres lettres tres-curieuses écrites au Roi & à la Reine, par le même Cardinal, pendant son voyage*. Amsterdam: Chez André Pierrot.

Molière, Jean Baptiste de, ed. G. Couton (1971). *Oeuvres Complètes*, Tome I. Paris: Editions Gallimard.

Motteville, Madame de (1723). *Mémoires pour servir à L'Histoire D'Anne D'Autriche Epouse de Louis XIII, Roi de France, par Madame de Motteville, Une de ses Favorites*, Tome V. Amsterdam: Chez François Changuion.

Relación (1959). *Relación del Casamiento de la Señora Infanta de España. Reina de Francia, Doña María Teresa*. Fuenterrabia: Ministerio de Educación Nacional.

Taar, Lázló (1969). *The History of Carriages*. Budapest: Corvina Press.

Van Gennep, Arnold, trans. M. B. Vizedom and G. L. Caffee (1960). *The Rites of Passage*. Chicago: Chicago University Press.

Vigarello, Georges (1985). *Le propre et le sale, L'hygiène du corps depuis le Moyen Age*. Paris: Editions du Seuil.

Webster (1977). *Webster's New College Dictionary*. Springfield: G. and C. Merriam Company.

Webster, John (1986). *Three Plays*. London: Penguin Books.

CHARLES T. WOOD

The First Two Queens Elizabeth, 1464–1503

As this paper will demonstrate, women in the Middle Ages experienced far more sovereign success as wives and mothers than they ever did as the direct possessors of sovereignty. Nevertheless, in order to understand this phenomenon one must first understand medieval assumptions as they pertained to women. For those assumptions were in this regard far more complex than the simple misogyny with which they are usually associated.

Since, in the Middle Ages, most relevant authors were members of the celibate clergy their assessment of the gender relationship tended to be dominated by themes of a feared sexuality. For example, St. Thomas Aquinas was confident that sexual relations had existed even in Eden; indeed, given the Aristotelian nature of his epistemology, he held that because the body in its "purer nature" must have had more corporeal sensitivity than it does in sin, sex in the Garden must have involved "even greater sensible delight" than it does at present. Moreover, since God had created Eve as a helpmeet for Adam, it followed that the divine plan must have intended her to have a sexual role from the very beginning since, of course, in all other respects a male helper would have been demonstrably preferable (Aquinas 1964–76 xiii: 154–56 [1a, qu. 98, art. 2]).

It should be noted, however, that this subordination of women was inherent in their very creation. It was not a consequence of, nor punishment for, Eve's sin. In point of fact, Adam bore far greater responsibility for the original transgression since, as Pope Gregory the Great put it,

all sin is committed in three ways, namely by suggestion, pleasure, and consent. The devil makes the suggestion, the flesh delights in it and the spirit consents. It was the serpent who suggested the first sin, Eve representing the flesh was delighted by it, and Adam representing the spirit consented to it (Colgrave and Mynors 1969: 100–1).

In other words, Eve's sin was secondary, one of no more than carnal delight that reflected her subordinate being as a creature made from Adam's flesh. Adam's, on the other hand, had been primary because it had involved his intellectual consent, a process that itself reflected his superior position as a being created directly in the image of God, whose mind was omniscient.

Still, if the male bore greater responsibility for that sin by which death entered the world, the female became the vessel in which God could mitigate some of the disastrous consequences of death. As Gregory the Great explained the phenomenon when responding to Augustine of Canterbury's query whether pregnant women could be baptized:

> Why indeed should a pregnant woman not be baptized, since the fruitfulness of the body is no sin in the eyes of Almighty God? For when our first parents had sinned in Paradise they forfeited by God's just judgment that immortality which they had received. And so because Almighty God had no desire to wipe out the human race entirely on account of its sin, He deprived man of immortality because of his transgression and yet in His loving-kindness and mercy He preserved man's power of propagating the race after him. For what reason then is that which had been preserved for human nature by the gift of Almighty God a cause for debarring anyone from the grace of holy baptism? (Colgrave and Mynors 1969: 88–91).

Widely shared beliefs such as these insured that the medieval outlook on women would be shot through with contradictions. They were secondary beings whose pure carnality made them a powerful source of sin via sexual temptation. Yet the sexual act was not itself necessarily a sin, and one of its principal consequences, motherhood, gave enduring witness to the unmerited mercy of God. As a result, dangerous though women might be when perceived as the daughters of that temptress Eve, they retained a capacity to transcend the natural inferiority of the female gender whenever their actions were perceived as flowing from their role as mothers. For, sexual though the road to motherhood may be, carnality has never been stressed by men as something to be feared in women in their role as mothers. On the contrary, because (in the formulation of St. Jerome) the *Eva* of the Old Testament had become the *Ave* of the New, even men as misogynistic as the Dominican authors of the *Malleus Maleficarum* were forced to admit that the maternal benedictions of Mary had taken away "the whole sin of Eve." As a result, they said, preachers discussing women "should always say as much in praise of them as possible" (Sommers 1928: 44).

Moreover, because things maternal can so easily be transformed into symbols of more abstract fecundity and creative powers, such imagery was frequently used in discussions of sovereignty. It was during the month of May 1483, for example, that John Russell, bishop of Lincoln and chancellor of England, wrote the sermon with which he expected to open the first parliament of Edward V, son of the first Queen Elizabeth and brother of the second. That Richard of Gloucester, the young king's protector and uncle, proved to have somewhat different plans for England's sovereignty need not concern us here. Rather, what is of note is the very way in which Russell frames his argument.[1]

Throughout the sermon he relies above all on Stoic imagery to describe the anthropomorphic way in which England functions. In his rhetoric, nobles become sense organs, the eyes, ears, and tongue that create the capacity for knowledge and communication on which government depends. By way of contrast, lesser subjects have more manual functions, for they are "the shoulders, arms, hands and feet of this great body of England." And, although the king himself is occasionally termed the head of this gigantic being, much more frequently he and his ministers are likened to its belly and womb. Indeed, there are times, as at the end of the following passage, when Edward's youth tempts Russell to use womb imagery that is far from metaphorical:

> That body is whole and strong whose stomach . . . is ministered by the outward members . . .; for if the feet and the hands, which seem to do most painful labour for man's living, would complain against the womb as against an idle and slothful part of the body, . . . all the other members should needs perish together. . . . What is the belly or where is the womb of this great public body of England but that and there where the king is himself, his court and his council? . . . In the midst of this . . . , the king our sovereign lord is called of God to reign upon his people . . . as a young creature coming out of the womb. . . . What . . . member . . . in this great body of England . . . cannot have compassion of the ache of his head?

Whatever Russell's faults as a rhetorician, his very maternal concept of sovereignty suggests that he—and, by extension, his audience—harboured little ill-will against the role of women as mothers. On the contrary, the very fruitfulness of the womb, a point so stressed in Marian devotions, insured that the reproductive functions of women would be highly regarded even by those, the overwhelming majority, who otherwise had little good to say about anything feminine. In the passage above, for example, it is the process of Edward V's birth that Russell praises, not Elizabeth Woodville herself, and it is surely noteworthy that if he also believes that the great body of England should show compassion, it is only for the resulting ache in his sovereign's head, not for that experienced by his mother in the birthing process. For the good bishop, one assumes, that pain was irrelevant, no more than one of those curses that God has so justly placed on Eve and all of her female descendants.

As a result, when one comes to examine the whole question of women and sovereignty more directly, one should not be surprised to find that the problems women faced were more the product of these general views than they were of more specific limitations such as their presumed incapacity to bear arms and hence to carry out the sovereign's supreme duty of defending the realm. After all, Shakespeare's Lady Macbeth becomes queen precisely by showing herself to be a true commander, adept in the use of arms, whereas her failure to gain widespread admiration seems profoundly rooted in her gender defects as a daughter of Eve, the one who, even more than Shakespeare's other women, achieves the worst in our first mother's potential. As one American scholar sums up the consequences:

> Feminist criticism undergirded by Psychoanalytic Deconstruction has opened the morality-play surface of *Macbeth* to reveal the anti-female . . . cancer that eats away at all the men in Scotland. This revelation helps account for the queasiness *Macbeth* evokes in perceptive, female-sensitive readers. . . . [T]he fear of females makes MacDuff as sick as Macbeth. (Lakin 1989: 27)

Whatever the case with *Macbeth*, though, the fact that women were presumed to be subordinate, inferior in their capacities, could prove devastating to their authority even when exercised as sovereigns ruling with an uncontested dynastic right. And here, surely, Mary, Queen of Scots, provides the perfect illustration. Like Lady Macbeth, Mary may have had a certain familiarity at least with the domestic use of arms—perhaps even of explosives— but she failed miserably every time she tried to persuade others of the correctness of her royal views. Thus, when she summoned John Knox to explain his appallingly low opinion of women as sovereigns, she found all her arguments summarily rejected. Most strikingly, after Knox attacks her church as "that Roman harlot

. . . altogether polluted with all kind of spiritual fornication," when she shrewdly replies with what is doubtless the one best Protestant response—"My conscience is not so"—her shrewdness is met with a curt: "Conscience, Madam, requires knowledge: and I fear that knowledge ye have none" (Knox 1952: 270). This is Knox's version, of course, and Mary's would have differed substantially from it, but in so far as theologians both Catholic and Calvinist knew that true knowledge depended on right reason, Knox had ample grounds for thinking that the arguments of his sovereign were no more than the products of woman's pure carnality—and hence that they were no match for the counter-arguments produced by his pure male intellect and spirit. He and other males had yet to hear of those "raging hormonal imbalances" so dear to the hearts of some twentieth-century misogynists, but the point involved was basically the same. If so, one sees more fully just why women sovereigns like Mary had so much difficulty getting their orders obeyed.

Mary's problems were, however, rather different from those experienced by the medieval queens of England, for without exception they were consorts, not sovereigns. Indeed, we do not even know whether a woman could have inherited the crown before the 1550s when, with a little help from parliament, the daughters of Henry VIII proved that even those who were technically illegitimate could do it (Wood 1988a: 27 and n. 80). With seeming baronial approval Henry I may have three times designated his daughter Matilda to succeed him, but in the event her claims were overmatched by those of Stephen, a king whose troubled reign would end not with the accession of Matilda, but, rather, of Matilda's son (Wood 1988b: 196–197). Similarly, Henry IV's act of succession may have included *all* heirs of his body as potential Lancastrian successors, thereby implicitly including women (Strachey et al. 1767–77 III: 582; see also Chrimes 1936: 24), but since the issue of an heiress never arose before the Yorkist Edward IV used force of arms and dynastic claims through the female line to depose Henry VI, the most that can be said is that by the end of the Middle Ages women had demonstrated the capacity to transmit rights of sovereignty even though they themselves had never possessed it.

It is in this context that the first two Queens Elizabeth take on their greatest interest. The first of them, Elizabeth Woodville, was deemed by contemporaries to be an upstart, and not without justice, given their values, but the second, her daughter Elizabeth of York, had a much better claim to the crown than did her husband Henry VII, a man whose dynastic rights rested on nothing more substantial than illegitimate descent through the female line

from the fourth son of Edward III. Nevertheless, with the notable
exception of the events associated with the deposition of her son
Edward V, Elizabeth Woodville proved a queen who enjoyed
considerable power, whereas her daughter was never to attain
even a particle of it. The difference is instructive, for it helps to
define the relationship between women and sovereignty as it
existed in the twilight of the Middle Ages or, somewhat old-
fashionedly, at the dawn of the Renaissance.

Elizabeth Woodville is surely one of history's better known
parvenus, the medieval counterpart of Mrs. Simpson. Already the
mother of children and the widow of a relatively minor partisan of
Lancaster, she possessed few of the qualities or qualifications one
might have expected in the wife of England's first Yorkist king. In
the words of Charles Ross, Edward IV's most recent biographer:

> Elizabeth had nothing to recommend her except her obvious
> physical attractions. Her rather cold beauty was not offset by
> any warmth or generosity of temperament. She was to prove a
> woman of designing character, grasping and ambitious for her
> family's interests, quick to take offence and reluctant to
> forgive. . . . This impoverished Lancastrian widow might
> have made a fitting wife for a member of the Northamptonshire
> gentry, or even for one of Edward's newly-created barons.
> She was far from suitable as queen. (Ross 1974: 87–89)

That, despite all, she became queen is almost universally
ascribed to those "obvious physical attractions," ones that caused
Edward IV, in Polydore Vergil's phrase, "to be led by blind
affection, and not by rule of reason" (qtd. in Ross 1974: 92). It
seems, then, that at least one king was prepared to abandon male
intellect for female carnality, but Edward's quest or courtship of
the lady proved far from easy. As J. R. Lander succinctly sums up
the problem: "It was said then, and later, that Elizabeth, thinking
herself too base to be the king's wife but too good to be his harlot,
was one of the few women who ever denied Edward Plantagenet
her bed" (Lander 1966: 144n). The result, probably unanticipated
by either party, was their secret marriage in 1464. The rise of the
Woodvilles had begun.

It goes without saying, too, that this rise was led by the new
Lysistrata (or at least the new Salome), a queen who was prepared
to use the allure of her sexual favours and her capacity to withhold
them to gain her ends. Note, however, that those ends reflected
more than pure personal selfishness, for they also encompassed
the whole of her remarkably extensive family. This is not to say
that Elizabeth Woodville was self-denying. Far from it. She

enjoyed every luxury that her newly royal status made possible, and she was fully prepared to feather her own nest even more richly by engaging in activities such as serving as the well-paid intermediary for the Mercers and Merchant Adventurers when they needed to gain the king's ear (Ross 1974: 101–2). But at the same time she seems almost automatically to have assumed that her own good fortune had to be shared by the rest of her family. Thus all her female relatives quickly found themselves married into the high nobility; secular males received the most honorific of titles (son Thomas Grey, for example, becoming the marquis of Dorset); and clerical brother Lionel became archdeacon of Oxford at nineteen, dean of Exeter at twenty-two, and bishop of Salisbury at twenty-nine. To these honours were added showers of income derived from newly acquired estates and newly acquired spouses.[2] The extent to which both Woodvilles and Greys began to prosper was truly remarkable, but their successes rested entirely on those of the queen. Though not a sovereign, it looked for the moment as though she were acting with the powers of one.

Although no one has ever claimed that the Middle Ages were a time of rampant individualism, Elizabeth Woodville's concern for the well-being of her several families underscores yet another aspect of women's differing relationship to sovereignty. If people of both sexes exercised political power more as members of families than as autonomous individuals, women found that, much more frequently than men, their place in the world was defined by a set of family allegiances that were both double and potentially contradictory. They were the daughters of one family but the wives and mothers of another, with the result that they understood themselves, and were understood by their society, within the context of a dual kinship relationship. By way of contrast, a man's place tended to be defined primarily by his membership in a single patrilineal family. And the position of Elizabeth was more than normally complex because, though she had been born a Woodville, by marriage she became the wife and mother not just of Greys but of Plantagenets. As a result, she assumed that her political ambitions had to be unrelentingly directed toward the betterment, as she saw it, of all three of her families, two more than were usually associated with men, the more political of whom reacted with patriarchal outrage.

The most obvious difficulty here is that some families are more equal than others, in her case the Plantagenets as compared to the Greys and the Woodvilles. As a result, her strategy caused resentment to grow among the royals and the high nobility even during Edward IV's lifetime—for example, Clarence's decision to support the readeption of Henry VI seems a case in point—but real disaster came only when Edward's early death in 1483 brought his twelve-year-old son to the throne. Seeking to protect both that son and her own position, Elizabeth tried to exclude Richard of Gloucester from power by attempting to crown Edward V immediately in a ceremony of which Richard was not to be informed. Unsurprisingly, too, the chief agents of this plan were to be Greys and Woodvilles. Richard's response, entirely understandable in terms of this threat to his protectorship, was to enlist the support of his cousin Buckingham so that the two of them could seize the king before his coronation. Something of the ire that Richard knew had been caused by Elizabeth's triple family ties comes through in the carefully crafted appeal that he dispatched to the city of York on 10 June:

> Right trusty and well-beloved, we greet you well. And as you love the weal of us and the weal and surety of your own self, we heartily pray you to come unto us in London in all the diligence ye can possible, . . . there to aid and assist us against the queen, her blood, adherents and affinity, which have intended and daily doth intend to murder and utterly destroy us and our cousin the duke of Buckingham and the old royal blood of this realm. . . . And as ever we may do for you in time coming, fail not, but haste you to us hither.[3]

The rest of the story is much too familiar to bear repetition, but one aspect of it does need stressing: the way in which the fate of Elizabeth's sons instantly transformed her reputation. As long as she was perceived as a woman who exercised a quasi-sovereignty only for the benefit of self and non-royal kindred, she was hated, but when, after the event, she was seen entirely as a mother, one who had bent every effort to save her royal sons, almost instantly she took on grandeur, not to say nobility. The Elizabeth Woodville of Shakespeare and More is hardly a villain, and in her will of 1492, drawn up only shortly before her death, she showed in her thoughts for her daughter, the new Queen Elizabeth, that she, too, had come to believe that her greatest virtues were those of a mother within a single family:

> Item, where I have no worldly goods to do the Queen's Grace, my dearest daughter, a pleasure with, neither to reward any of my children, according to my heart and mind, I beseech Almighty God to bless Her Grace, with all her noble issue, and with as good heart and mind as is to me possible, I give Her Grace my blessing, and all the foresaid my children.
> (qtd. in Kendall 1965: 574 n. 4)

Although no document records how this daughter responded to

her mother's death, the queenship of Elizabeth of York teaches further lessons about women and sovereignty, lessons which suggest that if a woman wanted to have influence and to exercise genuine power, then it was far better not to have any legitimate claim to them. Such claims were dangerous and a clear threat to male hegemony. Few males could ever have accepted them comfortably, least of all a man whose own rights were as dubious as those of Henry Tudor.

Elizabeth of York's greatest strength was also her greatest problem, the fact that with the deaths of her brothers she became the eldest possessor of whatever legitimacy the Yorkist dynasty may have enjoyed, and this was a point that was recognized almost instantly. The Croyland Chronicle reports, for example, that in the summer of 1483 those who had joined Elizabeth Woodville in sanctuary recommended:

> that some of the king's daughters should leave Westminster, and go in disguise to the parts beyond the sea; in order that, if any fatal mishap should befall the male children of the late king in the Tower, the kingdom might still, in consequence of the safety of the daughters, some day fall again into the hands of the rightful heir. (qtd. in Wood 1988a: 188)

By fall, moreover, plans became considerably more specific when the duke of Buckingham sent to the exiled Henry Tudor in Brittany,

> requesting him to hasten over to England as soon as he possibly could, for the purpose of marrying Elizabeth, the eldest daughter of the late king, and, at the same time, together with her, taking possession of the throne. (Croyland as qtd. in Wood 1988a: 190)

Richard III's incestuous wooing of his niece suggests that *he* may have had no qualms about sharing his throne with Elizabeth, but Henry Tudor proved a man of different character. Before the accession of William and Mary showed otherwise in 1688, true sovereignty could legally reside in only one person, and in no way did Henry want his title to be dependent on Elizabeth's since, as Bacon puts it,

> if he relied upon that *Title*, he could be but a *King* at *Curtesie*, and have rather a *Matrimoniall* then [sic] a *Regall* power: the right remayning in his *Queene*, upon whose decease, either with Issue, or without Issue, he [would have] to give place, and be removed. (Bacon 1622: 4)

One understands, then, why Henry's matrimonial arrangements took the form that they did. Shakespeare's version of Bosworth may have Richmond pledging to "unite the white rose and the red" through the marriage of "[t]he true succeeders of each royal house," but history's Henry did no such thing. Rather, he remained entirely silent on Elizabeth's prospects until he had entered London as king in his own right, at which point he finally announced to his council that he would indeed marry her—but only after his own coronation and the meeting of his first parliament, a parliament that would declare his title and silently remove the stain of illegitimacy with which Richard III's act of succession had so thoughtlessly burdened his intended bride. This plan of action thereby deftly avoided the dangers of a joint coronation, one that (in Bacon's phrase) "might give . . . countenance of participation of Title" (Bacon 1622: 8).

Thus it was that Henry VII married Elizabeth of York only on 18 January 1486, a full five months after he had laid claim to the crown at least partly through conquest. Her coronation as queen was then delayed another twenty-two months, until 25 November 1487, and for reasons that are instructive. Before a non-threatening coronation could take place, Elizabeth had first to produce a son, a male whose own rights would supersede her own. That requirement was met on 19 September 1486 when she gave birth to Arthur, but almost immediately thereafter Henry received word that Lambert Simnel had landed in Ireland. Dubious though everyone must have known his royal claims to be, they served nonetheless to rekindle Yorkish ambitions. As a result, both Queens Elizabeth became dangerous for Henry, a threat which he met by making a nun of the mother while leaving the daughter uncrowned. Only with Simnel's crushing defeat at Stoke, 16 June 1487, was the crisis resolved, thereby clearing the way for a safe coronation. Four months later, when Elizabeth of York rode from the Tower to St. Paul's for her investiture, her route was filled with "well-singing children[, s]ome arrayed like angels, and other[s] like virgins, to sing sweet songs as her grace passed by" (Leland qtd. in Withington 1918–20: I.161). Magnificent though the pageantry must have been, this was not, surely, the road to power. It was, rather, one that serves to underscore yet again the extent to which, before the accession of the significantly unmarried third Elizabeth, women's typically more complex family allegiances posed enormous obstacles to their being the successful wielders of sovereignty.

NOTES

1 Russell's sermon has been several times printed, but the most accurate edition is to be found in Chrimes 1936: 168–78.
2 See Ross 1974: 92–103, for a full discussion. Ross stresses that none of this cost the king very much, but that is to miss the extent of the resentment nonetheless engendered.
3 As quoted in Wood 1988a: 163–64; for the full story of Richard's protectorship and of Elizabeth Woodville's actions in it, see 152–74.

REFERENCES

Aquinas, St. Thomas (1964–76). *Summa Theologiae*, ed. Edmund Hill, O.P. New York: McGraw-Hill.
Bacon, Francis (1622). *The Historie of the Raigne of King Henry the Seventh*. London: W. Stanley.
Chrimes, S. B. (1936). *English Constitutional Ideas in the Fifteenth Century*. Cambridge: CUP.
Colgrave, Bertram and R. A. B. Mynors, ed. and trans. (1969). *Bede's Ecclesiastical History of the English People*. Oxford: Clarendon Press.
Kendall, Paul Murray (1965). *Richard the Third*. New York.
Knox, John (1952). *History of the Reformation in Scotland*, ed. William Croft Dickinson; reprint Harry Emerson Fosdick, ed. *Great Voices of the Reformation*. New York: Modern Library.
Lakin, Barbara (1989). (Abstract.) *Macbeth*: The Death of Feminist Critique? *British Studies Intelligencer* 4th Series 4, 27.
Lander, J. R. (1966). *The Wars of the Roses*. New York: G. P. Putnam's Sons.
Ross, Charles (1974). *Edward IV*. Berkeley and Los Angeles: University of California Press.
Sommers, Montague, ed. (1928). *Malleus Maleficarum* by Heinrich Kramer and Jakobus Sprenger. London: J. Rodker.
Strachey, J. et. al., eds. (1767–77). *Rotuli Parliamentorum*. London.
Withington, Robert (1918–20). *English Pageantry: An Historical Outline*. Cambridge, MA: Harvard University Press.
Wood, Charles T. (1988a). *Joan of Arc and Richard III*. New York: Oxford University Press.
—— (1988b). Les gisants de Fontevraud et la politique dynastique des Plantagenêts. *La figuration des morts dans la Chrétienté médiévale jusqu'à la fin du xive siècle* (*Ier Cahier de Fontevraud*, 26–28 mai).

CARLA FRECCERO

Marguerite de Navarre and the Politics of Maternal Sovereignty

In her introduction to a special issue of *Genre* on "Literature as Women's History," Nancy Armstrong (1986) argues for a necessary transgression of genres when studying the cultural work of women, for although the advent of new historicism has brought literature and history together as a new genre of literary criticism, it has not sufficiently questioned the category of history itself as political history, which renders invisible the largely "private" sphere of women's production. In the case of early modern France this division of history into public and private spheres may be itself anachronistic in that it adopts a framework of social organization derived from post-industrial Europe and inherits eighteenth- and nineteenth-century ideologies that served to maintain men and women in their separate spheres for economic and political purposes (Scott 1988: 15–27). Thus, in contradistinction to the political separation of public (state) and private (individual) interests in the modern European state, Sarah Hanley argues that "early modern monarchies were characterized politically by intertwined private-public (family-state) relations" (Hanley 1987: 54).

The political marketplace for state and family in sixteenth-century France is marriage. It is the keystone of state building, along with conquest and expansion. Parental consent is the issue over which church and state contend for power throughout the sixteenth century, leading to a series of legislative measures, culminating in the Parlement of Paris' 1556 civil statute overruling canon law on the matter of parental consent (Hanley 1987: 56–57). The enactment of such legislation and its accompanying corollates—a lengthening of the age of minority, an increase in the number of required witnesses to marriage, provisions for disinheriting those who married without consent, the definition of such marriages as *rapt*, a capital offense punishable by death, requirements to officially declare all pregnancies—suggest that marriage was, and not surprisingly, a zone of contention, not only in the litigations of church and state, but also in family practices. While the state was consolidating parental control, there were people opposing and contesting such control in their actual behaviors.[1]

In focusing on the specific individual Marguerite de Navarre and her self-inscription in a political economy of "a familial state within a political state" (Hanley 1987: 62), I hope to show how the subject position "mother,"—that genealogical building block of early modern state formation—articulates itself in relation to the currency of a patriarchal sociopolitical order, other "women," or in this case, "daughters." Much work has been done on the use kings made of marriages to consolidate state power, and thus on the interrelations of familial states from the point of view of masculine state-makers. This focus has reenacted the commodification of women by accepting their status as inert objects circulating among men. In practice, at least on the level of the "high politics of marriage" (Davis 1986: 62), women could to a certain extent negotiate their own exchange and the exchange of other women to consolidate power in their interests as the wives and mothers of monarchs but also perhaps in other ways as well.

One of the problems I set out to understand is how it is that an explicitly patriarchal political economy that constructs women as commodities for exchange interpellates its female subjects (how it is, in other words, that a system that does not serve the interests of women as a group enlists the collaboration of individual women whose interests seem to be served by that system). I am also interested in how that "position" (as commodity) becomes a "subject position," how human commodities articulate a "sense of self" in Natalie Davis' formulation, and how that "self" may resist or claim control over its own commodification, thus creating conditions of possibility for change. Davis points out that, in the sixteenth century, "a strategy for at least a thread of female autonomy may have been built precisely around this sense of being given away" (1986: 61). In the case of Marguerite de Navarre, "being given away" becomes an arena of contestation in which both opposition to and collaboration with the state are articulated.

The famous conflict between Marguerite de Navarre, acting on behalf of François I, her brother and king of France, and her daughter, Jeanne d'Albret, represents a case in point. Marguerite's proximity to the king and the consequent shift in the balance of power between herself and her husband, Henri de Navarre, complicate, in practice, the "official" ideology of patriarchy and place her in a crucial position of authority to negotiate. That authority, however, is not symmetrical to the authority exercised by the patriarchal state; it is mediated through it in specific ways. The *Heptameron* can illuminate this "maternal authority," its politics and practice, in the voice of one such subject. And, as it turns out, that "voice" has an interest in empowering the commodity of the exchange, Jeanne d'Albret, whose resistance to that position has also been documented for posterity.

Stanley Chojnacki, Natalie Davis, and others have shown how patrician women in early modern societies functioned as the sociopolitical cement of the aristocracy by maintaining strong kinship (horizontal) ties as they simultaneously participated in the lineage (vertical) construction of their families by marriage. Marguerite's position between kin and lineage produced a conflict which was carried out over the body of her daughter. Documents in the form of letters (by and to Marguerite) and declarations (made by Jeanne), as well as a report from the secret agent of the Hapsburg Empire, Juan Martinez Descurra, sketch a series of events leading to the marriage of Jeanne, Marguerite's daughter, to the duke of Clèves and its annulment four years later. Henri d'Albret (Marguerite's husband) seeking to recapture the part of Navarre that was under Hapsburg rule entered into secret negotiations with the emperor Charles V for a marriage between his son and Jeanne d'Albret. Meanwhile, François I, Charles' enemy, sought to use Jeanne in cementing his own alliances with the Germanies in order to further undermine Hapsburg control of Europe. Appraised of Henri's plan, he had Jeanne put under a "house arrest" of sorts from age ten onwards. In this context, Marot's famous reference to Jeanne as "the darling of two kings" seems particularly ironic. The primary source for the intrigues and conflicts that ensued between 1538 and 1541 (the year of Jeanne's marriage) is primarily a series of reports made by Charles' secret agent Descurra, who was responsible for negotiating the alliance between Charles and Henri. I will return to his speculations later.

Accounts of Jeanne's opposition to the arranged marriage between herself and the duke of Clèves (whom she married in 1541) are based upon a series of written declarations dated from the time of the marriage's annulment in 1545 (by which time, Charles had taken over the duke's territory and forced him to renounce his alliance with France, thus necessitating the dissolution of his marriage). Although verb tenses suggest that the declarations antedate the annulment and the marriage itself, there is no direct evidence from Jeanne that, in 1541, she actively opposed the marriage. There are allusions to her opposition, most notably in a letter from Marguerite to François written in 1540:

But now, Monseigneur, having heard that my daughter, knowing neither the great honor that you conferred upon her by deigning to visit her, nor the obedience that she owes you, nor as well that a girl should never have a will of her own, has had the utterly foolish notion to tell you that she was begging not to be married to M. de Clèves . . . I/we cannot imagine whence proceeds her great audacity in this matter, about which she has never spoken to us. (author's translation)

Mais maintenant, Monseigneur, ayant entendu que ma fille, ne connoissant ne le grant honneur que vous luy faisiez de la daigner visiter, ne l'obéissance qu'elle vous doit, ny aussi que une fille ne doit point avoir de voulunté, vous a tenu ung si fou propous que de vous dire qu'elle vous supplioit qu'elle ne feust point marié à M. de Clèves . . . je ne pouvons penser dont luy procede cete grande hardiesse dont jamais elle ne nous avoit parlé. (Genin 1842: 176–77, #105.)

In 1545, Jeanne d'Albret signs a declaration of the marriage's non-consummation and testifies to having written two earlier protests against the arranged marriage, stating that she did not consent to it. These other declarations are included in the 1545 document, prefaced by the royal notary's statement that "the said lady has presented two and a half sheets of paper, which she said were written and signed by her hand, and which contain the aforementioned declarations and protestations" (Genin 1842: 291).[2] Descurra (who was relaying messages between Marguerite's husband and the emperor Charles) reports that Marguerite, having capitulated to the king's will, devised a means to prevent the marriage in 1541 and so to promote her husband's plan. According to him, Marguerite writes the document that Jeanne then signs in order to fabricate non-consent and thus provide a basis for the marriage's annulment.[3]

Neither Marguerite's letter nor Descurra's account, not to mention Jeanne d'Albret's declaration, can be read straightforwardly given each interlocutor's position as subjects of a monarch articulating their actions to or for that monarch.[4] Literary historians and biographers, with the exception of Nancy Roelker, either assume that Jeanne's protests expressed her opposition to the contract, at the time it was proposed (rather than having been retroactively reconstructed), and that Marguerite desired nothing but her brother's will, or they unproblematically accept Descurra's account and assume that Marguerite put Jeanne up to it.[5] The latter supposition does not account for Descurra's access to such information (via Henri, who had an interest in representing the situation this way to the emperor) and includes the assumption that no twelve-year-old girl would be capable of mounting independent opposition to the king's will. The actors in this drama are all political subjects, two of which, Henri and Marguerite, have a relatively independent economic base that is nevertheless fragile, insofar as Henri's property is an object of contestation.

Marguerite, then, is at the center of a three-way negotiation: between her husband's and her brother's genealogical lines and property interests (a conflict between kinship and marriage), indirectly between the political interests of two monarchs (François and Charles), and finally between her daughter and these conflicting claims. It is to the question of Marguerite's interests, and perhaps to the more elusive (because historically unreadable) interests of her daughter Jeanne, that I will now turn.

Jeanne's declaration, then, reads as follows:

> I, Jeanne de Navarre, . . . declare and protest again that the arranged marriage between myself and the duke of Clèves is against my will; that I have never and will never consent, and that anything I might do or say from here on in, of which one might say that I consented, will have been by force, against my pleasure and my will, and from fear of the King, of the king my father and the queen my mother, who menaced me and had me whipped by my governess, who several times urged me by commandment of the queen mother, warning me that, if I did not agree to this marriage that the King wants, and if I did not consent, I would be beaten to death, and that I would be the cause of the loss and destruction of my father and mother and of their house; of which I am so greatly fearful, also for the destruction of my parents, that I do not know to whom to have recourse except to God, when I see that my father and mother have abandoned me, they who know well what I have told them, and that I will never love the duke of Clèves and do not want anything to do with him at all. (Author's translation)

> Moi, Jehanne de Navarre, continuant mes protestacions que j'ay cy-devant faictes, èsquelles je parsiste, dis et déclaire et proteste encoires par ceste presente que le mariage que l'on veult faire de moy au duc de Clesves est contre ma volunté; que je n'y ay jamais consenti et n'y consentiray, et que tout ce que je y pourray faire ou dire par cy-après, dont l'on pourroit dire que je y auroie consenti, ce sera par force, oultre

mon grey et voiloir, et pour craincte du Roy, du roy mon père
et de la royne ma mère, que m'en a menassé et faict foueter
par la baillyve de Caen, ma gouvernante, laquelle par plusieurs fois m'en a pressée par commandement de la royne ma
mère, me menassant que, si je ne faisois, au faict dudit
mariage, tout ce que ledit Roy vouldroit et que si je ne m'y
consentoie, je serois tant fessée et maltraictée que l'on me
feroit mourir, et que je seroie cause de la perte et destruction
de mes père et mère et de leur maison; dont je suis entrée en
telle craincte et peur, mesmement de la destruction de
mesdicts père et mère, que je ne sçay à quy avoir recours que
à Dieu, quant je vois que mes père et mère m'ont délaissée,
lesquelx sçavent bien ce que je leur ay dict, et que jamais je
n'aymeroie le duc de Clesves et n'en veulx poinct . . . (Genin
1842: 291–292)

These fragments of a narrative of conflict, mediated as they are
by their form and context (addresses to a patriarchal authority
with executive power over the narrating subject), bear a structural, thematic, and linguistic resemblance to more complete or
coherent narratives of mother/daughter and monarch/subject conflicts in Marguerite's text. Marguerite de Navarre inscribes a
mother-daughter relation into the prologue of the *Heptameron*,
and stages that relation, narratively as well as dialogically, in
several of her stories. Natalie Zemon Davis notes, in her study of
pardon tales as narrative models for Marguerite's novellas, that
there were no narrative models for female conflict except for the
"kind of female strife" that "pitted a young woman against a
stepmother or surrogate mother" (Davis 1987: 102). It is no
surprise that this should be the case, given the sociopolitical
significance of this particular relationship in patrician society, as I
have outlined it, and accepting the notion that filial aggression
would surface more readily when the legitimacy of maternal
authority was in question. Marguerite stages this conflict in a
particular way, using both narrative and discursive techniques, so
that each subject "speaks" its position within the fiction of her
tales. Furthermore, she explicitly situates the mother/daughter
conflict in its relation to matters of state. In other words, Marguerite
de Navarre articulates conflicts between the state and its subjects
as a matter of mother/daughter politics.

Davis' model (daughter and surrogate or stepmother) suggests
the daughter as privileged subject of the narrative.[6] In the *Heptameron*, the maternal also occupies the privileged subject position
in the text, although the narrating subject, Parlamente, poses as

a daughter. Authority is invested in the mother's voice and her actions, an authority confirmed both by narrative events and by the subsequent commentaries of the discussants. Marguerite's *Heptameron* is, then, a maternal text, maternal precisely insofar as it also enacts a praxis of mothering, construed as "legitimate" and privileging the daughter's "voice" as well. It is not in any sense *simply* the embodiment of (male) monarchic or state authority.[7]

In the prologue, Parlamente, a married woman whose husband also figures among the participating storytellers and whose name suggests a privileged narrative role as "porte-parole" and mediator (there are those who assert that she is the Marguerite persona of the *Heptameron*), invokes the mother-daughter relation in her address to Oisille.[8] Parlamente thus sets Oisille up as spiritual and maternal authority (Oisille is a post-menopausal woman, thus outside the sociopolitical economy of exchange and circulation) and figures herself as a daughter, mediating between Oisille's spiritual requirements and the carnal desires of her husband, Hircan. She does this in Shirazad-like fashion, proposing the deferring and communal activity of storytelling.

P.A. Chilton has noted that "these three, Oisille, Parlamente, Hircan, are at the apex of a miniature aristocratic society. They represent . . . a three-cornered antagonism that runs throughout the *Heptaméron*" (Chilton 1984: 13). It is interesting to note that this antagonistic triangle defies both Freud's and Girard's oedipal models for the structuring of desire and the novel, and announces the entry of feminine desire and feminine subjectivity as thematic preoccupations and structuring agents of prose narrative.[9] What implications might be drawn for literary theorists from the possibility that early novels include mothering in their motives (rather than "fathering" alone), and that the mother-daughter relation constitutes one of their founding paradigms?

The feminine subjectivity and desire constructed in this text operate explicitly within economic, political and social spheres where feminine desires constitute the objects of contention between subject and monarch and are circumscribed by patriarchal authority. In these spheres, the maternal figure speaks from the position of social authority, often in the service of a father, brother, or king, against the daughter's wishes, while the daughter transgressively speaks "in her own voice," a voice of resistance to that authority.

I choose to focus on two stories, novellas 10 and 21, the one delineating the predicament of maternal/filial conflict and the failure of daughterly resistance, the other telling a tale of success.

Both are narrated by Parlamente. The first involves a mother, her daughter, and a knight; the second a queen, Rolandine (her subject), and Rolandine's bastard lover. In each there is a conflict between a female authority, the mother or queen, and her daughter or subject. The men, with the exception of Rolandine's second husband, are eliminated in the course of the narrative. While in many respects these stories differ considerably, they both stage a conflict between the individual feminine subject and a sociopolitical authority that, while being marked as patriarchal, comes to be ambivalently (and not uncritically) upheld by a maternal figure.

Story 10 is about Floride, a girl, her mother, the countess of Aranda, and Amadour, a knight of a lower station who falls in love with Floride. In the course of the narrative the daughter is married to a count against her will. The narrative suggests that the countess (like Marguerite, in her letter to François) also has little choice in the matter;

> Pressed by the King to agree to the marriage, the Countess, as a loyal subject, could not refuse his request. She was sure that her daughter, still so young in years, could have no other will than that of her mother . . . (Chilton 1984: 137)

> ilz [the king and queen] prierent la contesse de faire le mariage . . . La contesse, comme celle qui en riens ne leur voulloit desobeyr, l'accorda, estimant que en sa fille, qui estoit si jeune, n'y avoit volunté que la sienne . . . (François 1967: 69)

Amadour, the knight, who cannot marry Floride because of their difference in social stations, insinuates himself into the countess' good graces and obtains free access to the house and to Floride. After Floride is married, he tries to rape her, whereupon the young woman, although in love with Amadour, resolves never to disclose her feelings or encourage the friendship between them. Amadour then appeals to the countess, who approves of his love and encourages him. While Amadour is away, she forces her daughter to write him letters. There is the suggestion in the narrative of an implicit antagonism between the countess and Floride's husband; when Amadour visits the countess he finds her "ailing and pining for her daughter" (144). Shortly thereafter the countess summons Floride, "in the hope that she might want to come back and live with her permanently" (145). Floride refuses, and one wonders how much the countess' indulgence toward Amadour is a function of her desire to reclaim her daughter and to negotiate a social compromise that will provide the daughter with "acceptable" pleasure, in true courtly love fashion.

Amadour despairs of ever recovering the favor of Floride and devises a scheme to rape her. He enlists the complicity of the countess in arranging a private meeting with Floride. This time Floride screams, and her mother rushes to the rescue. Amadour claims to have been trying to kiss her hand, while the countess, skeptical, asks her daughter for an explanation. Floride does not reply, and her silence provokes a seven-year estrangement between mother and daughter.

Floride does not succeed in mitigating her mother's anger until she learns deception; she finally tricks Amadour into courting another woman so that the countess may see that he is untrue and thus an unworthy object of her affection. He goes off to war a final time and dies. Then, "saying not a word either to her own mother or to the mother of her dead husband" (152), Floride retires to a convent.

Many modern readers of the tale (I'm thinking of my students in particular) side instinctively with the individualistic Floride against both Amadour and the countess. In the frame discussion however, both Hircan and Geburon justify the actions of Amadour, and the discussion ends with Geburon's extravagant praise of Amadour's knightly virtues. The women criticize or defend Floride. The countess is never mentioned, and yet it is she who conducts and directs the transactions and transitions of the tale. The countess provides Amadour with opportunities denied him by birth. Her travels provide the occasion for Amadour and Floride to meet; her influence facilitates Amadour's marriage to Floride's lady-in-waiting. The countess' affection for Amadour wins him a place in her household and in Floride's heart; the countess encourages his love and forces her daughter to reciprocate. She also forces her daughter to marry the duke of Cardonne. The countess provides the occasion for Amadour's attempted rape, and she also rescues Floride from its consummation. Finally, it is to the countess that Floride must prove herself by learning to dissimulate. Within the story itself then, she is clearly a contestant in a struggle for authority. That struggle, conducted in her (own) interests and those of her daughter, must be negotiated within patriarchal strictures that circumscribe her and her daughter's options. Constrained by the king to accept the marriage of her daughter to the Duke of Cardonne, she justifies her choice to the daughter, exercising her authority to silence Floride's complaints. Suffering the loss of her daughter and desiring to win her back, the countess subverts the husband-wife bond by encouraging and assisting Amadour in his courtship of Floride. In doing so, she nearly hands her daughter over to be raped. Finally, although Floride's opposition to her mother's wishes is, to some extent, justified in the tale—Amadour proves faithless and deceitful—her resistance results in estrangement, isolation, and separation from the social order.

The mother-daughter struggle in story 10 empowers neither, as the ending suggests. Instead, the narrative delineates a predicament whereby female conflict disempowers both mother and daughter. Sara Ruddick, in an essay analyzing maternal thinking as philosophy, theorizes the patriarchal predicament of mothers, offering a means by which to understand the simultaneous collaboration with, and subversion of, the structures of authority produced as givens in this text (Ruddick 1984: 213–30 and 1989). Ruddick, a philosopher, identifies three "interests" that govern maternal practice: preservation (ensuring the continued life of the child), growth (fostering the child's development), and acceptability (producing an adult who will be acceptable to her social group) (Ruddick 1984: 215). In the mother-daughter relation, the conflict among these interests may be particularly acute, since mothering takes place within the context of a patriarchal society that does not exist to promote the interests of women. Thus a mother is seen as constrained by the requirements of patriarchy to produce a cooperative and obedient woman, one whose desires will not conflict with the structures that govern her (and her mother's) life (in the case of these tales, the economic, political, and social alliances between the king and other men).

Ruddick's theory is helpful in providing a partial analysis of maternal collaboration with patriarchy but, while eliding the specificities of historical and cultural circumstance, it also does not account for the vested *interest* that is a component of collaboration. Nor does it account for the empowerment of resistance within the framework of collaboration. In Marguerite's text, this vested interest is maternal authority, the power of social and political decision-making granted to the woman in exchange for her collaboration. That authority, and its ambivalent interaction with the rebellious feminine subject, is the theme of story 21.

Rolandine's story is one of the most well-known in the *Heptameron*. It bears a striking resemblance to the story of Marguerite and Jeanne, including the presence of a *gouvernante* through whom the royal mother mediates her commands. This story symmetrically reverses the historical situation: instead of withholding consent from an arranged union, Rolandine arranges a union for herself without parental and royal consent. Rolandine is an unmarried thirty-year-old woman whose father's economic interests prevail over his daughter's desire to marry, and whose queen dislikes her because of a grudge she holds against the father. Rolandine eventually finds consolation in the company of a "bastard," whose illegitimate birth and physical unattractiveness have kept him unmarried as well. Eventually, the two hold a clandestine wedding ceremony, "in the church and in the sight of God, taking Him as witness of their vows" (240). They agree not to consummate their union (another parallel with Jeanne's situation) until Rolandine's father dies or lends his approval. When discovered together, the couple separate but continue to exchange letters through the intermediary of servants. The narrative details the queen's obsessive regulation of their speech and the eventual interception of a letter that reveals their marriage. At this point the narrator is highly critical of the queen's behavior ("The Queen was quite incapable of making a reasonable reply" [247]). In the lengthy confrontation that ensues between mistress and subject, Rolandine's calm reasonableness—"She [Rolandine] was as calm and composed as the Queen was violent and vehement" (246)—is repeatedly contrasted with the queen's rage.

Rolandine's transgression of the social order constitutes a threat in that she has not obtained "parental" or monarchic consent: "[The Queen] . . . far from addressing her as 'cousin,' she told her repeatedly, her face contorted with rage, that she was a 'miserable wretch' and accused her of bringing dishonor upon her father's house, upon her relatives, and upon her mistress, the Queen" (245).[10] The resemblance between this passage and what Jeanne says of her mother's reaction to her disobedience is striking. In one of the longest speeches in the *Heptameron*, Rolandine accuses the queen of injustice and claims the right to act according to her own desires. She appeals to a higher authority to justify her actions, in legal language that echoes Jeanne's declaration in a more assertive, and therefore subversive, fashion:

> "I have no advocate to speak in my defense. My only advocate is the truth, the truth which is known to me alone, and I am bound to declare it to you fearlessly . . . I am not afraid that any mortal creature should hear how I have conducted myself in the affair with which I am charged, since I know that there has been no offence either to God or to my honour." (248)

> ". . . puys que je n'ay advocat qui parle pour moy, sinon la veritee, laquelle moy seulle je sçay, je suis tenue de la

declairer sans craincte, . . . Je ne crainctz que creature mortelle entende comme je me suis conduicte en l'affaire dont l'on me charge, puisque je sais que Dieu et mon honneur n'y sont en riens offensez." (169–170)

Rolandine's claim is indeed outrageous ("audatieuse" is repeated twice in the text). In story 40, Rolandine's aunt is condemned, both within the story and by the discussants, for the far more modest transgression of marrying someone whom she thought would meet with approval. At the end of that story, story 40, both Parlamente and Oisille side with the social authorities: "'Ladies, I pray God that you will take note of this example, and that none of you will wish to marry merely for your own pleasure, without the consent of those to whom you owe obedience'" (370). Yet in story 21 the narrative works to justify Rolandine's claim. The state attempts to annul the union on grounds of non-consummation, while Rolandine appeals to scripture to uphold its validity:

> However, before they sent her [to the tower], they arranged for several men of the Church and some members of the King's Council to speak with her. These men made it plain to her that since her marriage was established by nothing more than exchange of words, it could quite easily be dissolved, provided that they gave one another up entirely. It was, they informed her, the king's wish that she should do so, in order that the honor of her house should be upheld. Her reply was that she was ready to obey the King in all things, provided there was no conflict with her conscience. But that which god had joined together no man could put asunder, . . . (250)

> Mais, avant l'envoyer, feirent parler à elle plusieurs gens d'Eglise et de Conseil, luy remonstrans, puisqu'il n'y avoit en son mariage que la parolle, qu'il se povoit facilement deffaire, mais que l'un et l'autre se quictassent, ce que le Roy voiloit qu'elle feit pour garder l'honneur de la maison dont elle estoit. Elle leur feit responce que en toutes choses elle estoit preste d'obeyr au Roy, sinon à contrevenir à sa conscience; mais ce que Dieu avoit assemblé, les hommes ne le povoient separer . . . (171)

Upon refusing to allow the dissolution of her marriage, Rolandine is returned to her father, who locks her in a castle in the forest. The bastard proves unfaithful and dies, whereupon Rolandine's father seeks to make amends. Rolandine marries a gentleman who "bore the same name and arms as her father" (252). When her brother tries to disinherit her because of her disobedience, God intervenes and the brother dies, leaving all the inheritance to her. God is indeed, as Rolandine asserts, on her side.

The queen disappears when Rolandine returns to her father, and the storytellers never mention her, although the dialogue between queen and subject occupies a significant portion of the tale. While the discursive confrontation with Rolandine works to discredit the queen, other events in the narrative, on the contrary, seem to justify her opposition to the union. The "bastard" proves an unworthy mate for Rolandine: "It was quite plain from his lack of constancy that it was not true and perfect love that led him to attach himself to Rolandine, but rather greed and ambition" (251), thus retrospectively justifying the queen's judgment on moral grounds. The unworthiness of the "bastard" reframes the queen's actions so that she appears to have been intervening in Rolandine's best interests. Earlier in the tale, the prince's mother, another queen, finds the "bastard" reading courtly romances, which serves further to undermine his moral standing.

In story 21 the moral justifications for opposition to Rolandine's choice ideologically mask the threat to the sociopolitical order represented by her claims, a threat mentioned by Dagoucin in the discussion of story 40: " 'in order to maintain peace in the state, consideration is given only to the rank of families, the seniority of individuals, and the provisions of the law, . . . in order that the monarchy should not be undermined' " (374). The exigencies of the "state," suggest these narratives, apply as much to the countess (story 10) and the queen (story 21) as they do to their daughters and subjects. Thus the countess in story 10 must marry off her daughter at the behest of the king, while the queen in story 21 serves the king and Rolandine's father in separating Rolandine and the "bastard." To the extent that they collaborate with or uphold the monarchy, they are invested with moral authority and the power to regulate the actions of less empowered feminine subjects, yet they do so, the narratives suggest, in the interests of those subjects as well.

The position of the aristocratic maternal authority-figure is contradictory indeed. It is a position from which a woman may exercise authority over other women in the negotiation of marriage contracts in the interests of the state. Yet for such controlling power to be successful, it must also at least appear to serve the interests of those daughterly subjects, for their resistance or rebellion threatens to undermine the hierarchy that constitutes the very basis of maternal authority.

There is simultaneously in these stories a subversion of the state through the privileging of daughterly resistance. In story 10 that subversion is disempowering; while it undoes patriarchal prerogative, it also undermines the countess' authority and results in Floride's definitive separation, both from her mother and from the social economy of exchange as a whole. In story 21, there is a more radical split between authority and its subversion because the mother-figure is queen, ersatz embodiment of monarchic authority. The daughterly resistance, in the assertion of the right to "give herself away," undermines the queen's power to control. In this story, however, the conflict is resolved by scapegoating the "bastard." Both desires triumph: the sociopolitical order is upheld (through a scapegoating of the "bastard" that justifies the queen's disapproval and defines it as "legitimate"), and Rolandine gets what she wants.

While the maternal figure is a collaborator, mothering is a praxis which, in the case of Marguerite and her text, is not solely based on political domination. A narrative such as story 21 provides a model of resistance, a precedent for other "daughters" to whom the *Heptameron* may be addressed, while it simultaneously provides a moral justification for the exercise of maternal authority. It is a praxis engaged in mediation. In the uneasy open-endedness of its dialogic structure and the inconclusiveness of the discursive confrontations between collaborator and rebel, Marguerite's text mediates between feminine desires, navigating those desires through patriarchal territory. Marguerite suggests this difference between her work and its male-authored counterparts, both in her condemnation of courtly romance (story 21) and in the anti-Boccaccian polemics of the prologue to the *Heptameron*. The Galeotto (Boccaccio's *Decameron*) mediates desire, but it does so exclusively in the service of a phallocracy, to the detriment of both the female subject and maternal authority. The *Heptameron* mediates in the interests of preserving a precarious, female, place of authority, whether it be the authority of the monarch's mother (which Jeanne d'Albret will become), or that of the women who manipulate the possibilities of consent and non-consent in marriage contracts to further their own interests.[11]

Natalie Davis suggests that some aristocratic women realized the economic and political importance of their bodies in contracting alliances and consolidating state power, and exploited that importance by "giving themselves away." She makes the point that "if women can think of giving themselves away, then they can also begin to think of having stronger ownership rights in their bodies" (Davis 1986: 62), rights for which many women today are still struggling. Marguerite's and her daughter's tales suggest some of the complexities involved in the concept of rights of ownership. Whom does it benefit when a woman accedes to the sort of power I have described as maternal authority, and how are we to understand that power? Did Jeanne refuse consent to her marriage to the duke of Clèves, or was non-consent created for the purposes of dissolving an unfortunate alliance? And, if Marguerite did indeed "set her up to it," in whose interests was she acting? If absolute resistance is self-defeating (as in the case of Floride), what does successful negotiation produce: another queen, a wife and mother to a king, but also perhaps an ardent Protestant in Catholic France? What sort of empowerment did Jeanne d'Albret's second marriage bring her? And what if, instead of maternal authority based on the exchange of daughters as commodities in the service of the "familial state," Marguerite's maternal praxis had been that of a traitor or a revolutionary? Would France have become a powerful nation-state?

NOTES

1 By "parental" the stricter term "patriarchal" (rule by the father) must be understood, since women were legally subject to their husbands. See Davis 1986: 55.

2 "ladite dame a presenté deux feuilles et une demie-feuille de papier, qu'elle a dict estre escriptes et signées de sa main et contenir lesdites déclarations et protestacions dont cy-dessus a esté faicte mention, desquelles les teneurs ensuyvent . . ."

3 For an account and partial translation (into French) of Descurra's report, which was written in Spanish, see de Ruble 1877: 80–110.

4 Pierre Bourdieu's 1982 study of the necessary linguistic negotiations of the colonized in exchanges with the colonizer seems particularly apt in this context.

5 The best biographical study I have read of Jeanne d'Albret, one that is judiciously cautious about interpreting documents, is Roelker 1968. For other interpretations of events I mention, see de Ruble 1877; Freer 1855; Ryan 1911; Jourda 1930; Putnam 1935; and Febvre 1944, as examples.

6 Hirsch 1989 points out that psychoanalytic models of subjectivity within the family romance privilege the child's point of view and that feminists, in revising such models, have nevertheless continued to privilege the child (now a daughter). Indeed she argues that much of feminism itself speaks from the position of the daughter. I would add that it is rare in general to find narrative structures that

centrally position the mother's voice and that Davis' research into pardon tales bears this out (with the added probability that the narrative structure of pardon tales themselves is shaped, in part, by family romances). Indeed, one could argue that psychoanalysis' privileging of the voice of the child is an extension of what is already, historically speaking, a narrative structure. Yet, for the daughterly voice to be privileged, and thus brought before the law and recorded in sixteenth-century France, the familial authority denounced must be, it would seem, "illegitimate." This may account for the preponderance of step-mother/daughter conflict rather than mother/daughter strife.

7 My use of the term maternal is specific; it implies a practice associated with a mode of sex/affective production which has "its own distinctive logic of exchange of the human services of sexuality, nurturance, and affection." See Ferguson 1984: 155. For the term "maternal text," a text that privileges the subjectivity or "voice" of the maternal subject position, see Hirsch 1989.

8 Chilton 1984, 65–66: "'Madame,' she [Parlamente] said, 'you have had much experience of life, and you now occupy the position of mother in regard to the rest of us women . . .'" For the French see François 1967: 6.

9 For critiques of Freud and Girard in relation to "woman," see Kofman 1980 and Moi 1982.

10 "La Royne . . . l'appella plusieurs foys malheureuse, en lieu de cousine, lui remonstrant la honte qu'elle avoit faicte à la maison de son pere et à tous ses parents de s'estre maryée, et à elle qui estoit sa maistresse, sans son commandement ne congé" (François 1967: 167).

11 Another important text by Davis that speculates about this issue is *The Return of Martin Guerre* (1983). Indeed, it is precisely the question of female agency that inspires Robert Finlay's attack on Davis' work and her rebuttal. See Finlay 1988 and Davis 1988.

REFERENCES

Armstrong, Nancy (1986). Introduction: Literature as Women's History. *Genre* 19: 347–69.

Bourdieu, Pierre (1982). *Ce que parler veut dire: L'économie des échanges linguistiques*. Paris: Fayard.

Chilton, P. A., trans. (1984). Marguerite de Navarre, *The Heptameron*. London: Penguin.

Davis, Natalie Zemon (1983). *The Return of Martin Guerre*. Cambridge, MA: Harvard University Press.

—— (1986). Boundaries and the Sense of Self in Sixteenth-Century France. In *Reconstructing Individualism:*

Autonomy, Individuality, and the Self in Western Thought, eds. T. Heller, M. Sosna, D. Wellbery. Stanford, CA: Stanford University Press, 53–63.

—— (1987). *Fiction in the Archives: Pardon Tales and their Tellers in Sixteenth-Century France*. Stanford, CA: Stanford University Press.

—— (1988). "On the Lame". *American Historical Review* 93, *AHR Forum: The Return of Martin Guerre*, 553–603.

De Ruble, Alphonse (1877). *Le Mariage de Jeanne d'Albret*. Paris: Adolphe Labitte.

Febvre, Lucien (1944). *Amour sacré, amour profane: Autour de l'Heptaméron*. Paris: Gallimard.

Ferguson, Ann (1984). On Conceiving Motherhood and Sexuality: A Feminist Materialist Approach. In *Mothering: Essays in Feminist Theory*, ed. Joyce Trebilcot. Totowa, NJ: Rowman and Allanheld, 153–82.

Finlay, Robert (1988). The Refashioning of Martin Guerre. *American Historical Review* 93, *AHR Forum: The Return of Martin Guerre*, 553–603.

François, Michel, ed. (1967). Marguerite de Navarre, *L'Heptameron*. Paris: Garnier Frères.

Freer, Martha (1855). *The Life of Jeanne d'Albret, Queen of Navarre*. 2 vols. London: Hurst and Blackett.

Genin, F. (1842). *Nouvelles lettres de la reine de Navarre adressées au roi Francois Ier, son frère*. Paris: Jules Renouard.

Hanley, Sarah (1987). Family and State in Early Modern France: The Marriage Pact. In *Connecting Spheres: Women in the Western World, 1500 to the Present*, eds. Marilyn Boxer and Jean Quataert. New York: Oxford University Press, 53–63.

Hirsch, Marianne (1989). *The Mother/Daughter Plot: Narrative, Psychoanalysis, Feminism*. Bloomington: Indiana University Press.

Jourda, Pierre (1930). *Marguerite d'Angoulême, Duchesse d'Alençon, Reine de Navarre 1492–1549: Etude biographique et littéraire*, vol. 1. Paris: Honoré Champion.

Kofman, Sarah (1980). The Narcissistic Woman: Freud and Girard. *Diacritics* 9: 36–45.

Moi, Toril (1982). The Missing Mother: The Oedipal Rivalries of René Girard. *Diacritics* 12: 21–31.

Putnam, Samuel (1935). *Marguerite of Navarre*. New York: Coward-McCann.

Roelker, Nancy (1986). *Queen of Navarre: Jeanne d'Albret 1528–1572*. Cambridge, MA: Harvard University Press.

Ruddick, Sara (1984). Maternal Thinking. In *Mothering: Essays in Feminist Theory*, ed. Joyce Trebilcot. Totowa, NJ: Rowman and Allanheld, 213–30.

—— (1989). *Maternal Thinking: Toward a Politics of Peace*. Boston: Beacon Press.

Ryan, P. F. William (1911). *Queen Jeanne of Navarre*. London: Hutchin Son & Co.

Scott, Joan (1988). *Gender and the Politics of History*. New York: Columbia University Press.

DIANA E. HENDERSON

Elizabeth's Watchful Eye and George Peele's Gaze: Examining Female Power Beyond the Individual

When Elizabeth Tudor ascended the throne in 1558, her sex was a source of anxiety and amazement for most of her subjects; forty years later, it had become a source of mythology, in one of history's most successful cases of political image-making. Her sex had a widespread and obvious impact on courtly art, be it the cause for eulogy in *The Faerie Queene* or the cause for frustration in the Petrarchan poetry of Gascoigne and Raleigh. Yet any major role for Elizabeth in improving the status of women, even those in the aristocracy, has usually been dismissed because of her unique position (an idea she promoted linguistically by blurring her own gender identity and stressing her exceptional role; cf. Heisch 1975, Marcus 1989). At the same time, many of the poems and dramas addressed to the queen by her male courtiers stress her gender as an aspect of her power over them. To what extent did the artistic veneration of Elizabeth extend into a cultural recognition of value in what was perceived as "the feminine"? More particularly, what was implied by representing her power as being distinctively female?

To represent the sovereign of a nation-state as female, given the sex-gender systems of western culture, upset central assumptions about hierarchical power and proper social order. Yet the continuing presence and success of the first unmarried queen regnant on the English throne forced her subjects to confront this union of woman and sovereignty. Recent criticism, perhaps replicating as well as documenting Elizabethan myth-making, has emphasized ways the Queen and her contemporaries represented her as anomalous and androgynous, a singular exception to the rule of female inferiority. Others note how the Queen skilfully manipulated traditional "feminine roles," those which define women relationally to men as mothers, wives, nurses, etc., thus legitimating her power through service to her "people" (the generalized subject tending, as usual, to presume "its" masculinity). Both these strategies work within the system of stereotypes based on sexual difference, and do not challenge the general assumption of female inferiority.[1] In a number of courtly works, however, the attempt to represent the Queen to herself and her courtiers leads to a re-vision of some aspects of the culture's stereotypes and can be read as (partially and tentatively) anticipating the modern project of conceiving a female subject.

In this paper, my exemplary case is George Peele's court drama, *The Arraignment of Paris*.[2] While this middle-class playwright wrote for a specific audience and may have intended to do no more than flatter his monarch, the representation of gender in his drama goes beyond mere recital of traditional praise for queens. His play reduces the erotic differentiation between the sexes typical of courtly Petrarchanism, and explicitly lauds the power of females in a political context, as bringing peace, cooperation, and wise guidance to an earthly kingdom—rather than keeping woman in distinct religious or private erotic realms, her common places of praise. Moreover, because *The Arraignment of Paris* was distributed in a published text, it (like many other discursive practices of the court) had an impact well beyond the bounds of the playing hall. Peele's play thus illustrates how Elizabeth's position as sovereign provided a specific occasion for, and indeed demanded, a reexamination of the proper places and power of women.

This gendered image-making complicates historicist analysis of the politics of sovereignty and subjectivity. As Teresa de Lauretis has observed, some of the most influential theorists of the subject in an ideological framework (Althusser, Foucault) "are either unconcerned with gender or unable to conceive of a female subject" (19). One result, observable in several new historicist studies of early modern England, has been to focus on the rebellious (male) courtier's resistance to the hegemonic power of the court system headed by a (female) sovereign as a desperate gesture at freedom for the subject. As soon as one attends to gender more than parenthetically, the limitations of such analysis become clear. To get past a single political model for situating the sovereign and the subject representing her, and for evaluating the significance of that representation, I invoke other connotations of the word "subject." This complication, I propose, more adequately places the text, its author and its audience within culture, as well as more fully accounting for the tensions and shifts within the play's script. Resisting a single perspective or monolithic concept of social power, I want to supplement an historical setting of the play within a Foucauldian political paradigm with a reading that is indebted to theorists who do foreground gender, allowing the partial truths each model reveals to put pressure on the others. Borrowing from feminist film analysis, I will touch on the relationship between the visual object of the gaze and the role of the viewer as subject; I will also investigate how Peele employs literary tropes and traditions as subject matter, primarily through a strategy of negotiation that allows him to "respond to the assumptions encoded into dominant cultural forms and systems of representation" (Jones 1990: 2). By considering these alternative analytic emphases, and acknowledging the dynamic complexity of defining power and privileged positions in dramatic performance, I hope to demonstrate how Peele's play innovatively represents female authority.

First, a preliminary placement. The text of *The Arraignment of Paris*, published in 1584, is most often remembered as the first English pastoral play and as a five-act drama unusual in its time for its poetic self-consciousness and metrical variety.[3] It presents the Judgment of Paris, but adds a legal twist to this familiar mythological scene: his subsequent arraignment before the Olympian gods on charges of corrupt judgment (due to bribery by Venus, who uses Helen of Troy as bait). The play also includes processions of country gods, a subplot involving the lovelorn Colin Clout and his shepherd friends, and a masque-like finale in which Queen Elizabeth receives the golden apple. Rather than separating exalted and lowly characters, Peele allows gods and shepherds to converse in a more fluid community, interweaving their stories to create a loose but coherent narrative about power and desire.

The Arraignment of Paris was performed at court by the Children of the Chapel Royal, most likely during the winter of 1581–82 on New Year's Eve or Shrove Tuesday.[4] The historical moment is suggestive, in that the play idealizes Elizabeth's power to create peace at the very time her religious and political policies were becoming more belligerent. By the end of 1581, the international situation for England was ominous. Philip II had annexed Portugal the year before; a Catholic resurgence seemed threatening, and the Parliament of 1581 reacted with repressive new religious restrictions. Avoiding military commitments on the continent grew all the more difficult; while Elizabeth still officially pursued neutrality and refused direct involvement in the Netherlands, she made hostile public gestures towards Spain.[5]

Most ironic, given Peele's representation of the Queen as a peaceful unifying force, were two recent enactments of torture, among the more famous cases of the crown's violent power over subjects who had not been implicated in any direct rebellion against Elizabeth.[6] The first victim was John Stubbes, whose book *The discovery of a gaping gulf* . . . (August 1579) warned the queen not to marry the Catholic French prince Alençon; Elizabeth was furious enough to demand his death, and settled reluctantly for a mild form of dismemberment, the axing of his authorial hand. Then in December of 1581, the Jesuit missionary Edmund Campion was dismembered in a gruesome public spectacle, which included hanging, removing his entrails before death, and quartering.

Although a standard punishment for heresy or treason in the sixteenth century, drawing and quartering was often commuted to beheading when the victim was a gentleman; Campion was not only of good social standing, but a moral scholar of great eloquence who had been praised by Elizabeth during her 1566 visit to Oxford.[7] International politics demanded some display of power from the Protestant sovereign and radical Protestants may have cheered, but this particular response ran counter to Elizabeth's tolerance of Catholics in earlier years. It may indeed have backfired, illustrating too clearly the violent power of the body politic over the body natural. Certainly it prompted a pamphlet war, including written accounts of Campion's bravery as well as a defense of the government's *Execution of Justice in England* from William Cecil's office.[8]

The spectacle of a wellborn Englishman dismembered provides an unsettling prelude, a necessary counter-image, to the complacent spectacle of peace and unity that resolves George Peele's *Arraignment*. In its famed final gesture, Juno, Pallas, and Venus endorse Diana's decision to give the golden apple to the Queen. Elizabeth is said to unify the strengths of many in her singular body, re-membering female virtues (obscured by the goddesses' earlier competition) as "shee,

> In whom do meete so manie giftes in one
> On whom our countrie gods so often gaze
> In honour of whose name the Muses sing.
> (5.1.1167–70)

The Queen embodies a happy, healthy state, a nation at peace. The juxtaposition of Stubbes' hand or Campion's bloody corpse with Peele's poetic tribute surely provides an illustration of an early modern state's mechanism for discipline and assertion of the crown's power over the body politic, fitting almost too neatly into a Foucauldian model.[9] The tendency in much recent analysis is to expose such historical tensions, suggesting the necessary connection between dismembering the unruly subject and incorporating state power in the sovereign, and furthermore implying alliance with the doomed subject struggling against monarchic authoritarianism.

But this is not the whole story. What may be discounted in these analyses is the double function of power to create as well as suppress (recognized by Foucault), and moreover to create several kinds of knowledge. The particulars of Peele's poetic representation lead us to attend to another aspect of power besides the state's atrocious apparatus of corporal punishment and control. In its play with patriarchal power, *The Arraignment of Paris* creates a new space in which to examine the Queen's two bodies, another way to "know" female sovereignty. This goes beyond conventional flattery or a counterstatement to the violent potential of Elizabeth's authority. The Queen's presence as judging audience prompts a final representation of female power as publicly *active* (rather than frustratingly distanced, as in the dominant Petrarchan poetic model) and *benevolent* (rather than exclusively death-dealing, through sexual rejection or the violence of an unruly "woman on top"—fears displaced onto two minor characters, Thestylis and Ate). Peele's response to Elizabeth's gaze ambitiously addresses the peculiar difficulties of venerating a female sovereign and imagining alternative views of female presence and power.

The Arraignment of Paris finally dissolves into a personal compliment to the queen, naming her as the "Nymphe Eliza" and aligning her with several goddesses represented onstage. It takes fully five acts, however, to reach this figure of the unified sovereign. En route, the play reexamines human desire and its frustrations from the perspectives of both male and female characters, in ways that reduce the emphasis on sexual difference common to myths and courtly love plots.

In the first four acts, *The Arraignment of Paris* exposes the inadequacies of objectifying women as the "cruel fair," that vision of the Other so familiar in Tudor poetry. By presenting equivalent stories of romantic cruelty and abandonment, the playwright suggests that the amorous behavior of the sexes is fundamentally similar. Paris's abandonment of his first-love, the shepherdess Oenone, takes place in scenes interspersed with the nymph Thestylis's indifference to Colin Clout, and both Oenone and Colin lament their rejection in song. The ability of Oenone to hold her own in the lyric lamentations alongside Colin Clout (who was at the time the surrogate for England's most impressive contemporary poet, Edmund Spenser) suggests a female as well as male version of voice and subjectivity.[10] Indeed, in the first scene between Paris and Oenone, it is she who commands language as well as song. Paris asks *her* to

> Tell me what shall be subject of our talke:
> Thou hast a sorte of pretie tales in stoore . . .
> In telling them thou hast a speciall grace.
> Then prethee, sweete, afforde some pretie thing,
> Some toie that from thy pleasaunt witte doth springe.
> (1.5.235–6, 239–41)

Although she will soon be rejected for a competing singer (Helen of Troy, crooning an Italian aria), Oenone's speech paves the way for a stronger and more successful assertion of female voices in the play's finale.

Of course, from the time of Ovid's *Heroides*, male poets have taken the voice of abandoned women in epistles, and Peele's drama negotiates with poetic tradition in portraying these lovers. Oenone becomes an abandoned lover, whereas Colin Clout's love is unrequited, so that in a sense she resembles her ancestress in *Heroides 5* lamenting bitterly after the fact, whereas he shares the thwarted desire for what has not yet been achieved characteristic of Petrarch and Spenser's lyric speakers.[11] But where Peele alters their representation, he does so in ways that stress similarity between the sexes. Thus, Oenone speaks well not only after but *before* her rejection; more broadly, the sequential juxtaposition of these two poetic stereotypes onstage serves to emphasize their *shared* experience rather than two different temporal modes or attitudes toward desire. Peele dramatically interweaves the two rejections: in adjoining scenes, Colin Clout's shepherd friends lament both his death and Oenone's abandonment.

The similarity between the romantic fates of men and women holds true as their stories conclude, superseding sexual difference. Colin Clout and Oenone remain faithful and loving even when hopeless, whereas Paris and Thestylis can both act heartlessly and also share the fate of being victims (perhaps scapegoats) of punitive gods. The distinction between men as active wooers and women as passive victims of love, so familiar in courtly poetry, does not materialize. Indeed, it is the utterly passive Colin Clout who, during the third act of the play, literally dies of a broken heart.

The stories of these lovers are poetically connected with the last act's paean to Elizabeth through the passing presence of Colin Clout, the shepherd-poet borrowed from Spenser's *The Shepheardes Calender* (published in the winter of 1579). Just as Oenone's song initiates the positive representation of female

voicing, Colin's appearance foreshadows explicit praise of the
Queen. Spenser's fourth eclogue, resembling Vergil's fourth in its
celebration of a messianic virgin, includes Colin's song "Of fayre
Eliza, Queene of shepheardes all" (1. 34), which according to the
Argument "is purposedly intended to the honor and prayse of our
most gracious sovereigne, Queene Elizabeth" (Spenser 1947: 431).
The eclogue links nostalgia and pastoral pain with praise of the
Queen through the personage of old Hobbinol, who, grieving at
his loss of the young man's love because of his passion for
Rosalind, recites Colin's happy song; not only is the song of female
praise doubly removed by speaker, but it is also a relic of a happier
past. By contrast, Peele moves his song of praise into a present
whose immediacy in time and place supplants the pains of Troy
and eros. Having killed off *his* version of Colin Clout in Act 3,
Peele uses his skills as a playwright to create a more spectacular
praise of the Queen, not from the nostalgic male poet's perspective
(or his male surrogate's, as in Spenser), but from the empathetic
viewpoint of female goddesses.[12]

Through this perspective shift and allied artistic strategies, the
play supersedes the competitive aesthetic of most male praise for
the beloved, epitomized in the choice demanded of Paris by the
Olympian goddesses. Petrarchan love poetry conventionally acknowledged some power of the lady over her suitor, her servant,
and so provided male courtiers with a vocabulary in one sense
appropriate for another kind of courtship, that of a female
monarch. But because Elizabeth's power was not merely a literary
fiction but a political truth, the use of this poetic language often
created as many tensions as it solved. In *The Arraignment of Paris*,
Peele counters the use of love poetry as a means to emphasize
male frustration with the distant female monarch, a device familiar
in the work of such courtiers as Gascoigne, Raleigh, and Sidney.
Instead, while acknowledging the pain of eros, Peele presents men
and women united in their experience of desire and disappoint-
ment. Moreover, by having Helen of Troy sing in Italian when she
appears as Venus's offering to Paris, Peele explicitly connects the
tongue of Petrarch and the sonneteers with the divisiveness and
tragic desire inherent in the story of the judgment of Paris.[13] The
playwright thus turns elsewhere to find terms of praise for his
female sovereign. He turns away from men and eros entirely.

Judgments based on male standards and desires are symbolically dismissed in the fourth act: first, after being arraigned by the
gods on charges of misjudgment, Paris is sent offstage; then, in
response to the demands of Juno and Pallas for a re-trial (an
appeals court ruling on who's the fairest of them all), the male

Olympian gods abdicate their authority in favor of Diana. The change to a female judge is defended on the grounds both of domain and gender: the initial decision was made "neere Dianas bowre" on Mount Ida, in the earthly realm where mortal queens also hold sway; and besides, these comically timorous Olympians admit, it would be folly for males to choose among powerful women. Thus Peele stresses the presence of an earthly space of female authority, before turning to the Queen.

By making Diana the arbitress and returning from the heavens to earth, Peele alters the Judgment tradition to create a final image that idealizes rather than displaces present-day England; that distinction would be reinforced by the immediacy of performance. It is not the arch-patriarch Saturn who restores this Golden Age, nor even heavenly Astraea, but instead the version of Diana who resides in the world of mortals.[14] In Act 2, Helen of Troy unwittingly called attention to the attributes of Diana that make her the appropriate goddess to preside over this happy ending: sovereign in all three realms (cielo, ferno, terra), Diana can create a vision of heaven *on earth*; as the chaste protector of virgins, she helps the other goddesses to dismiss the sexual rivalry caused by their competitive desire to be the fairest object of a male gaze. On a stage cleared of male characters, the fifth Act's praise of the nymph Eliza unites an unusual assortment of female deities, heavenly Olympians and infernal Fates combining to sing the praise of an earthly queen. Boundaries blur and realms merge in this paradise of women.

The traditional story of Troy, of male heroism and tragic desire, also recedes before a different image of human power in Troynovant, or London. The first Act's chorus to "Ida, happie hill," laden with dramatic ironies when it introduced the three goddesses to the disruptive judgment scene, is transmuted into a lofty Latin paean, "Vive diu foelix," purged of ambiguity, dissension, or doubt. The landscape regains floral abundance, recalling the world Flora "Bestrewed and deckt with partie collord flowers" in Act 1, before the golden apple caused a falling out; indeed, Pallas reminds us that when Elizabeth, here named "Zabeta," was born, "Flora with her flowers strewed the Earth."[15] Merging topical allusion with paradisiac imagery, England transforms into "Elizium," the people are "ycleeped Angeli," and the queen is hailed as "doctissima, candida, casta" (5.1.1150, 1155, 1215). She is idealized but also the woman in the audience:

> She giveth lawes of justice and of peace,
> And on her heade as fits her fortune best,

> She weares a wreath of laurell, golde, and palme:
> Her robes of purple and of scarlet die,
> Her vayle of white, as best befits a mayde.
> Her auncestors live in the house of fame;
> Shee giveth armes of happie victorie,
> And flowers to decke her lyons crowned with golde.
>   (5.1.1157–64)

In this transformation of a Petrarchan blazon, every line recalls Elizabeth's gender as well as her appearance and strengths. Other female figures speak of her and judge her fairest, extending Oenone's earlier powers of speech beyond the erotic into heroic portraiture. The Queen's body is decked colorfully, not to fetishize its parts but to compose a regal emblem. The gold and purple of State mix harmoniously with flowers and laurels, Beauty and Fame. Rather than erasing the woman to create a king, this passage weds the Queen's two bodies: the concluding couplet unites the giving of arms and flowers.

This catalogue of praise for Elizabeth, unifying stereotypically feminine traits with those of a good monarch, overgoes the Petrarchan blazon as "sparagmos," the objectification of the female body by a dismembering male gaze (see Vickers 1981). If all the world were a text, the rhetorical and actual dismemberment of female poetic and male political subjects might be grouped in antithesis to the Queen's unifying sovereign presence, but my only excuse for voicing this hypothetical equation is to call attention to its limits. Obviously, such sleight of mouth irresponsibly denies the pain of torture that Stubbes and Campion experienced. Less importantly except in the immediate context of this paper, it oversimplifies the relationship between the imaging of other female characters and the final image of the queen; she is not simply contrasted but related to them, extending their attributes of will and beauty into a political context and receiving their praise.

The tragic potential of the play, announced in the prologue by Ate, a goddess of discord, is finally solved by a very different female power—not only by the gesture of giving the apple to Elizabeth, but also by Diana's crucial role as the ultimate judge, with the endorsement of a female chorus.[16] Threatening versions of womanhood (earlier interspersed with male infidelity and violence) are gone, their appearance having worked against simple inversion of gender superiority, just as the erotic episodes worked against easy definition of sexual difference. Diana pacifies the three goddesses who competed earlier, initiating a compromise which does not deny the worthiness and fairness of any. In parallel couplets, as formal and ritualistic as the Latin song, Juno, Pallas, and Venus recognize the Queen as their apogee and verbally erase their differences. While most of the play diminishes stereotypical contrasts between the sexes, this public celebration of sovereignty occurs in a female realm exclusively—a reversal rather than erasure of usual gendering.

Perhaps the most remarkable aspect of this finale to *The Arraignment of Paris* is its attempt to represent a woman's-eye view, pleasing the queen as audience with praise appropriate from a female perspective. Nor is Elizabeth herself called on to speak, hence avoiding the problem of coercion or subjugation of the monarch to her playwright's script.[17] Through the Queen's presence in itself, but also through her representation in the goddesses' words, singing, and dancing, Peele associates Elizabeth with a vocal, harmonious community of powerful females. Thus he celebrates his monarch not as masculine or as an exceptional woman, nor primarily as a perpetual virgin, but instead as the epitome of femininity, the best of several female powers in the play. Indeed, in terms of the actual event, she was the only "true" woman in the play, the roles of the other goddesses being performed by boy actors.[18] As such, she marks the feminine extreme on a continuum of gender identity.

The Queen is certainly "different" from the other characters, as Inga-Stina Ewbank has remarked, noting that she defeats the dynamic and potentially tragic world of the play through her "simple, static presence"; to her analysis, I add the emphasis on the representation of this "wonder of monarchy" as explicitly feminine, and associated with fertility, peace, beauty, justice, and life itself.[19] All this is achieved only by representing her in language amenable to Elizabeth as female auditor and by offering a magic gesture amenable to her female gaze.

In so presenting this spectacle for the Queen, Peele in a sense supplants his own male perspective and takes what is traditionally the "woman's part." He does not present Elizabeth, as most of his and our contemporaries tend to do, by finding a relationship between her and his own subjectivity, his own male gaze. In its reflection of the Queen at twice her natural size, serving as a beautiful yet self-abnegating mirror, this play performs like a woman. In *A Room Of One's Own*, Virginia Woolf wryly observes that this traditional female role as flattering reflection, for all, or perhaps because of, its gross inequity, has boosted the confidence and achievement of men throughout history: "it charges the vitality; it stimulates the nervous system" (36). To the extent that Peele participated in a role-reversed version of this inflation of self, and to the extent that his printed play communicated and energized that image for his countrymen and women, *The Arraignment of Paris* participates in the counter-creation of a female subject as worthy sovereign.

By contrast, current scholarly tendencies to focus on the succession and Elizabeth's virginity as central to all representations of the queen, while certainly attending to major anxieties of the day, may replicate the cultural difficulty in looking beyond Elizabeth's sexual body when discussing her female sovereignty. Louis Adrian Montrose stresses Shakespeare's imagery of Elizabeth as mother, wetnurse, and virgin within *A Midsummer Night's Dream*, and intriguingly, in a recent historical study of Elizabeth, Christopher Haigh adopts the same rhetoric, dubbing Elizabeth a mother to the Church, a nanny to her Parliament, a nagging wife to her councillors, and a seductress to her court. The conventional labels are presented wittily and as sixteenth-century views, but aren't really superseded.[20] Yet Peele's play does not praise Elizabeth because of her relations to men or her ability to service them; he dismisses such labels of female power along with the gaze of his male characters. His representation of England as fertile and flowering while simultaneously chaste and virginal refuses the binary exclusiveness of succession discourse and, at least figuratively, blurs the categorization of women on the basis of sexual experience.[21] Here again Peele negotiates with traditional representations of his subject matter: while building an image of female sovereignty from terms and tropes familiar to a predominantly male audience as well as the Queen, his play represents her power as all-embracing and self-sufficient, not derived from men (not even her father) in any way. This fiction, applied to a human woman, can be read as both flattery of a sovereign and violation of the ideological basis for England's sex-gender system.

Such representation of Elizabeth is not confined to *The Arraignment*; it reappears in later works by Peele and other influential writers. In his Lord Mayor's Show for Wolstone Dixi in 1585, Peele praises the Queen as a figure of bounty and harmony, bringing to London "peace and calme" which now "Hath long bin such as like was never seene" (1952: 211). Again the reason for respect of the Queen's sovereignty goes beyond courtly veneration of a mistress's beauty, to more substantial political praise. Here London is gendered female, reinforcing the positive power associated with the Queen, her "regiment" not monstrous but "sacred."[22] Similarly, in 1589, George Puttenham was to write of Elizabeth, in a strikingly odd image, that "Out of her breast as from an eye, / Issue the rayes incessantly / Of her justice, bountie, and might."[23] Lacking the poetic delicacy of Peele, Puttenham's language nevertheless captures how the sovereignty of Elizabeth demanded new formulations of the linkage between femininity, the subjectivity of a royal "I," and the gaze of her "eye"; the female breast itself, often praised in the poetic form of the "blason du tétin" as an object for male desire, becomes not only a source of physical nourishment but a viewing eye, the source and subject of a different sort of "fairness," that of a just sovereign. Peele's play provides a fuller and more elegant precedent for the transformation of female fairness.

In later histories such as William Camden's, the image was perpetuated. His introduction begins with back-to-back praise of Elizabeth as the pattern of princes and the glory of womankind, epitomizing her achievement as a long-lived female sovereign in her own right; she is "The all-glorious, all-virtuous, incomparable, invict and matchless pattern of princes, the glory, honour and mirror of womankind, the admiration of our age, ELIZABETH, Queen of England. . . ." Despite cultural assumptions and actual hierarchies, Camden can see a prince mirroring a woman, now to be gazed upon by all who follow—including her male successor (who by implication would do better to gaze on her than be seen himself). The gaze is not one of gendered desire but of "admiration," the wonder appropriate to sovereignty.

Without the viewing eye of Elizabeth as the impetus for performance and simultaneously its ultimate judge, the vision initiated in *The Arraignment of Paris* would hardly have been realized. Sidney's "misunderstood" pageant, "The Lady of May," and Gascoigne's aborted Zabeta sketch attest to her shaping role in determining what would be—imaginatively and materially— shown. To recognize this does not automatically reduce Peele's play (and other such praise) to a thoughtless lackey's servile reflection, nor confine the critical enterprise exclusively to a search for the author's veiled but doomed marks of aesthetic autonomy in the shadow of political authority. It can also suggest a vision of political and aesthetic collaboration, with all the complex valences that word suggests when applied to *unequal* partners; collaboration, moreover, in creating an image of a woman's political power as self-sufficient and assertive.

In focusing on Peele's work and emphasizing its representations of gender, I have stressed Elizabeth's power as creative, counterbalancing the rebelliousness against central authority suggested by foregrounding the dismemberments of Stubbes and Campion, or indeed the poetry of Sidney and Marlowe. These poets have often been taken as a model of emerging individualism and modern subjectivity fighting a monolithic state power whose hegemony creates a compelling tragic vision (as in the work of Stephen Greenblatt, most influentially). In the process, critics often valorize, or identify with, masculine discontent as more mature and truthful than tamer tributes (just as antipetrarchan poets claim to have a more honest and accurate voice than their object of parody). Some recent studies of Tudor aristocracy and monarchy don't even mention gender as an issue complicating their discussion of political struggle, presuming rather than studying those aspects of "self" being asserted in challenges to the Queen's authority.[24] But the very amorphousness of the crown's power as a concept (as distinct from *de facto* force) was one of the central problems of Elizabeth's reign; this problem was aggravated by her gender. By discounting the complex nature of a female monarch's power, current readings can render state ideology in a much simpler way than contemporary art presents it. Dismissal of Peele's work as mere court propaganda to some extent reenacts the more rebellious courtiers' attitude towards female power.

Readings of *The Arraignment of Paris* that ignore the play's totality likewise erase complexity in favor of a single voice of assertion. Sometimes this voice is made explicitly male, as when Howard Baker focuses on Paris' fourth-act oration before the gods as the play's distinctive moment. As a result, he unironically calls this a "one-man play" prefiguring Marlowe's *Tamburlaine*, hence devaluing the importance and praise of feminine community in favor of masculine individualism.[25] The play becomes one moment in a narrative about the establishment of male subjectivity. Yet Peele's play, as I hope I have shown, examines subjectivity and power in quite another way. As do the works of Spenser, *The Arraignment of Paris* portrays numerous responses to female sovereignty, and by extension to other forms of female power in England, in its time, on earth.

Seeing the female as nurturing or peaceful is not in itself radical (especially when she's a queen), and Peele certainly praises Elizabeth's physical beauty as well; but *The Arraignment of Paris* melds these qualities with political praise for the Queen's justice and wisdom quite vigorously. It praises her as a peacemaker with power in the public, earthly realm rather than in the domestic or religious spheres exclusively. In watching this representation of herself, Elizabeth unifies the role of the female as the mediator or symbol of sovereignty, found in traditional ceremonies and pageants, with the direct, official power of the king. Thus the play indicates how Elizabeth's sovereignty sparked new interpretations of gender stereotypes, if only (or primarily) in works performed under her aegis and for her approval.

Because published works were increasingly important as a means by which subjects, especially those in the north and west, conceived of their monarch, the publication of Peele's own play in 1584 exemplifies the growing potential of court works to function as what Louis Adrian Montrose calls "shaping fantasies," creating as well as representing cultural attitudes. In the case of Peele's *Arraignment*, the fantasies include a bevy of powerful women ruling the universe and more immediately the state of England, and an ungendered, equal representation of the pains wrought by romantic love. The very real presence of Queen Elizabeth as viewing eye conditioned the playwright's own gaze, his own view of his artistic "subject"; in turn, the reality of her rule makes the published play more than mere fantasy. *The Arraignment of Paris* becomes a unifying aesthetic spectacle, and not only the converse of the political spectacle involved in punishing unruly subjects. It unifies ideal femininity with actual political power in what was for its time an innovative though not politically subversive performance. Seen in historical context, this court drama creatively confronts the double perspectives demanded by Elizabeth's gender and her sovereignty; in so doing, it substantiates her shaping role in the creation of resonant cultural images of women's political power.[26]

NOTES

1 These are only the strategies of praise; many historians, including some feminists, remark how "unsisterly" Elizabeth was in treating her ladies-in-waiting, although Bassnett 1988 defends her as a protective believer in chastity as a means of female power for both herself and her followers. A number of recent and forthcoming studies examine poetic tributes by women, stressing Elizabeth's importance as a model for female virtue *and* authorship. Less directly, Marcus 1986 and others have linked cross-dressing stage heroines with the androgynous Queen. My paper supplements these analyses.

2 See Horne's biographical sketch in Peele 1952: 3–146. I use the modern spelling of the play's title; otherwise I follow Benbow's edition (Peele 1970), with citations made by act, scene, and line.

3 See Benbow's introduction and Smith 1952 for standard views. Montrose 1980, while challenging Smith's reading, also discusses the play within the pastoral tradition; he

also anticipates some of my emphases. For unifying readings, see Von Hendy 1968 and Lesnick 1968.

4 Benbow (Peele 1970: 7–12) conjectured a version of the play prior to its 1584 publication date, but Greg 1906 placed it with "no doubt in 1581" (216) and Horne (Peele 1952) finds biographical evidence pointing to 1582. Daniel 1982 substantiated the dates I give through examination of the Master of the Revels' property lists for 1581. Nevertheless, my thesis does not rely on this dating.

5 For example, Elizabeth knighted Drake on board the Golden Hind, which returned from circumnavigating the world laden with Spanish gold. Jesuit-educated Englishmen had begun returning to their homeland in 1579 as missionaries. For more on the historical moment, see Haigh 1985 and MacCaffrey 1981.

6 Both gentlemen endured punishment gallantly. Elizabeth was not necessarily hypocritical in asserting a policy of peace and of religious toleration toward Catholics; as many historians note, it is a wonder she could withstand the militaristic and fervent religious pressures of her counsellors for so long.

7 On Campion's background and suffering, see McGrath 1967 and Meyer 1967. His "Brag" (a defense of his mission) was published before his sham trial.

8 Most notably, Thomas Alfield's *A True Report of the death and matyrdom of M. Campion* was secretly published before 1582, and Cecil's defense was countered by William Allen's *True, Sincere, and Modest Defense of English Catholics*; see Cecil 1965, Meyer 1967, McGrath 1967, Haigh 1988, MacCaffrey 1981.

9 See Foucault 1977, esp. 23–49; he cites Kantorowicz's analysis of the king's double body on 28–9.

10 Colin Clout was a character in Skelton's poetry, so Peele had Spenser's own precedent in "borrowing" him. Misattributing the choice of song to Paris ("In deciding what he should play, Paris has raised sinister topics" [91]), Von Hendy 1968 tellingly ignores Paris's own words, both those quoted in my text below and his admission to Oenone: "sith my cunning not compares with thine, / Beginne some Toy" (1.5.280–1).

11 Peele softens Ovid's portrait, replacing Oenone's anger after Paris's desertion with lamentation and song, sustaining unambiguous sympathy and pity for her as victim (as well as her resemblance to Colin).

12 King 1990 makes much of Spenser's distancing this song from his narrative voice. In the context of this paper, I can only call attention to this remarkable case of character-borrowing: Peele may be silencing his rival poet's voice, or he may be implying his own poetic

subjection and vocal erasure. In a longer study, I would stress the complications of Peele's subject position and the authority possible in different genres. Given the murderous subtext of male poetic competition, it makes even more sense that the play's happy ending is reached by pretending to erase the male gaze.

13 Helen claims to be a "Diana, dolce e rara" (2.2.506), putting herself in the unwise role of mortals who try to compete with goddesses. She courts Paris and disaster, but her song prefigures Diana's importance—not as "described," but as a sovereign power.

14 The use of Diana is not part of the Judgment tradition (see Anglo 1969, Ekeblad 1956, and Reeves 1954 for other instances of this device); rather, it derives from and transforms another pageant rivalry, between Juno and Diana (see note 17). I stress the earthly locale and immediacy as one significant shift from Mariology.

15 1.3.83; 5.1.1179. In another context, Montrose 1986: 333 notes that the verbal association of flowers with menstruation makes them an especially apt symbol of femininity.

16 The concluding transformation of Ate's vision is reinforced through the visual icon of the golden apple and through the shared use of blank verse (unusual in the play).

17 Recent studies have emphasized this tension between royal presentation and representation (cf. Montrose, Kastan 1986). Gascoigne's Zabeta sketch at Kenilworth exemplifies the dangers in instructive representation of the Queen; not coincidentally, Peele praises Elizabeth using the name "Zabeta" in a context that shows chaste Diana superior to married Juno (reversing the trope that got Gascoigne and several other proponents of a royal marriage into trouble during the 1560s and 70s).

18 The ironies of boys' company performances before the Queen are surely contributing factors to the overt concern with sexuality and queenship in the court drama. This emphasis is not exclusively attributable to homosexual titillation nor simply a result of more female parts (indeed, it does not necessarily correlate with the number of such parts).

19 138, 141. References to the fertile landscape and the Queen's virtues permeate Act 5.

20 Montrose 1986; Haigh 1988 frames his discussion by calling attention to the Queen's reliance on illusion, viewing her as an actress; he rightly notes that she "had a constant struggle to get men to do what she wanted" (125), but the labels of nanny and nag are surely his, not hers.

21 The current, perhaps exaggerated, focus on the Alençon

courtship (cf. Marcus 1989) may lead the impressionable to believe it polarized the culture into camps for and against the French marriage even into the early 1590s (when Elizabeth was obviously beyond marrying or child-bearing). Peele's work shows how mythological figures, images, and even "loaded" names such as Zabeta and Colin Clout could be transmuted, given complex new meanings that do not simply repeat or reverse earlier ones. Similarly, traditional attributes of the Virgin Mary signify differently when disconnected from God (Father and Son), and when located in England rather than in the heavens.

22 Peele does not always imagine London as female; see for example his "A Tale of Troy." The gendering here, then, implies a conscious choice to stress the kinship between City and Queen in a way that once again is not eroticized by male desire (despite the obvious occasion for such a trope, given the presentation before the new Lord Mayor, and the tradition of royal entries by kings as "marrying" the city). This pageant similarly ends with four nymphs praising the Queen—without reference to the Mayor. The female is not a symbolic mediator but rather the recipient of tribute, the surrogate for the real power of the sover-eign. Peele's phrase "the honor of her sacred regiment" (213) is a rebuttal to John Knox's 1558 *The First Blast of the Trumpet* which denounced "the monstrous regiment of women."

23 100; Montrose's mention of this passage in a footnote to his earlier version of "*A Midsummer Night's Dream* and the Shaping Fantasies of Elizabethan Culture" (1986) (*Representations* 1: 2, 88) spurred me to think about its significance.

24 For example, McCoy's (1989) analysis of the "militia" faction at court and chivalric "manliness" never addresses gender as a complicating term (odd given Elizabeth's double role as observing ladylove and active monarch). For tragic subjectivity see Greenblatt 1980, especially the Tyndale and Marlowe chapters (but see also his revised thoughts about "power" in 1988). Tennenhouse's intro-duction (1986) is straightforward about the desire to challenge the institutions of which he is an uneasy mem-ber. Reiss 1980 is equally frank about reading Marlowe through the lens of Foucault. Corthell 1989, citing Greenblatt and Althusser, distinguishes the subjectivity of Campion and other recusants: "Catholics were perhaps uniquely situated to experience the problem of the subject in Elizabethan England" (272).

25 Baker 1939 discounts Ate's Senecan prologue and Diana's

culminating praise of Elizabeth, other blank verse tonali-
ties just as crucial to the poetic whole.
26 Elizabeth's image became a positive influence or model
for many women, including poets such as Bradstreet. To
say this is not to fetishize royalty as a nostalgic form of
worship in a fractured culture. Thanks to all the Conference participants, and especially to Louise Fradenburg,
Lynda Boose, Carla Freccero, and Gordon Kipling, for
their responses. Special thanks to my colleagues Nancy
Coiner and Paul Monod for insights and advice. I gratefully acknowledge financial support from the ACLS, the
Ada Howe Kent Foundation, and Middlebury College.

REFERENCES

Anglo, Sydney (1969). *Spectacle, Pageantry, and Early Tudor
Policy*. Oxford: Clarendon Press.
Baker, Howard (1939). *Induction to Tragedy*. University,
LA: Louisiana State University Press.
Bassnett, Susan (1988). *Elizabeth I: A Feminist Perspective*.
New York: Berg.
Camden, William (1625–9). *Annales: The True and Royall
History of the Famous Empresse Elizabeth . . .* London.
Cecil, William (1965). *The Execution of Justice in England*
and *A True, Sincere, and Modest Defense of English
Catholics* by William Allen, ed. Robert M. Kingdon.
Ithaca, NY: Cornell University Press [for the Folger
Shakespeare Library].
Corthell, Ronald J. (1989). "The secrecy of man": Recusant
Discourse and the Elizabethan Subject. *English Literary
Renaissance* 19: 272–290.
Daniel, Carter A. (1982). The Arraignment of Paris. *Notes
and Queries* n.s. 29: 131–2.
De Lauretis, Teresa (1987). *Technologies of Gender*.
Bloomington: Indiana University Press.
Ekeblad, Inga-Stina [Ewbank] (1956). On the Background of
Peele's "Araygnement of Paris". *Notes and Queries* n.s.
3: 246–9.
Ewbank, Inga-Stina (1975). "What words, what looks, what
wonders?": Language and Spectacle in the Theatre of
George Peele. In *The Elizabethan Theatre V*, ed. G. R.
Hibbard. Hamden, CT: 124–54.
Foucault, Michel (1977). *Discipline and Punish*. Transl. Alan
Sheridan. NY: Pantheon.
Greenblatt, Stephen (1980). *Renaissance Self-Fashioning:
From More to Shakespeare*. Chicago: University of
Chicago Press.
—— (1988). *Shakespearean Negotiations*. Berkeley: Univer-
sity of California Press.

Haigh, Christopher, ed. (1985). *The Reign of Elizabeth I.* Athens, GA: The University of Georgia Press, 1985.

—— (1988). *Elizabeth I.* New York: Longman.

Heisch, Allison (1975). Queen Elizabeth I: Parliamentary Rhetoric and the Exercise of Power. *Signs* 1: 31–55.

Jones, Ann Rosalind (1990). *The Currency of Eros.* Bloomington: Indiana University Press.

Kastan, David Scott (1986). Proud Majesty Made a Subject: Shakespeare and the Spectacle of Rule. *Shakespeare Quarterly* 37: 459–75.

King, John N. (1990). Queen Elizabeth I: Representations of the Virgin Queen. *Renaissance Quarterly* 43: 30–74.

Lesnick, Henry G. (1968). The Structural Significance of Myth and Flattery in Peele's *Arraignment of Paris. Studies in Philology* 65: 163–70.

MacCaffrey, Wallace T. (1981). *Queen Elizabeth and the Making of Policy 1572–1588.* Princeton, NJ: Princeton University Press.

Marcus, Leah (1986). Shakespeare's Comic Heroines: Elizabeth I and the Political Uses of Androgyny. In *Women in the Middle Ages and the Renaissance*, ed. Mary Beth Rose, pp. 135–53. Syracuse: Syracuse University Press.

—— (1989). *Puzzling Shakespeare: Local Reading and Its Discontents.* Berkeley: University of California Press.

McCoy, Richard C. (1989). *The Rites of Knighthood: The Literature and Politics of Elizabethan Chivalry.* Berkeley: University of California Press.

McGrath, Patrick (1967). *Papists and Puritans.* London: Blandford Press.

Meyer, Arnold Oscar (1911/1967). *England and the Catholic Church Under Queen Elizabeth* [1911], trans. J. R. McKee. London: Routledge and Kegan Paul.

Montrose, Louis Adrian (1980). Gifts and Reasons: The Contexts of Peele's *Araygnement of Paris. English Literary History* 47: 433–61.

—— (1986). *A Midsummer Night's Dream* and the Shaping Fantasies of Elizabethan Culture. In *Rewriting the Renaissance*, eds. Margaret W. Ferguson, Maureen Quilligan, and Nancy J. Vickers pp. 65–87; 329–334. Chicago: University of Chicago Press.

Peele, George (1952). *The Life and Works of George Peele*, gen. ed. Charles Tyler Prouty. New Haven: Yale UP. Vol. I: *The Life and Minor Works of George Peele*, ed. David H. Horne.

—— (1970). *The Life and Works . . .*, gen. ed. Charles Tyler Prouty. New Haven: Yale University Press. Vol. III: *The Dramatic Works of George Peele.* ed. Mark Benbow et al., 1970.

Puttenham, George (1936). *The Arte of English Poesie*, eds. Gladys Willcock and Alice Walker. Cambridge: Cambridge University Press.

Reeves, John D. (1954). The Judgment of Paris as a Device of Tudor Flattery. *Notes and Queries* 199: 7–11.

Reiss, Timothy J. (1980). *Tragedy and Truth*. New Haven: Yale University Press.

Smith, Hallett (1952). *Elizabethan Poetry*. Cambridge, MA: Harvard University Press.

Spenser, Edmund (1947). *The Poetical Works of Edmund Spenser*, ed. J. C. Smith and E. De Selincourt. London: Oxford University Press.

Tennenhouse, Leonard (1986). *Power on Display: The Politics of Shakespeare's Genres*. New York: Methuen.

Vickers, Nancy (1981). Diana Described: Scattered Woman and Scattered Rhyme. *Critical Inquiry* 8: 265–80.

Von Hendy, Andrew (1968). The Triumph of Chastity: Form and Meaning in *The Arraignment of Paris*. *Renaissance Drama* 1 [n.s.]: 87–101.

Woolf, Virginia (1957). *A Room of One's Own*. New York: Harcourt Brace Jonanovich.

Yates, Frances (1975). *Astraea: The Imperial Theme in the Sixteenth Century*. London: Routledge and Kegan Paul.

MELINDA ZOOK

History's Mary: The Propagation of Queen Mary II, 1689–1694*

In December of 1688 James II fled his kingdom. While his flight removed a major obstacle from the path of England's "Glorious" Revolution, it also resulted in a constitutional crisis. England was left a kingdom without a king. The solution to the crisis hammered out by the nation's political elite in the winter of 1688/89 included a construction unique in England's constitutional history: the dual monarchy of William III and Mary II, a formula consisting of two sovereigns in name, but only one in power. Administrative power was vested in William alone. Consequently, historians past and present when examining the power politics of the 1690s have focused almost exclusively on the policies and person of William III. Queen Mary, submerged throughout history into her husband's identity, has for the most part vanished from our view. So much so, that her latest biographer, Elizabeth Hamilton, reminded readers of exactly "who" her subject was by entitling her 1972 book *William's Mary*.

Hamilton's book is a popular biography—the genre to which Mary II has been relegated in the twentieth century. Generally, current historical literature presents Mary II as a queen preoccupied with such traditionally feminine pursuits as knitting and moral reform. She has also been dismissed by modern scholars as "a docile and unassuming wife" or as possessing a "sluggish" mind (Zee 1988: 53; Smith 1988: 274). On the whole, her image today is of a powerless, ignorant woman, thoroughly dominated by her husband. Small wonder that she has generated little excitement even among historians of women's history. Only recently has a reevalu-

* I am indebted to Dr. Lois G. Schwoerer for her advice on an earlier draft of this paper and for sharing her knowledge of the subject with me in our numerous conversations.

ation of Mary's political talents begun, along with a reconstruction of her historical image (Schwoerer 1989a, 1989b; Speck 1991).

What follows is in part an effort to add to the reconstruction of Mary II. It differs from the previous work by Lois G. Schwoerer and W. A. Speck because it focuses on Mary's own writing, her own self-imaging. First and foremost though, this essay is an examination of the ideological functions which Mary's image has served in the various media in which it has been recreated: from satiric verse and song to history and biography. My concern is with the genesis and survival of the interpretative models in which Mary II has been traditionally placed. I argue that representations of Mary II—from the 1690s to the late twentieth century—have most commonly fallen into the prototypes of either the bad daughter or the good wife. These images originated with the propaganda campaigns that accompanied and followed the Revolution of 1688/89 and endured into the nineteenth century. They served the ideological needs of the political parties that used them, and entrapped Mary into familial models with expected patterns of behavior. Further, as either the betraying daughter of James II or the obeying wife of William III, Mary was safely paired with a male figure who dominated the narrative. Her character thus required little in the way of independent action and only (if any) the mildest of compliant voices. Only in the twentieth century, as ideological passions over the Revolution cooled, was Mary's image released from its more overt political functions. What remained was merely a stereotypic caricature: a bit of a guilty daughter, a most loving, loyal wife.

IMAGES OF MARY IN THE 1690s

The first representations of Mary II that long dominated subsequent historical understanding of her were a product of the political culture of the 1680s and 1690s. These images were cast during the violent party strife that accompanied and followed the Revolution of 1688/89. They were propagated by the defenders of the Revolution, mainly whig polemicists, and by the Revolution's most severe opponents, the supporters of the exiled James II, the Jacobites.

The very nature of the Revolution gave the Jacobites the propagandistic edge: not only because a legitimate king had been displaced, but because the deed was perpetrated by his own daughter and son-in-law. This revolution within the family was a glaring betrayal of patriarchal order. As Gorden Schochet has shown, royalist political and social thinking throughout the seventeenth century often revolved around patriarchal analogies. As the king was the metaphoric father of all his people, so fathers were like kings within their own households. In the 1680s and 1690s, patriarchal ideology was strongly reinforced by the publication of Robert Filmer's *Patriarcha* in 1680, and thereafter political patriarchalism ". . . very nearly became the official state ideology" (Schochet 1975: 193). Patriarchal discourse rested on Scripture, most commonly the fifth commandment, "honor thy father" (with the "and thy mother" part judiciously omitted). Disobedience to the father—on both the macrocosmic level of the king and microcosmic level of the male head of the household—was deemed a fundamental breach of both natural and divine law.

The Glorious Revolution, then, was none other than a violent disruption of the patriarchal ideal: James II as king, father of his people, was ejected from his kingdom; and James as father, king of his household, was overthrown by his own children. The Jacobite opponents of the Revolution seized upon William and Mary's violation of the fifth commandment and made it one of the major themes of their propaganda campaign. While King William's person and policies were viciously attacked through numerous devices, Jacobite publicists consistently satirized Queen Mary as the betraying daughter. This image struck at the heart of patriarchal structures and ideals and carried with it suggestions of treachery and infidelity, unnatural ambition, greed and lust. The daughter now married, cut loose from the relationship with the father, was now a sexual being. Jacobites represented her sexual relationship with her husband, William, as perverse or perversely nonexistent and transformed her into "the whore," unsatisfied, lusting for the phallus as she had lusted for power, the masculine domain.

The Jacobite image of Queen Mary as the betraying daughter and whore functioned as an "immoral" exemplar, and her story became a cautionary tale and as such explicitly linked to other cautionary tales. The tragedy of *King Lear* had familiarized English audiences with the specter of the evil, grasping daughter, and Jacobites capitalized on shock sensation produced by the image of an ambitious, disobedient and wanton daughter. As one 1690 Jacobite poem entitled the "Female Parricide" began: "Oft I have heard of impious sons before / Rebelled for crowns their royal parents wore; / But of unnatural daughters rarely hear / 'Till those of hapless James and old King Lear" (Cameron 1975: 157). Yet Mary's behavior was "worse than cruel lustful Goneril," and the Jacobites' favorite typology for Mary was the Roman matron, Tullia. Tullia had driven her chariot over the half-dead body of her kingly father, whose crown had been usurped by her husband.

She had the power immediately to evoke images of regicide and parricide.[1]

When Mary was not identified as Tullia, Jacobites referred to her in their poems and squibs as "Moll." A "Moll," in the colloquial usage of the seventeenth and eighteenth centuries, was a woman of ill repute (*OED* 9: 974–5). She might be a whore, such as Moll Hackabout in William Hogarth's *The Harlot's Progress* (1733), or she might be a professional criminal, such as Moll Cut-Purse, a character in two early Stuart plays, Middleton and Dekker's *Roaring Girl* (1610) and Nathan Field's *Amends to the Ladies* (1611). Defoe's Moll Flanders, of course, was both a thief and a whore (Blewitt 1989: 3). Thus by calling Queen Mary "Moll," the Jacobites identified her as a thief, who had stolen the crown, and as a whore, who had lusted for power and sold her soul as well as her body for three kingdoms.

At the same time, Jacobites continued to hope that Mary (a Stuart) would repent her disobedience to her father. Jacobite verse in the early 1690s often showed Mary as unhappy, lamenting her crime against James. In one poem, Tullia, with "weak reason" and a "debauched good nature" is said to have "crammed down remorse . . . Yet when she drunk cool tea in liberal sups / The sobbing dame was maudlin in her cups" ("Targuin & Tullia" in Cameron 1975: 52). In another Jacobite satire, Tullia is described as lying in bed next to her unresponsive husband, "a dull lump of Netherlandish clay," and dreaming of "the young gallants she'd seen" when her mother's ghost appears. The duchess of York sternly warns Mary to repent her betrayal of her father. After a long sermon from her mother, Mary is trembling, "drown(ed) in tears" ("The Duchess of York's Ghost" in Cameron 1975: 298–302).

William III, the victim of the most savage Jacobite satire, was portrayed in his relationship with Mary as a cruel, negligent husband, who used her merely as a tool to further his ambition. Jacobites represented William as either unable (impotent) or unwilling (homosexual) to satisfy his youthful wife's sexual appetite or provide the kingdom with an heir.[2] That the king should be impotent, "a dull lump of Netherlandish clay," signified a disfunctioning body politic. Again and again, Jacobites "dismembered" William, calling him "a churl to his wife without e'er a pintle" and asserting that "he's not qualified for his wife / because of a cruel midwife's knife" ("The Coronation Ballad" in Cameron 1975: 43–44). Another Jacobite poet compared James II, whose vigorous sexual appetite was well known and who had functioned appropriately and produced an heir,[3] to William's supposed inability to function sexually. The court ladies, the poet exclaimed, have traded kings for "one of less performing parts / For one that hadn't to show, God knows / So much to please them as a nose" ("The Campaign" in *Poems* 1702: 2:206).

When not imaged as impotent, the King was portrayed as a "shameless, buggering, sodomitical rascal" (*Dialogue* 1695: 5). The objects of his lust varied: from his Dutch favorite, Hans Bentinck, the earl of Portland, to young court Ganymedes, to noncoital relations with his mistress and even the Queen. In one of the more vulgar Jacobite ballads, Mary is described as having "a great arse instead of a great belly," which is just as the King prefers. In other words, he will not give her a "great belly" (impregnate her), but instead uses her body inappropriately. He is the Dutch foreigner debasing the English (Mary) nation. The same song concludes, "Let us pray for the sake of our nation and sake of his soul / He would put his Roger into the right hole" ("An Excellent New Ballad" n.d.). The King's body was represented as perverse, corrupt, disfunctional, preoccupied with non-productive behavior. Young, unhappy Tullia, unable to engage in natural relations with the king, "drives away sorrow" with other men. The Jacobites named as her lovers Charles Talbot, earl of Shrewsbury, William Cavendish, earl of Devonshire and even whig Bishop Gilbert Burnet, who, Jacobites claimed, was "well gifted with radical moisture." (The pun on "radical" is, of course, both political and sexual ["The Reflection" in Cameron 1975: 60]).

When Mary died of smallpox in 1694 Jacobite propaganda asserted that her death was divine retribution for her violation of God's law. In a satiric dialogue, published soon after her death, Mary's ghost appears to William crying, "Repent, for it's too late for me, not yet for you!" William cynically grumbles: "It shall never be said that she coming chanting from the dead shall move me, whom I never regarded in life." Later in the dialogue, William's favorite—and here lover—the earl of Portland, says of Mary: "She was a miracle in nature, if but for this, how so bad a daughter should be so good a wife" (*Dialogue* 1695: 1 and 4).

"So good a wife" was indeed the very message with which whig propagandists attempted to counteract Jacobite images of Mary as the betraying daughter. With the image of the obeying wife, whigs put the patriarchal model—which the image of the betraying daughter turned upside down—back on its feet. As a married woman, Mary obeyed her rightful master. The whigs countered Mosaic law with St. Paul: "wives, submit yourselves unto your own husbands as unto the Lord" (Ephesians 5:22). In whig literature,

Figure 1. William and Mary in profile—the official coronation medal.

Mary did not betray a father, she obeyed a husband: a husband with whom she was in perfect harmony in all things.

It was crucial to the success of the Revolution that Mary be shown in unity with William. She, after all, was a legitimate Stuart heiress, and her place on the throne next to William helped justify the exchange of kings. Early iconographic images of William and Mary emphasized the unity of the new dual monarchy. The royal cypher consisted of the letters "W" and "M" transposed over each other. Prints of the proclamation and coronation ceremonies pictured William and Mary seated together with joined hands or holding one crown (Schwoerer 1981: 248–63). Their coronation medals stressed the royal couple's unity while also suggesting William's ultimate superior authority since administrative power was placed in him alone. One of the most common coronation medals (see Figure 1) depicted the busts of William and Mary in profile, facing the same direction, with his bust eclipsing hers (Loon 1732–37: vol. 4:40–50). Her body as well as her identity were subsumed into his body, his identity. Mary's oneness with William was also stressed in political verse and prose. Even after Mary's death, a pastoral letter in memory of the late Queen claimed that William "stamped his own image on her soft mind. He was her husband, her father, her guide . . ." (Jurieu 1695: 10).

During Mary's four regencies, when she was empowered by Parliament to rule in William's absence, the whig press reflected the ambiguity of Mary's position as queen regent. Her power was only temporary and her decisions could at any time be overridden by William. For both domestic and foreign consumption, it was vital to portray Mary as a thoroughly empowered and able queen: "So Jove absenting, Juno rules the sky," exclaimed one court poet

(N. Tate 1691). Mary was also compared to Deborah, Elizabeth I, and "Cynthia, shining in the absence of Phoebus Apollo" (Minor 1974: iii–iv). At the same time, whig propagandists were sensitive to patriarchal anxieties over female sovereignty. They therefore continued to present Mary in the fashion of the good wife, confidently, but only temporarily, managing the kingdom in her husband's stead. As Noah's wife, a common whigite typology for Mary, the queen was simply a domestic care-taker and as such she soothed fears of a gynecocracy. She was, in effect, "queen and no queen."

Historians and poets alike in the 1690s and later most often described Mary's regencies as "prudently managed." In 1695, one of Mary's eulogizers wrote, "The Queen managed affairs at home with all the conduct which became a wife and a virtuous princess" (J.S. 1695: 81). Mary did not "reign," a masculine performance, she "managed" as "became a wife," a safe feminine performance. Her power was not to be feared, for it was merely that of a wife executing her husband's commands. As one poet explained, the Queen's regencies were a "Strange Paradox of Power, by love allayed / While the Queen governed, still the Wife obeyed" (P. Hume 1695). Similarly, while Bishop Burnet praised Mary's talent for government, he also confidently assured his readers that she "never affected to be masculine like Semiramis" (1695: 24).

The whig image of the regent Queen as a wife and domestic care-taker was meant to respond to the Jacobite image of Mary as the betraying daughter. Jacobites reacted in turn with what would become the most enduring image of Mary—as a fat, frumpy housewife, fit only to knit and "mold cockle bread." Picturing Mary on the throne surrounded by her counsellors appointed by William, one Jacobite scribbler exclaimed, "Pity the fat, round, pretty, blushing thing!" On her death, another wrote: "Her name shall never be forgot / For her houswifery and knitting knot." ("The Nine" 201; "The Litany" 219 in Cameron 1975).

Mary's sudden death from smallpox on 28 December 1694 solidified the propagandistic images of her as either the whig's obeying wife/managing queen or the Jacobites' betraying daughter-whore/housewife. With Mary's "live" person withdrawn from the political arena (her body lay in state for over eight weeks), her imagery no longer evolved.[4] The devices used by her friends and enemies to portray her in the remaining years of the seventeenth century were only repetitions of earlier representations. So one Jacobite epitaph played upon old strings: "Here ends, notwithstanding her specious pretences, / The undutiful child of the kindest of Princes, / Well let her lie, for by this time she knows / What it is such a father and king to dispose; / Between virtue and vice she parted her life, / She was too bad a daughter and too good a wife" (Strickland 1903: 14:222).

William and his supporters were profoundly shaken by Mary's demise. Her death was a severe blow to the Revolution: she had not only been the more legitimate half of the dual monarchy but also the more popular. The Williamite press responded by producing a deluge of literature in praise of the late Queen which also further glorified the King and often justified the Revolution once again. The numerous essays, elegies and sermons that poured forth from the presses reiterated familiar themes—Mary was virtuous, pious, beautiful, industrious, charitable—an excellent Queen, a devoted, loving and obedient wife. Among this literature, the most influential piece was Bishop Gilbert Burnet's *Essay on the Memory of the late Queen*, which became the fountain-head for subsequent whig portrayals of Mary II. Burnet's Mary had "no appetite for government"; its burdens were "unwillingly assumed" and "modestly managed." She was always in complete union in "thoughts," "designs" and "interests" with William. She was a true believer in basic whig principles of good government, and like a true whig, highly tolerant of religious dissent (Burnet 1695: 67, 92, 102). It was Burnet's Mary that dominated the whig-liberal vision of Mary II in the eighteenth and nineteenth centuries.

HISTORIOGRAPHICAL PATTERNS

In the eighteenth century, representations of Mary II continued to be divided along party lines. Yet with the Hanoverian succession in 1714 and subsequent whig hegemony over political culture, the obedient wife became the dominant image in eighteenth-century histories of William and Mary's reign. Likewise, as a result of the decline and demise of the Jacobite movement, the image of the betraying daughter receded more and more into the realm of folk culture. In Jacobite ballads and rhymes, prevalent in both English and Scottish folklore, Mary remained "the daughter." "Willie" was a "cheater" and Anne was an "eater," but Mary was simply "the daughter." Consistently, the theme of these rhymes was betrayal. One popular Scottish riddle asked:

> O' what's the rhyme to porringer?
> Ken ye the rhyme to porringer?
> King James the Seventh had ae dochter
> And he ga'e her to an Oranger. (Macquoid 1888: 20)

In an English rhyme all four of James' "children" were blamed:

William & Mary & Anne & George
Four such children had never a man
They put their father to flight & shame
And called their brother a shocking bad name.
(Opie 1951: 424)

In the world of official culture, eighteenth-century whig historians remained obsessed with justifying the Revolution and the
characters of William and Mary. Whig historians White Kennet,
John Oldmixon and Ralph James praised and defended Mary,
portraying her as an obedient wife and prudent queen. Each
responded to the controversy over Mary's joyful behavior upon
her 1689 arrival at Whitehall. Her mirth had been observed by
many and frequently censored as highly inappropriate for a
daughter whose kingly father had just fled his kingdom. Whig
historians excused Mary's behavior by following Bishop Burnet's
apologetic account of the incident, an account which attributed her
gaiety to the instructions of her husband. Ralph James praised her
actions which "consisted of obedience to her husband" (1744: 539).

One of Mary's most influential critics was Sarah Churchill, the
duchess of Marlborough. In her 1742 memoirs, the duchess retold
the story of Mary's arrival at Whitehall in 1689. She concluded
with a curt condemnation of Mary's character: "she wanted bowels,"
meaning Mary had not the courage to oppose her husband for the
sake of her father (26). Whig polemicists were outraged and
counterattacked with great ferocity, pointing out that the duchess's
account was motived by personal vendetta.[5] The author of an
anonymous whigite response wrote, Mary "did not want Bowels,
but the Boldness to disobey her husband" (*Review* 1742: 96).

In many nineteenth-century histories Mary's name was mentioned only in conjunction with William's. His policies and person
completely dominated the narrative. Images of Mary, as first
formed by the whigs and Jacobites of the 1690s, did surface
however. Historian John Heneage Jesse, writing in 1843, betrayed
his royalist (neo-Jacobite) bias in his portrait of Mary II. "The
great blot upon the character of Mary," he wrote, "was the
indecent zeal with which she espoused the cause of her husband
against that of her father" (1:198). Jesse echoed all the old
Jacobite propaganda: he described William's severe treatment of
Mary; he gossiped about Mary's supposed romance with the earl
of Shrewsbury; and he ended by condemning her for not repenting
on her death-bed her "former conduct toward her father" (1843:
1:230). Jesse's Mary II was a foolish, lascivious and unrepentant
woman, treated unkindly by her "phlegmatic Dutchman" (221).

Between 1840 and 1846, the Strickland sisters, Agnes and Elizabeth, began publishing their multi-volume history of the *Lives of the Queens of England from the Norman Conquest*. Here again Mary was condemned as the betraying daughter. But Elizabeth Strickland, who wrote the biography of Mary II, did not merely repeat Jacobite propaganda—although she was certainly aware of it and often quoted Jacobite barbs against Mary. Strickland was too good a historian to base her interpretation on Jacobite gossip and satire; in fact, she was the first scholar to pay serious attention to Mary's political abilities—something few have done since. But Strickland's interpretation of Mary also consistently revealed the author's strong royalist sympathies. Regardless of how skillful a queen Mary may have been, her behavior toward her father was, in Strickland's view, unforgivable.

In response to the panegyrical whig historians of the previous century, Strickland wrote: "The abilities of Queen Mary and the importance of her personal exertions as a sovereign, have been as much underrated as the goodness of her heart and Christian excellences have been overrated" (1903: 14:80). In fact, Strickland rarely praised Mary without at the same time condemning her for violating her filial duty: "There was but one spot of tenderness in the marble of her heart, and that was exclusively devoted to her husband" (113). But for Strickland the object of Mary's sole affection was unworthy of such devotion. Strickland's William III is a Jacobite caricature: an "insolent," "arrogant," "spoiled little manikin," who "neglected" Mary, "humbled her," and, prior to the Revolution, "persecuted her for her family attachments" (35 and 93). James II, on the other hand, was a deeply loving, affectionate father, whose heart was broken by his daughter's betrayal.

In the end, Strickland's Mary II was a portrait of a very talented, intelligent and politically astute queen, who, nevertheless, was an absolutely heartless "unnatural daughter" and "cruel sister" (218). Strickland condemned Mary for her violation of a Victorian patriarchal-familial ideal. At the same time, the royalist in Strickland had no sympathy with the Revolution; hence, Mary's devotion to her husband did not absolve her of her crime against her father, the legitimate Stuart King.

The liberal historian, Thomas Babington Macaulay, in contrast, did sympathize with the Revolution. He took a kind view of Mary II, but one which essentially relied on Burnet's whigite image of her. Not surprisingly, then, Mary returned once again in the guise of the obedient wife. Macaulay's Mary II was "naturally intelligent, but ignorant and simple" (1913–15: 2:822). Those who condemn her for a breach of filial duty, asserted Macaulay, should recall how James had first conspired to disinherit her after her marriage: "If to serve the cause of her religion, she broke through the most sacred ties of consanguinity, she only followed her father's example. She did not assist to depose him until he had conspired to disinherit her" (960). Moreover, she thoroughly believed in her husband's mission in 1688/89, understanding the Revolution to be both "just" and "holy." Had she not been willing to "take her seat on the throne from which her father had just been hurled," she would have violated "her duty to her God, her husband, and her country" (3:1056). Macaulay followed Burnet in his description of Mary's religious sentiment, calling it "latitudinarian" (1262), and he also recounted Burnet's apology for Mary's exuberance upon her arrival at Whitehall (1302-3).

Macaulay paid little attention to Mary's regencies, showing no interest in the queen as a political agent. Rather, his Queen Mary was thoroughly domestic. He admired her quick "feminine wit and shrewdness" in conversation, condemned her spelling (twice) and her taste in porcelains. She amused herself, he wrote, by forming a "vast collection of hideous images and vases on which houses, trees, bridges and mandarins were depicted in outrageous defiance of all the laws of perspective" (1362). Macaulay's Mary was simple, religious, virtuous, a loving, loyal wife, a non-political entity.

Mary II was not again the subject of a biography in English until 1913.[6] Between 1846 and 1913, however, there surfaced several remarkable documents written by Mary herself. In the 1880s, a small collection of letters by Mary, together with her memoirs written during her brief reign, were published (Bentinck). Then in 1911, Benjamin Bathurst made it known that his family owned a unique collection of letters written by James II's daughters, Mary and Anne, which he subsequently published in 1924. The majority of these letters, 93 in all, were written by Mary to a beloved friend, Frances Aspley.

These discoveries prompted new interest in Mary, and between 1913 and 1929 three new biographies were published (Sanders 1913; Waterson 1928; Bowen 1929). Unfortunately, the new material on Mary in the hands of the new biographers failed to yield a new interpretation of the life and reign of Mary II. These biographies were all long on narrative, while exceedingly short on interpretation. The events of Mary's life were reconstructed, but Mary herself never rose above them. Instead she was swept along by the desires and ambitions of the real historical agents in her life: her uncle, Charles II, who arranged her marriage, her father and her husband. Even William, while a prime mover, was trapped within predetermined conceptions of his character. Depending on the author's biases, he was either Mary's "indifferent lover" or her "dark young cavalier" (Waterson 1928: 59; Bowen 1929: 37).

None of Mary's new biographers was seriously interested in her as a political agent. In her biography of Mary, Marjorie Bowen stated in her preface that she would "only deal with politics where absolutely necessary," creating from the outset a non-political Queen Mary (Bowen 1929: x). All three of these biographies avoided a serious analysis of Mary's love letters to Frances Aspley. Mary's letters to William during her first regency in 1690 were cited, but only as evidence of her unfailing devotion to and dependence on him. Mary's memoirs, a thoroughly problematic source, were used simply as unquestionable evidence of Mary's insecure and suffering internal self.

Changes in the historical discipline in the 1960s and 70s failed to liberate Mary. The one sensitive portrait of her life and reign written in the twentieth century was published by Hester Chapman in 1953. Chapman alone pays attention to Mary's letters to Frances and to her regencies. But Chapman, who wrote twenty-two popular biographies and historical novels in twenty years, was far more interested in personalities than politics, emotions than motives, and her biography of Mary II is more a romance than a history.

In the 1970s, Mary was the subject of three new studies—two of which treated William and Mary together and which are rather more concerned with William than Mary (Zee 1977; Miller 1974). In Henri and Barbara van der Zee's 1977 portrait of William and Mary, Mary's affection for Frances was a result of the "decadent atmosphere" of the court of Charles II; and when Mary was a mature, married women living in Holland, the van der Zees asserted that when Mary proclaimed her love for Frances, she was really thinking of William (93 and 153–4). She was the perfectly feminine queen, employing that traditionally "feminine cure" for her occasional "low spirits," the purchasing of "plenty of new clothes." While Mary is described as having a "feminine love for the glitter of a silver ribbon, the gleam of a pretty satin slipper, the flash of a golden girdle," William, her perfectly masculine counterpart, is described as a true "soldier-king," a man with ideas and purpose (379 and 481). He was the most masculine king, she was the most feminine queen. He acted; she was acted upon.

The most recent biography of Mary in which she is the sole topic is Elizabeth Hamilton's book, *William's Mary*, mentioned earlier. Here Mary loses her identity to her husband in the very title of the book and remains a non-entity throughout. Hamilton's Mary is a colorless, dutiful bore, swept along by events. Her only lasting contributions to English society, according to Hamilton, were the mundane houses she had built. The last paragraph of Hamilton's biography begins: "Her virtues like her houses were homely and unspectacular . . . she was simple and unassuming though she lived in high places" (1972: 337). Mary's virtues (modesty, piety, charity) were entirely "feminine." Though a public figure, she had no virile pretensions. As Bishop Burnet had put it three hundred years before, Mary "never affected to be masculine like Semiramis."

RECONSTRUCTING MARY II

Regardless of whether Mary was portrayed as obeying or betraying or utterly passive, her attributions, behavior and scope of action (if any) were strictly circumscribed. Construction of an alternative representation of Mary II may begin with Mary's own presentations of herself through her writings. The corpus of her writing is small, but not insignificant. It includes the ninety-three letters to Frances Aspley, the largest single collection of her writing; her letters written from Holland to family and friends in England; twenty-one letters to her German cousin, Sophia, the electress of Hanover; thirty-seven letters to William written in summer of 1690; and finally a slim volume known as her "memoirs." Through these texts, Mary presents herself in relation to power and desire, dimensions that poets, polemicists and historians of the past have ignored.

But caution is also in order. Mary's life was entirely public. She grew up at the court of Charles II as a Princess of York, spent ten years at The Hague as the Princess of Orange, and held her own court in the five remaining years of her life as the Queen of England. She undoubtedly understood her own political significance. When she touched a pen to paper she was not only guided by the cultural protocol that governed all women's writing, but also by an ideal of how public figures should present themselves for the sake of posterity. Her concern with her own legacy was evident the night of 20 December 1694. Aware of her impending death, Mary stayed up the entire night, sorting through and burning many of her personal documents.[7] Those writings which escaped the flames, whether because they were in someone else's hands or because she chose not to destroy them, display different degrees of concern with a public image.

The ninety-three letters from Mary to Frances Aspley kept with the Bathurst family documents and unknown to historians for hundreds of years are undoubtedly the most "private" of Mary's writings. Since their publication in 1924, the letters' amorous content has generated little excitement or analysis, but has instead been dismissed as "adolescent daydreaming" unworthy of discussion (1977: 98). The letters are unpunctuated and, for the most part, undated; internal evidence suggests they cover the years from 1672 to 1688, meaning they begin when Mary is ten years old and Frances is nineteen.

The majority of the letters (only Mary's to Frances have survived) are very ardent, very passionate declarations of love. Mary and Frances adopted nicknames from various current dramas: "Clorine" for Mary and "Aurelia" for Frances.[8] Mary also refers to Francis as her "dear dearest husband" and to herself as "your most loving and obedient wife." In 1675, Mary wrote, "I only desire you will think of me as your faithful wife true to your bed" (Bathurst 1924: 54). Five years later, she impatiently protested, "In all your letters you complain of me as if I were a cruel mistress instead of a kind wife . . . (perhaps you) are grown inconstant yourself . . . take heed it does not prove so for tis dangerous to vex a lover and a woman for you know those are desparate things when they are angry" (122–3).

Mary's letters to Frances were written in the discourse of desire: replete with protestations and vows of eternal love, outbursts of jealousy and accusations of infidelity, lamentations over her lover's indifference, enticements and threats (see Kauffman 1986: 17–18). Mary wrote that she loved as had no lover before: "I love you with a love that was never known by man; I have for you excess of friendship, more of love than any women can for women" (Bathurst 1924: 60). Mary speaks of "violent love," "rude longing," and being carried away "in ecstasy" and "raptures of sweet amase when I think of you." She also threatens to give Frances a "pair of horns" (67, 58, 91). Mary's rapture and rhetoric suggest all the strenuous demands of romantic love: "Oh, have some pity on me and love again or kill quick with your unkindness for I cannot love in indifference. Dear dearest, loving, kind, charming, obliging, sweet Aurelia—kind husband remember your vows" (71–2).

How are these letters to be interpreted? Are they fictive, modeled on the love literature of the Restoration as some of Mary's biographers have suggested? And if the letters are— however crude—formulaic imitations, does it necessarily follow that their amorous content can be dismissed as meaningless? Or is the artifice not only in the form but also in the passion? I believe the Bathurst letters are the most sincere, least public-minded of Mary's writings—regardless of whether Mary was inspired by the popular novels and plays of the Restoration. Her poor education may account for their poor imitative quality (Schwoerer 1989: 217–18). But while her emotions were probably "genuine," they may well have been more inspired by the fictive world of Aurelia and Clorine, "dear husband" and "loving wife" than by Frances Aspley herself.

Yet their attachment was certainly more than a fleeting adolescent crush. They continued to play out their romance long after Mary's marriage to William in 1677 and departure for Holland the same year. Even after Mary's miscarriage in 1678, a traumatic and tragic point in Mary's life, she continued to write Frances letters filled with impassioned outpourings. It was only after Frances' marriage in 1682 that Mary's vows of fidelity and love began to sound stiff and artificial. Their correspondence continued for six more years, but Mary's ardour had evidently cooled, and her tone became more obliging and cooperative, although she was often irritated by Frances' demands that she write more often. Their relationship changed from a strenuous drama, described in terms of heterosexual love, to a more subdued homosocial friendship.

In literature as well as life, female friendship is often characterized by its cooperative, egalitarian nature. The friendship of two women also often articulates itself through a maternal, nurturing discourse—something we might have expected from Mary and Frances since Frances was nine years Mary's senior.[9] Instead, their passionate devotion played itself out in a "masculine" language of hierarchy and domination, in a world in which an "obedient loving constant wife" was continually pleading with her "cruel loved blest husband" (qtd. Chapman 1953: 41). Mary wrote in a language that not only expressed heterosexual (husband/wife) conflict, tension and desire, but also articulated positions of domination and submission, authority and obedience—a language which undoubtedly responded to the patriarchal world around her. Ironically, in these innocent, private moments, Mary imaged herself as a long-suffering and doggedly obedient wife, Frances' wife—an image not far removed from those the Jacobites and whigs would later draw of her as William's wife.

During Mary's ten years as Princess of Orange, when she lived in Holland, she also wrote in a much less regular fashion to family members and a handful of other friends. Not a trace of the romantically-inclined Clorine can be glimpsed in these much more serious letters. These letters reflect a woman fully conscious of her public position and political value. In the months preceding Prince William's invasion of England in November 1688, Mary wrote several letters to relatives and potential "friends" in England either seeking information for herself and the Prince or in an effort to line up possible allies in the Prince's cause. Three of these letters were written to Lady Rachel Russell.

Lady Russell's husband, William, had been a leading whig lord in the heady days of the Exclusion Crisis (1679–83), when the whig party had tried to pass a bill through Parliament excluding Charles II's Catholic brother James, duke of York, from the royal succession. The efforts of the exclusionist whigs ultimately failed, though not without much controversy and turmoil. In the summer of 1683 several whigs were tried and convicted of plotting to assassinate the King and the duke of York. Lord William Russell was executed for his part in the conspiracy, the so-called Rye House Plot. Since her husband's death, Lady Russell came to symbolize whig suffering at the hands of royalist tyranny, and around her developed a powerful network of family, friends and sympathizers (Schwoerer 1988). Mary's letters to Lady Russell flow with kindness and pity for her suffering. Mary assured Lady Russell that "(the Prince and I) should be very glad to lay in my power to do you any kindness. . . . (I wish) to be better known to you . . . (and) that you should be one of my friends" (*Letters* 1773: 81–2). For the Princess of Orange to promise friendship to the woman who symbolized the opposition to her father's throne was nothing less than a decisive political act. Mary certainly felt her own political prowess: an ability which "lay in her power" to grant favors, kindness, protection.

Mary's friendship with Lady Rachel Russell continued during Mary's reign as Queen of England and proved useful to both parties on several occasions (Schwoerer 1988: 196–97; *Letters* 1773: 175–76, 181–82, 190). During her five-year reign, Mary ruled as Queen regent for four separate periods when William was abroad. William was absent from England for a total of thirty-two months between 1690 and 1694, at which times Mary was empowered by Act of Parliament to exercise administrative authority (Schwoerer 1989a: 717). During her first regency, in the summer of 1690 when William was campaigning in Ireland, Mary and William were in almost daily contact. Thirty-seven letters from Mary to William have survived. The letters record Mary's transactions with the nine councilors William appointed to advise her. Mary judged the value of each of her councilors and described to William their various attempts to manipulate her and divide her interests from his. One expression, she told William, "I have heard often within these few days . . . is, that I have the power in my hands and they wonder I will not make use of it and why should I stay . . . for your return" (Dalrymple 1771–88: 142). Mary's loyalty to William proved unswerving and in his absence she defended his policies and prerogative with steady perseverance. She lost her temper more than once with those she believed to be challenging William's authority and taking advantage of his absence (142, 146). She was also acutely conscious of her public position. She wrote to William, ". . . all my motions are so watched and all so observed that if I eat less, or speak less, or look more grave all is lost in the opinion of the world . . . I must grin when my heart is ready to break" (167). And she reminded him, "either write me a particular answer yourself, or let Lord Portland do it for you; for you see the necessity of it for the public; do a little also for my private satisfaction, who loves you much more than her life" (150). Mary not only followed William's long-distance instructions, she also made a few requests of her own, asking him to take special care of the Protestant church in Ireland and to convert the confiscated estates into public schools (132, 141).

Like her letters to William, Mary's memoirs also resound with her devotion to him and his cause—a cause which she saw as inseparable from her own and from the cause of the Protestant religion. But her "memoirs" are a far more problematic source. They are not truly memoirs in the traditional sense, but rather an annual record, recording the events of the past year and written by her in one or two sittings at the end of each year. She seems to have written them with an audience in mind as a sort of presentation of her "side of the story." Despite their questionable nature as a genuine portrait of Mary's thoughts, her memoirs more than any of her writings have been used most lavishly and uncritically by historians and biographers.

This uncritical use of her memoirs is simple enough to explain. Mary's memoirs confirm the whigite portrait of Mary as the obedient wife and seem to resonate with the more recent feminine caricature of her. Mary presented herself as a devout Protestant and most of all as a devoted, loving wife. She feigned to have no head for business, no heart for a kingdom. Several times she asserted that she did not like "to meddle or trouble my head" with "public business" (Doebner 1886: 55, 56). Her memoirs also abound with traditional notions of the proper place of women. She was certain, for example, that women by nature of their delicate sex "should not meddle" in public affairs (23). Mary's memoirs reinforce patriarchal notions of the appropriate position of women as well as images of Mary as a loving simpleton, utterly dependent on her superior, heroic or tyrannical (depending on the historian's bias) husband.

The image Mary presented of herself in her memoirs is thus one of a most reluctant queen: a woman of leisure who suddenly had power thrust upon her. Reluctant perhaps, but she was not unwilling or ineffective. During her four regencies, Mary issued thirty-seven proclamations; ordered fasts; heard petitions; reviewed troops; censored the press; called and prorogued Parliament; made appointments to the church, navy and administration; pardoned, transported, imprisoned and executed criminal and treasonous subjects. She prepared for a French invasion; she ordered preparations for an invasion of France, and she dispatched British troops to Quebec. The queen regent could be severe and unyielding in defense of the King. In 1693, her mercy was invoked to save a printer, William Anderton, from execution for publishing some mild Jacobite literature. The crime was not unusual; the severity of the sentence was. Unhappy with the portrayal of the King in these tracts, Mary refused to transmute Anderton's sentence, and he was hanged (Howell 1812: xii–1246–67).

Friends and supporters other than the flattering Bishop Burnet commented on Mary's ability to rule. Dr. Hooper, Dean of Canterbury, believed that if William retained his throne, "it would be by her skill and talents of governing" (qtd. Strickland 1903: 14:81). Perhaps the man who benefited the most from Mary's abilities was the first to recognize them. When William left for the battlefield in June of 1690, his government was far from secure. He had had little success in inspiring devotion in the English and little reason to trust even those closest to him. Indeed, his continual absence over the next four years may have saved his government. Before he left in 1690, he remarked to Shrewsbury, "Though I cannot hit on the right way of pleasing the English, I am confident she will" (qtd. Chapman, 1953: 198).

If images of Mary II have been entrapped in politicized, familial models, it is because they have for so long been placed at the service of ideological needs. And if over the last three hundred years, Mary has been lost in the shadow of her husband, as if William-and-Mary were but one being, it is partly because of his status as the great Protestant defender of both England and Europe, and because of the brevity of her reign, and because she was a woman. And finally, it is because she herself participated so fully in the patriarchal world around her, projecting an image of herself which she undoubtedly believed to be the best possible public image, that of the loving, loyal wife. This she may well have been, but she was also a politically astute and effective queen regent.

NOTES

1 The classical tale of the ambitious husband-and-wife team, Tullius and Tullia, was widely familiar. Laurence Echard retold the story in the second volume of his *Roman History* published in 1695.

2 Shortly after her marriage to William in 1677, Mary suffered at least one, possibly two, miscarriages. Her inability to provide an heir was a great personal tragedy for her. William is known to have had one mistress, Elizabeth Villiers, whom he gave up after Mary's death in grief and guilt over the pain it had caused her. His relationship with Hans Bentinck, the earl of Portland, went back to their boyhood together. There was no doubt that their friendship was intimate, but whether it was sexual is unknown. Notwithstanding the rumors, especially concerning the earl of Shrewsbury, it is highly unlikely that Mary was unfaithful to William. See Chapman 195; Baxter 1966.

3 James II's second wife, Queen Mary Beatrice (Mary's Catholic stepmother), gave birth to a son, James Francis Edward, on 10 June 1688. This Prince of Wales naturally became the next heir to the throne. Soon after his birth, however, rumors circulated that the child was illegitimate or an imposter, snuck into the Queen's bedchamber in a warming pan. William cited James's attempt to alter the royal succession, displacing his wife, with a "pretended Prince of Wales" as one of his reasons for coming to England in November 1688. Mary Beatrice and the child escaped to France in December 1688. See Kenyon 1963.

4 William's grief over Mary's death has been described numerous times. See, for example, Burnet 1833: 4:245–9. Her death was a personal as well as a political tragedy for William. That he kept her body on display for such an unusually long time may have been a curious attempt to preserve the dual monarchy and remind the people of the "legitimacy" of the Revolution as long as possible.

5 In 1692, Sarah's husband, John Churchill, was accused of conspiring with the exiled James II against William and Mary. He was dismissed from all his duties. Regardless, the Princess Anne, Mary's sister, refused to be parted from her friend and confidante, Sarah. Sarah's continued presence in Anne's household was the source of friction between the two royal sisters. Mary not only ordered Anne to dismiss Sarah, but she also took away Anne's Guard of Honour as a punishment for her sister's refusal. Sarah apparently never forgave Mary for the whole incident, and she painted unflattering portraits of both Mary and William in her memoirs. For Mary's side of the story, see Doebner 1886: 24, 26, 27.

6 To the best of my knowledge, there are five biographies of Mary in languages other than English. Two French titles written shortly after her death, the anonymous, *La race et la naissance la vie et la mort de Maria Stuart* (1695) and F. Kaarsgietler, *Devices . . . fait sur la naissance, la vie et la mort, de Maria II* (1700). A German title by W. K. A. Nippold, *Die Regierung der Königin Mary Stuart II, 1662–1694* (1895); and two Dutch biographies: F. J. L. Krämer, *Maria Stuart, gemalin van Willem III* (1890) and Jacqueline Doorn, *De Vroww van de Stahhouder-Koning, Maria Stuart II, 1662–1694* (1967).

7 Included among those documents believed to be destroyed by Mary on the night of December 20 are her letters from Frances Aspley, James II and William. She also destroyed the various meditations and prayers she composed. Strickland 1903: 14:199; Chapman 250–1.

8 It is unclear from where exactly Mary and Frances derived the names "Aurelia" and "Clorine." Several popular plays contained a character named Aurelia. Where the name Clorine came from is a more difficult matter. One possibility is that both names were taken out of Philip Massinger's *The Maid of Honour* (first edition, 1632) which contains an "Aurelia, the Duchess of Sienna" and a "Clarinda, her woman." See the introduction to Bathurst 1924 which describes various other possibilities (30–1).

9 The various types of relationships between women in literature are described by Todd 1980, including the sentimental, the erotic and the female friend as surrogate mother.

REFERENCES

A Dialogue between KW & Benting (1695). London.
"An Excellent New Ballad," London: British Library, Sloane Manuscripts 1731a, #130.
Bathurst, Benjamin (1924). *Letters of Two Queens*. London: Robert Holden and Co. I have inserted punctuation and modernized spelling of the letters for reasons of clarity.
Baxter, Stephen B. (1966). *William III*. London: Longman Publications, 1966.
Blewitt, David (1989). "Introduction" to Daniel Defoe's *Moll Flanders*. New York: Penguin Books.
Bowen, Majorie (1929). *The Third Mary Stuart*. London.
Burnet, Bishope Gilbert (1695). *An Essay on the Memory of the late Queen, etc.*, London.
Burnet, Bishop Gilbert (1833). *History of His Own Time: with Notes by the Earls of Dartmouth and Hardwicke, Speaker Onslow, and Dean Swift*. 6 vols. Oxford.
Cameron, William, ed. (1975). *Poems on the Affairs of State*. vol. 5. New Haven: Yale University Press.

Chapman, Hester (1953). *Mary II, Queen of England.* Oxford: Alden Press.

Dalrymple, John (1771–88). *Memoirs of Great Britain and Ireland.* 3 vols. Edinburgh. See the appendix, vol. 2. I have modernized Mary's spelling.

Doebner, R. ed. (1886). *Memoirs of Mary, Queen of England.* London. I have modernized Mary's spelling.

Hamilton, Elizabeth (1972). *William's Mary: A Biography of Mary II.* New York: Taplinger Publishing Co.

Howell, Thomas B., ed. (1812). *Cobbett's Complete Collection of State Trials and Proceedings for High Treason.* 34 vols. London.

Hume, Patrick (1695). "A Poem dedicated to the Memory of Her Majesty, the Most Incomparable Q. Mary." London.

J. S. (1695). *A Brief History of the Pious & Glorious Life and Actions of the Most Illustrious Princess, Mary, Queen of England, Scotland, France, and Ireland, etc.* London.

James, Ralph (1744). *The History of England during the Reign of King William, Queen Anne, and King George I.* vol 2. London.

Jesse, Heneage James (1843). *Memoirs of the Court of England during the Reign of the Stuarts.* 4 vols. Boston: Chester F. Rice Co.

Jurieu, Peter (1695). *A Pastoral Letter on the Death of the Queen.* London.

Kauffman, Linda S. (1986). *The Discourses of Desire: Gender, Genre, and Epistolary Fictions.* Ithaca: Cornell University Press.

Kennet, White (1706). *A Complete History of England.* London.

Kenyon, J. P. (1963). The Birth of the Old Pretender. *History Today* June, 418–45.

Letters of Lady Rachel Russell; From the Manuscripts in the Library at Woburn Abbey, etc. (1773). London.

Loon, Gerald van (1732–37). *Historie Méttalique des XVII provinces des Pays-Bas, et de Charles-Quint, jusqúà la paix de Bade en MDCCXVI.* 5 vols. La Haye.

Macaulay, Thomas Babington. (1913–15). *History of England from the Accession of James II.* C. H. Firth edition. 6 vols. London.

Macquoid, Gilbert S., ed. (1888). *Jacobite Songs and Ballads.* London.

Marlborough, Sarah, duchess of (1742). *An Account of the Conduct of the Dowager Duchess of Marlborough from her First Coming to the Court to the Year 1710.* London.

Mechtild, Comtesse Bentinck, ed. (1880). *Lettres et Mémoires de Marie Reine d' Angleterre.* The Hague.

Miller, John (1974). *The Life and Times of William and Mary*. London: Weidenfeld & Nicolson.

Minor, Earl, ed. (1974). *Poems on the Reign of William III*. The Augustan Reprint Society Publications. #166.

Oldmixon, John (1735). *The History of England*. London.

Opie, Peter and Iona (1951). *The Oxford Dictionary of Nursery Rhymes*. Oxford: Clarenden Press.

Oxford English Dictionary (1989). 2nd ed. editors J. A. Simpson and E. S. C. Weiner. Oxford: Clarendon Press.

Poems on the Affairs of State. (1702). 4 vols. London.

Review of a Late Treatise entitled, An Account of the Conduct of the Dowager D – of M – etc. (1742). London.

Sanders, Mary F. (1913). *Princess and Queen of England: Life of Mary* II. London.

Schochet, Gordon J. (1975). *Patriarchalism and Political Thought: The Authoritarian Family and Political Speculation and Attitudes Especially in Seventeenth-Century England*. Oxford: Basil Blackwell, 1975.

Schwoerer, Lois G. (1981). *The Declaration of Rights, 1689*. Baltimore: John Hopkins University Press.

—— (1988). *Lady Rachel Russell*. Baltimore: Johns Hopkins University Press.

—— (1989a). "Images of Queen Mary II, 1689–94," *Renaissance Quarterly* 42, 717–48.

—— (1989b). "The Queen as Regent and Patron," in *The Age of William and Mary, Power, Politics & Patronage, 1688–1702*, eds. Robert P. Maccubbin and Martha Hamilton-Phillips. The College of William and Mary, VA, 217–24.

Smith, Lacey Baldwin (1988). *This Realm of England: 1399 to 1688*. 5th edition. Lexington: D. D. Heath & Co.

Speck, W. A. (1991). "William—and Mary?" In *The Revolution of 1688–89: Changing Perspectives, 1688–1702*, ed. Lois Schwoerer. Cambridge: Cambridge University Press.

Strickland, Agnes (1903). *Lives of the Queens of England since the Norman Conquest*. vols 13 and 14. Philadelphia: George Barrie and Sons.

Tate, N. (1691). "A Poem Occassion'd by His Majesty's Voyage to Holland." London.

Todd, Janet (1980). *Women's Friendship in Literature*. New York: Columbia University Press.

Waterson, Nellie (1928). *Mary II, Queen of England, 1689–1694*. Durham, NC: Duke University Press.

Zee, Henri and Barbara van der (1977). *William and Mary*. London: Macmillan Press.

—— (1988). *1688: Revolution in the Family*. London: Penguin Books.

ELIZABETH KRISTOFOVICH ZELENSKY

"Sophia the Wisdom of God": The Function of Religious Imagery during the Regency of Sofiia Alekseevna of Muscovy

The image of female sovereignty in early modern European political culture was intrinsically liminal[1]—this was its one irreducible given. The female sovereign's inability to achieve a "perfect fit" within the patriarchal paradigm which lay at the heart of absolutist theory resulted in her identification with the intertextual spaces between political categories and definitions. As the individual exception to the rule of male primogeniture, the regnant queen or female regent had to define herself, in terms of political imagery, through multivocal symbols which were capable of bridging the gap between her uniquely personal, and therefore liminal, position and the traditional hierarchic discourse of monarchical legitimacy. One such symbol was Sophia the Wisdom of God.[2]

I wish to examine this complex image and the role which it played in the political culture of Muscovy between 1682 and 1689. These were the years when Sofiia Alekseevna, a princess of the Romanov line, ruled as regent for her two younger brothers Peter I and Ivan V. An unmarried woman wielding the highest power in the land was an unprecedented phenomenon in patriarchal Muscovy—as such she could neither be represented nor acknowledged in political discourse. Thus, her first priority, semiotically speaking, was to establish a representational paradigm in which her right to wield political power could be accepted in conjunction with her obvious liminality. This she did through recourse to the image of "Sophia the Wisdom of God"—the root metaphor of her reign.

I perceive a vigorous attempt by Sofiia Alekseevna's government to change the focus of the integrating myth of Muscovy, to superimpose the image of Divine Wisdom over the traditional Christocentric iconography of the monarchy, and through this creative act to tap into a source of emotional sympathy and support for the regent's cause. The tangible evidence for this transformational activity may be found in numerous architectural, literary and iconographic artifacts, some of which will be examined below.

I have organized this essay around three problems: first, the interdependence of liminality and sovereignty in representations of female rulers; second, the specific role played by liminality in Muscovite monarchical discourse; finally, Sofiia Alekseevna's manipulation of religious imagery in her attempt to add a new element to the political discourse of Muscovy, one which would make it possible for her to be perceived as a legitimate political presence in the halls of government.

Most noble Princess Sophia,
You search for divine wisdom eyes raised to Heaven,
You lead your life according to your name,
Wise in word and wise in deed,
You habitually read church books
Seeking wisdom in the lives of our native saints.[3]
Simeon Polotsky (late 1670s; tr. E. Zelensky)

Oh how brightly does divine wisdom shine in your countenance,
How gloriously does honour sparkle in your lips and eyes
. . .

Thus Semiramis dwelt, on the banks of the Euphrates,
Her deeds will also be remembered, unto ages of ages.
Elizabeth of Britain, another sceptered monarch,
And Pulcheria, who was also blessed with wisdom
O Russia, you are now held in esteem by many kingdoms
Due to the prayers of our pious ruler.[4]
L. Tarasevich (1688; tr. E. Zelensky)

The first set of verses was addressed to Sofiia Alekseevna herself. Written by hand, in a stilted mixture of Ruthenian and Church Slavonic, on the frontispiece of a manuscript copy of Simeon Polotsky's catechism "Venets Very," poetically they are a modest effort; nevertheless, their very existence indicates that a social revolution had occurred in the women's quarters, the "terem," of the Kremlin by the late 1670s[5]—a revolution which was centered around Princess Sofiia. She was the first to rend the official veil of anonymity which masked the daughters of the Tsars of Muscovy, and her bid for political power was made possible by the fact that she had created an identity for herself outside the women's quarters prior to her elder brother Fedor's death (Semevsky 1859: 41).

The second set of verses was written in 1688, on an engraved portrait of princess Sofiia. Engravings were an important part of Princess Sofiia's campaign to create a legitimate political persona; in all, eleven engraved portraits of her, either by herself or with her brother, Ivan V, and half-brother, Peter I, were commissioned during her reign, both in Muscovy and abroad (Rovinsky 1886: 2: 1938–45). The political impact of these engravings may be gauged by the tremendous effort exerted by Peter I in having them destroyed—out of several hundred copies printed, only a handful survived to the nineteenth century. Copies of one particular engraving, the source for these verses, were used as evidence of treason against several of Sofiia's supporters during the trial of Fedor Shakhlovitii (see Truvorov 1884–93), which served as a purge of Sofiia's supporters from the government institutions of Muscovy.

I should like to draw the reader's attention to the sovereigns to whom Sofiia Alekseevna is being compared in the second set of verses. These are the mythical Semiramis, Queen of Babylon and architect of the Hanging Gardens; Empress Pulcheria (Holum 1982: 79–228), fifth-century Byzantine defender of Orthodoxy and regent for a younger brother; and Queen Elizabeth I (Yates 1985: 29–120), the virgin queen of England. These disparate female monarchs are linked solely by their aura of liminality; both Pulcheria and Elizabeth used their virginal status as the cornerstone of their political iconography, while the connotations evoked by the semi-divine Semiramis (Garrard 1989: 148) through the overlapping of her marital and maternal roles also placed her, as a symbol, outside the realm of regular social categories.

Jung has noted the special phenomenology connected with the child archetype, a common symbol of liminality. Its irrational, indefinite, potential quality allows it to serve as a symbol of redemption and unity, as a bridge between the Self and the World, Object and Subject. Its hermaphroditism makes it applicable to images of either sex (Jung 1958: 132–147). The unmarried woman or virgin carried many of the same connotations, and as such could be used as a popular and emotionally appealing symbol of state unity and inviolability—from the Vestal Virgins, through the Byzantine Princess cult (Holum 1982: 21–22), to Elizabeth I, in her identification with Virgil's Astraea (Yates 1985: 29–87). In far-off Muscovy, Princess Sofiia—as a single woman with no legal or traditional right to rule—was very much aware of this tradition, and used it to pursue her own political empowerment.

Sofiia Alekseevna's attempt to identify herself, in the eyes of the Muscovite political nation, with the principle of "divinely inspired monarchy" above and beyond any particular monarch (since this position was already occupied by her two brothers—the duly anointed Tsars Peter I and Ivan V) was anchored in a complex ideogram, a multivocal symbol capable of combining centrality and liminality. Sophia the Wisdom of God was the personification of the eternal principle of proportion or harmony between matter and spirit which was an attribute of the Incarnation in the New Testament and of God the Creator in the Old, but was never a self-sufficient manifestation of the Godhead.[6] By linking her political persona with the ancient Christian symbol of interstice or liminality, Sofiia Alekseevna presented herself as simultaneously marginal and vital to the well-being of Muscovy. By identifying herself emblemologically with the passive image of Creation as a reflection of the Creator, she transformed the most obvious physical impediment to her monarchic persona—the fact that she was a woman—into a source of strength: Wisdom as described in Proverbs 8–9 is a specifically feminine image. Simultaneously, by stressing her personal qualifications of education, intellect, and rationality, she made a practical case for remaining at the head of the government.

In short, Sofiia Alekseevna consciously created a political image which provided the most telling contrast with the adolescent pranks and drinking sprees of the "de jure" legitimate and obviously male monarch Tsar Peter I—but one which both reflected and amplified certain already existing tendencies within late seventeenth-century Russian political culture.

Liminality, as a positive characteristic, entered the Muscovite discourse during the reign of Fedor I (1584–1598). This tsar's other-worldly and child-like character served as an artistic and an emotional foil to the powerful, politically acute and ruthless figures of both his father, Ivan the Terrible, and his chief counselor and successor, Boris Godunov, as these two were portrayed in historical writings of the early seventeenth century.[7] This shift in political imagery came about, in my opinion, as a direct result of Ivan IV's totally erratic and unprecedented behaviour. The devastation which he wrought in Muscovy rendered political discourse meaningless and nullified the traditional identification of the monarch with the image of Christ. This opened the door for the popular deification both of his eldest surviving son, the feeble-minded Fedor I,[8] and of his youngest offspring, Prince Dimitri (canonized in 1606). The latter's mysterious death at nine years of age became one of the major political issues during the following three reigns.

Traditional monarchic imagery was no longer capable of expressing Muscovite reality, and this disorientation was reinforced by the political chaos and social devastation undergone by Muscovy during the Time of Troubles—the period between the death of the last Ruirikide, Fedor I, in 1598 and the first Romanov's election to the throne in 1613. At least half a dozen oaths of allegiance were made, and in turn broken, to a series of tsars and pretenders[9] by the political elite, with the final result of rendering meaningless the traditional discourse of legitimacy in Muscovy.[10] The official minutes ("Gosudarstvennaia kniga") from the Assembly of the Land which chose Michael Romanov to be tsar in 1613 make constant use of the terms "infant," "infant-like" or "orphan" in their self-descriptions—projecting a sense of amnesia and dissociation with their county's recent past (*Sobranie* 1828: 3: 2–3). The problem of who was a true monarch and why seemed, by 1613, to defy any rational solution, making a turn to liminality—to the spaces between set categories—a psychological necessity. It was the first Romanov monarch's youth and innocence, as well as his familial relationship to the feeble-minded Fedor I, which was most commonly stressed in the documents announcing his acceptance of the throne (*Sobranie* 1828: 3: 2).

Liminality remained a vital, if seldom overtly stated, value in Muscovite political discourse throughout the seventeenth century. This is suggested by a wide range of evidence. The liminal sobriquet "Tishaishii" or "Most Quiet or Still"—silence by nature being associated with the interstice—was rather inappropriately applied by seventeenth-century chronicles to Aleksei Mikhailovich, the second Romanov tsar. In 1668 the icon known as "The Tree of the Tsardom of Muscovy" (Smirnova 1968: 308) portrayed Aleksei Mikkhailovich and his wife Maria with their two eldest sons, praying in front of the Vladimir Virgin which hangs aloft in the branches of a heraldic tree upon which the tsar's spiritual and secular ancestors are portrayed. Among the spiritual ancestors, out of a total of ten images three are of saints who are Fools for Christ—traditionally marginal figures who represented the inversion of all social values in Muscovy (Fedotov 1975: 2: 316–342). The tenacity of the liminal image becomes apparent when one considers that in 1699, at a time when Peter I had already been firmly in power for ten years, a pattern *poltina* coin was issued by the State Armoury featuring Peter in full Muscovite royal regalia. At the time of this issue the monarch was twenty-eight years old, yet the image on the coin is that of a round-faced chubby child. This coin was scrapped, however, in favour of one portraying a laureate bust of a mature and triumphant Peter with mantle in the Western style—a graphic illustration of one set of values replacing another in a given political culture (Spasskii 1979: 143). Princess Sofiia bridged the gap between liminality and legitimacy which had widened considerably during the seventy years of stable Romanov rule preceding her reign (1613–1682) by identifying herself, in imagic terms, with the figure of Sophia the Wisdom of God. I should now like to examine the religious aspect of this image in greater detail.

Wisdom is most commonly portrayed in Byzantium as Christ Logos (See Fiene 1989 and Florovsky 1932); the scriptural source for identifying Wisdom with the Word is found in Paul's Epistle to the I Corinthians 1. 24, "But unto them which are called, both Jews and Greeks, Christ the power of God and the Wisdom of God." The complexity of this image is underscored by its position in the apostle's text—the verse is embedded in a chapter praising liminality as the highest of virtues—being preceded by I Cor. 1. 19 ("For it is written I will destroy the wisdom of the wise and will bring to nothing the understanding of the prudent") and followed by I Cor. 1. 25 ("Because the foolishness of God is wiser than men; and the weakness of God is stronger than men. For God has chosen the foolish things of this world to confound the wise; and God hath chosen the weak things of this world to confound the things which are mighty. And the base things of the world and the things which are despised, hath God chosen, and the things which are not to bring to nought the things which are." (I Cor. 1. 27–28)

The oxymoron found at the heart of the Pauline image of the Logos—"Foolish Wisdom/Wise Foolishness"—as well as the other major Biblical source for the image, the feminine figure of Wisdom in the Proverbs (specifically chapters 8–22, "The Lord possessed me in the beginning of his way before the works of old")—makes for a poetic symbol of remarkable flexibility and openendedness, one applicable to both Christ and the Virgin—these two subjects being the iconographic vehicles most commonly used before the fifteenth century to portray the Sophic aspect of Creation among the Balkan and Russian Orthodox Christians. Various dimensions of meaning overlapped in the image of Divine Wisdom for late seventeenth-century Muscovites. Its identification with the art of government in Russia was not an innovation of Sofiia Alekseevna's. It stemmed from Russia's Byzantine heritage, from the archetypal opposition of "Chaos" vs. "Cosmos," which took the Byzantine form of "Barbarian Pagan Hinterland" vs. "Christian City." The two oldest cathedrals in early medieval Russia, in Kiev and Novgorod, were dedicated to Divine Wisdom. In one of the earliest Russian sermons preserved, Metropolitan Ilarion's eleventh century "Sermon on Law and Grace," Prince Vladimir is praised both for founding the Christian Kievan state, and for his "wit" (rationality) in perceiving that God is the sole creator of all (Gorskii 1844: 42). Thus both statebuilding and true religiosity are perceived as different facets of the same God-given wit, i.e. Divine Wisdom. That the first written law code of Kievan Rus', the "Russkaia Pravda" (1056 A.D.), composed in the reign of Vladimir's son Yaroslav, earned this prince the title "the Wise" further confirms the existence of a link among the concepts of "Divine Wisdom," government and law in Kiev.

The meaning of "Sophia" for the medieval Rus' may be summarized by the main figure in the apse of the Sophia cathedral at Kiev. The Virgin as Oranta, arms uplifted in prayer—the traditional intercessor, protectress and even armed defender of Byzantine civilization against the forces of obscurity, paganism and disorder seething outside the city walls—floated over the Kievan worshippers, as the personification of divine order and harmony in Heaven, on earth and in their city.[11] The continuity of this motif in the seventeenth century may be seen in the special ceremony celebrating "The Triumph of Orthodoxy" performed by the Archbishop of Novgorod on the first Sunday in Lent, during the course of which he would kiss the image of Sophia the Wisdom of God, again reinforcing the connection between the idea of wisdom and proper religious and governmental order and observance (Iakovleva 1980: 291).

Beginning with the late fourteenth century, four concrete images of Sophia the Wisdom of God make their appearance on icons in medieval Rus', in addition to the earlier images of Christ Logos and the Virgin in their Sophic aspect; the Novgorod type (in which Sophia the Wisdom of God is portrayed as a fiery-faced angel), the Kievan type (in which a Winged Virgin or Woman of the Apocalypse is portrayed as Sophia), the Iaroslavl type (in which a crucifix, usually surrounded by the seven gifts of the Holy Spirit, stands for Sophia), and one entitled "Wisdom hath Builded her House" (an allegorical representation of Proverbs 9) (see Fiene 1989). All of these icons usually include a peculiar eight-pointed or star-shaped nimbus radiating around and marking the main figure in the composition.

Sofiia Alekseevna rebuilt the New Maidens Convent, a major fortress on the Western road leading out of Moscow, in the architectural style most frequently associated with her reign: the Muscovite Baroque. Her transformation of what had been an austere fortress-convent into an extravagant Muscovite Baroque ensemble of fairy-tale towers and gingerbread-trim was a powerful political statement. Princess Sofiia's renovations utterly destroyed the defense capabilities of New Maidens—gates were widened, watch towers which blocked pleasant views were demolished, white stone trim made it impossible to fire down from the crenellated tops of the walls. These innovative esthetic changes echoed the foreign policy of the regent; the Eternal Peace with Poland, signed in 1686, made a fortress guarding Moscow from the Smolensk road irrelevant. To understand the importance of the regent's effort to leave her personal imprint upon the New Maidens Convent two factors must be taken into consideration: first, the semiotic significance of this convent within the system of Muscovite political culture, and secondly, the general role played by religious imagery and architecture as a legitimizing device in Muscovite politics.

The New Maidens Convent housed the palladium of the ruling house of Muscovy—a copy of the Smolensk Virgin—and was often the final earthly and eternal resting place for various ladies both of the royal family, and of the Muscovite boyar elite. By the last quarter of the seventeenth century it also included a considerable number of Ruthenian nuns from the Ukraine, annexed by Muscovy in 1654. Thus, the convent may be seen as a microcosm of the ruling elite of the emerging Russian empire, containing within its walls both this empire's heart—the mothers and daughters of its most prestigious families, Muscovite and Ruthenian—and its soul, the Palladium of the Grand Princes of Muscovy (see Smirnov-Platonov 1885 for a history of the convent).

Prior to Peter the Great, Russia did not know triumphal arches or bronze monuments. Building or redecorating chapels, churches, and cathedrals were among the few ways by which one could impress oneself upon the consciousness of one's contemporaries. Visual religious imagery was a crucial element in the medieval Russian's universe, and one of the surest ways of communicating with the largest number of people was through church art and architecture.

Judging from the fact that Tsar Boris Godunov and Princess Sofiia were the two rulers who spent the most resources on church building and redecorating projects in the seventeenth century (Ovsiannikov 1968: 23), one could almost see money spent on non-military building activity as an index of anxiety concerning the status of one's legitimacy. Again, it was they who built the two highest belfries in Moscow. Tsar Boris added the top tier to the Ivan III belfry in the Kremlin, marking it with an inscription bearing the names of Boris and Fedor, his son and heir apparent. This addition made the belfry, at eighty-one meters, the tallest structure in old Moscow (Rodimtsev 1989: 63). The Princesses' bell tower, completed at New Maidens in 1690 after her retirement

Figure 1

(but, nevertheless, a major component of her renovation plans), was seventy-two meters tall (Ovsiannikov 1968: 63).

The interior of Our Virgin of Smolensk Cathedral, the main church in the New Maidens complex, offers eloquent testimony to Sofiia Alekseevna's attempt to identify herself with the image of Sophia the Wisdom of God. Three major works of art were commissioned in 1683 for the cathedral—an icon depicting the patron saints of the royal family, another one dedicated to the Seventh Ecumenical Council, and finally, a highly unusual Saviour. (For descriptions and histories of each icon see D. K. Trenev 1901.) I should like to describe each of these works in further detail.

The icon depicting the patron saints of all of the members of Tsar Aleksei Mikhailovich's family was a large painting which hung over the northern door of the cathedral (see Figure 1). On it fourteen saints are depicted—patrons of Sofiia's mother, father, aunts, sisters and brothers and of Sofiia herself. They stand in an intercessionary posture, arms uplifted in prayer to the central figure of the Virgin, floating over them, arms raised in the typical Oranta gesture of blessing. The Virgin is of the "Znamenie" type, associated with the palladium of Muscovy; in a medallion on her breast the infant Christ is depicted as the Logos or Eternal Word

Figure 2

against a background of stars, signifying creation and associated with the Old Testament image of Wisdom in Proverbs 8:27, "I was there when he prepared the heavens." Thus, all of the royal family is praying to the Virgin in her role as the rampart or shield of civilization, mistress of victory, and bridge through which Sophia the Wisdom of God enters the world.

The second major icon commissioned during Sofiia's reign was a depiction of the Seventh Ecumenical Council at Nicea, which was convened in 787 AD against the iconclasts (see Figure 2). This icon hung in the sanctuary, the most honorable place in church. The connection between Divine Wisdom and right order in religion and government which I have already mentioned is stressed in this composition, while its spatial placement underscores the princess' desire for the clergy's support. Shortly after taking over the regency Sofiia Alekseevna presided over a public debate with the Old Believers, or Schismatics[12] in July 1682. The debate itself was an inconclusive exercise in rhetoric, culminating in physical violence; nevertheless, the very fact that the princess was present and that she defended the Orthodox position became a major propaganda coup for her side. As a defender of Orthodoxy she could now join the ranks of righteous sovereign Byzantine

Figure 3

empresses, such as the already mentioned Empress Pulcheria, or Empress Irene.

The icon in question is quite unusual in its subject matter since, despite the fact that it is entitled "The Seventh Ecumenical Council at Nicea," it is a combination of two different iconographic subjects—the "Seventh Ecumenical Council" and the "Triumph of Orthodoxy." These two subjects commemorated historical events which took place in two separate Byzantine reigns. The major part of the icon is devoted to the council of 787, and Empress Irene and her son Constantine VI are featured prominently among the dozens of historical figures portrayed on the canvas. However, scenes from another church council, one which was convened in 842 AD during a brief revival of the iconodule-iconoclast controversy, are also included. This council proclaimed the first week of Lent to be dedicated to the memory of the iconodules and the "Triumph of Orthodoxy," which makes it possible to postulate a connection between this image and the Novgorod icon mentioned previously (see above, p. 198). The seven pillars of wisdom which figured prominently, in Sophia icons of both the Novgorod and Kievan type were associated with the

Seven Ecumenical Councils as well as Proverbs 9: "Wisdom hath builded her house, she hath hewn out her seven pillars." Thus, this peculiar combination of subjects, most unusual in terms of iconographic convention, was quite understandable in terms of Sofiia Alekseevna's political need to establish herself both as a living, historical defender of Orthodoxy, akin to such historical figures as Empress Irene, and as the embodiment of that Divine Wisdom which guided the Seven Ecumenical Councils to their preordained conclusion—the triumph of Orthodoxy in Muscovy during the regency of Sofiia Alekseevna.

The last icon which I wish to discuss is a full-length image of Christ Pantocrator, placed on the right-hand side of the bottom row of the icon screen in the Smolensk Cathedral (see Figure 3). He is depicted sitting on a throne, in the manner of Byzantine emperors, right hand held up in blessing, left hand supporting a Bible opened to an extensive quotation from John 3: 16–21. At Christ's feet, in the classical Byzantine posture of obeisance, kneeling with forehead flat against the floor, are two much smaller figures, identified by suprascripts as Saint John the Baptist and the Apostle Peter. The text of the verse begins "For God so loved the world that he gave his only begotten son," and continues "For God sent not his son into the world to condemn the world, but that the world through him might be saved . . . And this is the condemnation, that light is come into the world, and men loved darkness rather than light because their deeds were evil. . . . But he that doeth truth cometh to the light, that his deeds may be made manifest, that they are wrought in God."

The Byzantine identification of Christ-Logos with Sophia is clear; Christ as Pantocrator was also occasionally used in Sophic imagery, the most well-known example being a ninth-century mosaic in the Hagia Sophia Cathedral in Constantinople portraying the Saviour as Pantocrator enthroned, holding a Bible open to John 8:12, 20: 14, 26 ("Peace to you. I am the light of the world"). with the Emperor Leo VI kneeling in obeisance at his feet (Grabar 1979: 97; Oikonomides 1976). The parallels between this image and the Smolensk Cathedral Pantocrator are immediately apparent (see Figure 4). Both Biblical texts emphasize light and enlightenment, echoing the traditional literary connotations of Sophia the Divine Wisdom of God. The kneeling figures in the Smolensk icon are clearly the heavenly patrons of Sofiia Alekseevna's two brothers, Tsars Peter I and Ivan (John) V. A graphic representation of two anointed monarchs acknowledging the superiority of the institution of godly monarchy, as personified by the Word-as-Wisdom, this icon seems to be a clear statement

Figure 4

of Sofiia Alekseevna's view of her role in the government of Muscovy.

In conclusion, I would like to pose the following questions. If, as Weber says, "kingship represents a particularly important case in the historical development of the charismatic legitimization of institutions" (Weber 1958: 251), might not "queenship," specifically in the sixteenth and seventeenth centuries—at which time female rulers, both as queens sovereign and as regents, were particularly visible—have had a certain degree of influence on the development of the political imagery of the modern European state? Weber's description of the modern European monarch, "who gains a share in political power not by prerogative but by virtue of outstanding personal ability or social influence. . . . [and] Despite his lack of parliamentary power . . . [whose] mere existence and . . . charisma guarantee the legitimacy of the social and property order" (Weber 1958: 264) seems analogous to that of "de facto" female sovereignty. The circumstance of a female occupying the throne necessarily forced the monarchical discourse into channels of "feminine" or androgynous imagery, which tended to highlight the amorphous and implicitly "left-handed" interstitial values of mercy or "communitas," to the detriment of the specifically patriarchal "right-handed" sphere of justice, law and structure.[13] In a sense, the female ruler's unique power, which originated in her "liminality," may be likened to Weber's "charisma" (Weber 1958: 245–52). Both were, at least in some important ways, inimical to "patriarchal" and "bureaucratic" structures; both were inherently nontransferable; both could be used as symbols of social reintegration for marginal groups or at times of general social stress. I believe that the liminal nature of imagery connected with female sovereignty served to broaden the emotional basis of support for the early modern monarchy, and ultimately for the State itself, giving it semiotic access to the symbolism of human bonds above and beyond the structural ties of hierarchy and law, and furthering the West's non-contingent and almost mystical acceptance of the modern State as the ultimate arbitrator of all political and social values—as "that mortal god to which we owe, under the immortal God, our peace and defence" (Hobbes 1962: 132).

In the specific case of late seventeenth-century Muscovy, I see a clear connection between Princess Sofiia's reliance on liminal imagery and Peter I's political and cultural iconoclasm. Peter I was able, to some degree, to justify his disregard for tradition and precedent within the framework of late Muscovite political culture because of his half-sister's precedent-breaking regency. Her active promotion of an image of governmental power justified through rationality and order, rather than patriarchal right and tradition, altered the semiotic content of Russian political discourse. All of Peter I's reforms and official actions, including the barring from the throne and eventual execution for treason of his son and heir, Aleksei Petrovich, were justified in terms of political discourse through recourse to the paradigm of government by Divine Wisdom. In numerous engravings and portraits, the image of the Holy Spirit, enclosed in a Sophic eight-pointed star-shaped nimbus, is portrayed as Peter I's source of inspiration (Shchukin and Spasski 1979).

NOTES

1 By liminality I mean the state of being outside structured social categories, either temporarily or permanently. My understanding of liminality is primarily based on the work of Victor W. Turner. In this interim of "liminality" the possibility exists of standing aside not only from one's own social position but from all social positions and of formulating a potentially unlimited series of alternative social arrangements. That this danger is recognized by all tolerably orderly societies is made evident by the proliferation of taboos that hedge in and constrain those on

whom the normative structure loses its grip (Turner 1974: 13–14). Turner links liminality with "communitas"—a mode of social intercourse which stands in direct opposition to that of social hierarchy. Essentially "communitas" is a relationship between concrete, idiosyncratic individuals; these individuals are not segmentalized into roles and statuses but confront one another in the manner of Martin Buber's "I and Thou." Along with this direct, immediate and total confrontation of human identities, there tends to go a model of society as a homogeneous, unstructured communitas, whose boundaries are ideally coterminous with those of the human species.

2 Sophia the Wisdom of God is a complex, multivocal imagic theme in Eastern Christianity. Its complexity stems from the two mutually exclusive sets of associations which it evokes: the classical Greek and Roman sense of wisdom as something gained from observation of the world and experience, and the Early Christian sense of wisdom as being something revealed through divine grace. This tension is clearly felt in I Cor. 1: 22–24, the scriptural passage most often invoked in references to Divine Wisdom. St. Paul accuses the Greeks of seeking their classical type of wisdom but to no purpose since "Christ is the Power and Wisdom of God." For English language works on Sophia see Meyendorff 1987, and Fiene 1989. Sophia is the eternal proportion or analogy between matter and spirit; as such she is most often portrayed as Christ-Logos, since it is through the Incarnation that nature and grace, matter and spirit, rational observation and revelation are reconciled—and it is this interstice of reconciliation, in the spaces between the various elements of this dialectic, that Sophia the Wisdom of God reveals herself. The feminine pronoun traditionally given to New Testament Wisdom by way of analogy with the Solomeic Wisdom of the Proverbs is most revealing as another sign of the essential liminality of Sophic imagery.

3 Zabelin 1872: 174.

> O blagochestivaia tsarevna Sofiia
> Ishcheshchi premudrosti vidy nebesniyia
> Po imeni tvoemu zhizn' tvoiu vedeshi;
> Mudraia glagoleshi, mudraia deeshi
> Ty tserkovniia knigi obvykla chitati
> I v otecheskikh svittsekh mudrosti iskati.

4 Rovinskii 1886, Vol. II: 1940–41.

> Kakova v tsarskom litsu premudrost' siiaet,
> Kakova chest' v ochesekh i v ustakh blistaet.

. . .

Takova Semiramis u Efrata zhila
Eia zhe vveki pamiatno delo sotvorila.
Elisavet Britanska skipetroderzhashchi
Pulkheria takovym umom be smysliashchi.
Russio: Ashche tsarstvu mnogimi pochtenna
Predblagochestivoiu esi umalenna.

5 Koshikhin (Kotoshikhin) 1840: 12. "The sisters of the
tsar however, or his daughters, the princesses, have their
own separate chambers, where they live like anchorites,
seeing very few people, but always spending their time
fasting and praying and crying; for though they take
pleasure in their royal status, they are denied that pleasure which Almighty God gave to mankind, which is to
be fruitful and multiply. And they cannot marry their
subjects, neither princes nor boyars, since these are
considered their slaves, and it would be to their eternal
shame if a mistress should wed a slave; and they cannot
marry foreigners, since all of these belong to a different
faith . . . and also because, since the Muscovite princesses know neither the languages nor the politics of
other lands, they would be ashamed to marry abroad"
(Tr. E. Zelensky). This passage comes from the book *On
Russia during the Reign of Aleksei Milhailovich*, written
by a Muscovite diplomat who defected to the Swedes in
1666, and, therefore, may not have been the most
unbiased observer.
6 The elevation of Sophia to Divine hypostasis (essence),
or even usia (form) was invariably treated as a heresy by
the official Eastern Christian Church, whether in Late
Antiquity, or in the twentieth century; thus, the image's
liminality was assured within the system of Orthodox
semiotics, and, consequently, its strong emotional
appeal. For Sophic controversy during the early centuries
of Christianity see Eliade 1982 and, for a more partisan
view, Pagels 1981. For a twentieth-century slant on this
same theological problem see Newman 1978 on Father
Sergius Bulgakov.
7 Zenkovsky 1974: 388–389, quoting Prince Katyrev-
Rostovsky: "Tsar Ivan (IV) was cruel to his subjects given
to him by the Lord, being always ready to spill thir blood,
and both merciless and daring at killing. He ordered that
many people be slain, from infants to the aged . . . he
laid waste to his own cities . . . threw many clergymen in
jail . . . deflowered many girls and women in his lust . . .
Tsar Boris (Godunov) had two great shortcomings, he
used to go too much to doctors (i.e. sorcery, E. Z.) and
he was obsessed by an insatiable desire for power. And
he dared to slay those who should have been tsars before
him (i.e. Prince Dimitry, E. Z.). And for such deeds he

received divine retribution." In contrast, "the youthful
Fedor Ivanovich . . . was most humble, and greatly cared
after his soul, standing before icons and praying endlessly
he cared nought for worldly matters; and thus God gave
peace to his reign, brought his enemies in tow and
granted him a blessed epoch."

8 In a seventeenth-century icon manual Fedor Ivanovich is
listed as a national Russian saint, while in an eighteenth-
century manual he has been demoted to local status. See
Uspenskii 1910–1916: 1: 341.

9 A short chronology of oaths taken during the Time of
Troubles: Boris Godunov (1598); Theodore II (1605);
First False Dimitry (1605); Vasily Shuisky (1606); Second
False Dmitry (1607); Prince Wladislaw of Poland (1610).

10 "The mad silence of the nation," lamented by a chronicler of the Time of Troubles, Avramii Palitsyn, in my
opinion refers to the complete breakdown of the medieval Muscovite system of political semiotics (Palitsyn
1969: 489).

11 Averintsev 1972 perceives parallels in the function of the
image of the Virgin as Oranta with that of Pallas Athena
and the Muses.

12 Censor Savvatii wrote an eyewitness account of Sofiia
Alekseevna's debate with the Old Believers. Sofiia
Alekseevna became regent as a result of a mutiny
organized by the musketeers ("streltsy") in the name of
her brother, Ivan V, who was originally denied the
throne because of his mental and physical incapacity. The
musketeers as a group felt threatened professionally, due
to the army reorganisation begun under the Princess'
father, and the consequent influx of foreign soldiers and
military technology. Many of the musketeers belonged to
the Old Belief, and some of them supported its advocates
during the debate. The two "de jure" monarchs were not
present; in their places sat Sofiia Alekseevna—
significantly enough on the left-hand throne—and their
aunt Tatiana Mikhailovna on the right. Sofiia's sisters,
another aunt, the widowed Tsaritsa Natalia Kirillovna—
Peter I's mother—and members of the higher clergy from
the official Church were also present. See Kozhanchikov
1862: 120–133.

13 Here I must gratefully acknowledge new insights gained
from the papers given by Dr. Gordon Kipling and Dr. D.
A. Miller during the "Women and Sovereignty" Conference, from August 30–Sept. 5, 1990 at St. Andrews
University, Scotland. Dr. Kipling's association of queenship with mediation in "The Queen's Advent: The Ceremonial Civic Triumphs of Women Rulers, 1400–1550," in

combination with Dr. Miller's explanation of the importance of "left-handed" imagery for the Byzantine monarchical discourse, helped lend concrete features to my
originally rather amorphous conception of the relationship between female sovereignty and liminality.

REFERENCES

Averintsev, S. S. (1972). K uiasneniu smysla nadpisi nad
konkhoi tsentral'noi apseidy Sofii Kievskoi. *Drevnerusskoie isskustvo: khudozhestvannaia kultura domongol'-
skoi Rusi*, ed. V. N. Lazarev. Moscow: Nauka.

Eliade, Mircea (1982). *A History of Religious Ideas*. 3 vols.
Chicago: University of Chicago Press.

Fedotov, George P. (1975). *The Russian Religious Mind*. Vol
4 in *The Collected Works of George P. Fedotov*, ed.
John Meyendorff. Belmont, MA: Nordland.

Fiene, Donald M. (1989). What is the Appearance of the
Divine Sophia? *Slavic Review* 48, no. 3: 449–76.

Florovsky, Georges (1932). O pochitanii Sofii, Premudrosti
Bozhei, v Vizantii i na Rusi. *Trudy piatogo šezda russ-
kikh akademicheskikh organizatsii za granitsei*. Part I.
Sofia.

Garrard, Mary D. (1989). *Artemisia Gentileschi: The Image
of the Female Hero in Italian Art*. Princeton: Princeton
University Press.

Grabar, Andre (1979). *Byzantine Painting*, trans. Stewart
Gilbert. New York: Rizolli.

Gorskii, A. V. (1844). *Pamiatniki dukhovnoi literatury vremeni kniazia Iaroslava l-ogo*. Moscow.

Hobbes, Thomas (1962). *Leviathon: Or the Matter, Forme
and Power of Commonwealth Ecclesiaticall and Civil*, ed.
Michael Oakeshott, Intro. Richard S. Peters. New York:
Macmillan.

Holum, Kenneth (1982). *Theodosian Empresses: Women and
Imperial Dominion in Late Antiquity*. Berkeley, CA:
University of California Press.

Iakovleva, A. I. (1980). Obraz Mira' v ikone 'Sophia Premud-
rost' Bozhiia. *Drevnerusskoie isskustvo*: 388–404.

Jung, Carl G. (1958). *Psyche and Symbol: A Selection from
the Writings of Carl Jung*, ed. Violet S. de Laszlo. New
York: Anchor Books.

Kondakov, N. P. (1933). *Russkaia ikona*, 4 vols. Prague: Niva.

Koshikhin (Kotoshikhin), Griogorii (1840). *O Rossii v
tsarstvovanie Aleksei Mikhailovicha*, ed. Iakov Bered-
nikov. St. Petersburg: Tipografiia Eduarda Pratsa.

Kozhanchikov, D. E. (1862). *Tri chelobitniia-Spravshchika
Savatiia, Savvy Romanova i monakhov Solovetskogo
monastryia*. St Petersburg: D. E. Kozhanchikov.

Lossky, N. O. (1959). *Uchenie o. Sergeia Bulgakova o vseedinstve i o Bozhestvennoi Sofii.* South Canaan, PA: N. O. Lossky.

Meyendorff, John (1987). Wisdom-Sophia: Contrasting Approaches to a Complex Theme. *Dumbarton Oaks Papers* 41: 391–401.

Newman, Barbara (1978). Sergius Bulgakov and the Theory of Divine Wisdom. *St. Vladimir's Theological Quarterly* 22: 39–73.

Oikonomides, Nicolas (1976). Leo VI and the Narthex Mosaic of St. Sophia. *Dumbarton Oaks Papers* 30: 153–72.

Ovsiannikov, Iu (1968). *Novodevichii monastyr'.* Moscow: Nauka.

Palitsyn, Avramii (1969). Skazaniie. *Izbornik (Sbornik proiz-videnii drevnei Rusi),* eds. L. A. Dmitriev and D. S. Likhachev. Moscow: Khudozhestvennaia literaura.

Pagels, Elaine (1981). *The Gnostic Gospels.* New York: Vintage.

Platonov, S. F. (1913). *Drevnerusskiia skazaniia i povesti o smutnom vremeni XVIIv., kakistoricheskii istochnik.* St Petersburg: Tipografiia M. A. Alexandrova.

Rovinskii, D. A. (1886). *Podrobnyii slovar' russkikh gravir-ovannykh portretov.* 2 vols. St. Petersburg.

Rodimtsev, J. (1989). *Moskovskii kreml'.* Moscow: Moskovs-kii rabochii.

Semevsky, M. (1859). Sovremennye portrety Sofii Alek-seevny i V. V. Golitsyna. *Russkoie slovo* 12: 411–58.

Smirnov-Platonov, G. P. (1885). *Istoricheskoie opisanie Novodevich'igo monastyria.* Moscow.

Smirnova, E. S. (1968). *Moskovskiie ikony XV-XVIIv.* Leningrad: Avrora.

Sobranie gosudarstvennykh gramot i dogovorov khraniash-chikhsia v gosud, kollegii inostrannykh del. (1828). 4 vols. St. Petersburg.

Shchukin, E. S. and Spasskii, I. G. (1979). *Medals and Coins from the Age of Peter the Great.* Leningrad: Aurora.

Spasskii, I. G. (1970). *Russkaia monetnaia sistema: istoriko-numismaticheskii ocherk.* Leningrad: Aurora.

Trenev, D. K. (1901). *Ikony tsarskogo izografa Simona Ushakova v MoskovskomNovodevich'em monastyre.* Moscow: Tipografiia I. Efimova.

Truvorov, Askalon, ed. (1884–1893). Arkheograficheskaia Komissia. *Razysknia dela o Fedore Shakhlovitomiego soobshchnikakh.* 4 vols. St. Petersburg.

Turner, Victor W. (1974). *Dramas, Fields and Metaphors: Symbolic Action in Human Society.* Ithaca: Cornell University Press.

—— (1969). *The Ritual Process: Structure and Anti-Structure.* Ithaca: Cornell.

Uspenskii, A. I. (1910–16). *Tsarskiie ikonopistsy XVII-ogo veka*. 4 Vols. Moscow.

Weber, Max (1958). *From Max Weber: Essays in Sociology*, trans. and ed. H. H. Gerth and C. Wright Mills. New York: Oxford University Press.

Yates, Frances (1985). *Astraea: The Imperial Theme in the Sixteenth Century*. London: Ark.

Zabelin, Ivan (1872). *Domashnii byt russkih tsarits v XVI i XVII v*. Moscow: Tipografiia Gracheva.

Zenkovsky, Serge A., ed. (1974). *Medieval Russia's Epics, Chronicles, and Tales*. New York: E. P. Dutton.

SUSANNA ÅKERMAN

On the Impossibility of Abdicating: Queen Christina of Sweden and the Spiritual Crown

"To be a monarch without a throne is being like a God without a Temple," Christina wrote late in life when looking back on her varied fortunes. Memories of her abdication in 1654 and her subsequent journey through Brussels and Innsbruck to Rome, where she was received as the great convert of the age, had by then mingled with a bitter conviction that she could have attained even greater and much more substantive glory.

The Catholic image of Christina as a triumphant Queen who in Rome in 1656 lays down her Crown and Scepter in return for spiritual rewards and a celestial crown has been carved in monumental stone in the northern aisle of the St. Peter's Dome. Yet, this pious praise has a very peculiar relation to, and is also seriously questioned by, Christina's actual politics in Belgium during her year of exile and waiting in Antwerp and Brussels in 1654–55. Reactions to her public acts were tempered by contemporary ideology, and as I shall show, her strategy to differentiate herself after the abdication and the sequence of events that ended in her so-called murder of Monaldescho were to provoke wide international concern. Her acts were perceived as ambiguous crossings over boundaries of rulership and femininity, and stirred up the culture's need to publicly formulate the tacit rules of sovereignty.[1]

A TARNISHED IMAGE: THE SWEDISH QUEEN AS SPIRITUAL SAVIOUR

An English letter of intelligence from Dort on 13 June 1653 had exclaimed: "The Swede is the only politick prince, preparing and making herself ready against the day of change" (Thurloe 1742: ii). Then followed remarkable events; after Christina's abdication, "so much to despise the greatness of this world," and her secret flight "in habitu virilis . . . looked upon as a fantastic trick," came

Figure 1. Cromwell as the woman of the Beast

suspicion that along with her pro-Spanish politics, she was secretly negotiating with powerful pretenders such as the Prince of Condé, Cromwell, or Charles II. Her acts and impious ways led observers to believe that she had "some great design in hand," and that "a Generall Peace will suddenly be ushered in by the Queen of Swedeland" (Thurloe 1742: iv: 27, 39).

Catholics who observed the Swedish Queen in the Netherlands were convinced that great political change was to be expected. To enhance their belief they produced the Flemish pamphlet *Kort Beworp van de dry teghenwoordighe aenmerckens-weerdighe Wonderheden des wereldts* (Cologne 1656). Here Christina is pitted against the Protestant powers and their ally France in an apocalyptic scenario (Figure 1). The English Protector Cromwell is seen riding the seven-headed beast of the Apocalypse in an onslaught towards the Catholic Habsburg Emperor and the Spanish King, while Mazarin and Lucifer give him instructions. Alluding to the book of Revelations, the pamphlet shows Cromwell as "the bride" or woman of the beast, his long hair bound with braces. England's campaign threatens the whole of Europe, until Queen Christina through her unexpected conversion can

Figure 2.   Christina ushering in the day of judgment

make a pious plea in a direct parley with Christ, who, on his
Second Coming, is seen to cast Lucifer in chains together with the
English and the French masters—while the dead are rising from
their graves (Figure 2). The three notable and wonderful events
described on the title-page are, first, that it is certain that we live
in the last days of the world; second, that at this time "Crom-
ghewalt" has arrived as the promised Anti-Christ, and his party
has begun to play a vicious game with the Queen of Sweden and
"Mas-ruin"; third, that God through the holy conversion of the
illustrious Christina Maria Alexandra, has risen up a saviour in
the Theatre of the World, in order to overwhelm the schemes of
that shameful breaker of pacts, her successor—the new King of
Sweden Charles Gustavus, together with Crom-ghewalt, Masruin,
the Grand Turk and other godless rulers of these times.

In this popular and political context Christina was seen as the
classical saviour saint, but little was shown of her real personality.[2]
The pamphlet served a pro-royalist function and intended to show
resistance to the spread of the English revolution. The *Kort
Beworp* is staged as a dialogue between two Dutch merchants and
an English royalist refugee who warns of the rise of a Protestant
alliance under the aegis of the English Tyrant, while suggesting

the advantages of an English alliance with Spain. The edition even purports to have been supervised by the exiled Scottish Monarch Charles Stuart. When new Dutch converts that were to follow Christina to Rome were interviewed (among them the post Reyer Anslo), they revealed that they had been inspired by another small pamphlet by the self-educated peasant Arnold Gheluwen, entitled *Het licht op den Candelaar*.

The millenarian interpretation of Christina's abdication had been absorbed by Netherlands sectarians, whether Catholic, Quaker, or Mennonite. Thus, in the same year, other pamphlets were falsely spread in the name of the Dutch master poet Joost van den Vondel, arguing instead that Christina Maria Alexandra herself was the whore of Babylon. Her journey to Rome to kneel at the very feet of Pope Alexander VII in Rome was a sign corresponding to the apocalyptic claim that Kings shall kneel before the Anti-Christ (Becker 1973). The turns of pamphleteering became intense until the real Vondel, whose solemn hymns often are compared to Milton's and who was at work on his celebrated cycle *Lucifer*, emerged with a leaflet against the recent forgeries, asking: "To set a Crown of thorns upon her head—with what blind hatred have you thus Christina stung with thorns? When instead like Christ *she* wears a Crown as God's true sign." Vondel's poetic gesture emphasized Christina's background as divine monarch to set out the hope that her spiritual crown would provide for future graces.

In this way, Christina's abdication generated a belief, held up by public argument, that her sudden break with the Divine covenant involved in kingship had altered the normal pattern of Providence so to make it possible for her to help institute a new moral order, bringing in a new spirit for the age. This fantasy may have even suggested itself to Christina, as the Spaniards reported that in Belgium she read St. Bridget and Nostradamus for the first time; she spoke of Buckingham's five prophecies on England, Bohemia and Spain; and later she wrote in code that she had seen Pope Alexander VII's wheelchair in Joachim di Fiore's prophecies—hoping that he soon would pass "à l'autre monde," while lamenting that she could not say this straight out for fear of excommunication (Åkerman 1990b).

Her attitude was not exceptional. In 1655, Swedish diplomats at Cromwell's court could report that in the streets of London people were convinced that the prophecies of Daniel were soon to be fulfilled and the *Conflagratio Mundi* brought on (Roberts 1988: 142, 229). One saw the death of Gustavus Adolphus as God's wrath and "outpouring of the fourth vial." Similarly, in France, astrological pamphlets produced in the name of Andreas Argolin interpreted the Eclipse of 1654 and the Comet of 1652 as prefiguring the last days (Labrousse 1972: 16). The full import and utility of these expectations had grown all the more clear to European politicans, but especially to Christina through her talks in Antwerp with the secretary to the Prince of Condé, the heretic millenarian Isaac La Peyrère, after which his *Systema Theologicum ex hypothesi prae-Adamitae* (setting up a millenarian theology on the assumption that there were men before Adam) was speedily, but anonymously published with Christina's financial help (Popkin 1987: 197ff). Hence, the moment of her conversion was crucially conditioned by the critical stage of millenarian expectation—the renewal of Noah's convenant, thought to have been instituted 1,656 years before Christ and now to be repeated. The new dawn would be brought on by that politician who could unify the world for the thousand-year realm of peace expected to last until Judgement Day. It was thought that Christina had wanted to deliver a sign to the Church that now not only the most radical of the Reformed could adopt a scenario of universal salvation.

Queen Christina's secret diplomacy and hidden agenda in the Spanish Netherlands shows that in 1655 she aimed to act out popular millenarian expectations, by way of first helping the Prince of Condé storm Bordeaux and so in return gain influence in Brussels after the expected departure of Leopold Wilhelm—the Habsburg art collector who had made known that he had no wish to continue his governing. There were rumours that Count Fuensaldana, the Chief of Arms in the Spanish Netherlands, wanted to confer on Christina the rights of the Spanish Infanta. Then, when Brussels went out of reach with the rise of Don Juan José of Austria, Christina turned to a secret plan that would with the help of Mazarin establish herself as the future Queen of Naples—a Spanish domain (Åkerman 1990a, Weibull 1936). In Antwerp and in Paris, Christina sought out secret peace-negotiations with France and Spain and hoped that these would "threaten the world with a great calm." A new throne in southern Italy would enhance her claim to be a peace-loving female Prince. There are even some intriguing documents contesting that domains in Naples were offered to Christina, as early as in 1653, by the Spanish Ambassador Don Antonio Pimentel, suggesting that all along her aim was the Kingdom of Naples, not the City of Rome. Christina clearly expected that her spiritual Crown was soon to be exchanged for a throne where she could be the maker of providential kings—thus in the secret contract with Mazarin she said that as she would have no descendants, at her death she would hand over the crown to a French Dauphin.[3]

Her secret contract was, however, made entirely void in 1657 after the betrayal of her Neapolitan plot by her servant Marquise Monaldescho. After so many turns of intrigue in Belgium, Italy, and France, Christina had to revenge herself on his treason. This was done with unusual exactitude: since Monaldescho wore an ironside underneath his coat, his throat had to be cut (Figure 3). The blood stained a fifth of the floor at the *Gallerie des Cerfs*, the hunting hall on loan from Louis XIV at Fontainebleau. Because she was unable to relate the true reason for her act, the plan for Naples, Christina's public reputation now turned from praise and adulation to open contempt. The pamphlet *La Métémpsychose de la reine Christine de Suéde* (Paris 1657) summed up the public reaction (Weibull 1936: 96). It argued that the execution of Monaldescho revealed Christina to be as cruel and as lustful as Semiramis of Assyria, who used to bury her soldier-lovers alive. As it was believed that Christina's execution was a crime of passion, it was claimed that her soul must have transmigrated from Astarte, the ancient love goddess of the West-Semitic Orient. Also, as with Semiramis, it was believed that Christina cross-dressed so as to make it impossible to determine whether she was a woman or a man. While her cross-dressing in 1655 had been mystically hailed in the Spanish Netherlands through drinking glasses etched with Christina in male costume on one side and in female dress on the other, now in 1657 after the murder at Fontainebleau her masculine attire was regarded with suspicion as a sign of utmost disrepute.

Her crossing of boundaries, both in abdicating her throne and in her flight from traditional female roles, could at first be accommodated as a sign of Divine providence. As with Jeanne D'Arc, Christina's behaviour was so much out of the normal order that benign and sacred interpretations were attempted by many parties. But later, when expectations of the extraordinary were dashed, popular opinion started to bring her down. Observers in Sweden, for instance Axel Ivarsson Natt och Dag, had long been convinced that her abdication was not at all rooted in religious sentiment, since "everything religion denotes is alien to her" and in his view her act was "a mere desertion and the sign of a feeble and a volatile spirit" (Johannesson 1968). Hostile eyes on the Continent also found that her behaviour showed an illicit prefer-ence for a life as a "mondo vagabonda," thus invoking the threatening image of a vagrant cosmopolitan not in service to any

Figure 3.   "Frappez, répondit l'impitoyable Christine."

Lord. The traditional emphasis on virtue, on constancy, modesty, and a steadfast faith in nation, family, and office thus provided for a mythology of her independent state that simply negated all these common virtues, producing thereby the image of a Queen who mysteriously acted out a life both "mouvementée et scabreuse."

This image of "nomad vagrancy" caught on so well in France that in freethinking intellectual settings, like St. Evremond's libertine coterie at the Hague, the abdication of the Swedish Queen continued to be discussed. Had she not fooled herself? Had she not given away worldly power for existence in a political void? Was not an abdication in such young years the height of wastefulness? St. Evremonde's correspondent in Paris, Le Comte D'Olonne, in 1656 reported that the talk of the salons was that if only the Queen had used some self-restraint and had followed the customs of her country she would still be queen. Instead, she had now lost her dominion and *that* is all that her studies, science and "belles lumières" have produced. Yet, others replied that it was wrong to hold "les plus belles actions de sa vie" for a crime and that one still must regard her step as equal to that of Charles V or Diocletian, who both gave up their empires (that of Charles V was suggestive since he had abdicated in 1555 in Brussels for a spiritual retreat, thus nearly one hundred years earlier and in the very city in which the Queen had taken residence). Still, the skeptics continued their scorn, saying that then one could as well compare her to Alexander the Great or Caesar, and certainly, they never freely gave up their power and influence (St. Evrémond 1706: ii). Now, it was said, surely to be successful in France one needs no tomes of study: "Du Latin! De mon temps, du Latin! . . . Peu de latins, Vous dis-je, & et du bon François."

CHRISTINA'S DUBIOUS ACT EVALUATED IN THE COURT OF SCHOLARS

In a time less heated, a cooler debate took place among continental scholars, among them G. W. Leibniz, who took stock of the fact that Christina's status after the abdication had been heightened by her infamous execution of Monaldescho at Fontainebleau. The discussion displays not only the ideological and juridical assumption that an abdication hardly can be made at such an early age without a complete retreat from politics, but also the complexity of Christina's role as an unbound monarch—a role that still resonated with the equivocal words of John Milton's verse to her in 1654: "You may abdicate the Sovereignty, but you will never lay aside the Queen."

As time went on, the departure of monarchs from their thrones had become less fraught with apocalyptic trauma. For example, A. P. Chaussard's book of exciting fiction, *Les Antenors Modernes ou voyages de Christine et Casimir* (Paris 1806) could develop the case of abdicated monarchs with more nuance. In an appendix,

Chaussard summarizes the consequences of the legal debate on Christina's execution.

Jean Tesmar's *Tribunal Principis Peregrinantis* (1765) analyzed Christina's apology and the statement released by Father Le Bel, the priest present at *Gallerie des Cerfs* when the execution took place. Father Le Bel reported how Christina had told him that she had an indisputable right of justice over her servants. She "took God as witness that she was not aiming at Monaldescho's person, nor was she acting out of hatred, but had considered that the man's crime had no equal. His treason concerned all the world." In any case, she was master of her will to render justice over her domestics in every place and at all times and she would not answer for her actions to anyone but God himself. Father Le Bel had tried to appeal: "At least show some pity and hand him over to the justice of the King of France." But, Christina had replied: "What! Should I, in whom resides the absolute and sovereign justice over my subjects, see myself reduced to solicit for a domestic traitor, of whose perfidy and crimes I possess documents, written and signed by his own hand. No, I will made my decision known to the King of France when time seems fit" (Chaussard 1806: 490). Tesmar remarks that Christina thus herself appealed to "the character of an absolute Sovereign, who has an impenetrable shield towards every objection possible."

But, to most scholars her behaviour had shown a gap in legal doctrine and some rushed to point out that it was possible to see her execution as a crime: since no king or sovereign nation can calmly suffer that a stranger exercise justice within his territory (the most *éclatant* sign of sovereignty), it is clear that a Prince who lives in foreign territory cannot use his own jurisdiction, but at all times must comply with the law of the sovereign of the place in which he resides. If he commits a crime, he is not only responsible, but can also be justly punished.

In his *Mélanges Historiques* (Rouen 1699–1701), Vigneul de Marville was first to argue that Christina's execution of Monaldescho, an *Italian* nobleman, raises three levels of questions, two of which are not well handled by the explicit doctrine of sovereignty.

1. Whether a sovereign, in the kingdom of another sovereign who has given him hospitality, has the right to judge over the life and death of his domestics in case of their misdeeds. (Yes, this is quite conventional, Marville argues, and no-one would object.)

2. Whether a sovereign can put a criminal to death, i.e. when the criminal is his domestic, but also is a subject of the Prince in the place where he has taken residence, or the subject of

another Prince. (Monaldescho was not a Swede, but a Neapolitan nobleman, and the location of his death was France.)

3. And most importantly, whether a Prince who has renounced his Scepter and Crown can pretend still to have, irrespective of the abdication, a *jus gladii*, that is, a legitimate power to execute one of his domestics for reason of infidelity, or assault on his honour and person. (This consideration was apparently what was novel and exciting in Christina's case.)

Marville's problems show how the spatial dislocation of a Prince poses two alternative ways of locating the "root" of sovereignty: either in the concrete physical body of the Prince, or within his legitimate national boundaries. Yet, remarkably enough, the project of Tesmar's *Tribunal* (1765) was to save Christina, and he went to great lengths and considerable tedium to argue against Marville in defence of her act. Tesmar presented various arguments that place Christina squarely within the world of male sovereignty. If her bloody act was justifiable, it would have to be so irrespective of her female role, and certainly a crime of passion was no exception to the Princely role. First, the fact that a sovereign is given permission to stay in the territory of another does not mean that he therefore becomes a subject; becoming a subject requires submission to the right of the sovereign. Even if a sovereign wants to regard a foreign Prince as his subject, it is difficult to see how he circumvents the obligation to treat him as an equal, in the way custom has been in such instances, for example during the passage of the Habsburg Emperor Charles V through France.

Second, to have an obligation requires subjection, and although a monarch can forfeit his rights by lèse-majesté this is only a relation that holds between him and his nation. Thus, in cases of travelling monarchs one must take recourse to war or a decision by arms, which is the unique tribunal, sovereign to sovereign.

Tesmar's point is that these considerations show that if a sovereign is admitted by another sovereign to his territory, he constitutes immediately for him "an altogether separate society." The travelling monarch's subjects remain subjects and members of his state, although it is "ambulatoire ou voyagente." The very body of the monarch creates a nation around his court, even in foreign territory.

According to Tesmar, Christina had in fact observed all juridical requirements put on a travelling sovereign. She had instituted a successor (her cousin Charles Gustavus) and had thereafter determined the rules for his and her own role. Her resignation of the crown remained as laudable as that of Childeric or of Pepin of

France, who both had taken off their crowns and given their insignia to the priests (Chaussard 1806: 494). But, Christina had gone even further. She had continued to send her own ministers to foreign courts, and thereby she still enjoyed the dignity of royalty. Thus, the important point of the legal debate was that Christina's behaviour was considered to be successful because a) she had shown no signs of submission, and b) she received full royal recognition in the eyes of others; perhaps precisely because of her bloody revenge, she had proven herself worthy of an exalted status. Christina had acted as a Prince, she had taken every precaution not to let the betrayal destroy her status, and she did not even try to repent or excuse herself. Tesmar notes that the silence which the king of France has kept concerning the execution gives further authority to the queen. (Louis XIV was in fact wholly ignorant of her reasoning concerning the execution—and, indeed, to stage it in the very heart of France was a well calculated move. The King of France could not pretend not to allow what was going on in his own palace.) The whole case shows that one has to say with Tacitus: "With such a great example one has to elevate oneself over the normal rules of justice."

Yet, in an exchange with the Dutchman Cornelis Bynckershoek, the journalist Barbeyrac pointed out that at the court of France some still thought that if an abdication allows a queen to keep her sovereign rights, then one must wonder what kind of abdication she has admitted to. Was not the whole notion of abdication at risk? The learned Ambassador Abraham de Wicquefort (1981) similarly claimed that the rights of the sovereign clearly are cancelled by an abdication, especially after the time when the abdicated prince has no more *affair d'état* to negotiate. Also, Hugo Grotius' *De Jure Belli ac Pacis* (1625) asserts that a king who leaves his crown becomes a private person. Perhaps quite daringly, Wicquefort concluded that the King of France had refrained from intervening only because he wanted "to demonstrate to the infidels that his subjects are nothing but slaves and that Kings are proper Lords over their lives."

More detached from the politics at the court of France, the royalist philosopher Leibniz was determined to demonstrate that nonetheless there is no special vacuum cut open in the plenum or norms through Christina's unusual, but clearly accountable act. Normal jurisdiction holds, since her status was similar to that of an Ambassador travelling to another country: the punishment of his subjects belongs to him, or to his own sovereign. In his *Theodicée* (1709), Leibniz had noted with pleasure Christina's coin with a globe and her inscription "Ne mi Basta, ne mi Bisogna—

neither sufficient, nor necessary to me" and referred to it in arguing for the justice of her claim that God was her only sovereign. Leibniz contested that one can only reproach Christina on moral grounds for not respecting the *place* in which her justice was delivered—the Royal House at Fontainebleau. She had appropriated a place not belonging to her, but had done so quite effectively, thus maintaining her sovereign right in her displaced state. It would therefore be ridiculous to pretend that the Queen should leave to the *libre arbitre* of another the judgment of a crime of this sort. A transfer of rights could not be made without lowering her high dignity. If the Court of France finds her decision blameworthy, it is only because she did not want to trust them with such affection, and that the execution took place in the Palace of the King. The practical acceptance of her crime by the young French King was perhaps the factor that decided Leibniz's attempt to absolve her. On the other hand, the interest in the case was probably precisely due to the fact that Louis XIV's seeming acquiescence in her act threatened to show him weaker than her.

Another thinker, G. P. Marana, the famous Italian author of the early Enlightenment critique *The Turkish Spy at the Court of France* (London 1693), declared that as Christina was both sovereign and independent, and in addition had permission by the King of France to dwell in his Kingdom, one cannot contest her right over her subjects. All those in her service and in her pay have a standing unequal to the subjects of the state in which she chooses to reside. (Marana may in fact have been supported by Christina, since there is a letter to him from her in 1687, in which she lauds his talents. *The Turkish Spy* speaks of Christina in a tone and with details that indicate that she may have herself supplied the information.) It is true, Marana continues, that at her abdication, Christina gave up all immunities, liberties and independences due to her birth. But, in the abdication-statutes she had been given an independent appanage and her servants, including Monaldescho, had been obligated to swear her an oath of personal trust. As a matter of fact, she has continued to be received as a sovereign and she has her own foreign ministers at the most important courts.

Although many complained about her lack of royal civility, Christina managed to uphold the essential aspects of monarchical behaviour, and this was regarded as sufficient evidence that she had *not* alienated her monarchical rights. As her academies in Rome show, her Royal role still had a great deal of value and interest—she emblematically served as "Bassilissa" (a Byzantine title for a monarch with legal, sacred, and magical powers) to both the *Accademia Arcadia* and Ciampini's *Accademia physico-matematico*, even after her death in 1689. Books were thus typically offered to her with the dedication "Alla Sacra Real Maestà di Svezia." Summing up the debate, Marana exclaimed that the execution of Monaldescho was *un cas unique de monde*. This uniqueness was the result not only of her role as the convert of the age, and of the remarkable events surrounding her abdication, but also of the new perception that she was a female Prince with blood on her hands. Yet, Marana claims that it would have been better for her to dissimulate her resentment, since the world is bound to see all events from the worst angle. Clearly, a consequence has been that her act is regarded as a cruel deed. But if one looks at the case, Marana concludes, one sees that people's objections are only due to the fact that the execution took place so close to the Capital of France.

The crown of Absolutism again had asserted itself, even if, as here, at the cost of casting scorn on the courtiers circulating around its primary pillar in France. Affronted by these dispassionate conclusions, in 1806, Chaussard was inclined to reject any act of despotism and could only offer a last and public challenge: "the voice of nature, of humanity and reason raises itself against these subtleties and it would be an injury to common sense not to refute them."

In Italy, however, people with less philosophic minds thought that such a refutation could easily be made as they cleverly whispered:

> Regina senza Regno,
> Christiana senza fede,
> Donna senza vergogna.

Not so much queen without land, as

> Ruler without Reign,
> Christian without faith,
> Woman without shame.

In the popular jingle, Christina's gender was seen as parallel to those other riddling anomalies. As ruler is to reign, woman is to shame—a fabric of "proper" possession too well-knit not to devalue her exceptional status. Her acts now revealed a possibly mad lack of modesty. The landless Swedish Queen had been caught out of her female bounds and the spiritual crown began to slip off.

Yet, irrespective of her popular reputation, in 1668 Christina could enter as one of the official candidates for the elective throne in Poland. The election was staged to fill the gap after the departure of her relative Johan Cassimir Wasa, who, weary of government, had declared that he wanted a spiritual retreat at the monastery of St. Germain-de-Près in Paris. The campaign for the throne in Poland was carried on with much ingenuity on all sides. Christina cited the extraordinary precedents of Hedwig, on whom had been bestowed the formal regency of Poland in 1384, and Joanna Jagellonica who in 1574 had become Queen of Poland after the departure of the French king Henri. Christina even contemplated lying about her age when the Poles made known that they wanted to make the throne hereditary, so that it would be thought that she still could have children (she was by then forty-two) (André 1908). But, although Christina was both Catholic and of the family of Wasa, she was not chosen. Her disinformation concerning the weaknesses and violent minds of the other Princely candidates may, however, have determined the electors' decision finally to given the crown of Warsaw to a Pole less blue-blooded, Michail Wiesnowicki.

By 1761, in a review of Johan Arckenholtz' four grand and redemptive volumes of letters shedding light on Queen Christina's life, the Encyclopedist D'Alembert criticized its minute dwelling on monarchical paraphernalia and used the opportunity to consider the relation between sovereign power and the recent string of departures of rulers from their thrones:

> The love of debauchery, the desire to satisfy in peace all tastes violent and subaltern, are almost always the principle of their abdications. They believe that nothing are them wanting for rulership except the will; but then this will reigns supreme among them after their retreats until it becomes their greatest torment.

D'Alembert saw that the pursuit of power, and the fabric of praise that upheld royal prerogatives, did not even cease with abdications. In order to achieve an eclipse of popular affection, abdications are staged as personal sacrifices, D'Alembert continued, yet monarchs hardly would enjoy their isolation if rulership had not been an overbearing responsibility. Christina's bombastic coronation coin for her successor, Charles Gustavus (*A Deo et Christina*), then inspired d'Alembert to assert that legitimate royal authority never derives from God, but from the consent of the people, which is authority's visible sign and which solely justifies its exercise.

Christina's anomalous role may thus have had a lasting influence in strengthening those forces that strove to undermine the Absolutist world order, her case being a sure sign that sovereignty, under close scrutiny, is grounded in mortal and fallible flesh. Even the pro-royalist philosopher Pascal put this on record; when considering recent regicides and abdications, he exclaimed:

Whoever had the friendship of the King of England, the King
of Poland and the Queen of Sweden, would have believed it
possible to need a place of retreat or exile anywhere in the
world?

The enduring effect of Christina's career was neither to confirm
a Catholic worldview nor to safeguard aspirations for universal
peace. Rather it was to provide fuel for irreverence, a delight for
writers otherwise constrained to circulate around monarchs with a
decorum so elevated that one could mistake it for Divine Law. It
did not much help to alter this trend that a royalist like Arckenholtz in 1751 had added to his second volume an anonymous
enlightenment panegyric in which Christina is seen as the Queen
of the Parnassus, protector of "les Alexandrines et Philadelphes,"
i.e. of the cosmopolitan set of learned readers who revere the
Queen as "leur Déesse tutelaires et la souveraine de leur ordre."
As the eager readers of clandestine pamphlets were conditioned
to conclude, her role as monarch without a throne indeed had
become, as she wrote, suggestive of a God without a Temple, to
whom devoted subjects had ceased to pay their tribute. In
unforeseen ways, then, Christina's abdication, conversion, *and*
infamous execution of Monaldescho set forces in motion that
ultimately would facilitate the breakdown of the medieval world
of queens and kings: a world that she had tried both to challenge
and to uphold, but that she never dreamed would so rapidly
evaporate.

NOTES

1 I thank Louise Fradenburg for stimulating questions that
   have improved my paper. Fuller documentation of the
   turns in the secret diplomacy of 1653–1657 is being prepared, beginning with my recent thesis (Åkerman 1991).
2 The pamphlets arose in a popular and political context and
   their images, including many that denounce Christina's
   morals, suggest both bisexual activity and transsexual
   urges. This sensationalism may have been a factor in
   creating the later, more reflective treatment of her role in
   elite and scholarly circles.
3 Christina refused to marry the princes offered to her and
   there were rumors that she was more interested in women
   than in men. This is a difficult point. Recently, more of her
   loveletters from and to Cardinal Decio Azzolino have been
   found; they prove that, after their first meeting in Rome
   1656, Christina and the Cardinal had something of a life-
   long love affair.

REFERENCES

Åkerman, Susanna (forthcoming). *Queen Christina of Sweden and her Circle: the Transformation of a Philosophical Libertine*. Leiden: E. J. Brill.

—— (1990a). Queen Christina and Messianic Thought. In *Sceptics, Millenarians and Jews*, eds. David S. Katz and Jonathan I. Israel. Leiden: E. J. Brill, 142–160.

—— (1990b). Il momento profetico nell'abdicazione della regina Cristina. In *Cristina di Svezia—Scienza ed Alchimia nella Roma Barocca*, eds. Wilma di Palma and Tina Bovi. Bari: Neuva Biblioteca Dedalo 99, 207–43.

André, Louis (1908). La Candidature de Christine de Suéde au Throne de Pologne (1668). *Revue Historique* 2: 209–243.

Arckenholtz, Johan (1751–1760). *Mémoires pour servir à l'histoire de Christine, reine de Suède, pour servir d'éclaircissement à l'histoire de son regne et principalment de sa vie privée, et aux evenements de son tems civile et literaire.* 4 vols. Amsterdam & Leipzig.

Becker, Jochen (1973). "Deas supereminet omneis": zu Vondels gedichten an Christina von Schweden un der bildene Kunste. *Simiolus—Netherlands Quarterly for the History of Art.* 6: 177–208.

Chaussard, A. P. (1806). *Les Antenors Modernes ou voyages de Christine et Casimir*. Paris.

D'Alembert, J. R. (1821). Memoires et Reflexions sur Christine, reine de Suede. *Oeuvres de D'Alembert* 2. Paris.

Johannesson, Kurt (1968). *I Polstjärnans tecken—studier i Svensk Barock*. Uppsala: Lychnos bibliotek 24.

Labrousse, Elisabeth (1974). L'Entrée de Saturne au Lion—l'Eclipse de Soleil du 12 Août 1654. *Archives Internationales d'histoire des Idées*, series minor 14. The Hague: Martinus Nijhoff.

Popkin, Richard H. (1987). *Isaac La Peyrère: His Life, Writings and Influence*. Leiden: E. J. Brill.

Roberts, Michael (1988). *Swedish Diplomats at Cromwell's Court 1655–56—the missions of Peter Julius Coyet and Christer Bonde*. London: Camden Fourth Series 34.

St. Evrémond, de (1706). *Oeuvres Meslées* 3. Amsterdam.

Tesmar, Jean. (1765). *Tribunal principis peregrinantis, seu ex illustris facti specie disputata juris quaestio: an absolutae majestatis character possessori suo etiam in alieno territorio liberum jurisdictionis in suos excercitium praestet.* Marburg.

Thurloe, John (1742). *Thurloe State Papers* (1648–1667), ed. T. Birch. 6 vols. London.

Weibull, Curt (1936). *Drottning Christina och Monaldesco*. Stockholm: Natur och Kultur.

SHARON L. ARNOULT

The Sovereignties of Body and Soul: Women's Political and Religious Actions in the English Civil War

> "Every subject's duty is the king's; but every subject's soul is
> his own."
>
>   (*Henry V*, Act IV, Scene I)

The "sovereignty of the soul" describes the idea found in the
Christian tradition that all souls have absolute freedom and
autonomy. All souls are equal and therefore have liberty in regard
to each other. As one soul is not superior to another, one soul
cannot bind, or have authority, over another. The soul owes
obedience only to God and God's Law; therefore, because the
sovereignty of God is superior to any temporal sovereignty, no
temporal power which makes claims upon a person possessing a
soul, such as the family or the state, even if such temporal
authority is divinely instituted, can exercise any sway over the
soul, which is free, or sovereign, in regard to it. Moreover, all
possessors of souls, since souls are equal, are equally free of
temporal authority over their souls, however unequally their
bodies might be bound by temporal authority. Such a concept
could lead to the radical conclusion that the free and equal soul is
ultimately bound only by the free conscience of the individual.

Such a concept had explosive potential as a justification for the
individual's assertion of himself—or herself—against structures of
authority, whether social or political. Indeed, scholars have
recently demonstrated the challenging and even subversive character
of Christianity in its early centuries (Brown 1988; Pagels 1989).
The concept of the sovereignty of the soul remained a potentially
dangerous undercurrent in Christian thought, even during the
Middle Ages when the Church as the Body of Christ claimed the
authority of Christ's Law, and the Church itself had become part
of the social and political structure of authority, giving this a claim
to divine sanction. As Gordon Leff has pointed out, most heresy

in the Middle Ages was a result of taking some aspect of Christianity, such as apostolic poverty, too far. Heretical movements did not seek to create separate churches; they sought to renew the one true Church, only to find themselves thrust outside and persecuted by it. Caught between what they perceived to be Christ's Law and the claims of the Church, their response was "the taking of Christ's Law into their own hands" by denying the Church truly possessed it, and thus "to stress individual judgement and experience at the expense of ecclesiastical authority" (Leff 1967), in effect, reducing that authority to a temporal one.

This concept of the sovereignty of the soul—the absolute freedom of equal souls in respect of anything but God, and the ultimate authority of individual conscience—came increasingly into play during the Reformation. The one true Church was replaced by several churches, each claiming to be "true." Printing disseminated a wide variety of religious ideas. The sovereignty of the soul was appealed to both by individual groups against others, and by individuals against groups from which they dissented. At the same time, the establishment of national churches, such as the Church of England, made it harder to distinguish between religious and political dissent, between heresy and sedition.[1]

From this new situation, a new question arose: how far did the sovereignty of the soul extend? What could be claimed in the name of the equality and autonomy of souls in a world structured on the basis of inequality, where what one might do, or not do, in the interrelated orders of church, state and society was determined by one's place in those hierarchies?

Moreover, the sovereignty of the soul and its superiority over other sovereignties pertained to an aspect of humanity which was not gendered—the soul.[2] A woman could claim the sovereignty of her soul as equally as a man could his. But did that mean that when it was a question of conscience, when a religious matter was directly involved, a woman could use the sovereignty of the soul as a justification for challenging roles and realms which *were* gendered?

This is an examination of how some Englishwomen answered this question during the English Civil War, when the issue became particularly intense. What I hope to do is to shed some light on the circumstances and influences which determined how these women related the sovereignties of soul and body.

All women on the eve of the Civil War had been brought up to fulfill their traditional roles as wives and mothers, and to be always subject to male authority. A woman was to be "chaste, silent and obedient" (Hull 1982). However, as Protestants, Englishwomen were also brought up with the legacy of the Reformation, which

could provide another view of womanhood. An emphasis on
Bible-reading meant that women became very familiar with Old
Testament examples of women who had been charged by God to
take a more active role than was usual for their sex, such as
Deborah, Esther, and the woman of Tekoah who rebuked King
David; this could be very suggestive to a woman who was a
Puritan, given Puritanism's emphasis on the duty of the elect to be
active in the world, to bring in God's kingdom.[3] Englishwomen
were also raised with stories from the other book chained next to
the Bible in every English church, Fox's *Book of Martyrs*; here
also were examples, taken from the history of the Christian church
down to recent days, of women who had chosen obedience to God
before obedience to Pope or monarch.

It has been argued that the Reformation, with its emphasis on
the equality of souls, somewhat improved the regard in which
women were held (Hill 1972: 308–10). There were those who
wrote to defend "the worthiness and worth of women; both in
respect of their creation, as in the work of redemption" (Sowernam
1985: 76). The last of these apologia to appear before the Civil
War, *The Women's Sharp Revenge* (1640), was written by two
women and extolled the virtues of the female character as part of
a long tradition of justifications of the female sex, claiming respect
and dignity for women, but not challenging traditional female
roles or spheres. The Reformation's emphasis on women's spiritual
equality may have led some men to take a more positive attitude
towards women, or increased women's valuation of themselves,
but in this patriarchal age a woman's sphere remained restricted—
indeed, in some ways was contracting—and her ecclesiastical, legal
and political status remained the same: a virtual non-status.

On the eve of the Civil War, however, there were some women
who were ready to challenge this invisibility, at least in the church.
They were women who had associated themselves with the most
radical of the religious movements to spring out of Puritanism.
Puritans believed themselves to be the elect—God's saints on
earth—who had a special relationship to God (Christ died for
them, not everyone). Belief in one's election could be a powerful
source of confidence, even boldness, and perhaps a sense of
superiority. In religious matters, the Puritans rejected the authority
of the "un-elect," both in terms of institutions (the established
church) and persons (the ungodly minister). The more extreme
this sensibility, the more likely the open challenge, on the grounds
of conscience, to the government's authority to compel obedience
to an ungodly church. The more radical sects, such as the
separatists and others which splintered off from mainstream

Puritanism, came to deny government authority in religion altogether. Scripture and the holy spirit were the only true religious authorities for the saints; if the established church was ungodly, they could separate from it and "it is not schism" (Chidley 1641: 21) but the fulfilling of God's command to forsake false worship. God's law was above the kingdom's; Christ was the "king of kings." For the radicals, the sovereignty of the soul meant they could—nay, must—defy the social and political order when it conflicted with their conscience, by denying that structure any legitimate authority to keep them from fulfilling their obligation to obey God's call to them.

In 1641, some radical women demanded a public voice by deciding that God had called them to preach, despite the prohibition by the apostle Paul. Probably because of Paul, most of the women forbore to use the actual word "preach"; in her gathered congregation, a woman usually claimed to be speaking "only to exercise her gifts,"[4] even if the exercise was exegesis on a text and went on from one to four hours. This fooled nobody, especially male clergy and others who were appalled by the women's audacity. But it did allow the women to justify themselves with the Bible, which forbade the hiding of spiritual gifts, and tied them into the tradition of female prophetesses in the church. One woman actually claimed the prophetess Anna appeared to her in a dream and gave her charge to preach.[5] If the holy spirit could inspire female souls to prophecy, why couldn't it empower them to preach? Moreover, the women made a direct claim to the superiority of the elect and their duty to battle the Antichrist, by stating that the male preachers available expounded on Scripture in "the language of the Beast, but they themselves would preach nothing, but such things as the spirit should move them" (Irwin 1979: 212).

In January, 1646, the mayor and aldermen of London, in their petition to the Commons for the suppression of unauthorized religious assemblies, pointed to the number of women preaching in these assemblies as proof of their danger. Later that month, several women preachers were imprisoned and others examined (Williams 1929: 563–564). But despite hostility and ridicule, female preaching did not stop, if the works published by their male condemners are any indication.

The 1640s also saw a modest explosion in the number of women appearing in print. Between 1600 and 1640, only 39 first editions by women were published but between 1641 and 1650, 109 were printed (Crawford 1985: 269). It may have become easier for women to publish after Parliament inadvertently eliminated censorship when it abolished Star Chamber in 1641 (Siebert 1965: 165–70), whereas the extraordinary nature of the times also moved women to risk modesty to speak out in print. The prophecy of Joel, that in the last days God would "pour out my spirit on all flesh/your sons and your daughters shall prophesy,"[6] was often mentioned in the books in which women printed their prophecies. Such works, which made up over half of all first editions by women between 1641 and 1650 (Crawford 1985: 269), often had political overtones.

Except for prophecy, women's religious writings were almost all of the mother's blessing/daily devotions type.[7] But during the Civil War some women began to write in the undisputed male territory of theology and ecclesiology, an area which, at the time, was also political territory. Katherine Chidley had been involved with radical religion for almost twenty years when, in 1641, she published *The Justification of the Independent Churches of Christ*, a plea for toleration of gathered churches in response to the Presbyterian minister Thomas Edwards. Chidley made it very clear that the ungodly had no religious authority over the godly, whether they be magistrate, master or husband. She asked "what authority this unbelieving husband hath over the conscience of his believing wife; it is true he hath authority over her in bodily and civil respects, but not to be a lord over her conscience," for this was entirely outside his power; in matters of conscience, godly women were free in relation to their husbands for "it is Christ the king of kings that reigneth over their consciences" (26).

Chidley limited her autonomy for godly women to their consciences, but in the name of conscience, she herself had ventured into the public arena of print to dispute with a clergyman about religious matters considered off-limits to women. In 1645 she took on Edwards again as well as Presbyterianism itself (Chidley 1645a, 1645b). Chidley was also known both as a preacher and an interrupter of clergymen's sermons (Williams 1929: 566). Hers was the assurance—if not the humility—of a saint. By her actions, Chidley indicated that, on religious issues, the sovereignty of the soul could lead to more than a wife's defiance of a husband; a woman could also defy the authorities of church and state, at this time in England so intertwined as to be inseparable. The sovereignty of the soul, for a woman like Chidley, justified not only the breaking of traditional female domestic roles (obedience to husbands) but also traditional female public roles (keeping quiet and acquiescent to male authority figures like ministers).[8]

Chidley's supreme confidence in her election by God gave her a public confidence most seventeenth-century women lacked. The few women who published in the seventeenth century almost always seemed uneasy at doing so, even when they were writing in an accepted woman's genre such as motherly devotions. Sensing their modesty and reputations at risk, they went beyond the usual pro forma humility of seventeenth-century writers in justifying their appearance in print (Crawford 1985: 216–21). Chidley, however, made no apologies about writing, nor even dredged up a bunch of biblical precedents for her actions, but proceeded to lecture Edwards and refute him point by point, with even an occasional touch of sarcasm.

As with the women preachers, the majority of the women who published, especially on religious/political topics, were associated with radical religion. These sects and movements attracted mainly urban women—and especially London women—of the artisan and middle classes, who made up most of the radical women (Thomas 1985; Fraser 1984: 244–64). The artisan and middle-class women of urban areas often took a share—equal and sometimes greater—in running businesses with their men; a few ran their own businesses (Stone 1979: 139–41; Clark 1919/1968).[9]

The London women were also well-positioned, geographically, to move into another public, more overtly political, role: demonstration petitioning of Parliament. By late 1641 this tactic was being used regularly by groups of "many hundred citizens" to call for suppression of the bishops and reform of the church (*The Heads* 1641). That December, a certain MP made a speech complaining of the tumults around the House of Commons and the number of petitions being proffered, many from "abrupt & disordered persons" (*Mr. Smith's* 1641).

Women had presented petitions for redress of grievances to Parliament before, but their petitions had been private ones, seeking remedies from powerful men in their weakness as women. They were like the petition read in Parliament in mid-December, 1641, from the legally-separated wife of the clerk of St. Boltolph Algate, seeking Parliament's help in securing alimony from her husband (*Diurnall Occurrences*1641). But in the fervor of the time, some women began to present petitions publicly, in groups, whose "grievances" were religious/political issues.

On January 31, 1642, a company of women delivered a petition to the Lords complaining of the decay of trade and the Lords' opposition to peace between the two houses of Parliament (*The True Diurnall* 1642). The petition also advocated the settling of the religious establishment and aiding the oppressed Protestants in Ireland. On Tuesday, February 1, the women—now numbering about 400—tried to deliver another petition to the Lords, and also tried to present a petition to the Commons which complained of a lack of satisfaction from the Lords. The latter petition urged the Commons to abolish the oppressive bishops, establish pure religion, place learned teachers in the ministry, rid the House of Lords of the Popish peers, remember Ireland and make ready for war (*The Humble Petition of Many* 1649).

The women were very aware that "it may be thought strange and unbeseeming our sex to show ourselves by way of petitions" and that many did "scoff and deride our good intent." The next petition presented by a group of women (very possibly the same group), on February 4, used more conciliatory language; the women stressed that they looked to Parliament to protect them, including protection from "the thralldom of our souls and consciences in matters concerning God, which of all things are most dear unto us." They justified their actions on religious grounds, "the right and interest we have in the common and public cause of the Church." They had this right and interest because Christ died for women as well as men, the free enjoyment of Christ was women's greatest happiness as well as men's, and women, as well as men, suffered and were martyred, in the common calamities when church and commonwealth were oppressed. They stressed they were not "seeking to equal ourselves with men, either in authority or wisdom. But according to our places to discharge that duty we owe to God, and the cause of the church." On this occasion, Parliament thanked the women and assured them of all possible satisfaction, but also urged them back into their proper places, "to repair to your houses and turn your petitions into prayers at home for us" (*A True Copy* 1642). The equality of women's private prayers with men's in God's ears did not, in the eyes of Parliament, entitle women to the public voice of petitioning, with its implied share of rights in the sovereign body politic. Parliament needed showings of popular support against the king, but it was dangerous to allow into the public political arena those whose duty it was to wait outside that arena and do what they were told. Once a public voice was given to those whose duty was to be silent, that voice could also be used to challenge.

On Tuesday, August 8, 1643, a group of women showed up at the Houses of Parliament and began to clamor for peace. By now the war had been in progress for a year, and its economic effects were being seriously felt, especially by poorer women whose husbands were in the armies, and it was a group of these that had come to cry for peace. They were chased off, but returned the next day, in greater numbers, once again demanding peace (*Parliament Scout* 1643; McArthur 1909: 701–4; Fraser 1984: 228–9). This time, they not only clamored, but carried a petition which they desired to present, trying to articulate their discontent through the political process. The petition, worded respectfully, declared the women's only desire was for the reformed religion preserved, the just prerogatives and privileges of king and Parliament maintained, true liberty and the property of the subject restored by known laws, and an "honorable way and means for a speedy peace endeavored." They begged Parliament for a "speedy means for the settling of religion and the restoration of trade" (*Mercurius Civicus* 1643). Eventually, the women's frustrations erupted into a riot that afternoon which two troops of horse and the trained band finally broke up, with many women hurt or imprisoned, and at least three deaths.

In the reports in the Parliamentary newspapers that followed, the women were increasingly vilified and their actions linked with the enemy, the Royalist "Malignants." The first paper to come out, on August 11, was the *Parliament Scout* (1643), which characterized the women as "all of the poorer sort" of whom "some say" a few were whores. The *Scout* blamed the deplorable incident on the disorders caused by civil war. *Mercurius Civicus* (1643) came out the next day, August 12. Its writer, Richard Collins, described the women as "most of them of the inferior sort" but stated he "should not have much misliked" the content of their petition, which he printed; their behaviour, though, was completely unacceptable, especially their "insolent abuse of divers men of quality." When *Certain Informations* (1643) came out on August 15, however, it called the women "Oyster wives and other dirty and tattered sluts," and presented them as a much greater threat to the Parliamentary cause, claiming the women cried out against and assaulted "roundheads" and threatened to "tear Mr. Pym in pieces and to pull the House of Commons down about their ears." Finally, *The Kingdom's Weekly Intelligencer* (1643), which was written by the same Richard Collins of *Mercurius Civicus*, came out on August 16. By now the women were "for the most Part, whores, bawds, oyster-women, kitchenstuff women, beggar women, and the very scum of the suburbs, besides an abundance of Irish women," and the entire thing was declared a Royalist plot.[10]

The reason for the increasing vilification and association with the royalists was that the women's public and violent action had to be not only suppressed, but firmly separated from the Parliamentary cause. This was all the more important because a favorite argument against Parliament and the Puritans was that such tumults—and such outrageous things as women trying to participate

in the public political process—were the natural result of overthrowing the authority of bishops and king. There is some
evidence that the women were encouraged by "some men of rank
and quality," probably of the Lords' peace party, and egged on at
the scene by a few men in women's clothes who joined them. But it
is doubtful this event is properly characterized as a "Royalist
plot." The Commons themselves seem to have had no objection to
the content of the women's petition, as it was accepted, and six
members carried a conciliatory answer to them (McArthur 1909:
702–4). The women themselves seem to have acted primarily out
of economic and personal reasons; the *Parliament Scout*'s assertion
that "most have their husbands in one or other army" seems to
support this. They had had the example of the public petition by
women only eighteen months earlier, and in the meantime there
had been petitioning by groups of men who were newly come to
the public political arena, such as apprentices and laborers. Yet
the women were repressed much more severely than any male
group claiming a right to public discourse, and contemporaries had
no doubt that the reason was their sex.[11]

Actually, any public support by women for a cause could be
problematic for it. It was a favorite tactic of political attack to
satirize what one opposed by associating it with women, especially
sexually rapacious women. Numerous ballads and scurrilous tracts
of the time used this tactic.[12] Others explicitly relied for effect on
the incongruity of associating women with the forms of political
process. In 1641, possibly even before women had presented their
first petition, an Anglican had ridiculed all petitions for church
reform by producing a "women's petition," in which the usual
reform requests were mocked, such as the women objecting to
surplices because starching them hurt their hands and to choir-
singing in church because the voices of the young boys aroused
them sexually (*The Petition of the Women* 1643). Three pamphlets
in early 1643 claimed to be "petitions" from virgins, wives and
widows, respectively, the gist of all of them being that women
wanted peace in order to get the men home to satisfy their lusts.[13]
At least seven tracts throughout the period are variations on the
"parliament of ladies" satirical theme.[14] Such works not only made
clear a widespread derogatory view of women in general, but in
particular showed the complete contempt in which men held any
idea that women could participate, in any way, in the political
sovereignty of the commonwealth.

After 1643, public petitioning by women as a group seems to
have ceased for a while. But in 1646, Elizabeth Lilburne submitted
a petition to Parliament demanding the release of her imprisoned

husband, John (E. Lilburne). Lilburne's petition was not unlike the private petitions of women which continued to be presented to Parliament, such as the petition of the army widows in 1648 for their husbands' arrears of pay (*Kingdom's Weekly* 1648). But Lilburne's petition, with its elaborate legal proofs of the injustice of John's imprisonment, was printed and widely circulated. It was not only a wife's petition for the release of her husband, but a vindication of the cause of the Levellers, a radical group of which John Lilburne was one of the leaders. The Levellers had their roots in radical puritanism, but in the mid-1640s they developed a transition from the absolute moral religious value to the absolute moral political value of the individual. They did not mean, as almost everyone thought they meant at the time, that order of government or hierarchy of degree and property should be abolished, but that each member of the commonwealth had a right, by virtue of membership in the commonwealth, to a voice in that polity. In June of 1646, John Lilburne fully articulated the linking of the sovereignty of the soul to the sovereignty of the political individual: "God . . . gave man . . . a rational soul or understanding and thereby created him after his own image . . . every particular and individual man and woman that ever breathed . . . are and were by nature all equal and alike in power, dignity, authority and majesty, none of them having (by nature) any authority dominion or magisterial power, one over . . . another. Neither have they or can they exercise any, but merely by institution or donation, that is to say . . . by mutual consent" (J. Lilburne 1646: 11–12). In other words, Lilburne claimed that women not only possessed an equality and sovereignty of soul with men, but *because* they did so, they also possessed a natural political sovereignty in themselves, any limitation of which must be with their consent. Thus if, as the Levellers held, the political sovereignty of the commonwealth resided ultimately in the people who had consented to it, women, consenting just as men did, were members of that polity fully sharing in its sovereignty.

At least three of the radical women were clearly tied to the Leveller movement: besides Elizabeth Lilburne, Mary Overton was the wife of Richard Overton and Katherine Chidley the mother of Samuel Chidley; both men were Leveller leaders. In January and February, 1647, Mary Overton and then Elizabeth Lilburne were arrested for their activities regarding "seditious pamphlets." At the bar, Elizabeth Lilburne railed against her "unjust and unrighteous judges" (Fraser 1984: 234–43); Mary Overton printed and circulated an argument against her arrest, and her husband's, in a "Petition" to Parliament (Overton 1647).

In 1649, with her husband and other Leveller men again imprisoned, Elizabeth Lilburne led a petition movement on their behalf which was quite different from her earlier petition. In this movement, she was joined by many hundreds, perhaps thousands, of London women (McArthur 1909: 706). Their Petition of late April, 1649 stated that, due to Parliament's indifference and the great general calamity and distress, "we are so overpressed, so over-whelmed in affliction, that we are not able to keep in our compass, to be bounded in the custom of our sex." These women, unlike the women in 1642, addressed themselves not to matters of religion but politics: "for indeed we confess it not our custom to address ourselves to this house in the public behalf, yet considering, that we have an equal share and interest with men in the common-wealth," they were resolved "to suffer and perish," if necessary, "for upholding the cause of the people in their native freedom and right" (*The Humble Petition of Divers* 1649). In 1642, women had used sovereignty of the soul to justify their speaking out for change in the church, but in 1649, the Leveller women spoke not at all about religion, but demanded Parliament give the people their political rights. They not only asked for the release of Lilburne, *et al*, and due process of law, but went further, advising Parliament on how it should govern and legislate. They almost seemed to be issuing a warning when they said "God hath wrought many deliverances for several nations from age to age by the weak hand of women" (*The Humble Petition of Divers*).

These women had moved completely out of any acceptable sphere, and Parliament told them so in no uncertain terms. When, on their third attempt to present their petition, the Commons finally sent the women a reply, they were informed that "the matter . . . was of a higher concernment than they understood, that the House gave an answer to their husbands, and therefore desired them to go home and look after their own business and meddle with their housewifery" (McArthur 1909: 707).

The women reacted with a petition which was full of fury. "Can you imagine us to be so sottish or stupid," they demanded, "as not to perceive, or not to be sensible when daily those strong defences of our Peace and welfare are broken down and trod underfoot by force or arbitrary power?" They claimed their right to a political voice by explicitly linking it to their religious equality: "since we are assured of our creation in the image of God and of an interest in Christ, equal unto men, as also of a proportionable share in the freedoms of this commonwealth . . . Have we not an equal interest with the men of this nation in those liberties and securities contained in the petition of right and other the good laws of the land . . . and are we Christians, and shall we sit still and keep at home . . ." (*To the Supreme Authority of England* 1649).

With the Levellers, radical women had gone from claiming an equality of sovereign souls with men, and public voice in defense of conscience and true religion, to claiming an equal share in the political sovereignty of the commonwealth and an equal public voice in the polity. They had directly challenged the traditional "compass" of women. But the ideas of the Leveller women were rejected by the majority of Englishwomen, and none did so more strongly than Mary Pope, the only Anglican/Royalist woman to publish a defense of her religious/political position during the war.

Pope clearly saw the link between the sovereignty of the soul and political sovereignty, and she condemned it. In her *A Treatise of Magistracy* 1647, Pope condemned "some teachers, that have taught our women to follow their new found out truths, without their husbands" (39). Pope argued that allowing free conscience and religious autonomy led directly to the breakdown of all authority, and political and social chaos.[15] She denied "what the radicals say, that there is rational reason in man, to direct for the ordering of the discipline of civil affairs" (A3). Instead, God, as revealed in Scripture, had clearly given secular and religious authority over sinful man to the magistrate, and arranged a hierarchy of authority to govern him. To this female Filmerian, the equality and autonomy of souls could not justify the sin of disobedience, because the structures by which one was governed were divinely ordained.

Yet, in their own way, Anglican women like Pope believed in a sovereignty of the soul just as Puritan women did. They certainly refused to give up their religion. Lady Anne Clifford refused to give up her faith when her husband joined the Parliamentary side; she established Anglican chaplains at her residences and held Anglican services in her own room, if necessary, despite threats of sequestration (Williamson 1922/1967: 305). Alice Wandesforde informed her Presbyterian fiancé that she would not marry him unless he would agree to let her keep her religion (A. Thornton 1975: 78). In this regard, Anglican women agreed with Katherine Chidley that "It is Christ the king of kings who reigneth over their consciences." Even Mary Pope's advocation of obedience went "no farther than is according to God's commission" (1647: 42).

However, while radical Puritanism had challenged the right of a lawful government to determine the religious life of the saints, Anglican women saw themselves as maintaining loyalty to the lawful church which was being overturned and oppressed by an unlawful government. Therefore, their acts of defiance in defense of that church were really defenses of the traditional order and were traditional ones for women in a time of war and tribulation: they sheltered deprived bishops and clerics, acted as spies, defended their manors if attacked while husbands and sons were away, and tried to salvage family estates when their menfolk fled into exile after defeat.[16] A Royalist women's petition to Parliament humbly begs it to remember the suffering women and children and provide them with what portion of the sequestered estates they were granted by law. It is a petition touching not on political matters but charitable ones, not demanding rights but begging succor and kindness (*To the Supreme Authority of this Commonwealth* 1650).

Anglican women's acts of defiance also were more quiet, private, and stayed more strictly within the sphere of religion; they attended clandestine Anglican services, and sought out "underground" Anglican clergy to marry them and baptise their children, although their church was proscribed and such actions were criminal.[17] But they left the public political challenges to men. Pope treated of politics only by firmly planting political ideas in the realm of religion. Her work was primarily a defense of the established church, shrouded in much of the language of prophecy. Pope, who, unlike Chidley, apologized all over herself for publishing, claimed that God had "directed this speech . . . overpowering my Spirit, and as it were forcing me on"; she was merely God's instrument and "I desire God may be only seen, who hath wrought in me to will this, and enabled me to do it" (1647: C, C2, 108).

As was true of the radical women, what Anglican women did in the English Civil War was heavily influenced by their religious identities. But Anglican religious sensibility was different from that of Puritanism, and especially radicalism. There was an emphasis on fitness and order in the established church of the seventeenth century, both in church government and worship. Indeed, three times Pope declared that God was "a God of order" (1647: 4, 89, 96). Anglicanism's chief focus was on corporate worship and prayer. The Anglican women of Charles I's court, who had Dr. Cosins draw up for them a Protestant breviary of offices to perform throughout the day, exemplify this desire both for order and corporateness in worship (Bedford 1904: 190–91). Anglican households attended church or chapel twice a day for Morning and Evening Prayer, and even as fairly unpious a woman as Anne Halkett was "seldom or never absent" from these services (Loftis 1979: 11). Martin Thornton has summarized this Caroline religious attitude as a sense that corporate worship was "the most perfect praise we can offer because it is the prayer of Christ, through his Church, to the Father" and "the Common Prayer, shared with saints and angels, is that prayer in which our frailties and infirmities are made up by Christ himself" (1986: 268).

Anglican religious sensibility, although just as intense as Puritan religious sensibility, was more passive in nature, more meditative, even a touch mystical. It was a sensibility that led, not to action in the world, but to withdrawal from it; and at least one group of Anglican women did just that at Little Gidding (Bedford 1904: 210–13; Ferrar 1912). Preaching was important to Anglicanism, but not as important as it was to Puritanism, and seemed less essential as a form of religious expression. With her prayer book, an Anglican woman participated in worship equally with lay men. The role accorded to her by her church was to inspire others by living an exemplary life and, as a devoted mother, to nurture young Christian souls. "Though Paul forbids her sex to preach/yet may her life instruct, and her death teach" (Duncon 1649: n. pag.)[18] Many Anglican women clearly felt that their place in the religious order was an honored one which they found fulfilling. Anglican religious sensibility helped to reinforce the belief of Anglican women, as expressed by Mary Pope, that the order of church, state and society had been divinely ordained by God and was proven by Scripture. The sovereignty of the soul could not, for Anglican women, justify challenging their given place in church, state and society on the grounds of conscience, for to challenge the order of things was to challenge God himself.

And while Puritan women would have disagreed with Pope's stand in favor of the divine right of bishops or her charge that the root of all present evils was the slighting of the Book of Common Prayer, most of them would have agreed that God established lawful authority and that a woman's proper place was in submission. The Puritan Elizabeth Warren, unwillingly and apologetically, "yet conscious to my mental and sex-deficiency," in 1645 published a defense of the ordained ministry. She specifically condemned "those which intrude into this weighty work, having neither due calling, nor fit abilities . . . who leap from the limits of their lawful station" (15).

The trial and execution of Charles I in January, 1649, may have encouraged radical women; when an MP told one of them that it was strange women should petition, she is said to have replied, "Sir, that which is strange is not therefore unlawful; it was strange that you cut off the King's head, yet I suppose you will justify it" (McArthur 1909: 706–7). These events also emboldened both Pope and Warren to write openly in the area of politics, but their motivation was the fear and horror of great blasphemy. Pope called those deposing the King the slaves of Satan (1649: 19). Both denounced the sin of disobedience in no uncertain terms, for "God's sacred word commanding our reverence unto all he hath placed in lawful authority, prohibited Rebellion and acts of violence, both in children to their parents, and in subjects to their prince" (Warren 1649: 40). England's misery was God's wrath upon "rebellious sinners . . . trampling contemptuously, with audacious insolence, upon all sacred and civil authority . . . nor can any be infranchised with a glorious liberty, by involving themselves in a labyrinth of sin" (8, 13).

Because they believed that mankind's sinfulness made obedience to authority necessary, and that the authority embodied in the order of society and government was either divinely instituted, or at least divinely sanctioned, Anglican women and most Puritan women did not believe that the sovereignty of women's souls meant women could claim an equal share of political sovereignty and the right to a voice in the public arena of political debate; their place in the English polity was not the same as men's, it was subordinate, and their share in the commonwealth derivative, through the men who had charge over them. To demand otherwise was to commit the sin of disobedience. The subordination of women was too firmly entrenched in seventeenth-century England. The women who subscribed to the most radical religious ideas had used the justification of the sovereignty of the soul to challenge the traditional religious and political roles of women. But even the most radical women never got completely away from the idea that their political identities were subsumed in men's; they demanded a voice, but not, for example, a vote.[19]

And yet, every subject's soul was *her* own, and the sovereignty of the soul had led some women to a new view of both religious and political society. Despite overwhelming male hostility, they demanded a voice, challenging their traditional places, as women, in these structures. For others, their religious sensibilities and beliefs, and the degree to which they accepted the traditional role of women and the order of the world, limited their interpretation of the sovereignty of the soul. The English Civil War had shown that the idea of the sovereignty of the soul carried a latent threat to the structures of the English religious, political and social establishment. That some women during the war had pushed its claims to challenge their role in the English polity may have been condemned, but it also was not forgotten.

NOTES

1 For a good general overview of the Reformation, see Chadwick 1972. Spitz 1985 is a more recent work focusing on the crucial first generation of the Reformation, while Ozment 1980 ties the Reformation to its late medieval roots. For the specifics of the Reformation in England, see Dickens 1964.

2 St. Paul's "There is neither Jew nor Greek, there is neither slave nor free, there is neither male nor female; for you are all one in Christ Jesus" (Galatians 3:28 [Revised Standard Version]) is but one expression of spiritual equality. Of course, St. Paul did not think spiritual equality implied any other sort of equality, as he makes clear in his First Letter to the Corinthians.

3 Esther was used by the women petitioners of 1642; however, Mary Pope, an Anglican, also used the woman of Tekoah to justify expressing her political/religious views.

4 So claimed the female preacher Mrs. Attaway, as reported in Thomas Edwards' *Gangraena* (1646). The sections on women preaching are reprinted in Irwin 1979: 214–22.

5 This was Anne Hempstall, who lived near London (Anonymous, *A Discovery of Six Women Preachers* London: 1641; Thomason Tract E. 166[1]; rpt. in Irwin 1979: 210–14). In these excerpts, and in all quotations from sixteenth- and seventeenth-century sources, spelling and punctuation have been modernized.

6 Joel 4:28 (Revised Standard Version). This was used by Sarah Jones, *To Sion's Lovers* (1644), among others.

7 This was a type of religious work in which women recorded their daily devotions and/or their prayers for and religious instructions to their children. This pious genre was not considered out of bounds for women, especially as it was linked to their maternity.

8 In many ways, Puritans and radicals were less moved by Christ than God, if such a thing can be said; this is what lends an Old Testament flavor to their religion. Even though both God and Christ are male images, Puritans and radicals emphasized their power rather than their gender. Anglicanism, in contrast, focused not only more on Christ, but on Christ as a male, through its emphasis on the Incarnation. Since Anglican women tended to see Christ as male, this may have tended to reinforce the sense of dependency and passivity which is a part of their religious sensibility.

9 Mary Pope's second book was sold by "Mrs. Edwards, the book-binders widow in the Old Bailey." It may be possible that the degree to which men were able to exert patriarchal authority in their own families was tied to their status in society. For example, Ralph Verney, a

member of the gentry, exercised considerable authority over not only his wife and children, but his sisters as well, but Ralph Josselin, a country vicar, experienced marriage as more of a partnership. See Verney and Verney 1907 and Macfarlane 1970.

10 Frank 1961 is the best history and evaluation of the quality of the Civil War newspapers. They are surprisingly reliable, especially the best of them such as *Parliament Scout*, *Mercurius Civicus* and *The Kingdom's Weekly Intelligencer*.

11 Simonds D'Ewes noted in his diary, "many had just cause to wonder that when those great multitudes of mean and factious people being men and not women which came down and offered so much violence . . . had no course at all taken against them, and yet that such severe cruelty was used against these women, who were only misled by their wicked and unlawful example" (McArthur 1989: 703–4). D'Ewes was a Member of Parliament and probably an eyewitness to the event.

12 An example is the ballad "The Four-Legg'd Elder or, A horrible Relation of a Dog and an Elders Maid" (Thomason Tract 669.f.14).

13 The three tracts, most likely by the same anonymous author, are *The Virgins' Complaint* 1643, *Petition of Many Thousand Wives and Matrons* 1643, and *The Widows' Lamentation* 1643. "You have them press upon the enemy when they should be pressing upon us" is a paraphrase of the general theme.

14 These are spread out over ten years, from 1646 to 1656. An example is *The Parliament of Women* 1646.

15 The same point is made by "Filodexter Transilvanus," the pseudonymous author of *Church-Members Set in Joynt* (1648: 13), who asked "A woman may possibly have more wisdom than her husband in the family, or more knowledge and grace than a minister in the church, may she therefore usurp authority over her husband in the family, or over her Pastor in the church?" If the answer was yes, then were hurled "all things into black confusion" and one had "almost all government, in church and state, blown up."

16 For the sheltering of bishops and clerics, see Hardacre 1956: 44–45, 88; Duncon 1649: A3–A4; Reynolds 1920: 67. The newspaper *Mercurius Civicus* mentioned the capture of Royalist women spies and couriers. The Countess of Derby, while holding Lathom House under siege, was personally present at public prayer four times a day (Bedford 1904: 244). Fraser (1984: 205–21) has many examples of Royalist women as pleaders for their estates and menfolk.

17 Alice Thornton and Anne Halkett were so married (Thornton 1875: 81; Loftis 1979: 85). Virtually the only time Mary Verney defied her husband was over baptising their child "in the old way" (Verney 1907: 355).

18 Quiet inspiration and gentle instruction in the private domestic sphere, rather than public exhortation, were obviously more in line with traditional ideas about women, yet the example of a virtuous woman was thought to have a power of sorts of its own. Lady Grace Mildmay (1552–1620) remembered in her memoirs that her father used to say that the mere sight of a virtuous woman would drive away "a wicked and evil disposed man" (Northampton Central Library, Film #25273).

19 Seventeenth-century English political thought, however, did not equate the vote with representation. Even though all members of the commonwealth could not vote, nonetheless they were all held to be represented in Parliament and other elected bodies. Franchise rights, like political rights in general in English thinking at this time, were bound up with property rights; thus the linking so often of liberty and property in the petitions. The gist of the idea was that a certain amount of property was necessary both to insure one's "vested interest" in the commonwealth, and to enable one to vote "freely," i.e., without being influenced by a landlord or employer. But how much of this "interest/property/freedom" was required could vary depending upon the office for which an election was being held; one could be entitled to vote for some offices and not others. At the local level, a few women who owned property in their own right, such as widows, voted through the early seventeenth century, although later in the century the trend was to deny them this (Fraser 1984: 230–32). The Levellers challenged this idea in demanding universal manhood suffrage at the Putney debates (1647) but even they, who most clearly articulated the idea of inalienable individual rights, were willing to keep the vote from those who, being "under authority," were not completely "free," such as male servants, even though such servants, as part of the people, shared fully in the sovereignty of the people. Needless to say, since women's legal rights were wholly subsumed by their men's and they were always assumed to be under some sort of male authority, the issue of female suffrage never came up, even among the women themselves, who nonetheless could—and did—hold themselves to be full members of the commonwealth, equal sharers in its sovereignty and entitled to some part in the political process. For more on this complex and often confusing subject, see Sommerville 1986 and Thomas

1972. Aylmer 1975 is the best guide to the whole body of
Leveller thought. Two books focusing on the electoral
process in early modern England are Hirst 1975 and
Kishlansky 1986.

REFERENCES

Aylmer, G. E. (1975). *The Levellers in the English Revolution*.
London: Thames and Hudson.
Bedford, Jessie (1904). *Social Life Under the Stuarts*.
London: Grant Richards. (Published under the pseudonym
Elizabeth Godfrey.)
Brown, Peter (1988). *The Body and Society in Late Antiquity:
Men, Women, and Sexual Renunciation in Early
Christianity*. New York: Columbia University Press.
Certain Informations. 7 August to 14 August 1643. Thomason
Tract E. 65.
Chadwick, Owen (1972). *The Reformation*. London: Penguin
Books.
Chidley, Katherine (1641). *The Justification of the Independent
Churches of Christ*. London. Thomason Tract E. 174(7).
—— (1645a). *Good Counsel, to the Petitioners for Presbyterian
Government*. London. Thomason Tract 669.f.10(39).
—— (1645b). *A New-Year's Gift, or a Brief Exhortation to
Mr. Thomas Edwards*. London. Thomason Tract E.
23(13).
Clark, Alice (1919/1968). *Working Life of Women in the
Seventeenth Century*. London: Geo. Routledge & Sons,
Ltd.; reprint New York: Frank Cass & Co., Ltd.
Crawford, Patricia (1985). Women's Published Writings,
1600–1700. In *Women in English Society, 1500–1800*, ed.
Mary Prior. New York: Methuen.
Dickens, A. G. (1964). *The English Reformation*. New York:
Schocken Books.
Diurnall Occurrences. 13 December to 20 December 1641.
Thomason Tract E. 201(3).
Duncon, John (1649). *The Returns of Spiritual Comfort and
Grief in a Devout Soul*. Second Edition. London.
Ferrar, Nicholas (1912). *The Story Books of Little Gidding*.
London: Chas. J. Thynne.
Frank, Joseph (1961). *The Beginnings of the English Newspaper
1620–1660*. Cambridge, MA: Harvard University Press.
Fraser, Antonia (1984). *The Weaker Vessel*. New York:
Alfred A. Knopf.
Hardacre, Paul H. (1956). *The Royalists During the Puritan
Revolution*. The Hague: Martinus Nijhoff.
The Heads of Several Proceedings. 29 November to 6
December, 1641. Thomason Tract E. 201(2).

Hill, Christopher (1972). *The World Turned Upside Down: Radical Ideas During the English Revolution.* London: Maurice Temple Smith.

Hirst, Derek (1975). *The Representative of the People: Voters and Voting in England under the Early Stuarts.* Cambridge: Cambridge University Press.

Hull, Suzanne W. (1982). *Chaste, Silent, and Obedient: English Books for Women, 1475–1640.* San Marino: Huntington Library.

The Humble Petition of Divers Well-Affected Women. 23/24 April 1649. Thomason Tract E. 551(14).

The Humble Petition of Many Hundreds of Distressed Women. 1 February 1642. (Misdated 4 February.) Thomason Tract 669.f.4(57).

Irwin, Joyce L., ed. (1979). *Womanhood in Radical Protestantism, 1525–1675.* New York: The Edwin Mellen Press.

Jones, Sarah (1644). *To Sion's Lovers.* London. Thomason Tract E. 16[7].

The Kingdom's Weekly Intelligencer. 8 August to 15 August 1643. Thomason Tract E. 65.

——— . 19 September to 26 September 1648. Thomason Tract E. 464.

Kishlansky, Mark (1986). *Parliamentary Selection: Social and Political Choice in Early Modern England.* Cambridge: Cambridge University Press.

Leff, Gordon (1967). *Heresy in the Late Middle Ages: The Relation of Heterodoxy to Dissent c. 1250 – c. 1450* (2 vols). New York: Barnes & Noble, Inc.

Lilburne, Elizabeth (1646). *To the Chosen and betrusted knights, Citizens, and Burgesses, assembled in the High and Supream Court of Parliament.* Thomason Tract 669.f.10(86).

Lilburne, John (1646). *The Free Man's Freedom Vindicated.* London: 1646.

Loftis, John, ed. (1979). *The Memoirs of Anne, Lady Halkett and Ann, Lady Fanshawe.* Oxford: Clarendon Press.

McArthur, Ellen A. (1909). Women Petitioners and the Long Parliament. *English Historical Review* 24: 698–709.

Macfarlane, Alan (1970). *The Family Life of Ralph Josselin, a Seventeenth Century Clergyman: An Essay in Historical Anthropology.* Cambridge: Cambridge University Press.

Mercurius Civicus. 3 August to 11 August 1643. Thomason Tract E. 65.

Mr. Smith's Speech in Parliament Concerning the late Tumultuous Assemblies about the Parliament Houses. 29 December 1641. Thomason Tract E. 199(46).

Overton, Mary. *To the right honorable, the knights in*

Parliament assembled. 24 March 1647. Thomason Tract E. 381(10).

Ozment, Steven (1980). *The Age of Reform 1250–1550.* New Haven: Yale University Press.

Pagels, Elaine (1989). *Adam, Eve, and the Serpent.* New York: Vintage Books.

The Parliament Scout. 3 August to 10 August 1643. Thomason Tract E. 63.

The Parliament of Women. 14 August 1646. Thomason Tract E. 1150[5].

Petition of Many Thousand Wives and Matrons. 4 February 1643. Thomason Tract E. 88[13].

The Petition of the Women of Middlesex. 8 December 1641. Thomason Tract E. 180(17).

Pope, Mary (1647). *A Treatise of Magistracy.* London. Thomason Tract E. 417(13).

—— (1649). *Hear, hear, hear, hear, a Word, or Message from Heaven.* London. Thomason Tract E. 537(10).

Reynolds, Myra (1920). *The Learned Lady in England 1650–1760.* New York: Houghton Mifflin Co.

Siebert, Fredrick S. (1965). *Freedom of the Press in England, 1476–1776.* Urbana: University of Illinois Press.

Sommerville, J. P. (1986). *Politics and Ideology in England, 1603–1640.* New York: Longman.

Sowernam, Ester (1985). *Ester Hath Hang'd Haman.* 1617; rpt. in *First Feminists: British Women Writers, 1578–1799*, ed. Moira Ferguson. Bloomington: Indiana University Press.

Spitz, Lewis W. (1985). *The Protestant Reformation 1517–1559.* New York: Harper & Row.

Stone, Lawrence (1979). *The Family, Sex and Marriage in England, 1500–1800.* Abridged Edition. New York: Harper Torchbooks.

"Tattle-well, Mary and Joane Hit-him-home" (1640). *The Women's Sharpe Revenge.* London.

Thomas, Keith (1985). Women and the Civil War Sects. *Past and Present* 13: 42–62.

—— (1972). The Levellers and the Franchise. in *The Interregnum: The Quest for Settlement 1646–1660*, ed. G. E. Aylmer. New York: Macmillan.

Thornton, Alice (1975). *The Autobiography of Mrs. Alice Thornton.* London: Surtees Society.

Thornton, Martin (1986). *English Spirituality.* Cowley Publications.

To the Supreme Authority of England the Commons Assembled in Parliament. 5 May 1649. Thomason Tract 669.f.14(20).

To the Supreme Authority of this Commonwealth, the

Parliament of England. August 1650. Thomason Tract 669.f.15.

"Transilvanus, Philodexter" (1648). *Church-Members Set in Joynt*. London. Thomason Tract E. 422[3].

A True Copy of the Petition of the Gentlewoman and Tradesmen's Wives. 4 February 1642. Thomason Tract E. 134(17).

The True Diurnall Occurrences. 31 January to 7 February 1642. Thomason Tract E. 201(13).

Verney, Frances Parthenope and Margaret M. (1907). *Memoirs of the Verney Family During the Seventeenth Century, Volume I: 1600 to 1659*. London: Longman's, Green, & Co.

The Virgin's Complaint. 31 January 1643. Thomason Tract E. 86(38).

Warren, Elizabeth (1645). *The Old and Good Way Vindicated*. London. Thomason Tract E. 311(33).

—— (1649). *A Warning-Peece From Heaven, against the Sins of the Times*. London. Thomason Tract E. 581(5).

The Widows' Lamentation. 8 February 1643. Thomason Tract E. 88(26).

Williams, E. M. (1929). Women Preachers in the Civil War. *The Journal of Modern History* 1:561–69.

Williamson, George (1922/1967). *Lady Anne Clifford: Her Life, Letters and Work*. Reprint Yorkshire: S. R. Publishers Ltd.

DEAN A. MILLER

Byzantine Sovereignty and Feminine Potencies

The Byzantine Empire (that is, the East Roman, or to its citizens and its enemies, simply the Roman Empire) does not at first glance provide much evidence for "feminine potencies" working through or in its conception of sovereignty and sovereign rule. During its millennium of existence the oecumenical empire was ruled, in theory, by a single God-chosen monarch who was also the politico-ideological descendant of the Roman Imperator, Caesar and Augustus. In this Roman tradition, with its military and patriarchal roots, signs, and affects, the male ruler was a given. More, other elements fused into the later Byzantine model of imperial monarchy, derived from the so-called Hellenistic pattern of kingship, released the emperor from most "constitutional" mediatory or amendatory constraints, and left or lifted him to a posture of towering isolation, singular, omnipotent on earth—and male.

This was the accepted image. In the Byzantine system's own extrapolated political symbolism, it led to such conceits as the "family of princes," where the East Roman ruler declared himself to stand as a "father" to other rulers within his ideological hegemony (for example, the Balkan Slav lands, in Kievan Rus' or the Caucasus), who were termed "sons" or, occasionally, "younger brothers" (Ostrogorsky 1956; Grabar 1954). In terms of my own view of the imperial office, I admit to a long-standing suspicion about the suppositious dominance of this imperial masculine singularity, and nearly twenty years ago I published a paper (in the *Annales E.S.C.*), the title of which, translated as "Kingship and Sexual Ambiguity," pretty well betrays the thrust of my argument (Miller 1971). What I will lay out below begins with that argument for ambiguity and, similarly, tries to reorganize our perceptions of the *structure* of imperial kingship itself, so as to include the element of the feminine. I will not—except in one instance—be dealing with what we might call Great Consorts, that is, imperial consorts such as a Theodora or a Theophano, who managed to achieve considerable personal power and prestige (or a proven notoriety among their contemporaries) on the basis of personal characteristics. Nor will I try directly to address the points recently raised by Kenneth Holum, whose *Theodosian Empresses* puts forward the possibility that in the fourth and fifth centuries AD a concept of the "sacred *basileia* of empresses" emerged in the eastern part of the empire, though I will suggest an eastern influence as it may have appeared much later; I will be passing over the confused flux of the Theodosian centuries to concentrate on the developed, fully mature "Byzantine" system (Holum 1989: 66).[1]

In that *Annales* essay, in general outline, I dealt with certain signs and significations that seemed to moderate the dominant symbolic masculinity of any king not stigmatized as a tyrant—which is another if associated problem—and even of *the* emperor, the man atop the Byzantine system of rule. These included the Christian monarch's *imitatio* of Christ (and his related Adamic persona), and the concept of the childless king. More importantly, there is superadded to the Byzantine model a series of images adapted from the Iranian (Sassanid) ceremonial worldview and system. This adaptation followed on the nearly Pyrrhic victory won over East Rome's enemy and mirror image, the Persian Empire, in the early seventh century AD. The prime mark, as I saw it, of the victorious Roman emperor, the now truly oecumenical Lord of the Earth, is the double title, invariably used from this point, of *autokrator kai basileus*, which I interpreted as projecting two balanced modes of power, *administrative* and *magical* (Miller 1971: 640).

This double imperial title, and the different potencies that underlie each component of it, can be made to connect Byzantine political ideology to the wider network of conceptions of Indo-European sovereignty postulated by the late Georges Dumézil, and specifically to his division of the social, political, religious dimensions of the *fonction* of Indo-European sovereignty into what he called, borrowing on the Indic context, *Mitraic* and *Varunaic* modes (Dumézil 1988). It must be said that Dumézil himself never delved into the complicated scenarios of East Roman political ideas, preferring more archaic patterns of human thought and social action; nevertheless, his ideas are both provocative and, often, directive.

Of particular value is his description of these two, the Mitraic and the Varunaic, modes of expressing power as, respectively, representative of the *overt, organized, predictive and prescriptive* aspect of sovereignty *en plein air*, and the *indirect, covert* aspect, ambiguous and even mysterious in its workings. Dumézil's bifurcation of sovereignty leads to a number of possibilities both within, and exterior to, his Indo-European *idéologie*, but for my purposes, in the context I am now examining, I want to make a further connection to another kind of dual systematic, of Right and Left—and to examine as well the possibilities of masculine and feminine signs and forces encased in this duality.[2]

The significance of Right Hand and Left Hand (investigated in a number of cultures in *Right and Left: Essays on Dual Symbolic Classification*, a volume edited by Rodney Needham) can be decanted or re-formed into the general transcultural perception, especially apparent in "traditional" (pre-modern) cultures, that the "right hand" tends to be seen as expressive of masculine (in Dumézil's term, Mitraic) force and predictable authority, at base because it is the warrior's "spear-hand" or "sword-hand" (Needham 1973). The ethnographic evidence in Needham's volume often assigns the "left" aspect or orientation to the feminine, but can the left hand of the Byzantine royal figure then be made expressive of feminine or feminized powers? Dumézil himself made no clear attempt to connect his Varunaic mode to the "left hand"; the Varunaic is simply the "darker" or immeasurable modality in sovereign force and, in fact, there may be a perceptible gap between Varunaic (or Odinnic) *grande magie* and any feminized potency (Dumézil 1988: 143). Yet this gap *can* be closed, to the extent that Dumézil's Varunaic force suggests and can be read by us as organizing and displaying a different mode of creative force: one having an active, especially a harmonizing or reconstructive power, not merely "sinister" in effect, and with a symbolic identification activating the feminine gender. More to the point, we are aware of a perceptual shift in Byzantium itself, in that the potency of the "left hand" can be seen to fit with a series of dualized, or matched, powers with which the Byzantine king-emperor is invested. I limit myself here to two examples: first, the dealing out of *justice* (on the right hand), an authority that can be delegated, while the "miraculous" proffer of *mercy* (projected, by default, from the left hand) only the emperor himself has the power to extend (Miller 1971: 637, 647). Again, a twinned power appears in the expectation that the emperor must be *nikephoros*— "victory-bearer"— and *eirenopoios*—"maker of peace"—that is, be at once overbearer of the enemy, and harmonizer of the disturbed political cosmos (Treitinger 1938: 230). In brief, the Byzantine imperial figure expresses, makes concrete, the juncture of two bifurcate plans: the Dumézilian Mitraic/Varunaic, and the more widely recorded division of activated "power" into Right and Left orientations.

My use of the term *invested* in the previous paragraph also carries an assumption that the king-as-emperor received his doubled powers (together with a number of others) at the time of investment or coronation: that the signs and attributes of investment with regal authority and power can be construed into two groups with more or less clear, though certainly symbolic, gender associations. In brief, we seek to organize the masculine instruments of scepter, sword, staff or lance toward one hand; the feminine ring, crown, robes and, arguably, the throne itself toward the other, and we look for this organization in shapes, orientations, and archaic or traditional significances. The ruler's stance—standing or sitting—may act as an important indicator as well. It may even be claimed that the famous "imperial purple" (actually a deep blood red) associated with this high office could be parsed as both a deadly color, of war and bloodshed, and a color related to acts of birth, and so to life-giving and creation.[3] My conclusion is that the full *persona* of the king-emperor combined male and female signs and symbols: that "he" expressed and contained paternal *and* maternal valences, though both must have been denatured of any sexual connotation—that is, we will see no Byzantine representations of an androgynous ruler, for here sexual signs and potencies will be throughly abstracted, removed to a symbolic level, that is, iconized.

In addition to reorganizing our thinking about the nature and roots of royal and, *a fortiori*, imperial power, this kind of explanation perhaps helps us to understand an episode in the history of the empire when, in 790 AD and from 797 to 802 AD, Byzantium was ruled by Irene, a woman who styled herself, as the surviving documentary record shows, "emperor." The incident has been used to indict the Byzantines as absurdly bound by sclerotic usage and tradition.[4] In fact one can say that Irene understood full well both the singularity of the imperial title ("empress" to the Byzantines read only as "consort" and carried no possible political connotation) and the dual significances enclosed in it, that is, as emperor "she" was in fact "he," and surely held both paternal and maternal modes of creative power. We know nothing about her own, private maternal posture, though she had her own son deposed and blinded, and so might be regarded as bridging between the mythic and the historic, between the Jungian Terrible Mother—"if she could silence the voice of conscience" (we recognize Gibbon's inimitable tone) "she neither heard nor regarded the reproaches of mankind"—and the historical realities of female rule (Gibbon 1898: 191). It may have been important for Irene's psychic or subconscious development that she was one of the handful of imperial consorts chosen by means of the Bride Show, that is, she was "created" as an imperial consort from the assembled eligibles of the empire.[5] But Irene's political career, and the symbols that commanded it, was itself only understandable in terms of the great ideological (and necessarily, theological) quarrel that dominated the empire in the eighth and ninth centuries AD: the Iconoclastic controversy. It is in this tremendous rift in the historical fabric of the empire, and particularly in the eventual reconsolidation and triumph of icon-venerating Orthodox theology, together with some new views of the icon and the iconic, that I believe some most important data for "sovereignty and feminine potencies" can be found in Byzantium.

Iconoclasm can be and has been variously considered and analyzed in terms of patterns of cause and effect, following the usual historiographical process. At one time the "breaking of icons" was read as showing a popular, puritanical, perhaps Moslem-influenced spirit rising in the powerful armies of the Eastern (Anatolian) provinces (or themes) of the empire; now the best scholarship emphasizes the consolidation of power in the imperial office, the ambitions of that office in terms of controlling a powerful monastic community, and other political, ideological and social elements. The historical record is not at all without problems, in any case, because the victors in this confrontation—as usual—controlled and wrote that historical record. It *is* worth noting that despite the fact that the iconoclastic emperors failed to achieve their wider political goals, the Eastern Roman oecumene emerged from this drastic test to enter on the most potent and prestigious two centuries of its existence (see Jenkins 1966).

The triumph of the icon, which is firmly and finally recognized as a material representation of a spiritual reality, was accompanied by (and I am adducing no cause-and-effect relationship running either way) a consolidation of the system imaged in the imperial office, readjusting, for example the emperor's position in respect to the Byzantine bureaucracy or civil service (Bury 1911/1948; on imperial bureaucracy, see Miller 1969). The appearance of, or the new emphasis on, certain symbolic or, in a better definition, *iconic* representations of "power" (iconic signifying the clearly defined perceptual relationship between human observer and divine substance) flows naturally as well from the victory of the icon.

From theory to particularity: let us look at some especially significant examples of this new imaging of power, the first of these the magnificent Theotokos (that is, "God-Bearer," the Virgin), a mosaic installed in Haghia Sophia, the ceremonial and administrative center of imperial Orthodoxy, in Constantinople. This large and impressive work, fortuitously discovered in the late 1950s (almost exactly five hundred years after it was covered over by Ottoman whitewash) is one of a number of mosaics in the Great Church dated to the late ninth century (after 843 AD) and it is certainly the most impressive of the Haghia Sophia mosaics to survive to us.[6] Located in the choir of the apse, it shows the Theotokos enthroned, holding her Son, both facing front, Christ shown in the austere "miniature" mode (that is, with no specifically childlike features or gestures). Even with the aid of the best and most percipient students of Byzantine iconology, it is not always easy to decode all of the symbols and their meanings being radiated by a particular icon, but it seems at least arguable that here the Theotokos, the Bearer of God, has taken over and now commands the "place" of Haghia Sophia, that is the sacred structure dedicated by the Byzantines to the Holy Wisdom. This particular concept, of Sophia as Wisdom, is not easy to disentangle from the complex web of Orthodox—and not only Orthodox—theology and iconography.[7] As an example of the complexity, a narthecal mosaic in the same church (Haghia Sophia) shows an enthroned Christ "investing" the emperor Leo VI with that same Holy Wisdom; in two roundels on either side of Christ appear a Theotokos (making a "receptive" gesture similar to that of the emperor, below her) and an archangelic figure, presumably Gabriel. This "investiture" mosaic thus shows the confluence of several metaphorically related ideas: the flow of divinity through (by means of) the Virgin of the Annunciation to Christ; the simultaneous or parallel incarnation of Holy Wisdom *in* Christ, and the investiture of the emperor with that transmitted Sophia, as well as the delegation of rule in the *saeculum* to the emperor, living "icon" of Christ on earth: ". . . this mosaic defines and celebrates in terms of art the supreme power in the Byzantine Empire, governed by Christ through his vicegerent on earth, the Emperor" (Grabar 1955: 97).

Another instructive mosaic, located in the south vestibule of the church, shows another set of combinatory iconic significances: here Constantine and Justinian offer models of the city and of Haghia Sophia, respectively, to the enthroned Virgin and Son. The central or commanding image here is the *chōra*, the sacred place within the Virgin where humankind's salvation was formed into flesh, but also signifying the City as container (under the vigilant guard of the Theotokos) and, within the city, the Great

Church, synecdochal of the City and equally reverberant of
enclosed guardianship—both womb and "sacred fortress" (in Otto
van Simson's [1987] phrase, as he describes an earlier imperial, in
fact Justinianic, monument). The place and power of the emperor
is implicitly conflated with the Theotokos (and with the "feminine"
Holy Wisdom). For once we are not limited to iconological
speculations; the symbolic parallelism between emperor and
Theotokos is also stressed in the text of the emperor Constantine
VII's tenth-century compilation usually titled *De ceremoniis aulae
byzantinae (Ekthesis tes basileiou taxeōs)* where the emperor is
given charge of salvific *space* (again, the *chōra*)—of church, city
and empire—while, like the Virgin, he is called *euergetes* or
"producer of good" since he defends against that chaos exterior to
imperial order (8.53–54; Miller 1969: 21–28). As a last point in this
regard, it is clear why the icons of Christ and of the Theotokos
would dominate the post-Iconoclastic artistic propaganda of
Byzantine Orthodoxy, since both figures are compact of flesh and
divine Spirit, and both act as intermediaries between humankind
and the divine; though it should be stressed that Eastern
Christianity did not, and could not, move as far as the Mariolatry
of the medieval West (Mayendorff 1979: 147ff). It is also clear that
the emperor did, in symbolic and ceremonial terms, engage in a
mimesis of both, of Christ and of the Mother of God (*De cere.*
2.35–38).

The emperor, then, may display a syncretic power partially
derived from and imitative of an abstracted and desexualized
maternal figure. It is quite a stretch from this conception to my
next, where I will suggest that some other mosaic representations
in Constantinople's Haghia Sophia show another possibility in the
theme of power and feminine potencies, that is, hints of the theme
of the "marriage to sovereignty," wherein the ruler's legitimacy is
authenticated by his marriage to a feminine figure who represents
"both [the kingdom's] abstract sovereignty and the physical reality
of its territory" (Mac Cana 1979: 448–49). The "marriage to
sovereignty" motif is most clearly apparent in the archaic Irish
Celtic tradition, both in an actual ceremony associated with the
assumption of royal office (the *banfeis rígi* or "marriage of
kingship"), and in the literature surviving to us, describing the
legends of such king-heroes as Niall of the Nine Hostages, Cormac
mac Airt, Lugaid Laigde, Conaire Mor (Mac Cana 1979; Rees and
Rees 1975: 73ff.). The tradition has been identified in the Indic
context, the Roman and probably in the Homeric Greek, with
specific reference to Odysseos (Rees and Rees 1975: 75, 369 n.123).
In other words, we probably have an Indo-European motif, and I

have come around, or back, to Dumézil and his *idéologie indo-européenne*.[8]

What has this to do with Byzantium, or for that matter, with the mosaics created for Haghia Sophia? Some background is necessary: at the apogee of East Rome's political and ideological renaissance in the early eleventh century the ferocious soldier-emperor Basil II died, and his brother, Constantine VIII, ruled briefly. Thereafter, for almost thirty years, the imperial office was to be granted, in turn, to the three husbands of Constantine's aged daughter, the *porphyrogenita* Zoe.[9] This extraordinary dynastic continuity-in-marriage has been the subject of much discussion. Dynastic succession was not at all the earlier Byzantine practice. Basil I (called "the Macedonian" because of his birth-province; his descent was in fact Armenian) took the imperial office and founded the so-called Macedonian dynasty after overthrowing his predecessor, thus following the usual Byzantine pattern by showing that the office was God-chosen, rather than dictated by man—that is, through inheritance or familial connection. Why did the shift toward inheritance of the office occur? Some have cited the overextension, even the "burning out" of the imperial monarchy with Basil II; others look to the increasing dominance of the capital's civil aristocracy, who stood behind, and thought to control, the decadent Macedonian house and its relict princesses, remnants of a great dynasty. But perhaps there is something more.

The last imperial mosaic to which I will refer is the "Zoe panel," located in the south gallery of Haghia Sophia. It shows the empress Zoe on the right, the emperor Constantine IX Monomachos (her third imperial husband) on the left, and an enthroned Christ Pantokrator—All-Ruler—in the center. The important feature of this "offering" by the imperial couple is that Constantine's portrait is not original; at least one and possibly both of Zoe's previous consorts were depicted here. We have a striking physical record, in fact, of the motif called "marriage to sovereignty."[10]

How and why did this theme come to Byzantine politics—and iconic art? The possibility at least exists that it emerged from that storehouse of archaic Indo-European themes and practices, the Caucasus, and passed into East Rome by way of the Armenian presence so marked from the ninth through the eleventh centuries of the empire's history (see der Nersessian 1944; Charanis 1963). The possibility of Armenian influence in the mosaic panel I have just discussed was raised by Grabar (1955: 102). The Armenian migration into the empire had, we know, introduced an aristocratic (sometimes called a "feudal") ideology into the civil and even more into the military elite of the empire (Vryonis 1959: 161ff.).

Certainly one element of this ethnic consciousness was the reliance on "dynastic" descent and affiliation by blood. There is the further point that what we might call "vital" aristocracies often regarded their inborn, blood-carried excellence as potent regardless of gender. However, the Caucasian-Armenian nexus and the origin of the concept of "marriage to sovereignty" (if that is what we have seen) is certainly problematical and perhaps unprovable. The peculiar turn taken by the Byzantine imperial dynasty, the new importance of dynastic succession, remains a puzzle, and I will make no strong claim to solve that puzzle.

In sum: the system of sovereignty embodied in the Byzantine emperor makes room for significant modifications in the model of simple patriarchal rulership, that is, as the simple model would delete, ignore, or marginalize the signs and affects of feminized power. The "true" emperor, *autokrator kai basileos*, operated in a symbolic universe that was bifurcated, and on his "left hand," in a symbolic perception, he wielded powers that were partially expressive of the nurturing, the merciful, and the covertly-miraculous, that is, of the feminine or the feminized zone. Whether or not the "left hand" of the ruler is actually (iconically) involved in signing and so externalizing this feminine potency might be discovered from a wider and more thorough look at the iconography, but I suggest that as the imperial "right hand" may exercise the juridical power of God-as-Father, the left hand expresses the potentiality of the salvific power associated with God's Mother. As we have seen in the imperially-sponsored art of the post-Iconoclastic period, the emperor is invested with the mysterious Holy Wisdom, and though this power descended from Christ and was exercised as part of the emperor's Christomimetic character, the parallel intervention of the Theotokos is plain enough, and "investment" is strongly allied with "incarnation" as process. The emperor is also required to imitate the God-Bearer as he, like her, is guardian of *chōra* or sacred space—the empire itself is sacred space writ large (Miller 1969: 23). Finally, Byzantium *may* have been infiltrated by an idea of great antiquity and interest to us, so that the imperial office itself, if briefly, was passed on and authenticated by marriage to a "sovereign" woman. So signs and aspects of the feminine, and especially of feminine "creativity," were surely built into, and remained significant in, the overtly male-centred structure of the Byzantine imperial office.

Why should East Rome have created or evolved the singular but doubled, symbolically bi-gendered imperial figure? Let me suggest two intersecting ideas, drawn from the possibilities inherent in our understanding of *myth* and of *ritual*.

(1) In terms of political-theological *myth*, the physical, human characteristics (including gender and age) of the imperial figure are dissolved into the Sovereign necessarily involved in that *imitatio* of Christ I mentioned early on, so that the emperor's masculinity has proportionately less significance, in parallel with the theologically occluded masculinity (and humanity) of Christ, the model. The second, very "Byzantine" theological (mythic) current invests the Sovereign, again as imitator, with the salvific powers of the Mother of God, both through his guardianship of sacred space (*chōra*) and through his investment with the powers of Holy Wisdom. Iconically, the emperor is feminized, though at a very high level of abstraction.

(2) In terms of the affective net of *ritual*, the Byzantine urge toward balance and symmetry, and the *combinatory* aspect of their perception of the Sovereign acting in ritual, leads to a figuring of two kinds of operations, following the Right Hand and the Left Hand in orientation. In this process the emperor intercepts other, reinforcing, "archaic" patterns whereby Right is conceived as masculine, Left as feminine or feminized, but both must operate as two parts of one body.

A comparison with another system or society may be in order. In the medieval West, despite attempts to borrow or recreate a true imperial mode (as with the Ottonian house and later), and though the rituals of coronation and the regal iconography might contain the symbolic gender-signs to which I referred, monarchy in the West kept the essential force of the *war-king* or *sword-king*. In the Dumézilian schema such a figure might not stand even for the Mitraic side of sovereignty, but hold his powers from the Second (or Warrior) Function.[11] In any event, he would or could be balanced by another, separate figure—perhaps the queen as arbiter or expression of solicitude and mercy. At base, we see an idea-system in which *division* rather than *combination* is the dominant trait.[12]

In terms of a further comparative effort, the Byzantine system might well be set against other "oecumenical" imperial systems, including the Persian, the Chinese, and the Ottoman Turkish, where some sort of balancing, feminized potency was evidently felt to be necessary to the full or completed structure of sovereignty. Each of these imperial constructions is a possible subject for further research along the lines I have suggested.[13]

NOTES

1 Whether or not these ideas of the "*basilea* of empresses" remained as a hidden element or sub-motif in the "mature" Byzantine system is worth investigating.

2 See Needham 1980: 63–105 for a brilliant investigation of the wider permutations of the idea of "dual sovereignty."

3 For Byzantine "color-coding" see Mathew 1963; Lopez 1945.

4 Gibbon (1898), oddly enough, has nothing to say about the title, though a good deal to say about Irene; see below. Brehier 1948: 93 says "cette situation était sans précédent."

5 Miller 1971: 649. According to the Byzantine *Book of Ceremonies* (the *Ekthesis tes basileiou taxeōs* or *De ceremoniis aulae Byzantinae* attributed to the emperor Constantine VII Porphyrogenitus), the empress was also "Chosen of God" (Corpus Scriptorum Historiae Byzantinae, ed. Niebuhr 1829: 89.206).

6 Robert Van Nice, who knew and had plotted every brick in Haghia Sophia, was certainly of the opinion that this mosaic was created just after the victory of Orthodox icon-worship; more recently Cormack 1985: 146 gives a later date. In my opinion Van Nice is probably closer to the truth, but the great representation is, in any case, a product of the new Orthodox iconic sensibility.

7 A monograph on the "Iconography of the Holy Wisdom" by Marie-Thérèse d'Alverny is mentioned by Grabar in his masterful text to the Skira publication (1955: 97), that is, is cited as a work that will be published "shortly," but this never appears to have happened. For an intriguing instance of the transmutation of the Holy Wisdom in the medieval West see Gold 1985: 49 ff. and Pl. 3.

8 For Dumézil's own brief remark on the motif see Dumézil 1954: 3–8.

9 For a fuller picture of the complications in this pattern see Ostrogorsky 1957: 283 ff.

10 In fact "marriage to sovereignty" may have two scenarios. One is marked by the choice of the king's daughter (or widow), but in the second "sovereignty" is disguised as a Hag, and it is by embracing the Hag that the true king is made known. See Ó Cathasaigh 1977.

11 Though the Dumézilian *idéologie* of trifunctionality is revived in the medieval West; see Grisward 1981 and Duby 1983.

12 Students of the Byzantine thoughtworld are aware of the fact that no division between Church and State is, in theory, possible there, and the secular headship of both, combined into one *oecumene*, is vested in the emperor. The divisibility of the royal *persona* in the West may be seen to continue, along slightly different lines, with the phenomenon Kantorowicz (1957) so carefully and eloquently described; that is, the king seen as possessing two

bodies, one his ordinary "natural body," the second the *corpus mysticum.*

13 At the time this essay was being written, I had not received the most recent volume of the *Journal of Indo-European Studies* in which appears Puhvel's "Hittite Regal Titles" (1989). Puhvel has uncovered a Hittite (Old Kingdom) royal personage, the Tawanannas, "a daughter of the sovereign who served as intermediary to succession whenever direct male descent failed" (353). We thus have early evidence of an Anatolian (and indubitably Indo-European) usage with intriguing parallels to the Celtic world (359–60). How this institution might relate to Armenian royal custom, and by extension to East Rome, is a matter for more investigation—possibly by re-connecting to Holum's work on the Theodosian empresses, noted above.

REFERENCES

Brehier, L. (1948). *Le monde byzantin*, vol. 1: *Vie et mort de Byzance*. Paris: Éditions Albin Michel.

Bury, J.B. (1911/1948). *The Imperial Administrative System in the Ninth Century*. New York: Burt Franklin (reprint).

Charanis, Peter (1963). *The Armenians in the Byzantine Empire*. Lisboa: Livraria Bertrand.

Cormack, Robin (1985). *Writing in Gold: Byzantine Society and Its Icons*. New York: Oxford University Press.

(1829). *De ceremoniis aulae Byzantinae* (*Ekthesis tes basileiou taxeōs*, the *Book of Ceremonies*). *Corpus Scriptorum Historiae Byzantinae*, 1: 7, ed. Niebuhr. Bonn: Imp. Ed. Weberi.

der Nersessian, Sirarpie (1944). *Armenia and the Byzantine Empire: A Brief Study of Armenian Art and Civilization*. Cambridge, MA: Harvard University Press.

Duby, Georges (1983). *The Three Orders: Feudal Society Imagined*, trans. E. A. Goldhammer. Chicago: University of Chicago Press.

Dumézil, G. (1954). *Meretrices* et *uirgines* dans quelques légendes politiques de Rome et des peuples celtiques. *Ogam* 6, 3–8.

——(1988). *Mitra-Varuna: An essay on Two Indo-European Representations of Sovereignty*, trans. D. Coltman. New York: Zone.

Gibbon, L. (1898). *A History of the Decline and Fall of the Roman Empire*, 5, ed. J.B. Bury. London: Methuen; New York: MacMillan.

Gold, Peggy Schine (1985). *The Lady and the Virgin: Image, Attitude and Experience in Twelfth-Century France*. Chicago: University of Chicago Press.

Grabar, Andre (1954). God and the "Family of Princes" Presided Over by the Byzantine Emperor. *Harvard Slavic Studies* 2, 117–23.

—— (1955). *Byzantine Painting*, trans. S. Gilbert. Geneva: Éditions Skira.

Grisward, J. (1981). *Archéologie de l'épopée médiévale: structures trifonctionelles et mythes indo-européenes dans le cycle des Narbonnais.* Paris: Payot.

Holum, Kenneth C. (1989). *Theodosian Empresses: Women and Imperial Dominion in Late Antiquity.* Berkeley: University of California Press.

Jenkins, Romilly (1966). *Byzantium: The Imperial Centuries, AD 610–1071.* New York: Random House.

Kantorowicz, Ernst (1957). *The King's Two Bodies: A Study in Medieval Political Theology.* Princeton: Princeton University Press.

Lopez, R.S. (1945). Silk Industry in the Byzantine Empire. *Speculum* 20, 1–42.

Mac Cana, Proinsias (1979). Regnum und Sacerdotium: Notes on Irish Tradition. *Proceedings of the British Academy* 65, 443–79.

Mathew, D. (1963). *Byzantine Esthetics.* London: Oxford University Press.

Mayendorff, J. (1979). *Byzantine Theology: Historical Trends and Doctrinal Themes.* New York: Fordham University Press.

Miller, D.A. (1969). *Imperial Constantinople.* New York: J. Wiley.

—— (1971). Royauté et ambiguité sexuelle. *Annales E.S.C.* 26, 639–52.

Needham, R., ed. (1973). *Right and Left: Essays on Dual Symbolic Classification.* Chicago: University of Chicago Press.

—— (1980). Dual Sovereignty. *Reconaissances*, 63–105. Toronto: University of Toronto Press.

Ó Cathasaigh, Tomás (1977). *The Heroic Biography of Cormac mac Airt.* Dublin: Dublin Institute for Advanced Studies.

Ostrogorsky, G. (1956). The Byzantine Emperor and the Hierarchical World Order. *Slavic and East European Review* 35, 1–19.

—— (1957). *History of the Byzantine State.* New Brunswick, NJ: Rutgers University Press.

Puhvel, Jaan (1989). Hittite Regal Titles: Hattic or Indo-European? *Journal of Indo-European Studies* 17, 351–61.

Rees, A. and B. (1975). *Celtic Heritage: Ancient Tradition in Ireland and Wales.* London: Thames & Hudson.

Treitinger, O. (1938). *Die oströmische Kaiser- und Reichsidee nach ihrer Gestaltung im höfischen Zeremoniell.* Jena.

von Simson, Otto G. (1987). *Sacred Fortress: Byzantine Art and Statecraft in Ravenna.* Princeton: Princeton University Press.

Vryonis, S. (1959). Byzantium: The Social Basis of Decline in the Eleventh Century. *Greek, Roman and Byzantine Studies* 2, 159–75.

MÁIRE HERBERT

Goddess and King: The Sacred Marriage in Early Ireland

In early Ireland women were not sovereigns, but sovereignty itself was conceived of as female. The mythic model of royal rule which the Celtic world shared with many other ancient cultures was that of the *hieros gamos* or sacred marriage. According to this model, successful and prosperous government of society was the outcome of union between female and male elements, between the goddess of the land and its sovereign. Sacred marriage imagery has been a constantly-recurring theme in Irish literature through the ages (Breatnach 1953: 321–36). Eighteenth-century poets, for instance, still referred to the ruling of Ireland in terms such as "the bride wed in bliss . . . to the King" (Ó Tuama-Kinsella 1981: 189). Yet we must distinguish between the durability of the image as a literary *topos* and its survival as a constituent of royal ideology in Ireland. By the eighteenth century, the country was no longer ruled over by a native sovereign and the whole traditional institution of kingship had long since been attenuated. At this period, therefore, the image of the sacred marriage had poetic rather than political resonance. But did the mythic representation of female sovereignty retain active political force for as long as native institutions remained in Ireland?

It has been suggested that the theme of female sovereignty espoused to male sovereign "exercised an influence on recorded history as late as the eleventh century" (Mac Cana quoted by Trindade 1986: 153).[1] But what was the nature of this influence? Did the myth persist in Ireland unchanged in its lineaments and in its influence even as the practice of sovereignty changed and developed? The present enquiry will seek to address the question.

We must begin, however, by focusing on the mythic image itself. The sacred marriage originally seems to have been a myth of agriculturally-based communities, reflecting a belief that the earth, no longer a self-fecundating *generatrix*, required human intervention to ensure successful harvesting of its fruits. Thus, energy or natural forces, represented by the female principle, combined with social forces represented by the male principle. The ritual counterpart of the myth, the mating between the surrogate female divinity of the natural world and the male who was representative of human society, seems originally to have been associated with New Year festivals and seasonal renewal. Over time, however, both myth and ritual appear to have acquired more specific associations with royal rule, so that sacred union with the goddess of the land was seen to initiate the fertility and prosperity of a sovereign's reign.[2]

In its Celtic setting, the myth is represented primarily in sources from both Gaul and Ireland. Neither material presents an unmediated view of pagan Celtic antiquity. Ireland's substantial literary evidence referring to the pagan past survives by virtue of its having been redacted in writing by Christian *literati* from about the seventh century AD onward. Gaulish epigraphic and iconographic evidence belongs to the period between circa 500 BC and 400 AD. Yet despite its greater antiquity, this material was produced, for the most part, at a time when Celtic society in Gaul was being greatly subjected to Roman influence. Written sources referring to Gaulish society were produced by Greek and Roman observers (Mac Cana 1970: 16–17, Green 1989: 1–8). Despite disparities and limitations in the evidence, however, discernible correspondences between Gaulish and Irish representations still allow us to trace basic features of the early Celtic gendered representation of societal well-being and government.

Gaulish iconography depicts many paired deities, divine couples whose partnership seems designed to promote an image of fertility and prosperity. While the male appears in many guises, the dominant imagery of the female is that of well-being, human and animal fertility, and earthly productivity (Green 1989: 72–73). Epigraphic evidence reveals that the male is occasionally given a Roman name, while the female is always a native divinity (Green 1989: 45). The iconographic imagery of a foreign consort of the goddess of the land finds a literary reflex in the foundation-story of Massilia (Marseilles). This relates that the Gaulish king's daughter, in the act of proffering a symbolic marriage libation to her intended spouse, bestows the drink on the newly-arrived foreigner. Thus the outsider is incorporated into the native belief system by his being accepted by, and ritually espoused to, the female epitome of the territory.[3]

In early Ireland, we find that literary representations similarly depict the goddess as spouse, and therefore validator, of a

succession of rulers. In the redactions of Christian scribes, myths
were transferred from sacred time into history, and transformed
into narratives of the past. Yet since narrative had been the vehicle
of transmission and preservation of myth in the first place, the
transmutation of oral myth into written story did not obliterate the
themes constitutive of the myth (Bolle 1970: 27).

We find in early Irish literature many euhemerized and
historicized representations of sovereignty, though these have not
always been recognized as such. Zimmer, writing in 1911 (*art. cit.*
Ó Máille 1927: 129), used the example of story depictions of queen
Medb of Cruachu as evidence of the moral laxity of the pagan Irish
period. He was drawing on narrative material, titled in one of its
versions "Medb's Husband-Allowance" (Meyer, "Ferchuitred
Medba"), which details the liaisons between the queen and a series
of royal spouses. In the narratives, rivalries and jealousies abound
amongst the male suitors. Ultimately, however, the choice of
spouse is the prerogative of the female. The narratives relate of
Medb, for instance, that while married to the third of her husbands
she noted a young man who was active in protecting her province.
Thereupon she loved him, took him as her husband, and "with
Medb's consent," the former husband was ousted and her new
spouse installed as king (O'Neill 1905: 182–85).

Read as historicized myth, it is evident that the depiction of
Medb should be viewed, not as that of a promiscuous Celtic
queen, but rather as the realization in human terms of the goddess
of sovereignty who chooses as partner the most fitting of royal
candidates. Statements attributed to Medb that she had never
been "without one man in the shadow of another," and that she
required a partner without "jealousy, fear nor niggardliness,"
further reveal the sexually-assertive queen as the disguise of
female sovereignty requiring properly-qualified rulers in unbroken
succession. That it was originally the female role to select and
validate her royal spouses is underlined in narratives of another
Medb, called Medb Lethderg of Leinster. She too is serially
wedded to a line of kings, and it is stated of her that "she tolerated
no king at Tara without his having herself as a wife" (Ó Máille
1927: 136–43; Dumézil 1973: 85–107).

What do we know of the interaction between the foregoing myth
and the practice of sovereignty in early Celtic society? A
generative link between mythic image and contemporary social
reality is discernible in the Gaulish evidence. As the sacred
marriage originally seems to have been associated with the
engendering of earthly and human fertility, so too in Gaul,
symbols of fertility are a feature of the iconography of the paired

deities (Green 1989: 73). However, the variety of partners of the native goddess, and specifically the introduction of a new Roman partner for her, thereby shifts the signifying emphasis of the image from the prosperous outcome of the sacred marriage to the marriage union itself. In an era of change in political rule, the permanence of the land and its sovereignty was represented by the goddess, to whom all aspiring sovereigns were to be espoused. The same myth in another medium, the foundation-story of Massilia, which portrays the female bestowing the symbolic marriage drink on the foreigner, reinforces this significance. In political terms, foreign overlordship was mitigated as the intrusive ruler was himself represented as the object of active intervention by the native goddess.

We do not have the same degree of access to the politics of the pre-Christian Irish society from which surviving literary representations of sovereignty derived their origins. In the versions of the early Christian period which we have just examined, the chosen spouses of both Medb of Cruachu and Medb of Leinster are all figures from the Irish prehistoric or legendary past. None has historical status. Is the preservation of the myth in literary sources of the early Christian period, therefore, simply the outcome of the survival of its narrative realization? Is it a fossilized story element, dissociated from contemporary Irish political life?

Other instances of the myth in Irish literature make this conclusion less clear-cut. The text *Baile in Scáil*, dated to the early eleventh century AD, portrays a vision of the pan-Celtic god-king Lug enthroned in iconic fashion beside his female consort.[4] She is instructed to bestow the drink of sovereignty on a succession of rulers destined to be kings. The imagery is strongly reminiscent of the Gaulish representations. Yet we note that in the Irish text the rulers to whom the female sovereignty figure dispenses the symbolic drink include not only prehistoric kings of Tara, but also the succession of historical kings extending to the writer's own time, the beginning of the eleventh century (Dillon 1946: 11–14).

Can it really be concluded from this that the concept of female sovereignty bestowing the right to rule on male sovereigns did, indeed, remain as an active factor in Irish political ideology even to this late date? What has been most lacking from scholarly discussion is any full scrutiny of the interactive association between the historical practice of sovereignty and its literary representations. Before addressing the question of the survival of the myth, therefore, we must focus on Irish sovereignty in its historical rather than in its literary setting.

Contemporary historical records date from about the late sixth century AD onward, while archaeology and other ancillary sources illuminate the period from the early centuries of the millennium. All the evidence indicates that, even in the early centuries, Irish rulers did not function as sacral figures in a cultural backwater, but rather functioned actively in a society which had a good deal of contact with the outside world, in particular with Roman Britain (Stevenson 1989: 127–33). By the beginning of the historical era, the sources portray rulers in pursuit of real, rather than symbolic, authority. From the seventh century there is evidence of the increasing power of major royal dynasties, and the growth of territorially-based kingdoms. While the Viking wars of the ninth and tenth centuries may have been a complicating factor in the power struggles of Irish rulers, they may well have served also to hasten development towards national consciousness and national institutions. By the late ninth century, we find the over-king of the Uí Néill, Ireland's premier royal dynasty, claiming the title of "king of all Ireland." Yet, though it had been rulers of this dynasty in particular who dominated Irish political life and were in the forefront of the aggrandizement of royal power through the centuries, the culminating achievement of national sovereignty slipped from their grasp. It was a ruler from a comparatively obscure Munster dynasty, Brian Boruma, who finally converted the aspiration to the kingship of all Ireland into demonstrable reality at the beginning of the eleventh century.[5]

In the practice of Irish sovereignty, therefore, rulers actively seized power and shaped their own destinies. Yet was contemporary theory still in thrall to the myth that the ruler acquired authority and legitimacy only through his espousal to the female figure of sovereignty? It must be noted that the expression of political theory in early historical Ireland was by no means univocal. In the early centuries of Christian conversion, clerical writers sought to promote a Christian ideology of sovereignty in which the overseer and legitimator of royal power was not the goddess but the male god of Christianity (McCone 1990: 138–45). Some seventh-century churchmen campaigned to have this change affirmed in public ritual by substituting royal inauguration by clerical unction for the traditional rite based on the sacred marriage (Enright 1985: 5–78).[6] Yet in the following centuries, the ever-closer merging of the interests of church and state meant that the clerical voice grew less distinct and separate. A survey of the source-material reveals subsequent expressions of sovereignty-ideology with direct reference to contemporary Irish political life which seem to have been produced in the period from around the beginning of the eleventh century onward, and which are couched in the traditional imagery of goddess and king.[7] Is it the case, then, that tradition ultimately triumphed over innovation at the level of theory, while the direct reverse seems to have happened at the level of practice? Is there, in fact, a fissure between representations of ideology and of actuality? To seek further to resolve the matter, we must redirect attention to the later realizations of the myth.

The binary system of the sovereignty-myth is based on gender difference. Yet up to now its gender component seems to have been viewed merely as an unproblematic given, and there has been little scrutiny of the relationship between the paired terms. While iconography alone seems to point to equality of status between the female and male partners in the Gaulish system (Green 1989: 73), the combined evidence from Gaul of iconography, epigraphy, and traditional legend privileges the female. It is the goddess who is the constant, whose presence in the partnership legitimates even intrusive rulers. This configuration of gender relations is repeated in early Irish *mythologie littérarisée*, as in the representations of Medb in all her guises. Here, again, the female is the constant, and the initiator of relationships with her male partners. The dominance of female over male in the Gaulish sovereignty-representations has a societal correlative in a political system in which kingship had become demonstrably weak (Chadwick 1974: 57–58). While the Irish material about Medb can be less securely anchored in a historical context, it seems reasonable to conclude that it originated in the period before the expansion of kingly power in Ireland.

What of the eleventh-century *Baile in Scáil*, which refers to historic as well as legendary Irish sovereignty? In this text, it is the king-god, Lug, who instructs his female companion regarding the bestowal of the drink of sovereignty on successive kings. It is his action rather than that of the goddess, therefore, which ultimately designates the ruler. The locus of power has shifted from female to male. In its gender asymmetry the mythic image reveals itself in dialogue with the Irish historical era, when royal rule had become a matter of achievement by male sovereign rather than of assignation by female sovereignty. What Barthes (1973: 127) describes as the ideographic quality of the myth still seems to be maintained.

Yet *Baile in Scáil* is not simply a later model of sovereignty expressed in traditional gendered discourse. The compiler of the text does not allow the myth to speak itself but rather forecloses interpretation by explicit intervention. When the goddess, at Lug's behest, offers the drink of sovereignty to a line of kings, we read, in terms of the myth, that each of these kings "will be wedded to Lug's consort, and in that sense take Lug's place and be his

surrogate for the time being in the kingship of Tara" (Ó
Cathasaigh 1989: 31–32). The compiler, however, overrides this
implicit signification by identifying the goddess-figure as "the
Sovereignty of Ireland." She now stands, therefore, not as the
bestower of symbolic power on holders of the ancient kingship of
Tara, but rather as a new political concept which was the goal of
contemporary rulers. While retaining the image of partner in a
sacred marriage, the female role is, in fact, relegated from that of
subject to that of object. Royal rule is not now conceived of in
terms of partnership but rather in terms of a relationship in which
the male appropriates the female.

Moreover, as the female is a specific political objective, so too
the male kings in *Baile in Scáil* have particular political significance.
In the text, the recipients of the drink of sovereignty are a
succession of kings of Tara in a continuum of prehistory and
history, from the era of Conn Cétchathach through to the
beginning of the eleventh century (Dillon 1946: 12–14). As the
legendary kings of Tara were regarded as Ireland's premier rulers,
so too historical holders of the title, the Uí Néill dynasty, claimed
primacy among Irish kings. As we have seen, the Uí Néill were
set fair to convert this primacy into authority over fellow rulers
from about the late ninth century. Yet ultimately it was a ruler
from a hitherto-obscure Munster dynasty who overtook them in
attaining this goal (Byrne 1973: 70–105, 254–69). In the king-list
of *Baile in Scáil*, the final identifiable figure is the author's own
contemporary, Maél Sechnaill, the Uí Néill dynast who had to
cede the kingship of Ireland to Brian of Munster at the beginning
of the eleventh century. Read against the background of this
upheaval in sovereignty, therefore, the compilation of *Baile in
Scáil* reveals its full contemporary signification. It is a statement
of advocacy on behalf of the Uí Néill dynasty.[8] It seeks to counter
the achievement of *parvenu* might by proclamation of long-
established right. The myth is co-opted to serve the purpose of
projecting the dynasty's claim to the sovereignty of Ireland back
to primordial time.

From around the same era at which this literary activity was in
progress there appears a further literary instance of the sacred
marriage theme. This occurs in what is perhaps the best-known of
Irish sovereignty-tales, that of the so-called "Loathly Lady." Its
earliest surviving redaction is found in a verse text of the beginning
of the eleventh century (Joynt 1908: 101–7). A corresponding
prose version not far removed in date from the verse also survives
(Stokes 1903: 190–203).

The sovereignty episode forms part of a biographical account of king Niall of the Nine Hostages, whose reign may be assigned to the period around the beginning of the fifth century, just before the beginning of recorded history in Ireland (Byrne 1973: 70–86). The texts set out to show that Niall's right to kingship was evident in the heroic pattern of his whole life. The central core of the biography, however, concerns the manner in which he became king. This relates how Niall and his four brothers went to hunt, and, having consumed their captured prey in the wilderness, they needed drink to quench their thirst. The brother who volunteered to search for water came upon a well guarded by a hag of hideous appearance. Her offer of water in return for a kiss led him to flee in repulsion and terror. The hag's encounter with the three other brothers followed the same pattern. Finally, it was Niall's turn. He too was greeted by "that hideous shape, thin-shanked, grey-headed, bushy-browed." Yet, instead of fleeing, "around her he closed his arms . . . he strained her to his breast and bosom, as though she were for ever his own spouse." Thereafter when he looked on her she was transformed utterly. She had become a beautiful maiden, "the fairest in human form" (Joynt 1908: 102–5). Niall's immediate query regarding her identity brings the response "I am sovereignty."[9] Moreover, in the verse text, she provides an allegorical interpretation of what had occurred. Just as "the direness of her foul form" had been transformed by Niall's action, so too would be his kingship: "rough its beginning . . . smooth its mid-course, . . . peaceful . . . its final close" (Joynt 1908: 107 §56).

Ostensibly, the story of Niall presents an image of the mating of female sovereignty and male sovereign, the dyad which the myth deems necessary to ensure societal rule. In gender terms, there is marked asymmetry favouring the male. Yet again, however, the female is not simply demoted to weaker ruling partner. Rather, she functions once more as object to be appropriated—in this instance her appropriation being the necessary condition for the recuperation of her form and appearance. As in *Baile in Scáil* there is authorial interpretation projected onto that disclosed by the mythic image. The feminized political status and power which the ruler assumes may present an initially unpromising face, but the perspicacious rightful king could convert disorder to harmony. Moreover, lest there be any doubt about the nature of sovereignty represented in female terms, the verse text, in its following account of the return of Niall and his brothers to their father, explicitly states that what Niall had attained was "the kingship of Ireland" (Joynt 1908: 109 §66).

The royal hero of this story was not simply a famous ruler of the past. He was also the founding father of Ireland's premier royal dynasty, the Uí Néill, whose name literally means "the descendants of Niall." The redactor of the poetic version of Niall's story, Cuán Ua Lothcháin, whose death is recorded in the year 1024, elsewhere in his compositions reveals himself as a servitor of the dynasty, in particular, of his contemporary, Maél Sechnaill, the ruler supplanted from the kingship of Ireland (Joynt 1908: 91). The political sub-text revealed in *Baile in Scáil*, therefore, is again in evidence here. Uí Néill's right to kingship is reasserted, in this instance, by demonstrating its acquisition by the dynasty's eponymous ancestor in an era of antiquity reaching back before Christianity.[10] Female sovereignty's transformation from ugliness to beauty by Niall's action suggests a link between the state of Ireland and the holding of the kingship by the Uí Néill, while at the same time the overt allegory presents a paradigm of hope for the poet's contemporary ruler. Sovereignty might be rough in the beginning as indeed the reign of Maél Sechnaill undoubtedly was, but the inheritor of rightful kingship had the capacity to embrace adversity and to transform it into prosperity and success.

It is evident that for the Uí Néill propagandists of the early eleventh century the mythic past provided a defensive strategy in a threatening present. The depiction of the designation of rulers by the sovereignty-goddess linked sacred time with historical time, and accorded to the former legitimating status for the latter. In the use of the sacred marriage myth, there is now a lateral shift of signification such as Barthes describes as having occurred in the case of myth itself (1973: 115). In its original semiological system, the sacred marriage myth was the sign, the associative total of signifying divine couple and signified societal rule. Now, however, the myth itself functions as signifier, signifying present aspiration in terms of past accomplishment, in the new signification of politically-inspired eleventh-century composition.

We may conclude, therefore, that in this historical era in Ireland we are to view the representation of the sacred marriage not as functional myth, but rather as metamyth. Yet as signifier in this system, the gendered union of natural and social forces, of female sovereignty and male sovereign, retains evidence of its own historicity and intentionality. The sum of our evidence over time presents a diachronic view of the inter-relationship between power and gender. Female sovereignty is privileged in the era of prehistoric *rois fainéants*, but in the androcentric culture of kingly power, her role as partner is diminished. Ultimately, the metaphoric view moves toward the metonymic.

NOTES

1 For instances of suggested "action of myth on history" in the ninth century and later, see Mac Cana 1970: 121, also Byrne 1973: 225, 273; Doan 1984: *passim*.

2 This general discussion is indebted to the article *Hieros Gamos* in Eliade 1987: 6, 317–21; as well as to Lerner 1986 and Neumann 1963: *passim*.

3 The original text from the fourth century BC is translated by Murphy (1937: 143). On the symbolism of the libation and its role in the Irish Sacred Marriage material, see Murphy 1937: 144; O'Rahilly 1943: 14–21.

4 I agree with Murphy (1952: 150 n.1) that there is an earlier stratum in the text, possibly of the ninth century. The final surviving version, the subject of present study, I take to be a revision and updating of the early eleventh century.

5 On these developments see, in particular, Binchy; Byrne 1971, 1973; Ó Corráin; Wormald.

6 The question of ritual merits separate study. For a survey of evidence regarding inauguration ceremonies, see Simms 1987: 21–40.

7 I base my conclusions on evidence available, noting, for instance, that so-called "King Tales" which have particular reference to this theme date from the eleventh and twelfth centuries. For discussion of some of these, see McCone 1990: 145–48.

8 The conclusion which I have reached regarding this material was suggested in Bromwich 1960–61, but without any accompanying discussion. Her article also contains valuable discussion of the "Loathly Lady" theme in medieval literature.

9 The printed version of the verse text (Joynt 1908: 105, §53a) contains the question but lacks the answer. This, however, is supplied in the corresponding prose (Stokes 1903: 200–1, §15).

10 This suggestion is made by Mac Cana (1980b: 104), but without any accompanying discussion or elaboration of how this view integrates with his other published views on the subject.

REFERENCES

Barthes, Roland (1973). *Mythologies*, trans. Annette Lavers. Frogmore: Paladin.

Binchy, D.A. (1970). *Celtic and Anglo-Saxon Kingship*. Oxford: Clarendon Press.

Bolle, Kees W. (1970). In Defense of Euhemerus. *Myth and Law among the Indo-Europeans* ed. Jaan Puhvel. Berkeley: U. of California Press, 19–38.

Breatnach, R.A. (1953). The Lady and the King: A theme of Irish Literature. *Studies* 42, 321–36.

Bromwich, Rachel (1960–61). Celtic Dynastic Themes and the Breton Lays. *Études Celtiques* 9, 439–74.

Byrne, Francis John (1971). Tribes and tribalism in early Ireland. *Ériu* 22, 128–66.

—— (1973). *Irish Kings and High-Kings*. London: Batsford.

Chadwick, Nora (1974). *The Celts*. Harmondsworth: Penguin.

Dillon, Myles (1946). *The Cycles of the Kings*. London and New York: Geoffrey Cumberledge and Oxford University Press.

Doan, James E. (1984). *Sovereignty Aspects in the Roles of Women in Medieval Irish and Welsh Society*. Boston: Northeastern University Working Papers in Irish Studies 84–5.

Dumézil, Georges (1973). *The Destiny of a King* trans. Alf Hiltebeitel. Chicago: University of Chicago Press.

Eliade, Mircea ed. (1987). *The Encyclopaedia of Religion*. New York: Macmillan.

Enright, Michael J. (1985). *Iona, Tara and Soissons: The Origin of the Royal Anointing Ritual*. Berlin, New York: Walter de Gruyter.

Green, Miranda (1989). *Symbol and Image in Celtic Religious Art*. London and New York: Routledge.

Joynt, Maud (1908). Echtra mac Echdach Mugmedóin. *Ériu* 4, 91–111.

Lerner, Gerda (1986). *The creation of Patriarchy*. New York and Oxford: Oxford University Press.

Mac Cana, Proinsias (1955–56/1958–59). Aspects of the theme of king and goddess in Irish literature. *Études Celtiques* 7, 76–114, 356–413; 8, 59–65.

—— (1970). *Celtic Mythology*. London and New York: Hamlyn.

—— (1980a). Women in Irish Mythology. *The Crane Bag* 4.1, 7–11.

—— (1980b). *The Learned Tales of Medieval Ireland*. Dublin: Dublin Institute for Advanced Studies.

McCone, Kim (1990). *Pagan Past and Christian Present*. Maynooth: An Sagart.

Meyer, Kuno (1901). Mitteilungen aus irischen Handschriften. *Zeitschrift für celtische Philologie* 3, 457–66.

—— Ferchuitred Medba. *Anecdota from Irish Manuscripts* 5: 17–22.

—— (1918). Das Ende von Baile in Scail aus Rawl. B 512. *Zeitschrift für celtische Philologie* 12, 231–38.

Murphy, Gerard (1937). Rev. of *Fontes historiae religionis Celticae*, ed. J. Zwicker. *Béaloideas* 7, 143–45.

—— (1952). On the dates of two sources used in Thurneysen's Heldensage. *Ériu* 16, 145–56.

Neumann, Erich (1963). *The Great Mother: An Analysis of the Archetype*, trans. Ralph Manheim. London, Boston: Routledge & Kegan Paul (2nd ed.).

Ó Cathasaigh, Tomás (1989). The Eponym of Cnogba. *Éigse* 23, 27–38.

Ó Corráin, D. (1972). *Ireland before the Normans*. Dublin: Gill and Macmillan.

—— (1978). Nationality and kingship in pre-Norman Ireland. *Nationality and the pursuit of national independence*, ed. T.W. Moody. Belfast: Appletree, 1–35.

Ó Máille, Tomás (1927). Medb Chruachna. *Zeitschrift für Celtische Philologie* 17, 129–46.

O'Neill, Joseph (1905). Cath Boinde. *Ériu* 2, 173–85.

O'Rahilly, T.F. (1943). On the Origin of the names *Érainn* and *Ériu*. *Ériu* 14, 7–28.

Ó Tuama, Seán and Thomas Kinsella (1981). *An Duanaire 1600–1900: Poems of the Dispossessed*. Dublin: Dolmen.

Simms, Katherine (1987). *From Kings to Warlords: The Changing Political Structure of Gaelic Ireland in the Later Middle Ages*. Woodbridge: Boydell Press.

Stevenson, Jane (1989). The Beginnings of Literacy in Ireland. *Proceedings of the Royal Irish Academy* 89C.6, 127–65.

Stokes, Whitley (1903). Echtra mac Echach Muigmedóin: The Adventure of the Sons of Eochaid Muigmedón. *Revue Celtique* 24, 190–203.

Trindade, W.A. (1986). Irish Gormlaith as a sovereignty figure. *Etudes Celtiques* 23, 143–56.

Wormald, P. (1986). Celtic and Anglo-Saxon kingship: some further thoughts. *Sources of Anglo-Saxon Culture*, ed. P.E. Szarmach. Kalamazoo: Western Michigan University Medieval Institute, 151–83.

EMILY LYLE

A Line of Queens as the Pivot of a Cosmology

In this study I develop a thesis I have been working on for some time concerning a specific old world cosmology, the society that lived in terms of it, and the deities in its pantheon (see Lyle 1990; forthcoming a). The society is marked by the presence of sovereignty, and I have already outlined a process of alternate succession by which a king of one generation comes from one of two segments of society and a king of the next comes from the other (1990: 119–33). It appears, too, that in a sense each king rules jointly with his predecessor of the previous generation who has been transformed into a king of the dead. The human kings mirror and are mirrored by the kings of the gods who are, in the Greek instance, Zeus and Hades.

What of the queens, both human and divine? I have found that the female aspect in the cosmology is an all-encompassing one and that it is manifested as a mother-daughter pair (1990: 16–23, 113–14). Here I shall argue that both the females are queens and that the line of descent from mother to daughter is the pivot of the system of sovereignty which is central to the society and its cosmology.

I shall concentrate especially on Ireland, which is particularly fruitful ground for an enquiry into the question of the power of queens. Georges Dumézil was moved to comment on the place of women in his structure—which is the basis of my own—after exploring stories about the Irish queen Medb and an Indian parallel figure called Mādhavī (1973: 106–7):

> Will it be possible to propose a sociological or psychological interpretation of this structure? Today such an attempt holds only risks. But even now, precautions can be taken against one risk: to judge from the vocabulary of kinship, the oldest Indo-European societies were composed of families defined strictly in relation to the males, to fathers, and sons, and

husbands. Accordingly, there is little chance that the
conduct of the proud queen Medb, and that of her humble
Indian sister Mādhavī, will carry us back to the nebula of
matriarchy.

It would now be generally agreed that matriarchy is not an
appropriate concept, but we might debate whether or not a society
with a cosmological structure that gives an important place to
queens is a "gylany", in the word coined by Riane Eisler (1990:
105) to denote a society with an equal balance between men
and women. Dumézil's comment on the Indo-European male-
oriented kinship terms could apply to the general population—
which could have had patrilineal or cognatic descent—without
necessarily being relevant to the royal house—which could have
had matrilineal descent—for, as Wendy James has noted in an
article on "Matrifocus in African Societies" (1978: 143), "the two
apparently alternative modes of unilineal descent" may be present
together.

In the same article James has some interesting comments on
matrilineal descent and on how the presence of matriliny affects
the way women are viewed (149):

We . . . mean by "matriliny" a principle whereby, in the
thinking of the people under discussion, a connection between
one generation and the next is made, for whatever purpose,
systematically through females. This can be represented
diagrammatically (and interestingly, in contrast to diagrams
of patriliny, the females cannot be left out of the diagram!).
Even in the sketchiest of matrilineal diagrams, the females are
clearly more than unmarked links between men; they are
nodal points. Even on the diagram, the "position" of every
individual, men no less than women, is definable only with
reference to females, and the continuity of the society as a
whole, through the generations, must be represented through
them. Now society is more than a diagram; and where the
matrilineal principle is enshrined, for whatever practical or
symbolic purpose, the nodal position held by women must be
more than a diagrammatic matter. There must surely be
evaluative connotations, even a theory of the central focus
provided by women in the definition of social relations
stemming from the matrilineal principle. The granting of a
key position to women in the logical, formal ordering of wider
relations surely invites us to look further, not necessarily for
"female rule" in a crude power sense, but for equally strong
affirmations of the central qualities, even the primacy, of
women's position.

In Figure 1, kinship diagrams of the kind referred to by James are used to express the link between one generation and the next. Figure 1a shows a son succeeding his father without any representation of the female, and Figure 1b shows a nephew succeeding his mother's brother, that is, a male succeeding through a female. Another way for a male to succeed through a female involves affinity as well as descent, and Figures 1ci and 1cii show a son-in-law succeeding his father-in-law. This is a not uncommon form of inheritance but generally it is only when a man lacks a son that the succession passes to a daughter's husband, and so it occurs sporadically (see, e.g., Goody, Thirsk and Thompson 1976: 10, 44, 122, 125–6, 131).

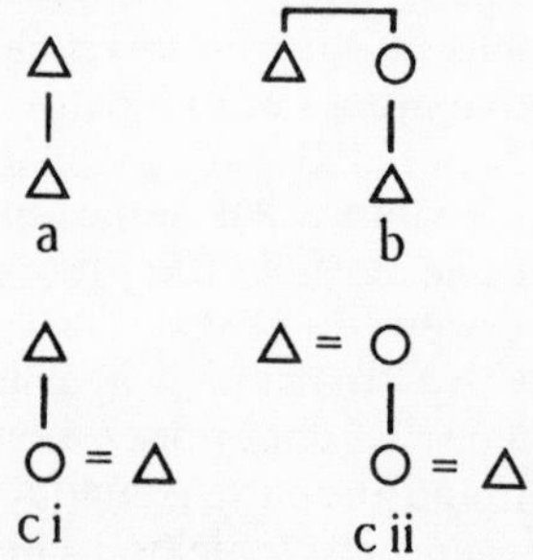

Figure 1

Inheritance obviously passes by means of the female in both the nephew and son-in-law cases but it is as well to be cautious about placing emphasis on the female line. Keesing warns (1975: 63) that "because men control key political power in a matrilineal system, it is misleading to speak of descent as passing from mother to daughter; instead, one can better think of descent as passing from a woman's brother to her son" or, comparably, one might add, in the son-in-law case one can think of succession as passing from a woman's father to her husband as shown in Figure 1ci. It seems, however, that it would be unduly clumsy not to express descent as from mother to daughter in a situation where inheritance by son-in-law was the regular practice instead of an option occasionally called into play. In that case, steadily, throughout the generations, daughter would succeed mother[1] while a man could inherit only through marriage into the female line as shown in Figure 1cii.

Perhaps there would be less debate about whether such a

pattern should be expressed as mother-daughter descent than about whether this form of inheritance occurs at all, for, although it was explored at the beginning of this century in the context of history and legend by J.G. Frazer who speaks of a system of royalty where "the kings are elective and the queens hereditary" (1905: 257), it does not seem to have attracted much current interest. However, it is certainly a conceivable form of inheritance, and it is one that makes complete sense in the context of alternate succession to the kingship: where a son *cannot* succeed his father since the succession must pass to a segment which does not include the son, direct royal succession can be secured only through the female line. Each king would then be an inmarrying affine (cf. Schneider and Gough 1961: 8–29).

Now that the notions of descent from mother to daughter and son-in-law succession have been considered, it will be possible to model a society which had this type of succession in its royal house and see how it can be understood as having arisen from a society operating in terms of kinship rather than sovereignty. As a first step, we can explore the place of the mother-daughter pair in the cosmogony.

It is generally thought that the Irish cosmogony has been lost (cf. Mac Cana 1970: 132–4; Condren 1989: 222) but this is perhaps to paint too gloomy a picture, since the method I have been using does appear to have succeeded in eliciting at least some parts of the cosmogony. The method rests on recognition of the point that, where there is a network of correspondences, there is a high level of redundancy with the result that, if a piece of information is not available in one register, it may be recovered through reference to another. So far as the surviving record goes, Ireland does not, like Greece, have a story of the birth of a god, sky, from a goddess, earth, and the subsequent birth of their descendants, but it does have an exceedingly interesting complex centred on the figures of Boand and Clothru which appears to offer the outline of a comparable theogony.

The story of the birth of the sons of Boand seems to be an expression of the creation of time rather than of space, as in the Greek myth. Boand, whose name is that of the River Boyne, gives birth to three sons whose names are those of the three types of music a skilled harper was expected to be able to play: Súantraige, Gentraige and Goltraige—music that induces sleep, music that provokes laughter and music that provokes sorrow. I have argued from other Irish material and from Greek parallels that these three types of music can be associated with the three Indo-European seasons of spring, summer and winter (1990: 26–32) and it is on

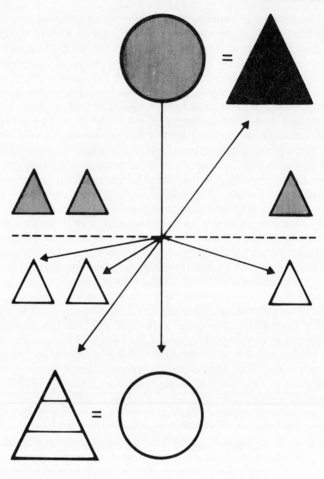

Figure 2

these grounds that I would say that Boand gives birth to the three
components of the period of the year, which is generally to be
regarded in cosmological studies as an analogue of the whole of
time. According to the theogonic structure I have already studied
(1990: 111–15), the birth of three sons to the primal goddess
completes the number of the old gods, and to bring the young gods
into existence all three of the males must have intercourse with the
one female. Although there are other scattered indications of this
unusual begetting, the story of Clothru is a key one of this type

that I have used in building up my general picture of old world theogony. I suggest that we set the stories of Boand and Clothru side by side and see them as giving different names to the same deities, with the Boand aspect of the goddess giving birth to the three males in the first part of the theogonic sequence, and the three males lying with the Clothru aspect of the goddess in the conception story that precedes the culminating birth which brings the young gods into existence.

The males are first identified as kinds of music and, if I am correct in my inference, are identified at the same time as spring, summer and winter. The males who lie with Clothru are her brothers called Nar, Bres and Lothar, names which Bruce Lincoln has translated as Noble, Combat and Washing Vessel (1986: 160–1). The son born of the multiple conception, Lugaid of the Red Stripes, has a head like Nar, body from neck to waist like Bres, and body below the waist like Lothar, so that we can say that in the microcosm of the human body Nar relates to head, Bres to body above the waist and Lothar to body below the waist. When we draw on microcosmic-macrocosmic correspondence, the three males can be seen as relating also to the three cosmic levels, and this is in keeping with comparative material which indicates that the first phase of the cosmogony brings the cosmic levels into existence. Time and space, then, can be seen as having emerged from the Boand/Clothru goddess who also conceives through intercourse with her three sons and gives birth to the young gods.

The entire pantheon is illustrated in Figure 2. Above the dashed line is the domain of the old gods, and the primal goddess is shown here along with her first three sons. Below the line, the large triangle represents the triple king figure who is Lugaid in the Clothru story. Parallel birth narratives, including a Welsh one in the Fourth Branch of the *Mabinogi* (Lyle 1989a), indicate that there are four other sons, three corresponding to the three fathers and one especially tied to the triple king as a twin king who rules the dead. This son is a maverick who joins the old gods in their domain instead of being grouped with his siblings to whom he is linked only by birth (cf. Lyle 1990: 62–5), and it is assumed here that he joins the old gods through marriage with his mother. This god brings darkness into the world and his siblings bring light, and this is indicated by the use of black and white in the figure for these gods, while grey is used for the gods of the earlier generations.

When we turn attention to the daughter who corresponds to the mother just as three of the sons correspond to their fathers, Irish legend also provides a figure who can be identified as this goddess—the Queen Medb referred to by Dumézil. The man she takes in marriage, she says, must be without jealousy, without fear and without avarice, and, as Dumézil has shown (1973: 86–7, 90–2, 106–9, 114), this indicates that the man she marries will have the virtues appropriate to each of the three functions of the sacred, physical force and prosperity, and that he will accordingly be the triple Lugaid figure. Although Medb is said in Irish pseudo-history to be a sister of Clothru (Dumézil 1973: 101–3), this marriage with the triple king places her among the young gods, and so we should see her as daughter rather than as sister of the Boand/Clothru goddess.

The bizarre happenings outlined here cannot directly reflect human family relationships, and I see the theogony as a means of expressing social relationships, rather than family ones, within a society which has a specific form of sovereignty with two queens, the younger of whom is married to the living king and the older of whom has a symbolic marriage with the dead king who was formerly her husband. My previous work on the encompassing female has indicated that the place of the female is at a mid-point (1990: 23, 86–91), so how is it possible for two queens to be placed in the structure? The answer seems to be that there are two mid-points, each of which is the location of a palace where a queen resides. It may seem odd to have two "centres" but this is actually what turns up in the Irish material, as is amply demonstrated by Alwyn and Brinley Rees (1961: 146–63), and I think we are now in a position to extend our understanding of this feature.

The two centres are Uisnech and Tara. Uisnech, which means navel and is at the geographical centre of Ireland, is associated with the female and with beginnings and so is appropriate to the old queen, who has no living consort, and to the primal goddess, Boand/Clothru. Tara I would see as at the mid-point of a circuit of the periphery. Going clockwise round the western and northern provinces of Connacht and Ulster at the top of the diagram, which correspond to the summer part of the year (Lyle 1990: 80), one arives at Tara before traversing the eastern and southern provinces of Leinster and Munster. Tara is well known as the place of the king's inaugural wedding feast (cf. Mac Cana 1970: 92–4; 1979: 448–53), and it is clearly appropriate to the young queen, whom the king marries, and to the young goddess, Medb.

In Figure 3, the two centres are shown in the approximate locations of Uisnech and Tara on the map of Ireland. It should be mentioned, however, that it is unlikely that prehistoric Ireland ever had a king ruling from Tara (Byrne 1973: 57). What we have is a conceptual pattern which may have applied in reality at the level of small-scale tribal kingdoms, but is available to us through

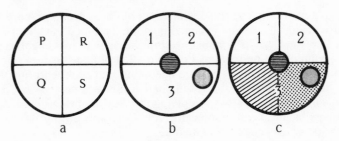

Figure 3

written documents that refer to the whole island, which is a bounded entity well adapted for ideas of totality to be inscribed upon it. The diagram based on the map of Ireland is used here for the expression of ideas about a whole community, of whatever size. The kinship relationships discussed below can legitimately be set out on a spatial plan, since the people belonging to tribal units can, when they choose, convey these relationships by disposing themselves spatially, as, for example, in a camp or on a dancing ground (cf. Needham 1962: 254–5; Maddock 1989: 47–9).

Now that we have traced the mother and daughter goddesses in the theogony and seen how the human queens that correspond to them can relate to two centres in a territory, we can return to the matter of the line of descent from mother to daughter and regular son-in-law succession and see how this exceptional form of inheritance could have arisen when a type of society held together by bonds of kinship was modified in such a way that the bonding was provided by the marriages of kings and queens alone (Lyle 1989b). The same transformation could also account for the conceptual division of Indo-European society into the three groups consisting of priests, warriors and cultivators that Dumézil has studied in terms of his three functions of the sacred, physical force and prosperity (cf. Turner 1982 and Allen 1987).

The type of society referred to is the segmentary one consisting of four patri-groups known today in Australia, which is characterised by fluidity as marriage exchanges are carried out and the different segments interact also in ritual and economic terms. It seems as if sovereignty came into being simultaneously with a loss of fluidity when a society like this was "stopped" in the way I shall outline below.[2]

As part of an interchange of services, at a particular time men belonging to two patri-groups, called here P and R (see Figure 3), may engage in ritual on behalf of the community, men of the P group performing the ritual while men of the R group prepare for and manage the event. When things are "stopped" in the way I referred to, a group remains fixed in the activity it is engaged in, the group of the performers becoming that of first-function priests and the group of the managers becoming that of second-function warriors. The men of the other half, QS, become the group of third-function cultivators, supplying the wealth of the community, perhaps having been responsible for provisions during the ritual occasion when society "stopped".

It seems that, while the three male deities among the old gods and the three corresponding young gods relate to the three differentiated groups formed in this way, the sovereign deities relate to the marriage-exchange function of the community. At the time of "stopping," a woman in the S quarter marries, and from this time on the queens come from this quarter, or rather from the palace now associated with it, which corresponds to Tara. This woman's mother is in the Q quarter and has the role of old queen. Men of the QS half are not eligible to be the husbands of the queens since they belong to the same kin group. The P and R quarters take it in turn by generation to present young men as candidates for kingship, one of whom marries the princess who becomes queen on marriage.

A major change in structuring is that the society now has a superior core instead of a system of exchange between equals, and this is symbolised apparently by the creation of centres. Kenneth Maddock has recently shown (1989) how fours and eights are typical of non-hierarchical societies, as illustrated in Figure 3a, while uneven numbers relate to hierarchical ones, and here we have a fivefold system doubled into the tenfold one we have seen in the pantheon. There are three regions and two palaces, one of which, the palace of the king and the young queen, is at Tara at the mid-point of the periphery, and the other, that of the old queen and the dead king, is at Uisnech at the centre, as indicated in Figure 3b. However, the connection of a palace with the segment from which the prototypical queen came appears to have been maintained, as indicated in Figure 3c, and this accounts for some of the associations of the provinces of Leinster and Munster as discussed by Rees and Rees (1961: 118–40). Of the sovereign deities, Medb and the Lugaid figure (the god Lug) relate to the peripheral palace at Tara, and Boand/Clothru and the god of the dead (Donn) relate to the central palace at Uisnech.

On the human level, a princess becomes queen when she marries the man who defeats her father in a contest and kills him (cf. Lyle 1990: 130–3). Eventually her husband the king is killed in turn and she moves, as if to a dower house, to the palace at Uisnech, leaving possession of Tara to her daughter and her daughter's husband. The whole pattern is the stuff of romance, and that is no wonder when romances, especially those of King Arthur, were built from this material. The primary narratives in the case of the old queen appear to deal with birth, like those of Boand and Clothru noted above. The primary narratives in the case of the young goddess appear to be, firstly, that of the contest through which she is won in marriage, of which one example is the story of the winning of Hippodamia by Pelops (Lyle 1990: 130–1; cf. de Pontfarcy 1987: 204), and, secondly, that of her abduction by the king of the otherworld and the dead, of which the famous Greek version is the story of Persephone, and of which there are many instances in early Celtic tales and their analogues in romance (cf. Schoepperle 1960: 417–30; Lyle 1979; 1981).

Although I found it convenient to speak of society "stopping" as a graphic way of capturing the transition from one social mode to another, it will be as well to articulate this idea also in other terms before turning finally to a brief consideration of the balance of power in the newly-formed society. In the earlier, pre-class society, an individual performs various roles.[3] For example, to take the three roles relevant to the present discussion, a man could have from time to time the role of performer of a ritual, the role of manager of a ritual, or the role of provider of a feast. The change consists in applying these familiar individual roles analogously to society in such a way that it is now only society as a whole which has the capacity to perform ritual, undertake guardianship and provide the necessary wealth. The individual man belongs to a specific group which is tied to, or has a particular association with, one of these three roles.[4] The important roles in relation to marriage and the life cycle that have been adopted by the sovereigns of the society are wife, widow, husband, and dead man, although naturally these life-cycle stages continue to relate to non-royal individuals also. There is no question, I think, of one of the two transitions discussed above taking place without the other; they are interlocked. The queens are supplied by the half of the cultivators, and the segments of the priests and warriors in the other half take turns to supply the living king, the husband of the young queen. The two halves are welded together by the royal marriage.

What can be inferred about gender relationships in the society that has been modelled? Women, through the queens, are symbolically connected with the cultivators, and their half, by an analogy I have studied previously (1990: 33, 86–91), is related to the below while the "male" half of the priests and warriors which supplies the kings is related to the above. Since it seems that above is universally perceived as superior to below, I think we must say that there is a certain hierarchy here and that queens and cultivators are regarded as inferior to kings and priests/warriors in certain respects. At the same time the whole structuring implies a necessary complementariness of the "male" and "female" halves (cf. Lyle 1991), and due weight should also be given to the primacy and centrality of the female. On the whole, it seems rather likely that any superiority ascribed to the male in the society with this balanced structure was a relatively slight one.

It should be observed that, since women are linked with the cultivator class, a drop in the value of one would potentially be paralleled by a drop in the value of the other. The matrilineal succession of the sovereigns with a line of queens into which the kings married probably guaranteed an important place in the system to the group of cultivators which developed from, and was analogically associated with, the kin of the women who became queens. While matrilineal royal succession continued, the group of cultivators which stood in the place of the queen's kin would have been assured, I suggest, of a certain status and, conversely—if we can draw an analogy from the results of Alice Schlegel's researches in the domestic sphere—the strength of the cultivators vis-à-vis the priests/warriors would have guaranteed a degree of freedom to the queens. Schlegel found that "domestic power declines as it disperses" and that a woman has greater autonomy when neither her husband nor her brother is dominant than when either of them is dominant over the other (1972: 134–5). Similarly, as long as the cultivators, corresponding to the brothers, counterbalanced the priests/warriors who provided the husbands, the queens (the sisters and wives) would have had autonomy, and perhaps we can see this reflected in the position of the "proud queen Medb" mentioned above. Clearly, the rise of class distinctions is a vast topic that cannot be explored here, but it may be noted that a tipping of the balance in favour of the kings could have led simultaneously to the subjugation of the cultivator class and of women, and that such a change could have been brought about by a shift to patrilineal royal succession.

In the cosmological society in which old world culture was shaped, the human and the divine reflected each other in such a way that we can read its messages, including those about gender, on both levels. The two goddesses in the pantheon do not have the range of roles that the more numerous gods do, but both are central, the primal goddess being the source of everything, and her daughter motivating the actions of the gods as she is battled over, abducted and rescued. Similarly, in the human sphere, the sequence of queens forms an unbroken line that serves as the pivot of the sovereignty and provides the continuity between generations for the whole of society.

The present article is a sketch only and is necessarily speculative since the field of cosmological studies as it relates to the archaic old world is in an early stage of development. However, it clearly raises important issues, and I hope that these can soon be debated in the light of increased understanding of how cosmologies operate and of how theoretical structures can best be related to the historical record.

NOTES

1 This mode of succession would apparently involve both unigeniture—the selection of one daughter when there was more than one—and also the possibility of drawing on a wider pool of female relatives when no daughter was available.

2 For detailed discussion of the proposed transition, see Lyle forthcoming b, and also an earlier formulation (Lyle 1989b) which it partly supersedes.

3 I was made aware of the importance of roles in this connection by some remarks in Turner 1984: 360, which I quote in Lyle 1990: 132.

4 The three groups may have fulfilled the roles on the everyday level of practice or on the symbolic level.

REFERENCES

Allen, N.J. (1987). The Ideology of the Indo-Europeans: Dumézil's Theory and the Idea of a Fourth Function. *International Journal of Moral and Social Studies* 2, 23–39.

Byrne, Francis John (1973). *Irish Kings and High Kings*. London: Batsford.

Condren, Mary (1989). *The Serpent and the Goddess: Women, Religion, and Power in Celtic Ireland*. San Francisco: Harper and Row.

Dumézil, Georges (1973). *The Destiny of a King*. Chicago and London: University of Chicago Press.

Eisler, Riane (1990 [1987]). *The Chalice and the Blade*. London: Unwin, Mandala.

Frazer, J.G. (1905). *Lectures on the Early History of the Kingship*. London: Macmillan.

Goody, Jack, Joan Thirsk and E.P. Thompson (1976). *Family and Inheritance: Rural Society in Western Europe, 1200–1800*. Cambridge: Cambridge University Press.

James, Wendy (1978). Matrifocus on African Women. In *Defining Females: The Nature of Women in Society*, ed. Shirley Ardener, pp. 140–62. London: Croom Helm.

Keesing, Roger M. (1975). *Kin Groups and Social Structure.* New York: Holt, Rinehart and Winston.

Lincoln, Bruce (1986). *Myth, Cosmos, and Society: Indo-European Themes of Creation and Destruction.* Cambridge, Mass., and London: Harvard University Press.

Lyle, Emily (1979). *Sir Orfeo* and the Recovery of Amis from the Otherworld in *Guy of Warwick. Neuphilologische Mitteilungen* 80, 65–8.

—— (1981). Orpheus and Tristan. *Medium Aevum* 50, 305–8.

—— (1989a). A Theogonic Interpretation of the Fourth Branch of the *Mabinogi. Cosmos* 5, 142–50.

—— (1989b). Two Triads and a Revolution. *Shadow* 6, 66–74.

—— (1990). *Archaic Cosmos: Polarity, Space and Time.* Edinburgh: Polygon.

—— (1991). Markedness and Encompassment in Relation to Indo-European Cosmogony. In *Perspectives on Indo-European Language, Culture and Religion: Studies in Honor of Edgar C. Polomé.* ed. Roger Pearson, 1.38–63. McLean, Virginia: The Institute for the Study of Man.

—— (forthcoming a). Broadening the Perspective on Dumézil's Three Functions. In *Indo-European Religious Studies after Georges Dumézil,* ed. Edgar C. Polomé. McLean, Virginia: The Institute for the Study of Man.

—— (forthcoming b). From Kinship System to Tripartite Political Structure. *Shadow* 9.

Mac Cana, Proinsias (1970). *Celtic Mythology.* London: Hamlyn.

—— (1979). *Regnum* and *Sacerdotium*: Notes on Irish Tradition. *Proceedings of the British Academy* 65, 443–79.

Maddock, Kenneth (1989). Numerical Schemes in Society and the Cosmos. *Shadow* 6, 43–53.

Needham, Rodney (1962). Genealogy and Category in Wikmunkan Society. *Ethnology* 1, 223–64.

de Pontfarcy, Yolande (1987). Two Late Inaugurations of Irish Kings. *Études Celtiques* 24, 203–8.

Rees, Alwyn and Brinley (1961). *Celtic Heritage: Ancient Tradition in Ireland and Wales.* London: Thames and Hudson.

Schlegel, Alice (1972). *Male Dominance and Female Autonomy.* HRAF Press.

Schneider, David M. and Kathleen Gough (1961). *Matrilineal*

Kinship. Berkeley, Los Angeles and London: University of California Press.

Schoepperle, Gertrude (1960 [1913]). *Tristan and Isolt: A Study of the Sources of the Romance*. New York: Burt Franklin.

Turner, David H. (1982). Caste Logic in a Clan Society: An Aboriginal Response to Domination, In *Aboriginal Power in Australian Society*, ed. Michael C. Howard, pp. 32–54. St Lucia, London and New York: University of Queensland Press.

Turner, Terence (1984). Dual Opposition, Hierarchy, and Value: Moiety Structure and Symbolic Polarity in Central Brazil and Elsewhere. In *Différences, valeurs, hiérarchie: textes offerts à Louis Dumont*, ed. Jean-Claude Galey, pp. 335–70. Paris: École des Hautes Études en Sciences Sociales.

M. C. JEDREJ

Rain Makers, Women, and Sovereignty in the Sahel and East Africa

It is now generally recognized that in reports about sovereignty and power in non-Western societies we may be discovering little more than our own assumptions and discourse about the "male" nature of political power (Moore 1988: 133). Anthropological research has been biased not only because the researchers and their informants are frequently men but also because of the colonial circumstances of the fifty-year period of modern anthropological research, roughly from the early twenties to the late sixties. This was a period of normalizing colonial rule which worked to amplify anthropological research as the classification of types of social structure and the codification of a supposed customary law of the subjugated peoples. The work was done with the approval of colonial authorities, sometimes by their own personnel after anthropological training, but often at their invitation and with their material support. The government's interest was in identifying in the indigenous societies points where bureaucratic controls might be engaged (Asad 1973). In this setting it is to be expected that the representation of women and alternative idioms of power, and especially supreme power, will, in Ardener's (1975) terms, be muted, or classified under some other category such as magical techniques. In Africa this has, to some extent, been the fate of so-called rain making rituals, although there is considerable evidence pointing to the prominence of women in such institutions and therefore to their participation in power and sovereignty. Perhaps the most renowned is the Lovedu queen, described by the Kriges in their monograph *The Realm of a Rain Queen* (1943). However, I want to begin with the experience of weather of certain African people and with how this experience is articulated as a language of political power.

The first point that needs to be made is that there is no useful correlation between rainfall distribution and the distribution of rain making institutions. Thus rain making institutions are to be found not only in the Sahel and even Sahara (Dieterlen 1951, Chapelle 1957, Holy 1974) but also among people of eastern Zaire whose land is blessed with rich soils and plentiful rainfall, averaging over 1300mm per annum (Packard 1981: 25). It is also evident that the unreliability of rainfall is not a sufficient condition for the emergence and persistence of rain making institutions. Thus people who used to inhabit an area of rainfall scarcity and unreliability may continue to practice the art of rain making after migration to an area of adequate and reliable rainfall (Akong'a 1987: 72).

All writers point to the ambivalent attributes of rain as experienced by subsistence agriculturalists in this region of Africa. This is evident in Packard's study of Bashu and their ritual leaders. Here despite the high annual average rainfall in a zone characterized by two rainfall maxima per annum Bashu have to contend with variations from year to year affecting quantity, quality and periodicity of rainfall. However, the total annual amount may be of less concern than the periodicity of the rains—starting too late and/or not finishing on time. Here the break between the two maxima is very important for the ripening and harvesting of certain crops, notably pulses. The quality of rain is also very important. The Bashu require what they call in their invocations "soft rain" (*mbula nzolo*). The same amount of rain, but arriving as a thunderstorm sometimes even accompanied by hail, can destroy a crop of millet in minutes. As Packard notes, despite the apparent lushness of their environment the Bashu live in a world in which plenty and famine can and do follow one another unpredictably (Packard 1981: 25–6).

Another notable feature of the experience of rain is the localised nature of precipitation. For instance, for Uduk dwelling in the upper Nile region near the Ethiopian borderlands, rainfall showers, though averaging about 1000mm pa, are not only irregular in terms of frequency, but are often highly localized and geographically erratic. The region is a fairly uniform plain draining to the White Nile swamps in the west, but it is broken by numerous hills rising perhaps 300 metres above the plain, and this results in localized showers in the vicinity of the hills. During the rainy season it seems that the hills are often under cloud and that rain spreads out from them into the surrounding plain. These named hills are associated with particular settlements. It is in this setting that a farmer can see rain falling on the fields of a neighbouring village while the crops in his own fields wilt from lack of water. Moreover, the rain, when it does fall, rarely falls as a gentle continuous precipitation soaking a grateful earth. Most of it comes in short intense downpours accompanied by wind, thunder and lightning. Such storms may cause a good deal of damage to crops and houses and people may even be killed. Thus, though rain is vital and beneficial, it cannot be dissociated in the experience of the people from danger and destruction (James 1972).

Therefore individuals who are recognized as having an ability to control rain are attributed with a highly ambivalent power which, in subsistence economies, impinges on the lives of everyone. What is striking is that such individuals, unlike people with extraordinary abilities in other areas of life, such as healing or divination, almost always exercise political power and authority. Moreover, to the extent that the weather is experienced as benign or malignant and therefore indicative of the general state of the community, its moral well being, then all persons embedded in relatively dense networks of social relations are of some influence in the community and are believed to have some effect over the weather in general and rainfall in particular.

It is, therefore, the political quality of indigenous meteorological institutions which accounts for their distribution and persistence rather than the physical properties of the climatic environment with which people may have to contend. In a study of the way one ethnic group, the Alur, have extended their domination over adjacent peoples, Southall has noted that rain power is an aspect of political power and that the efficacy of rain making is inherent in the lineages of the ruling group. Political authority abstracted from the institutional complex and idiom of rain making does not exist among Alur (Southall n.d.: 94–5). In Zimbabwe the role of chiefs does not cease after their death when they become *mhondoro* (lion); indeed it appears to become more onerous, as they are now considered to be the source of the fertility of the land itself and the provider, or withholder, of rain. *Mhondoro* participate in the affairs of the living through spirit mediums who are addressed by the title *samvura*, "owner of the rain" (Lan 1985: 72). By the same token, those enjoying sovereign powers which are not expressed as a rain making cult appreciate the threat posed by the appearance within their domains of such techniques and their practitioners. For example, a definite boundary to the spread of rain making techniques can be detected along the Nile-Zaire watershed. The Azande ruling houses deliberately discourage the importation of rain magic. Azande chiefs and princes look upon rain magic with grave suspicion and anyone suspected of having acquired such magic will be harshly dealt with if a drought occurs (Seligman 1932: 521; de Schlippe 1952: 159–60).[1]

That rain magic is an idiom of political power rather than applied meteorology is also evident in the fact that invariably each rain maker is embedded in a power hierarchy (Wagner 1949; James 1972; Lan 1985). Moreover, though rainmaker is the usual term, the connotations of this gloss are misleading since the vernacular expressions describe the individuals as using their power to "hold up the rain" and are therefore supplicated and begged to cease doing so and thereby allow the rain to fall. If, after a rain maker has been approached in this manner and tribute paid, the rain does not fall, that is because a more powerful rain maker is continuing to withhold the rain and so supplication accompanied by greater tribute must be made. If the rain still does not fall, then approaches may have to be made to a yet more powerful rain maker. Such hierarchies frequently extend to embrace several different ethnic groups.

The failure of rains is then a real test of the political weight and relative authority of leaders in the community and wider society. In the course of this process the political credit of leaders may collapse completely; the people may turn against them and it is not unknown for rain makers to be killed. On the other hand, the power and authority of other rain makers may be enormously enhanced, as is their command over material resources through tribute payments, fees, placatory gifts and the like.[2]

Given that these hierarchies may transcend ethnic boundaries, it is hardly surprising that rain magic is widely diffused, and, while variations in technical details may be found within one culture area, remarkably similar techniques have been reported from regions which are geographically and culturally quite distant. Packard has drawn attention to the similarity between Bashu rain making techniques in Eastern Zaire and those of the Madi in southern Sudan (Packard 1981: 211). The cultural complex involving rain stones (sometimes referred to as thunder stones), metal objects, horns and the like extends west across the Sahelian zone (Keletigui 1948). Consistent with this are myths and local histories of origin identifying the first rain magician as a stranger, someone from outwith the community or ethnic group (Wagner 1949: 153–4; Seligman 1932: 247 n.1). The rain stones characteristically possessed by a rain maker are categorized as male and female, the latter bringing soft, gentle rain and the former storms, thunder and lightning. Stones are fed on the blood of sacrifices, and they gain in power and effectiveness the wider the area from which the sacrificial victims are contributed.

Male and female are also evident as regards the important theme of the hereditary nature of the virtue with which the rain makers are attributed and which makes their manipulation of the rain stones or other objects efficacious. In the Upper Nile this frequently involves dogmas of bilateral filiation, so that only a person whose father and mother are themselves descended from rain makers can be recognized as a rain maker. In some instances this may require inter-ethnic marriages between rain makers to ensure a successor (Seligman 1932: 328). Women rain makers or women as prominent actors in such processes are found in the Sahel, the Upper Nile and throughout East Africa.

For example, among the Lotuko on the east bank of the upper Nile in the Sudan each territorial group comprising several villages is represented by a rain maker who is referred to in colloquial Arabic as "sultan." The vernacular term is *kobu* (masc.) or *nobu* (fem.), since the rain maker may be either a man or a woman. In order to be a *kobu*, the rain maker must be born of parents who were themselves both rain makers. However, it is not only a matter of an inherited quality but is also a function of social relationships. A man so qualified succeeds to the office on the death of his father or elder brother, and a woman who is born of rain making parents can perform the rain making ceremonies when she has married a rain maker. A rain maker can only exercise his or her power on achieving social maturity, which for a woman means becoming a wife and mother and for a man means taking the place of his father. Female rain makers are not uncommon among Lotuko. Indeed the Seligmans' most important informant was such a female rain maker.

Lotuko mythology also testifies to the significance of women in rain making. Rain makers trace descent back to a figure who appeared on earth near a pool as rain and, taking the form of a man, married a woman called Colobus Monkey. When she was pregnant the personification of rain smeared saliva on her navel and then, leaving behind what are now recognized as the rainstones, disappeared back into the sky, where he is associated with thunder. Her child is regarded as the first rain maker. Today the crocodiles in the pool are believed to be the deceased rain makers, and gourds of this water are used in the rain-making rites. According to legend, a child born to a rain maker would be taken to the pool and left for three days. It remained unhurt because it was of the same clan as the crocodiles.

Since every rain maker should be the child of a woman "having rain" as well as of a rain maker father, and as clan exogamy is enforced, a *kobu* may have difficulty as regards an heir, and so marriages are frequently made with the daughters of Lokoiya and Acholi rain makers. A girl descended on both sides from rain makers is called *nongoti*, but as has been noted she takes no part in rain making ceremonies and has no power until she marries a rain maker. If she marries a man without rain, her children have no rain making powers.

The key features of the Lotuko rain making procedures may be worth describing since they are typical of what may be found throughout Sahelian and eastern Africa. The shrine containing the bones of the previous rain makers can be approached only by the rain maker and his/her assistant at the time appropriate for the ceremonies. A goat is killed and the stomach contents and some blood are thrown over the bones and skulls in several pots. Then the rainstones are smeared with stomach contents and blood. The stones are kept in clay pots at the side of the rain maker's house under a small roof of thatch. No one dare touch them. The party then proceeds to the sacred pool where another goat is killed, and a gourd of water is taken from the pool back to the rain stones. A third goat is killed and the stones are anointed with blood, stomach contents and fat. The rain makers spit into the water before pouring it over the stones. They also drink some water and then wash the stones in their hands before returning them to the pots. The gourd of water is then left beside the stones, and some ten days later the rain maker will pour the water over the stones. The rain makers then proceed to other houses where spears considered to be the relics of former rain makers are similarly rubbed with blood and stomach contents and aspersed with water from the sacred pool. All of this may seem bizarre and without meaning, but if it is recalled that rain makers are asked to cease withholding rain, to release it, so that the celestial and terrestrial may be in conjunction through rainfall, then these rites objectify and make concrete such abstract notions. The killing of the goat releases its life, and the residues of this separation, blood and stomach contents—the latter being part of the victim and also not yet part of the victim—represent transition in a state of being. They are brought into association with the rainstones—which are themselves residues from a mythological time of the fecund conjunction of the celestial (the personification of rain) with the terrestial woman—and with the relics (the bones) and spirits (the crocodiles, or rather the water from the pool in which they dwell) of the previous rainmakers, which are the links between the past and the present.

David Lan has described how, in Zimbabwe, sovereignty over land is associated with a vocabulary of rain making so that "the people whose ancestors bring the rain own the land" (1975: 98). Consequently, the spirit mediums through whom the spirits of the dead chiefs, *mhondoro*, speak became crucial in the war of liberation from colonial rule, which was in this respect a recapitulation of the late nineteenth-century wars in defense of their land from European settlers. In northern Zimbabwe, one particularly renowned spirit, Nehanda, a woman, was prominent through her female mediums both in the nineteenth-century wars and in the recent struggle for liberation. Guerrillas told Lan that "the medium was doing her command work, directing us in Zimbabwe . . . She led us in the war of liberation" (1975: 5).

In the Zimbabwe case, the male and female components are not imaged through notions of bilateral descent but expressed in terms of marriage and affinal relationships, of autochthonous people and subsequent conquering immigrants who find their wives, and so the ancestral mothers, among the former. A considerable amount of myth and ritual is concerned with the manipulation of the contradiction between the power of the conquerors and their dependence upon the rather different power of autochthons, so that a chiefly lineage is represented both as autochthon and conquering stranger. *Mhondoro* are usually men, but there are four powerful female *mhondoro*, and the most powerful male *mhondoro* have what Lan calls a "female aspect"; individuals are often referred to as the "woman who has the power. That is the one who makes the rain fall very heavily" (1975: 88). According to Lan, "Recent male lineal ancestors conquer. Distant female affinal ancestors bring rain" (1975: 89). But these distant female affines, wives, are of course also the mothers of the chiefly lineages, their source of life in a different sense.

A report from Kenya details a relatively unusual form in which women, among the Kamba of Kitui District of the Eastern Province, contribute to the domestication of weather. This District falls within the semi-arid region of Kenya with up to thirty inches of rain per annum in two rainfall maxima. The farmers practice a mixed agricultural and pastoral regime in which livestock form the basis of cash incomes. The district has experienced droughts and famines since at least the beginning of the colonial era, and food relief is an important means of survival for many familes during famine periods. In this region a women's spirit possession cult, though ostensibly addressed to the welfare of the individual members who have been called by the female spirit Nzambi, in fact also works for the general welfare of the community. Individual members of the cult may be informed through spiritual agency of the need to anticipate inadequate rainfall, and will be advised about the appropriate drought-resistant crops to plant. Moreover, since the weather is, it seems, some kind of indicator of the moral state of the society, the cult members may also learn the reasons why the rainfall will be poor that year. The cult members sacrifice a goat, and the head and skin are presented to an influential person of standing in the community selected by the members, which person must then undertake to provide a goat for the sacrifice the following year. It seems that such public activities of the cult are directed at the moral well being of the community, with the consequence of ensuring an adequate rainy season (Akong'a 1987: 77–81).

However, the most renowned instance where women, sovereignty and rain are linked in an institutional complex is that of the Lovedu queen in the Transvaal, as it was described in the nineteen thirties by the Kriges (Krige and Krige 1943). Various groups subordinate themselves to the Lovedu queen and to the ruling Lovedu nobility by supplicating the queen for rain and sending as tribute their sisters and daughters. These women, after a period at court, are then distributed by the queen as wives among the nobles who are her lineage brothers and among the chiefs of various subordinate groups. These marriages constitute the structure of political ranking and allegiances. Though the queen is known by such titles as "Transformer of Clouds and Changer of the Seasons," such powers are not enacted through dramatic rituals which switch on or off the rain. Rather, the weather is a matter of the queen's disposition and her careful and continuous attention to her conduct throughout the year. It is to the disposition of the queen that the people address themselves. For instance, when the people "dance for rain," as it is called, this is done for the queen in order to alter her feelings. The feelings of the queen and the quality of meteorological events seem to be aspects of a totality. At the same time, the queen works with several "rain doctors" who have special techniques to release rain, and they are often consulted in this capacity in their own right. But the queen may "stay their hands," as Lovedu say, and this can account for their lack of success. Similarly, the queen's effectiveness may be countered by the spirits of her dead predecessors. However, the queen does have secret magical substances kept in "rain pots" which, when correctly used, will release rain. The application of these substances seems to function as a kind of ritual purification, so when some procedure, such as a burial, has been identified by diviners as having been incorrectly and carelessly carried out, the substance may be aspersed on the grave. Sometimes the whole country is judged to have been spoiled, and so all fires are extinguished with water containing material from the rain pots and are then rekindled.

The rain queen, as a result of her allocation of wives to her noble kinsmen, stands in relation to them as cattle-linked sister, and accordingly embodies, at the level of the whole society, supreme sovereignty. The institution of cattle-linked sister is part of the social life of all Lovedu. According to Lovedu, the household and homestead of a brother has been created by the sister whose bridewealth cattle made possible that brother's own marriage. She was the means by which he acquired a wife. Consequently, such a sister has considerable authority over the affairs of her brother's household. Specifically, the sister has the power to protect the household from witchcraft, protection which she can, of course, withhold if she is so disposed. She also functions as a priestess who makes offerings to the household gods on behalf of her brother, and her displeasure may result in the spirits causing harm to the household. The sister is responsible for the division among his heirs of her brother's personal property when he dies, and during his lifetime is keeper of the emblems of any offices he may hold. For instance, if her brother is installed as a chief, then at the installation ceremony the emblems of office are presented to her, not to her brother. The web of asymmetrical links between households and lineages culminates in the households of the ruling nobles and ultimately in the figure of the queen, their cattle-linked sister.

The argument of this paper has been that political authority and political sovereignty are in many parts of Africa expressed through what may be called a meteorological idiom, and that in practice they are realized through institutional complexes loosely described as rain making rituals. However, the relationship to the political structure of any given society where these institutional complexes are found is not always straightforward. In general, they may either be constituted as an intrinsic capacity or quality of the prevailing rulers, or where rain making is not a component of a ruling group's powers, be perceived as a threat to the rulers and received with hostility by them. In this case, rain makers will appear from time to time among subordinate classes and groups. The role of women in these institutions in either of the two manifestations is by no means uncommon. Indeed, it may well be the case that the prominence of men in political affairs may be more apparent than real and due perhaps to a rather ethnocentric perspective on the part of the ethnographers as regards idioms of political domination and resistance to subordination.

NOTES

Some of the reports referred to in this paper detail observations made up to eighty years ago, and it is sometimes difficult to assess their contemporary relevance and significance. However, there are no theoretically compelling reasons to suppose that the institutions and techniques will have fallen into desuetude, and there are some reasons to suppose that recent historical developments might even favour their persistence. In southern Sudan, both the departure of the Christian missionaries and virtual breakdown of local authority constitute circumstances in which a reversion to traditional political-ritual leaders would seem to be predictable. Moreover, even in relatively stable and modernizing environments such as Kenya, there is empirical evidence of the enduring nature of at least some rain-making institutions. In the Kakamega District of western Kenya among the Banyore, there is recent confirmation of the persistence of a rain-making institution and its continued control by the same family. Wagner, conducting research in this part of Kenya more than fifty years ago, recorded an oral tradition explaining how one Nganye learnt from a stranger, a woman said to be from Nandi, how to make rain. Akong'a, carrying out field research in the same district in 1982, confirmed both the oral tradition and that the descendants of Nganye are still the only family in Banyore associated with rain making. Beattie (1964) found that rain makers were still busy a generation after Roscoe's (1923) observations in eastern Uganda. David Lan's (1985) study also confirms the persistence of such institutions in Zimbabwe.

1 The association of rain-makers with subordinated, even oppressed, groups is also indicated in Roscoe's observation that among the Ankole rain makers were to be found only among what he described as "the serf class" (Roscoe 1923). Similarly, among the neighbouring Baganda, women have the power to prevent storms and heavy rain (Roscoe 1911: 432).
2 The Zimbabwe instance is slightly different. "Each year offerings for rain are made at each *mhondoro's* shrine but the *mhondoro* is unable to produce the rain for his province by himself. The request must be sent up a chain of *mhondoro* until it reaches the most senior, the *mhondoro* who is in charge of the realm as a whole . . . to the 'head office' ", as it was explained, in an apt modern idiom, to Lan (1985: 74).

REFERENCES

Akong'a, J. (1987). Rain making rituals: a comparative study of two Kenyan societies. *African Study Monographs* (Kyoto) 8, 71–85.

Ardener, E. (1975). Belief and the problem of women, in J. la Fontaine (ed.) *The Interpretation of Ritual*. London: Tavistock.

Asad, T, (1973). *Anthropology and the Colonial Encounter*. London: Hurst.

Beattie, J. (1964). Rainmaking in Bunyoro. *Man* 64, 140–1.

Chapelle, J, (1957). *Nomades Noirs du Sahara*. Paris: Plon.

de Schlippe, P. (1956). *Shifting Cultivation in Africa. The Zande System of Agriculture*. London: Routledge and Kegan Paul.

Dieterlen, G. (1951). *Essai sur La Religion Bambara*. Paris: Plon.

Holy, L. (1974). *Neighbours and Kinsmen: the Berti people of Darfur*. London: Hurst.

James, W. (1972). The politics of rain control among the Uduk. In I. Cunnison and W. James (eds) *Essays in Sudan Ethnography*. London: Hurst.

Keletigui, M. (1948). Croyance soudanaise relatives a "pierre de foudre". *Notes africaines* 40, 27–29.

Krige, E.J. and J.D. Krige (1943). *The Realms of a Rain Queen*. London: Oxford University Press.

Lan, D. (1985). *Guns and Rain: guerrillas and spirit mediums in Zimbabwe*. London: Currey.

Madden, J.F. (1940). The exhumation of a Lotuka rain chief. *Sudan Notes and Records* 23, 351–4.

Moore, H.L. (1988). *Feminism and Anthropology*. Cambridge: Polity Press.

Packard, R. (1981). *Chiefship and Cosmology. An historical study of political competition*. Bloomington: Indiana University Press.

Roscoe, J. (1911). *The Baganda*. London: Macmillan.

—— (1923). *The Bakitara or Bunyoro*. Cambridge: Cambridge University Press.

Seligman, C.G. and B.Z. (1932). *Pagan Tribes of the Nilotic Sudan*. London: Routledge and Kegan Paul.

Southall, A. (n.d.). *Alur Society*. Cambridge: Heffer.

Wagner, G. (1949). *The Bantu of North Kavirondo*. London: International African Institute.

ANDREW DUFF-COOPER

Women and Sovereignty in Balinese Lombok and in Japan

The present chapter is intended as an empirical contribution to the study of women and power that explores some of the ways in which two "forms of sovereignty produce and are produced by the cartographies of gender relevant to their cultural circumstances," as Fradenburg puts it in her Introduction to this collection of essays on *Women and Sovereignty*. These forms of sovereignty derive from the ideology of the Balinese of western Lombok and from Japan.[1] Before we proceed, though, "women" and "sovereignty," as I understand them below, require short comment.

"Women," as a category, is of course usually contrasted with "men." Adult Balinese, however, can be either transvestites (*bantong, banci* [Duff-Cooper 1986b]), men, or women. These three categories are related non-transitively: depending upon the context, any may be assessed as "superior." In the present chapter, mainly women, and necessarily (cf. e.g. Rivière 1971: 64) but to a far lesser extent men, are focussed on.

"Sovereignty" brings to mind Dumézil's theory of the three social functions, priest, warrior, and farmer, that set the tone for archaic Indo-European society. This theory has been broadened by a further look at Dumézil's conjoined idea, that the powers to which the Indo-Europeans were subject were divided between the first two functions. For Needham (1980, chap. 5; 1985, chap. 8), this complementary governance (also dual sovereignty or diarchy) is an aspect of a globally incident partition of powers. It can be recognized under such pairs of labels as mystical/jural, religious/political, sacred/profane. The Balinese distinction *niskala/sakala*— what is generally essential, invisible, and timeless, and what generally material, visible, and in time respectively—can be assimilated to these dichotomies.

All the examples considered by Needham are public institutions (if the term is not pleonastic). But Japanese ideology suggests that a person's thoughts and feelings (*honné*) are as real as what is seen and heard (*tatemaé*), which is far more immediate and public. Balinese ideology, also, in distinguishing what is generally invisible from what can generally be seen does not suggest that either is less real than the other (though arguably in terms of closeness to a physical and/or ideational reference point, for instance, the former is to be treated more finely than the latter).[2]

This response to what is generally unseen is akin to the situation in Japan, where one should try to determine the *honné* behind the *tatemaé* so that in responding with propriety to appearance one does not inadvertently compromise what is "behind" it in some way.[3] "Sovereignty" is thus understood below as referring to some of the situations where Balinese and Japanese women exercise authority, are influential, or are otherwise of social significance in ways that are not always supposed to be seen, at least by outsiders.

Various such situations could on the face of it be described. Different reasons make it impossible to consider them all, though, so below the house, marriage, and mystical ideology alone are addressed. These are sufficient for the present purpose.

Our procedure is, first, to set out details concerning Balinese and Japanese women and houses, marriage, and aspects of mystical ideology. These two sets of data are then compared, through instances of specific relations.[4] Ideally these should range from symmetry, asymmetry, modes of partition, reflexivity, and transitivity, to alternation and other periodic modes, reversal (inversion), to analogy and homology. Only the first three just mentioned, though, are employed below, for reasons given there.[5]

Now, in the context of Balinese ideology "house" refers to the institution of the compound, *gria*, *puri*, *jero*, or *pakarangan*, depending upon the estate (*bangsa*, *varna*) of the local descent group (*seturunan*) holding rights in and residing in it. The empirical forms of the institution are variations on the theme of a group of brothers, their wives, and their married or unmarried sons and their unmarried daughters, and the married sons' wives and children. All honour forebears and other gods in a compound temple, but have separate living-quarters, cook on different fires, draw water from one or more wells, and bring goods including cash and/or services into, and dispose of them from, their respective families (but cf. Duff-Cooper 1986a) without consulting (the heads of) the other families residing in other living quarters sited, systematically (Duff-Cooper 1990b, chap. 4), in the compound.

The compound and the living quarters in it are the focus for work, both in the ricefields and gardens and in activities connected with the five kinds of rites (*yadnya*, sacrifices) that all Balinese should hold at the appropriate times.

In activity connected with rice-growing—the cultivation of the female deity Sri, which, however, in the *nini*, one of the goddess's representations, is made from more male than female stalks (e.g. Duff-Cooper 1987a; 1989)—and in the cultivation of such secondary crops as tobacco and cucumbers, women play an important role. Many of the activities they perform, such as weeding and harvesting, can also be done by men. Other activities connected with rice-growing, especially making offerings and planting the seedlings, are not properly done by men.

The reference to offerings re-introduces the sacrifices because all sacrifices require offerings. These are properly made only by women and transvestites. Women, as aspect of "female" (*pradhana*), are thus crucial to "work," including rites, as it is currently organized. This is especially so because whereas on Bali offerings can be bought, on Lombok they are not, nor are they exchanged for other goods and/or services.

Men also work in the fields. The only task they appear to have to carry out in rice-growing, as opposed to tasks they or women may carry out as it suits them, is fertilizing. During rites, men prepare the special food for guests and other people attending them.

Both offerings and this food are items of exchange. These items are thus made by both women and men, who have particular roles also in rice-growing. Men are an aspect of "male" (*purusa*). As in the bisexual icon Ardhanārīśvara (an icon exemplary of Balinese ideology [Duff-Cooper 1988c], and a representation of the conjoined female and male principles, *pradhanapurusa*, and also of Ida Sang Hyang Vidhi, the high or highest Balinese god), women as well as men constitute a necessary aspect of "work."

The duties of a woman include providing food and sweetmeats for her husband and children or grandchildren or siblings, as the case may be, and then afterwards for herself and her (women) helpers. This is particularly clear when a male or high status female guest is entertained by a family: its men socialize with the guests, the women provide refreshments and retire. When my friend Pak Care's father did the family cooking, Pak Care said his father was "like a woman."[6] A woman can thus cause chaos in a household if she withdraws these services, and married men, only half-jokingly it seems to me, often recall times in the past when they angered their wives, who stopped cooking for them, and relate what difficulties it caused them.

Women contribute to their families' economies in other ways. It

might be thought that what a woman contributes depends upon, or
is correlated with, her freedom to move outside the compound,
but this is not so. What a woman contributes in bringing goods,
cash, and/or services into a compound and her family are in my
experience much the same whether she has relatively much
freedom of movement (as a Sudra, non-"caste," married woman
has) or little (like a "caste," Brahmana, Ksatrya, or Vésia, married
woman).

The goods brought into a compound in this way comprise food-
stuffs and drinks in the main, but may also include cloth in various
forms, and other items like crockery. Women may also contribute
cash to the domestic economy (as implied in the last paragraph).
The money comes from selling the produce of the dry and wet
gardens and the pig(s) they husband. Women sell this garden
produce at markets or in more or less permanent stalls in their
compounds; pigs are sold—when not used by the women who rear
them as items of "ritual" exchange—*in situ* and then transferred to
the buyers for sacrifice. Other goods and services like cooking,
washing clothes, looking after children, and helping to make
offerings, are not sold but are usually exchanged within the
compound for other goods and/or services either at the same time
or on a deferred basis when women help others in (tacit) exchange
for help later in their compounds. In the former cases, I think that
a woman obtains the approval of her husband or father, and
perhaps her father's brother(s), to trade or to work outside the
compound, as must Islamic Sasak women in more commercialized
villages on Lombok (Krulfeld 1986: 198).

Women who introduce services into a compound are usually
fairly old, that is, with two or more children, or are senior by
virtue of relative age and/or estate. They may also be of means.
Women do not differ from men who give work (work is a "gift"
from employer to employee [Duff-Cooper 1991e]), for which
women and men both receive labour in return. Men do so as men,
women as women. Some men do not find such women congenial
either as marriage partners or in the abstract. These responses
confirm, though, that such women act as women and not as what
Rich (1986: 150) calls "honorary men."

Women's authority over the disposal of the goods, cash, and
services introduced into a family by them and by its men operates
in three main areas. First, women look to the needs of their
children, buying them clothes, books, and toys (if they can afford
them), paying for their schooling if they go to school (cf. Duff-
Cooper 1990d, sec. I), and giving them pocket-money. The
compound must be kept up, and the money found for offerings,

furnishings, and cooking and other utensils. In caring for the compound, men residing in it are responsible, but women are too; and in the other areas just mentioned, women are virtually their own mistresses. Finally, a woman has the right to keep some of what she is given by men for the expenses mentioned or so that she can buy herself or others clothes and jewellery, say; and she may want to put some cash aside for the marriage of a son (which his father and mother and his father's brothers and wives are mainly responsible for), or a later cremation. But saving is not much cared for by the Balinese because it smacks of stinginess, a characteristic much disliked in other people by most Balinese.

Looking after children, in whose bringing-up the women of a family have more authority than men, weighs most heavily with a woman, then her duties to the compound and village, and finally her duties to herself. This is not only altruism, though doubtless for many Balinese women, and men, as perhaps for most people "the really dominant concern is . . . just . . . to keep their children alive and safe" (Needham 1970: xxxiv n.62). Children, who will look after one in one's old age and in death, are a most important part of the rationale for marriage. They are worth looking after well so that they grow up to be healthy, hard-working ("capable," *mampuh*) Balinese able to care for one and later to fulfill their other responsibilities as Balinese. As for the compound and village (*Kaklianan*), these and other allegiances comprise the main socio-political-cosmological entities within which one lives materially, and after death, essentially. This is *dharma*, a form of Balinese life (*patra*) in one place (*désa*), at one time (*kala*), and also an aspect of Vidhi. It is hence to be cared for and put above one's own interests: without it, one could not exist.

All men should marry, and they should marry a woman who accords well with Balinese ideas about marriage, which favour some unions and not others.[7]

Various decisions have to be made before a marriage is contracted. The woman proposed to has to decide to accept the offer. Even if it and its acceptance are more or less common knowledge, the woman usually runs away from her natal compound to a place where the prospective husband is waiting. Here, the union is blessed and the couple sleeps together for three or four more days before returning to the man's compound for the rites of marriage (*ngantén*). The woman relies upon close women friends, often close agnates, to put her side of the arrangements (i.e. to run away) in train. Before proposing marriage, the intending groom usually makes sure that his father and his father's brother(s) concur in the proposed union. A man often approaches these men through his mother, who can use her good offices on her son's behalf, if necessary—as indeed does a woman who asks permission to marry and then does not elope if her father and his brother(s) consent to the union. Or a mother may be against the union and urge the men to withold their consent to it. Either way, for one does not lightly so offend a woman that she withdraws her labour from such tasks as making offerings, etc., a woman exercises an influential role in marriage. The prospective wife, of course, may also use various stratagems to get the expected proposal from a man. One used by Pak Care's wife (he told me) was to hint broadly that if he did not propose quickly she would accept a proposal from one of the other (two) men who used regularly to visit her compound.

Like all rites, "marriage" comes in three degrees of elaboration, small, medium, and large. A groom's family must decide at what scale to pitch the rites that follow the elopement and return of the couple. A woman's voice can here again be influential, for she is intimately concerned in the holding of the rites; and although it is hardly imaginable that a woman would refuse to take part in such ceremonies being held for her son or for her husband's brother's son, she could make life very difficult for the men were she not to co-operate in the preparation and holding of the ceremonies, if she had not agreed to them but they were held nonetheless. This power to disrupt the harmony of ceremonies (and of normal, non-ceremonial life mentioned before) may not constitute sovereignty and/or authority, but it clearly sets limits to the autonomy of others, which *is* an aspect of sovereignty and authority.

Ideally, a couple whose union has been sanctified in the rites of *ngantén*, which are replete with allusions to cosmology and to the couple's daily life and their well-being and prosperity, should remain together for the rest of their lives; and "before" (*sané dumun*) at least at their deaths, if the first to die is the husband (Duff-Cooper 1983, chap.IX). But divorce is permitted, and is taken advantage of by women as well as by men. It is a particularly difficult decision for a woman. It involves her leaving her children with their father, or else taking them back to her natal compound (if their father agrees) but having to support herself and the children with no material contribution from her ex-husband. A woman may, of course, divorce one man to marry another, but there is no guarantee that her new husband will support children from the earlier marriage. But women can and do decide to divorce their husbands.

Women, that is, have this right of self-determination (and the others already alluded to). This ability to choose, and the choices made, do not rest on the exploitation of others. They thus prefigure at least one aspect of the social/personal relationships and reordered priorities that one socialist-feminist suggests "we want to achieve . . ." (Brenner 1989: 258).

"Cosmology" and "daily life," just mentioned, correspond with the ideological division of everything into what is *niskala* and what is *sakala* (above).

Temples, generically *pura*, are the places in Balinese agglomerations (such as villages and realms) that are set apart from what is *sakala*. Here people may come into contact with aspects of the essential, invisible side of the partitioned whole that, under one aspect, the universe constitutes. These places are not the only ones where one comes into such contact, though: no matter where one is and what one is doing, one is in contact with aspects of the universe that are essential and invisible, because everything derives from the gods or, to adopt the language of Balinese metaphysics (*sarva-surya*), Vidhi is pervasive (*sarvagatah*) in the world. But temples are the finest such places and one's actions, including thoughts and words, are (or should be) equally fine (e.g. Duff-Cooper forthcoming).

The female as a concept pervades this mystical (essential, timeless, invisible) domain. All gods, for instance, have "consorts" (*sakti*), their female, often destructive, aspects, rather as Pedanda (Brahmana "priests") and, before them, kings should have a wife before taking on the position.[8] Demons, by contrast, are often seen as female and as alone, as are witches (*léak*) who are often widows. (One of the Balinese words for widow is *rangda* [below].) Witches have a queen, Durga, the *sakti* of the god Siva. Witches and Durga are contrasted with practitioners of white, right-handed, curative magic. This kind of magic is associated with what is high, to the north and east, and with sunrise and life; the black, left-handed magic of witches is in contrast associated with what is low, maleficent, to the south and west, and with darkness and death. In all these cases, male is contrasted with female. In Baturujung, where I lived for about half the fieldwork mentioned in note 1, the priest in charge of the middle and inside (*dalem*) courts of the village temple (*pamaksan*), associated with northeast and the highest gods, is male, whereas the priest in charge of the outside (*jaba*) court, associated with south and low, is female. "Caste" Balinese, also Dalem, are superior to Sudra, also Jaba.

"Aloneness" may be associated with non-cultivated areas, such as forests. Such areas are ambivalent, being associated with such beings as demons, but also with mystical power (*sakti*).[9] What might be termed consortship, by contrast, is not ambivalent, but is a state to which all (should) aspire. Conjointedness is life-giving and -promoting, whereas separation is associated with processes that can be destructive of life. Conjointedness, further, replicates Vidhi as a unity that is dyadic. There is no higher value in Balinese ideology.

"Female" is an integral part of all creation; but only in such matters as the conception and birth of baby girls, in which the female seed (*kama bang*) predominates over male seed (*kama putih*), is "female" ultimately superior: female is in all other respects ultimately inferior to "male." "*Pradhanapurusa*," the conjoined female and male principles (above), shows this relative evaluation: in the mystical realm, what is lower and more impure precedes what is higher and purer. Ardhanārīśvara also shows it: the left side of this bisexual icon is female, the right side male. Right is superior to left (e.g. one eats with the right hand but washes the genitals and anus with the left). These associations are apparent either directly or in analogue throughout Balinese life.[10]

We may therefore summarize as follows: "female" is an integral aspect of any context whatsoever within the bounds of Balinese ideology, except in Sunya, the Void, though here "male" is also absent. In some contexts, this aspect is clearly visible; in others, closer inspection is required to tease it out. In some contexts, female is superior to male, but ultimately male is superior to female. These remarks apply to both the material and the essential realms.

A possible objection should here be met, before we turn to Japanese ideology. Durga is the queen of witches. For witches, and others, she is superior to Siva and other high gods, let alone village and compound gods that include undifferentiated male and female ancestors. But this evaluation is made from the viewpoint of those who are interested only in wrongdoing. The right-minded, who are not congenitally interested only in harming others, and are associated however distantly with the best things (pragmatically speaking) of Balinese life, should not and generally do not adopt this attitude, which like witches' formulas (*mantra*) reverse (invert) the proper order of things. Such reversal is associated with misfortune and/or death (e.g. Goris 1926: 59ff.; Weck 1937: 47ff.).

What about women, too, who become Pedanda on the deaths of their husbands, and the fact that there are, for instance, women musicians (Sanger 1985) and shadow puppeteers (Dalang) (Zurbuchen 1987: 120 n.12)? Do these facts suggest that in very important everyday aspects of the mystical, the female *qua* women can predominate? The operative word here is "can." The significance of these facts derives in large part from them being so relatively uncommon. On Lombok, Pedandas are all male, while shadow puppeteers and musicians are overwhelmingly men both on Bali and on Lombok, and are usually succeeded by males (when succession occurs); where this is not so, the facts do not contradict the relative evaluation of male as ultimately superior to female. In the matter of female Pedandas, Dalangs, and musicians, that a Pedanda or a Dalang is female is less important than that she is a person of such a status which she has usually attained through relationship with some male, be it husband or teacher. In such elevated statuses, anyway, women can be deferred to by men and women, as men defer to women of greater years or of higher estate than they. Whether a musician is male or female is an indication not of female superiority, but, like the female Pedanda and Dalang, an affirmation of the ubiquity of "female"; and in the relative dearth of such instances, an affirmation of the social fact that male is ultimately superior to female but that in certain contexts female can be (is) superior to male. Metaphysically, male and female, like all other concepts, become less and less differentiated one from another the higher and thus the more abstract and essential they are. It may be that this idea is also at work in the acceptance of female Pedanda and Dalang. That it did not operate among kings çould be accounted for by the latter being more associated with the jural, what is of the middle world (*madyapada*); and Pedanda, Dalangs, and even musicians, or at least the music they produce, being associated more with the highest world, heaven (*sorga*) or the sky (*akasa*), and the mystical.

These data could be lengthily extended, but we must now turn to Japan. In present-day Japan, women are the legal equals of men. Children inherit equally, after a man's widow has received one third of her husband's estate (Hendry 1981: 26–7). Yet Nakane remarks (1984: 33 n.) that although Japanese women are usually ranked as inferior to men, this is not because femininity is assessed as inferior to masculinity but because women seldom hold higher social status than men. Dale (1986: 31) suggests that Nakane's assertion is tautological, but this is questionable: reasons other than gender could have resulted in women's general lack of social status higher than men's. But Yoshida Teigo (e.g. 1989) suggests that femininity as a concept is inferior to masculinity in Japanese ideology; and in any case the general asseveration about women's inferiority is supported by Hendry (1981: 21), while

Smith shows (1978: 129) that, qualified by such matters as relative age, "status in the household, and position in society," women's inferiority continues after death.

What follows renders these general remarks more precise and amplifies them. In Japan generally, there once obtained a thoroughgoing division of authority over the powers to which the Japanese, or their rulers, considered themselves subject: the division created a realm of the jural and one of the mystical (Frédéric 1973: 16; Morris 1975: 43; cf. Yamaguchi 1977: 173; 1987). In the Ryukyus, this division still obtains (Yoshida and Duff-Cooper 1989). Bell warns (1984: 122 n.6) that this division "into spiritual and temporal . . . is not supposed to be clean-cut. Males do have a (small) part to play in ritual affairs, and women have a very large part to play in household economics." Still, men were and are mainly concerned with temporal welfare, women (mothers, sisters) with spiritual matters. But even in the Ryukyus, where women "command a comparatively high degree of respect and power" (Maretzki and Maretzki 1966: 53), they are nevertheless disvalued relative to men (cf. Bell 1984: 135, 123, 126).

It is not only in the Ryukyus that women command some power. Hendry reports (1981: 94–5) that "since women in Kyushu are usually able to support themselves economically, men are actually more dependent for their daily needs upon women than vice versa." Bell goes further: "without their (women's) labour, survival in the Ryukyus would probably have been impossible" for men (1984: 122 n.6). Nonetheless, Nakane writes (1984: 74 n.) that in "traditional morals the ideal man should not be involved in an affair with a woman," an attitude consonant with the way in which an employee only, or overly, concerned with his family ("my-home") was in a "humiliatingly weak position in the past and remains so in the present" (Tada 1978: 208): the proper company man should be, and often (in the great cities at least) is, a modern Samurai (e.g. Masatsugu 1982), a person whose energies should be expended in devotion to his master (sc. employer(s)).[11]

"Household" and "family" as used here refer to the *ie*, "the household at a given point in time (but cp. Kitaoji 1971: 1036) and a more durable entity, the 'house' which exists over time and is composed of only one house in each generation—that household headed by the male who is the legal successor to the household and household head. It is this succession of households down through the generations that is the basic and ideal meaning of . . . ie; the extant household is merely the concrete but transient form of the latter" (Pelzel 1970: 229). We may also be concerned therefore with people, called *shoutai*, "all who live together under one roof and *share a common budget*" (Johnson 1964: 839). Some *ie* include a household whose members are *shoutai*, some do not.

Within a household a woman may have her own disposable income. This is more likely in rural areas than in urban areas, though even in the latter a woman, once married, may continue working until she and her husband start a family, returning to work, perhaps, when the children are away at high school or college. Most would (I think) make some contribution to the household budget for food, services, gifts and offerings, and for leisure, which is very often administered by women. Many women who do not work outside the house also administer this budget, their husbands handing over their pay-packets or monthly salaries to their wives, who in return give them daily or weekly pocket-money and, of course, a well-stocked freezer, a well-run house, and clean, well-brought-up children. One way or another a woman clearly exercises a variable degree of authority within the household through control of its finances; and in doing so, she can usually put together a larger or smaller cache of money (*heisoukuri*) for herself.

Though a woman disposes of cash and/or goods and services either on behalf of the household or on her own account, it is not easy for her to accumulate services. Often when the men of the household work away from home, they acquire services outside the house. These services remain outside to be disposed of by the men, to whom they accrue through their work and other outside relationships, though to the benefit, perhaps, of the household as well as of themselves.

The distinction just implied between inside (*uchi*) and outside (*soto*) is extremely important in Japanese ideology (cf. e.g. Bachnik 1986: 67–8). "Inside" and "outside" are not exclusive: what is inside in one context may be outside in another. Thus wives, mainly associated with "inside"—the house, and particularly within the home, its innermost parts (cf. e.g. Duff-Cooper 1991d, chap.1)—are also a part of an "outside" world. It is important for a man in business to be married for advancement in his work; and the deportment of his wife with the wives of his colleagues, especially his senior colleagues, can affect his advancement positively or adversely. But this is only a particular example of a fact generally agreed about Japanese life, that marriage is a major preoccupation of young women and men and of their parents. In the arrangement of a marriage, "the choice of the object of a relationship is to a high degree conscious and deliberate, and instrumental to perceived socio-economic interests" (Pelzel 1970: 238).[12] A wife, that is, in any sphere has an important and powerful role to play in the advancement of her husband and of his, and her, household.

Nevertheless, women are most associated with the inside of the household, men with the outside. This symbolic and practical association, to which Bestor (1989: 190) alludes, but which, like perhaps all such distinctions, is not absolutely clear-cut (cf. e.g. Needham 1985: 179), extends even to leisure activities usually followed outside the house: it is "somewhat uncommon" for men and women to follow these activities together, though spending Sunday with their wives and children has become "almost a norm" for some Japanese men (Linhart 1976: 208).

Men and women are not only separated by being associated with different activities outside the house, and with the outside and inside of the *ie*, but also within it. This separation could be called a public one, for there are of course times, especially at night and in sleeping and other intimate matters (as *The Makioka Sisters* and *Some Prefer Nettles* [Tanizaki 1958; 1985] demonstrate) when a husband and his wife are very close. This closeness is extremely private, though "privacy" refers mainly to visual and not auditory privacy, the latter being hard to achieve in traditional and in many modern Japanese houses and apartments.

Within a household women run the house, look after the garden, and take care of the children. They also attend to the ancestors in the *butsudan* and the *kamidana* (the places of the ancestors of a house). Women are pre-eminent in these ways in all these spheres, in line with the "nurturing" role that women are ascribed in Japanese ideology (cf. Bestor 1989: 167), though I cannot say whether they exercise what might be called "final authority" in these spheres: sometimes their husbands might concern themselves with them, in which case women would probably defer to their wishes and directives, though sometimes not. But in general it is correct to say, I think, that women's authority here consists in making decisions and executing them.

Women are not, though, confined to activity within the house. In rural areas, women often work (as noted), and there are other groups to which they can belong both in towns, suburbs, and in villages. Housewives' Associations, which organize annual outings and events of interest, also look after the cleaning of the village hall and public ("religious") areas such as those around temples and Buddhist images. "Same-age" groups, for older and other women, organized and run by women, provide their members with social activities and with aid and support when they are needed. Women who are mothers, also, are usually members of their children's schools' Parents-Teachers Associations. These are open to both parents, but often women attend alone, sent as substitutes for their husbands by them (Hendry 1981: 61, 68–9, 71). One should not overestimate the social importance of such groups of women; but combined with the ways in which women can accumulate "private" funds and usually have at least some control over the household budget, they are of significance especially as the senior members of such organizations command respect, not just within their group but also outside it, in the village at large and beyond it, and from men as well as from women.

One of the arenas in which senior women can command respect is in politics, national and/or regional. There are very few women in Japanese politics as politicians (e.g. Pharr 1981); but as voters, women are courted, usually by men through senior women who have relationships (such as membership in one of the groups just mentioned) with them. Curtis (1983: 159–77) goes into this courting of women voters' support in detail. These reports, and Japanese political life over the past two years or so, especially in relation to the sales tax and to ex-Prime Minister Uno's "private" life, show that once mobilized the women's vote can have a dramatic effect on Japanese politics both through the ballot-box and more informally, a fact which Japanese politicians and their supporters and commentators on the Japanese political scene are clearly aware of.

One small fact that Curtis reveals (p. 175) is that the organizers of political rallies pitch their rhetoric at women's hearts (so to say) rather than at their heads, as when it is intended for men. This is an aspect of the system of dual symbolic or analogical classification that is evinced by Japanese ideology (on which see e.g. Duff-Cooper 1991d, chap. 2): the opposition between men and women, associated with the head ("reason") and the heart ("emotion") respectively.

One of the ways in which this opposition is overcome is through marriage, which, rather like other aspects of Japanese life such as the balcony (*engawa*) of a house, which unites its inside and outside, and the periods of silence (*ma*) that in Japanese theatre unite periods of activity, unites a man and a woman.

Hendry (1981) goes into the details of Japanese marriage in admirably detailed clarity. Women are essential to marriage in Japan in various ways. Before, men took women as wives and as concubines (e.g. Wynd 1988); now fewer men than before have concubines, but nearly all men—including male homosexuals, many of whom want to marry, or feel that they must marry to appease family, work, or other pressures—view marriage as an important and inevitable part of their lives.[13] They also often want to be entertained, so that women are in demand as bar-women and as *geisha*.[14]

Women also play an important role in the events leading up to a marriage. Families, especially a young person's parents and grown-up brothers and sisters, play important parts in deciding whether a child or sibling should be married, and if so, to whom. Men and women take part in making these decisions, but it depends upon the circumstances of each case whether men or women predominate in making a particular decision. *Black Rain* (Ibuse 1985) and *Some Prefer Nettles* (Tanizaki 1985) depict men as pre-eminent in such contexts; *The Makioka Sisters* (Tanizaki 1958) and *Beauty and Sadness* (Kawabata 1979) show women predominating in initiating a marriage and a divorce. I have as yet not been able to discern any patterns in the circumstances depicted in these novels that would cast light on this differential influence of women and men. All four authors are male, so that their gender would not appear to be significant here, though their social circumstances and personal histories, which are widely divergent one from another, might be. However, in old Japan, "the mother had a stronger say than the father in the matter of their daughter's marriage" (Seki 1963: 280).

A still common way of initiating the investigations and nego-tiations that can lead to a marriage, i.e. an alliance between two *ie* and even perhaps two corporate groups (*douzoku*) of *ie* (Duff-Cooper 1988b), is through a go-between (*nakoudo*) (e.g. Vogel 1961). Women and men may act as go-betweens more or less full-time, but women predominate over men in that the latter tend so to act ancillary to their main occupation (doctor, university or school teacher, etc.), women if they are such more professionally, one might say more determinedly. These go-betweens play im-portant parts in the wedding ceremonial that follows, if the use made of their services by parents succeeds in producing a couple. Women also play important roles in marriage "celebrations" (*yorokobi*) (Hendry 1981: 140, 185).

Altogether, then, it can be seen that women's lives are such as to make acceptable the claim that not only in Okinawa but throughout Japan women can command a comparatively high degree of power; prestige and respect are its shadows. Yet, as in Bali and Balinese Lombok, women are finally subject to the authority of men. True, the highest Japanese deity is the sun goddess, Amerterasu-Oo-Mikami; and the Emperor of Japan, Tenno Heika: The Son of Heaven, is by some accounts a descendant of this goddess. Women still exercise much spiritual authority in the Ryukyus, and probably once did in pre-Buddhist Japan. But the Emperor was subject for much of Japanese history to a political authority—Yamaguchi, indeed, suggests (1977: 173; cf. 1987) that it was always so—and is so subject now. Japanese women, equally, have been and are subject to men's authority, in spite of women being, like the Emperor to whom the political authority deferred and defers, more powerful in many contexts than men. The association of the mystical with femininity, and with passivity, has long and often been noted, by Gordon (1950) and many others. The present case is one more instance of the association.

The facts about women and mystical ideology in the Ryukyus have already been noted; and reading just a few recent sources about women and mystical ideology (e.g. Mabuchi 1980; Bell 1984; Segawa 1984; Yoshida and Duff-Cooper 1989) impresses one with the extent to which women are much in evidence in this sphere in Japanese life. But too much reliance should not be put on materials from "island" Japan: they are only a part of a complete picture. Indeed, part of the large interest shown in "island" Japan by Japanese anthropologists and others is, I think, based to a great extent on these areas being perceived by them, and by other Japanese (though on perhaps different grounds), as unlike present-day and earlier life in mainland Japan.

What, then, of mainland Japan? In that part of the literature consulted, very little mention of women arises. This ignoring of women could truly reflect their position in Japanese mystical ideology; or it could be that this position has not been truly seen, perhaps because most students of this aspect of Japanese ideology, indeed of Japanese ideology in general, have been men, and because only relatively recently has feminist theory and historical scholarship alerted us to the social importance of the female (cf. Fradenburg, Introduction to this volume). But the fact is that in this mystical sphere, the female is ubiquitous—be it in (hi)stories like the *Kojiki* and *Nihon Shoki* and in articles by scholars like Ackroyd (1959) and Wada (1978); in metaphysical ideas about the male and female principles (e.g. Yamaguchi 1977); in ideas connected with, and the ways in which, Japanese people honour their forebears of varying removes from the *ie*; in Shinto, "The way of the *Kami*" (*kami*: high, divine, sacred, god, goddess), and Buddhist sects admitting women to the priesthood and to other positions in shrines and temples; and in demons of various kinds, the mediums who act as channels through which one can contact and appease or otherwise try to satisfy the needs of such demons, and, often, supplicants, being female; or in martial arts such as *kendo*, *judo*, and *kyudo* (but not *sumo*) where disciples of a particular master may be either women or men, though the masters are most often men.

That is, the female does appear both in the literature and in the ideas and practices referred to. Even the repertoire of the Noh Theatre, in which all the actors and musicians are men, represents women and includes "women plays"; and just as the "young woman masks" (*Ko-omote*) are considered representatives of Noh masks in general, so the women characters' costumes are considered "central" to Noh (Komparu 1983: 231, 241).[15] Such "spiritual" activities, also, as flower-arrangement, the tea ceremony, calligraphy, and poetry-writing, are open to women and include ideas that link the mystical and the feminine. In most cases, the female is ultimately subordinated to the male, even where, as in the Ryukyus and other parts of island Japan, male is in some contexts subordinated to female—except in such institutions as convents. Even in these, though, since there is always a male authority above a convent or group of them (as in village associations and "same-age" groups), women are arguably ultimately subordinate to men. I think that probably this subordination is not amenable to explanation, in the common acceptation of this word. Rather, I follow Wittgenstein and would suggest that we wrongly expect an explanation, "whereas the solution of the difficulty is a description": "What is needed for (an) explanation? One might say: a culture" (1967, secs. 314, 164).

The matter of the primacy of the goddess Amerterasu must be considered in this context. Here, the female is clearly of first importance: for instance, Amerterasu bestowed the imperial regalia on her grandson, Ninigi-no-Mikoto, who was induced to descend and rule Japan by his grandmother. His great-grandson, the Emperor Jimmu, was the first human emperor of Japan. Since his reign, Japan has nearly always had an emperor, not an empress. This association of the imperial line with the female, however, well accords with the ways in which political action has properly been outside the responsibilities of the emperor. It is also consonant with the generally passive role that a Japanese woman, whether a specialist in things mystical or not, is expected to, but does not always, take, both in regard to such matters and more generally. Other things, such as the encarceration of the sun goddess by gods and not by goddesses, reported in the *Kojiki*, might be taken to suggest that even at this height of purity and sacredness the seeming superiority of "female" over "male" and what is associated with it would be only a part of the complete picture. But, as in Balinese ideology, this does not mean that the female in various guises is not significant and noteworthy in Japanese ideology. Usually, and expectedly, situations where this significance is most manifest involve women of relatively great age; and the greater this relative age and concomitant status, the more significant and noteworthy in "official" ideology is the female, though this significance does not mean that the practices of younger women are analytically insignificant. To the contrary— but this disjuncture cannot be further gone into here.

Let us now turn to some comparisons of these data. From among the formal notions mentioned above, "symmetry," "asymmetry," and "modes of partition" are here employed to compare the social facts that have been described. Only these notions are used because space precludes the use of the others mentioned. They were chosen in preference to the others because in an ordered list of those notions (Duff-Cooper 1991c), "symmetry," "asymmetry", and "modes of partition" stand near and at the head of the list. Both in Japan and in Balinese Lombok, such positions indicate (among much else) relative importance and priority.

One of the ways in which symmetry and asymmetry can be discerned is through the idea of interchangeability: two entities A and B, for instance, are symmetrically related when A/B is equivalent to B/A. When A and B are not interchangeable in a particular context, so that A/B is not equivalent to B/A, an asymmetrical relation holds between A and B in that context.

In Balinese life, fathers and sons and mothers and daughters are in certain contexts interchangeable one for another of the same sex. In those contexts, fathers and sons and mothers and daughters are symmetrically related. In Japan (we saw), women can sometimes stand in for their husbands, though I am unsure whether sisters and brothers can stand in for a sibling of the same or opposite sex in other contexts. In any case, in the former instance male and female are symmetrically related.

Symmetry is not otherwise absent from Japanese life: it is evinced, for instance, in relationships called *yui* that involve the equal exchange of labour between *ie* (Duff-Cooper 1988b). Plain membership of a group such as a house is such that a symmetrical relation holds between the members of the group by virtue of membership of it. This symmetry, though, is "broken" by the relative ages and the genders of the members (Duff-Cooper 1990b, chap. 5). Likewise on Lombok: members of a local descent group and of families are symmetrically related one to another by virtue of their membership of these groups, but relative age and gender again "break" the symmetry. However, the contexts in which symmetry is evinced appear to be far fewer in Japan than in Balinese Lombok.

Instances of asymmetries, though, pervade our materials. Balinese and Japanese women may predominate in relation to the house over men. In both ideologies, women may be pre-eminent in relation to "inside," men to "outside," but in both ideologies there are "outside" contexts that are mainly female domains. Where the female is pre-eminent, ideas about relative age and status interact to make the situation thus. However, the male is ultimately superior to the female. How all this is worked out in daily life differs both from (parts of) Bali and Lombok to Japan, and differs in different parts of Bali and Lombok and in different parts of Japan.

In Balinese ideology, female may be a part of a triad; in Japanese ideology, it is usually an aspect of a dyad (male/female). The three aspects of that triad may also be seen as two (i.e. "transvestite" is excluded), and each of these two aspects may be represented by up to as many as eleven female and male aspects. In Shinto, further, there is no One like Vidhi, only numerous gods and goddesses (and demons) which may be located in natural phenomena like mountains, trees, and waterfalls. These phenomena constitute classes that can be subdivided into their constituent members. But classification by division (partition) of this kind is far less thoroughgoing systematically than in Balinese ideology. However, diarchy (bi-partition) may be considered thoroughgoing in both Balinese and in Japanese ideology (Duff-Cooper 1986a; 1990d, chap. 2).

Balinese and Japanese marriage both evince symmetry. The relation holds between the people who give and those who take a bride, though in Balinese ideology there are indications that wife-takers may be superior to wife-givers. Symmetry also holds between the bride and a groom as aspects of the couple to be blessed and created by the marriage rites. Japanese go-betweens may be male or female, and here again, male and female are related symmetrically. Nevertheless, as above, asymmetries are here more discernible than symmetries. The asymmetries hold between the couple and all others involved in the rites. There is also a great disparity between the predominance of the group that gives a woman, both in Japan and among the Balinese, who fund and otherwise are responsible for the marriage rites, and the wife-givers, who are only marginally involved in Japan and in Lombok and may well play no part in the rites. As to the decisions surrounding a marriage, the influence that women can exercise in this area of social life was noted, as were the crucial parts that they play, both on Lombok and in Japan, in all the other aspects of marriage considered. Yet "male" is formally predominant in all these matters, as it is in the rites and in the couple that they create or affirm.

Modes of partition, to conclude the present comparison, are not greatly in evidence. However, duality is discernible in all aspects of marriage, the rites of which overcome the division of people into male and female and create a unity that has a male and a female aspect. In both ideologies, new life properly emerges from this "everlasting" unity.

When it comes to the mystical, symmetry is evinced in Balinese mystical ideology by Vidhi, which may be conceived of as a whole that is equivalent to each of its two constituent aspects (Duff-Cooper 1990a). These three aspects of Vidhi are interchangeable in any context whatever, because they are devoid of content. In the material about Japan surveyed above, though, it is hard to locate one instance of symmetry that can be set beside an instance of the relation from Balinese mystical ideology. But by contrast, again, asymmetries abound. These are evinced in various ways that females are subject to males, that they predominate in some contexts over males, but that males are ultimately superior to females.

Modes of partition, like symmetrical relations, are barely discernible in Japanese mystical ideology, except of course in the fact that females and males are ubiquitous and are the two aspects that "gender" possesses. It should, though, be mentioned that Yoshida Atsuhiko has it (n.d.) that "in the Japanese myths recorded in the *Kojiki* and the *Nihonshoki*, we find a large number of expressions, in various forms, of a tripartite conception, which is very similar indeed to this (Dumézilian) Indo-European trifunctional system." In Balinese ideology, modes of partition abound (though they are not specially in evidence in the data presented above), but only as they abound in all analyzed aspects of Balinese life, and probably in the others (Duff-Cooper 1990b; 1990c).

The consideration, anyway, of some of the situations in which Balinese and Japanese women are significant leads to a number of findings. First, substantively, women are superordinate to men in some contexts, subordinate to them in others (as more general studies (e.g. Moore 1988: 35, 201 n.16) show). Ultimately men, and more broadly "male," are predominant over women, "female." "Male" may include the biologically female, i.e. women.

Second, considered formally, the materials from Lombok and

from Japan evince symmetries, asymmetries, and modes of partition as a means of classification. Symmetry is far less prevalent numerically as a principle of order than asymmetry in both ideologies. It is more prevalent in Balinese ideology than in Japanese. That it is discernible in the latter is consonant with Hendry's view (1987: 205) that "equality" is one of the principles that order Japanese life.[16] Modes of partition, again, are far more prevalent in Balinese life than in Japanese, though both ideologies have recourse to duality as a mode of classification. This recourse is not surprising in the light of the global incidence of this mode of classification by division, e.g. Needham (ed.) 1973, and more particularly in the light of "dual sovereignty," structurally, being characterized by "bipartition, opposition, and complementarity" (cf. Needham 1980: 89).

Symmetry was noted to be more prevalent numerically in Balinese ideology than in the Japanese materials examined. Asymmetries abound in both. The latter are more discernible in what can be termed the social sphere, the symmetries in the symbolic and mystical spheres. But both kinds of relation are discernible in all these spheres. Whatever else these findings indicate, they tend to support Dumézil's contention, insofar as its terms are clear, that "sovereignty aligns itself on two planes, at once antithetical and complementary" (1970: 55); and they show that asymmetry is not a necessary aspect of any social relationship. Unfortunately, in the exercise of authority by women and in the wider schemes in which they do so, women do so in relationships that are largely asymmetrical.[17] It is understandable that in Bali and Balinese Lombok and in Japan, where women exercise authority over other women (and over women and men), the symmetrical relations that feminists in the East and West aim for are not much in evidence, even in those all-female institutions considered: "It is . . . commonly found that dyadic terms (such as male/female, men/women) in a binary system are of unequal value, and that one term is assessed as 'superior' in some respect or another to its opposite" (Needham 1980: 57), and it can be argued that "the social domination of men over women . . . is virtually coextensive with the history, not only recorded but even inferrable, of the species (*homo sapiens*) itself" (Anderson 1983: 89; but compare e.g. the Indonesian Communist Aidit's view of the wholly egalitarian form of life that existed there 3–4,000 years ago [Feith and Castles (eds) 1970: 312]). Since humankind is a mainly traditional animal,[18] it would have been cause for reflection if those symmetrical relations had been evinced. Had they been, though, they would naturally have made the quasi-axiomatic insistence on the necessary asymmetry of social relationships even less tenable than it anyway is (on this insistence and reasons for doubting it see e.g. Duff-Cooper 1988a). More important, perhaps, they would have been a powerful encouragement to those feminists' aspirations and programs of action and to their supporters.

To conclude, I should perhaps mention that I have designedly not ended this chapter by suggesting some of its theorectical implications for the many students and scholars of women and sovereignty in a wide range of cultures *via* an equally wide range of methodologies. I should prefer it, and would be gladdened by it, if scholars working in fields other than social anthropology discern problems and questions in the empirical data presented in this essay that can help them frame their own scholarly and, perhaps, political approaches to this important topic.

NOTES

1 The Balinese materials in this chapter derive from about twenty-one months' fieldwork in Pagutan, western Lombok, in 1979–81. I am indebted to my hosts in Pagutan and to the then Social Science Research Council of Great Britain, the Emslie Horniman Anthropological Scholarship Fund of the Royal Anthropological Institute, and to the Philip Bagby Fund, University of Oxford, as also to the Indonesian Academy of Sciences (LIPI), for making this work possible. "Balinese" refers to the Balinese of western Lombok unless it is specified or otherwise clear. "Japan" refers to mainland Japan (the four main islands) and to the islands south from Amamioshima to Okinawa when it is helpful. A demonstration that the polity of Japan comprises some culturally and socially very different entities which, however, share some common values (about e.g. inside and outside, good and bad, and life and death) that are equally important throughout Japan and which here constitute these different entities as one, must wait upon another occasion. At the time the first draft of this essay was prepared and written out (December 1989), I had been living and researching in Japan for about four years. Thanks are due to Joy Hendry and to Louise Fradenburg for their comments on and criticisms of the first draft of this essay.

2 The relative fineness of any two entities is gauged by assessing their relative closeness to a physical and/or ideational reference point. Such points take different forms in different contexts. On these forms and the implications of relative closeness to reference points see e.g. Duff-Cooper 1984a, 1986c.

3 Wikan (e.g. 1990: 93) argues that a prime Balinese concern, also, is to avoid giving others offence.

4 Various ways of going about this are open to us. The "field of anthropological study" approach (e.g. de Josselin de Jong, ed., 1984) is too narrow. "Metaphors for living" (e.g. Fox 1981; cp. 1988) is unlikely to be helpful in the comparison of aspects of two such radically unconnected forms of life as those addressed in this chapter. That there is "an interesting correlation . . . between 'peacefulness' as a moral value and gender equality" might frame an approach that could usefully be pursued (cf. Howell and Willis 1989: 24, 25)—but not as it stands: the crucial terms of the proposition, viz. "peacefulness," "equality," need clear unambiguous definition before it can be assessed. This requirement is not met by these writers, nor by e.g. Howe (1989: 102). Then our data could be compared by reference to the functions that they seem to perform, but the results of such comparisons are usually not very interesting nor revealing. Or else, very respectably, the aspects could be considered from the angle of the archaic society or societies (e.g. Lyle 1990) that perhaps underlie present-day and earlier life on Lombok and in Japan; but this is a huge topic to which not even the beginnings of a satisfactory answer could here be given.

5 The particulars should also be compared through forms, iconic (e.g. darkness), spatial, and institutional, but lack of space precludes these comparisons being made below. They will be done elsewhere. Comparison through values (e.g. superiority, passivity, fertility) is not adopted either, although it is advocated by one authority (Needham 1985: 186). "Superiority" is almost empty, and returns analysis to the materials being analyzed. "Passivity" and "fertility" are unlikely to prove useful if proper regard is had for the meanings of these concepts in Balinese and Japanese ideology. Comparing through these values might lead to a suggestion akin to that of Howe (1989: 103), which is to be avoided: Howe has it that the Balinese and Chewong (Howell 1979) are comparable because "the Chewong theory of human nature stresses that the health and well-being of the person is achieved ,when his being is in balance" while "there is abundant evidence that the ideal nature of the Balinese cosmos and the notion of the person is structured by ideas of balance, order, and equilibrium"; also, because the Balinese "experience emotional states similar to the Chewong and valued in the same way." Such suggestions can be made only if, here, Chewong and Balinese concepts of e.g. balance, order, and equilibrium, and their "emotional states" and the

ways they value them are so honed that, as in these opinions of Howe, one is told next to nothing about the ideologies of the peoples whose concepts are lumped together. The ways in which this is done at once deform the ideologies in question and demonstrate scant respect for the data, i.e. the details of the lives of the peoples that are the object of analysis.

6 Pak Care's father, who sold palm-wine from his living quarters, had arranged with his wife, who sometimes worked as a day-labourer away from the village, that he would cook for the family while she was away. I should not want to use this or any other example, however, to support Geertz's view that "Bali is a rather 'unisex' society" (1973: 417). I tend rather to concur with Wikan whose judgement is (1990: 67) that Balinese forms of life evince "extreme gender differentiation both in ritual and symbolic activity and in more mundane life."

7 These practices are discussed in Hobart 1980 and Duff-Cooper 1984b, 1985, 1987b. See also Boon 1977 and 1990 (both *passim*).

8 The consecration of Dewa Manggis (van der Meij 1986) does not include his wife as is the practice with Pedanda, but the Dewa clearly has one (pp. 265 1.106, 263 1.41).

9 *Sakti* is itself doubly ambivalent: it is a quality that is an aspect of certain places, objects, substances, or persons and also a force at the command of deities, ancestors, and demons. It is morally neutral and may work good or evil (cf. Wikan 1990: 242, 315 n.8).

10 White is to (:) red as (::) male : female :: North : south :: sun : moon :: day : night :: life : death, for instance.

11 But see Ebara 1981 for other directions in which traditional Samurai expended their energies.

12 "Six Japanese Novels under an Anthropological Aspect" (Duff-Cooper 1991d, chap. 3) argues that marriage is a main theme of the novels it considers, unexpectedly but revealingly: the novels were selected for analysis randomly.

13 As for gay women, opinions of Japanese diverge: some say that it is harder for women than for men to remain unmarried, especially as they approach about 40, others that it is easier for them to do so. Again, others cogently say that it depends upon where the people live and what their social status is. All agree, though, that for a woman (or a man) to remain unmarried is unusual and a cause for (adverse) comment and gossip.

14 See Linhart 1986 on this demi-monde, also Ishiguro 1986, one of the novels considered in the study mentioned in note 12 above.

15 The exclusion of females from the Noh theatre probably

has to do with its historical connections with "sacred drama" (*kagura*) and with the relative impurity of women according to Shinto to which e.g. Bestor (1989: 310 n. 11) alludes in the context of the recent decision to allow women to carry shrines in festivals. Various questions are raised by the matters mentioned in this paragraph— whether the kinds of cultural work being performed and the practices/rituals engaged in exclusively by men that represent "the female" and those in which women themselves engage, for instance, evince significant differences. Space precludes addressing these and other important matters here.

16 As in Japan one encounters few and certainly not "frequent" outbursts of anger, emotional display, and quarrelling, one can presumably expect more "gender equality" in Japan than in Bali (cf. Howell and Willis 1989: 24). Allowing "symmetrical relations between male and female" as equivalent to "gender equality," the "correlation" between " 'peacefulness' as a moral value and gender equality" is not apparent: Japan is more peaceful than Bali, but there is less gender equality (sc. fewer symmetrical relations between men and women) there. But by what criteria, in any case, is one supposed to determine that "peacefulness" is more "morally valuable" in one ideology than another?

17 These relations may be less asymmetrical, arguably, than those between men and men and men and women. This would depend on the question, at least, of whether "asymmetrical" is a predicate of degree or an absolute predicate, admitting of no qualification, on which see e.g. Duff-Cooper 1991b. These relationships among other things are recognized by the Japanese pronouns (so-called) *watakushitachi* ("we," women and women and very formal), *ware-ware* ("we," men and men, men and women), and *bokutachi* ("we," men and men). Bestor, interestingly, discusses the way in which status in a male domain is more finely graded than in a complementary female one (1989: 191, 316 n. 8). It may, finally, be helpful to mention that in the last two sentences and in the next paragraph I equate "asymmetrical relations" with relationships of social domination, an unequal distribution of power, and usually a concomitant unequal distribution of the status and wealth that accompany it, between related classes of people. The equation is made by Anderson (e.g. 1983: 89–90), and by many others.

18 Cf. e.g. Hocart (1938). It is probably prudent to say that the judgment made at this point in the text should be taken to imply neither that classes of people within a

tradition all subscribe to a uniform dogma, nor that within classes, divergences etc. do not occur, nor, indeed, that the constituents of a tradition do not change. Classes of people, and within them individuals, clearly do disagree, and traditions patently do change.

REFERENCES

Ackroyd, Joyce (1959). Women in Feudal Japan. *Transactions of the Asiatic Society of Japan* 7, 31–68.
Anderson, Perry (1983). *In the Tracks of Historical Materialism*. London: Verso.
Backnik, Jane M. (1986). Time, Space, and Person in Japanese Relationships. In *Interpreting Japanese Society; Anthropological Approaches*, eds Joy Hendry and Jonathan Webber, pp. 49–75, Oxford: JASO Occasional Papers.
Bell, Rosamund (1984). Women in the Religious Life of the Ryukyu Islands: Structure and Status. *Journal of the Anthropological Society of Oxford (JASO)* 15/2, 119–36.
Bestor, Theodore, C. (1989). *Neighborhood Tokyo*. Tokyo and New York: Kodansha International.
Boon, James A. (1977). *The Anthropological Romance of Bali, 1597–1972*. Cambridge: Cambridge University Press.
—— (1990). *Affinities and Extremes*. Chicago and London: University of Chicago Press.
Brenner, Johanna (1989). Feminism's Revolutionary Promise: Finding Hope in Hard Times. In *Socialist Register 1989*, eds Ralph Miliband and others, pp. 245–63, London: Merlin.
Curtis, Gerald L. (1983). *Election Campaigning Japanese Style*. Tokyo: Kodansha.
Dale, Peter N. (1986). *The Myth of Japanese Uniqueness*. London: Croom Helm.
Duff-Cooper, Andrew (1983). A Study of the Collective Ideas of a Community of Balinese on Lombok. University of Oxford: D. Phil. thesis.
—— (1984a). *An Essay in Balinese Aesthetics*. University of Hull: Centre for South East Asian Studies, Occasional Paper 7.
—— (1984b). Principles in the Classification, the Marriages, and Some Other Relations of a Community of Balinese on Lombok. *Anthropos* 79, 485–503.
—— (1985). Notes about Some Balinese Ideas and Practices Connected with Sex from Western Lombok. *Anthropos* 80, 403–19.
—— (1986a). The Family as an Aspect of the Totality of the

Balinese Form of Life in Western Lombok. *Bijdragen tot de Taal-, Land- en Volkenkunde (BKI)* 141/2 & 3, 230–52.

—— (1986b). Twins and Transvestites: Two Aspects of the Totality of the Balinese Form of Life in Western Lombok. *Zeitschrift für Ethnologie* 111, 205–29.

—— (1986c). Living with the Structure of a Balinese Form of Life in Western Lombok. *Philosophy* 84, 193–226.

—— (1987a). The Balinese Rice-planting Rite of *Nuasén* and the Magic Square of Three. *Cosmos* 3, 41–57.

—— (1987b). Incorporation and Alliance among a Community of Balinese in Western Lombok. *Zeitschrift für Ethnologie* 112, 45–69.

—— (1988a). Reflexive Relationships in Aspects of the Ideology of the Balinese on Lombok. *Philosophy* 87, 219–55.

—— (1988b). *Aspects of Japanese "Exchange": A Conspectus.* Free University, Berlin: East Asian Institute, Occasional Paper 68.

—— (1988c). Paradigmatic Scenes in Balinese Ideology on Lombok. *Man and Culture in Oceania (MCO)* 4, 129–51.

—— (1989). Aspects of the Aesthetics of Rice-growing in a Balinese Form of Life on Lombok. *JASO* 20/2, 123–47.

—— (1990a). The Formation of Balinese Ideology in Western Lombok: Inspection, Change of Aspect, Assessment. *Sociologus* 40/2, 133–57.

—— (1990b). *Shapes and Images.* Denpasar (Bali): Universitas Udayana.

—— (1990c). Models and Modelling: Sculpting Balinese Ideology. *JASO* 21/3, 283–302.

—— (1990d). The Multilingualism of a Balinese Community in Western Lombok. *Anthropos* 85, 329–44.

—— (1991a). Remarks on Some Systematic Aspects of Forms of Life. *Philosophy* 93, in press.

—— (1991b). For and Against "Degrees" of Asymmetry: Culture and Science 2, in press.

—— (1991c). Analogical Classification in Balinese Ideology on Lombok. *MCO* 7, 39–61.

—— (1991d). *Three Essays on Japanese Ideology.* Tokyo: Seitoku University, Occasional Publication.

—— (1991e). Balinese Exchange: Replication and Reaffirmation of "The One." *Southeast Asian Studies* 29/2, in press.

—— (forthcoming). Remarks on Balinese Invocations. In *Prières et invocation en Asie du Sud-Est,* ed. S. Headley, Paris: C.N.R.S.

Dumézil, Georges (1970). *The Destiny of the Warrior,* trans. A. Hiltebeitel. Chicago: University of Chicago Press.

Ebara, Saikaku (1981). *Contes d'amour des Samourais*, trans. Ken Sato. Paris: J. Damase.

Feith, Herbert and Lance Castles, eds (1970). *Indonesian Political Thinking 1945–65*. Ithaca: Cornell University Press.

Fox, James, J. (1981). Review of Cécile Barraud, *Tanebar-Evav; Une société de maisons tournée vers le large* (Cambridge and Paris: Cambridge University Press and Editions M.S.L'H., 1979). *Man* (n.s.) 16/3, 483–4.

—— (1988). Review of de Josselin de Jong (ed.), 1984. *BKI* 144/1, 178–81.

Frédéric, Louis (1973). *Daily Life in Japan at the Time of the Samurai, 1185–1603*, trans. E.M. Lowe. Tokyo: Tuttle.

Geertz, C. (1973). Deep Play: Notes on the Balinese Cockfight. In *The Interpretation of Cultures*, pp. 412–453, New York: Basic Books.

Gordon, Pierre (1950). *Le Sacerdoce à travers les âges*. Paris: La Colombe.

Goris, R. (1926). *Bijdrage tot de Kennis der Oud-Javaansche en Balineesche Theologie*. Leiden: Drukkerij A. Vros.

Hendry, Joy (1981). *Marriage in Changing Japan*. London: Croom Helm.

—— (1987). *Understanding Japanese Society*. London: RKP.

Hobart, Mark (1980). *Ideas of Identity; The Interpretation of Kinship in Bali*. Denpasar (Bali): Universities Udayana.

Hocart, A.M. (1938). In the Grip of Tradition. *Folklore* 49, 258–69.

Howe, L.E.A. (1989). Peace and Violence in Bali. In *Societies at Peace*, eds S. Howell and R. Willis, pp. 100–16, London: RKP.

Howell, Signe (1979). *Society and Cosmos*. Singapore: Oxford University Press.

—— and R. Willis (1989). Introduction *Societies at Peace*, eds *idem*, pp. 1–28, London: RKP.

Ibuse, Masuji (1985). *Black Rain*, trans. John Bestor, London and New York: Bantam Books.

Ishiguro, Kazuo (1986). *An Artist of the Floating World*. London: Faber.

de Josselin de Jong, P.E., ed. (1984). *Unity in Diversity; Indonesia as a Field of Anthropological Study*. Dordrecht and Cinnaminson, NJ: Foris.

Johnson, E. (1964). The Stem Family and its Extension in Present Day Japan. *American Anthropologist* 66, 839–51.

Kawabata, Yasunari (1979). *Beauty and Sadness*, trans. Howard Hibbett. Harmondsworth: Penguin.

Kitaoji, Hironobu (1971). The Structure of the Japanese Family. *American Anthropologist* 73, 1036–57.

Komparu, Kunio (1983). *The Noh Theater; Principles and Perspectives*. New York and Tokyo: Weatherhill/ Tankosha.

Krulfeld, Ruth (1986). Sasak Attitudes Towards Polygamy and the Changing Position of Women in Sasak Peasant Villages. In *Visibility and Power; Essays on Women in Society and Development*, eds L. Duke and others, pp. 194–208, Delhi: Oxford University Press.

Linhart, Sepp (1976). The Use and Meaning of Leisure in Present-Day Japan. In *Modern Japan: Aspects of History, Literature, and Society*, ed. W.G. Beasley, pp. 198–208, Tokyo: Tuttle.

—— (1986). *Sakariba*: Zone of "Evaporation" Between Work and Home. In *Interpreting Japanese Society: Anthropological Approaches*, eds Joy Hendry and Jonathan Webber, pp. 198–210, Oxford: JASO Occasional Papers.

Lyle, Emily (1990). *Archaic Cosmos: Polarity, Time and Space*. Edinburgh: Polygon.

Mabuchi, T. (1980). Space and Time in Ryukyuan Cosmology. *Asian Folklore Studies* 39, 1–19.

Maretzi, T.W. and H. Maretzki (1966). *Taira; An Okinawan Village*. New York: Wiley.

Masatsugu, M. (1982). *The Modern Samurai Society; Duty and Dependence in Contemporary Japan*. New York: Amacom.

van der Meij, Th.C. (1986). A Balinese Account of the Royal Consecration of I Dewa Manggis of Gianyar in 1903. In *A Man of Indonesian Letters*, eds C.M.S. Hellwig and S.O. Robson, pp. 257–70, Dordrecht and Cinnaminson, NJ: Foris.

Moore, Henrietta L. (1988). *Feminism and Anthropology*. Cambridge: Polity.

Morris, Ivan (1975). *The Nobility of Failure; Tragic Heroes in the History of Japan*. Tokyo: Tuttle.

Nakane, Chie (1984). *Japanese Society*. Tokyo: Tuttle.

Needham, Rodney (1970). Editor's Introduction, A.M. Hocart, *Kings and Councillors*, pp. xiii–xcix, Chicago and London: University of Chicago Press.

—— ed. (1973). *Right & Left; Essays on Dual Symbolic Classification*. Chicago and London: University of Chicago Press.

—— (1980). *Reconnaissances*. Toronto: University of Toronto Press.

—— (1985). *Exemplars*. Berkeley, Los Angeles, and London: University of California Press.

Pelzel, John C. (1970). Japanese Kinship: A Comparison. In

Family and Kinship in China, ed. Maurice Freedman, pp. 227–48, Stanford: Stanford University Press.

Pharr, Susan J. (1981). *Political Women in Japan; The Search for a Place in Political Life*. Berkeley: University of California Press.

Rich, Adrienne (1986). *Blood, Bread, and Poetry*. New York: Norton.

Rivière, P.G. (1971). Marriage: A Reassessment. In *Rethinking Kinship and Marriage*, ed. Rodney Needham, pp. 57–74, London: Tavistock.

Sanger, (1985). Music, Dance, and Social Organisation in Two Balinese Villages. *Indonesia Circle* 37, 45–62.

Segawa, Kiyoko (1984). *Onna no Minzoukushi (The Ethnography of Women)*. Tokyo: Tokyo Shouseki.

Seki, Keigo (1963). The Spool of Thread: A Sub-Type of the Japanese Serpent-Bridegroom Tale. In *Studies in Japanese Folklore*, eds R.M. Dorson and others, pp. 267-88, Bloomington: Indiana University Press.

Smith, Robert J. (1978). *Ancestor Worship in Japan*. Stanford: Stanford University Press.

Tada, Michitaro (1978). The Glory and Misery of "My-Home," trans. R. Wargo. In *Authority and the Individual in Japan; Citizen Protest in Historical Perspective*, ed. J. Victor Koschmann, pp. 207–17, Tokyo: University of Tokyo Press.

Tanizaki, Junichiro (1958). *The Makioka Sisters*, trans. E.G. Seidensticker. Tokyo: Tuttle.

—— (1985). *Some Prefer Nettles*, trans. E.G. Seidensticker. London: Pan.

Vogel, Ezra F. (1961). The Go-Between in a Developing Society: The Case of the Japanese Marriage Arranger. *Human Organization* 20/3, 112–20.

Wada, Yoshiko (1978). Woman and Her Power in the Japanese Emperor System. *Feminist (Japan)* 1/4, 15–7.

Weck, W. (1937). *Heilkunde und Volkstum auf Bali*. Stuttgart: Enke.

Wikan, Unni (1990). *Managing Turbulent Hearts; A Balinese Formula for Living*. Chicago and London: University of Chicago Press.

Wittgenstein, Ludwig (1967). *Zettel*, eds. G.E.M. Anscombe and G.H. von Wright, trans. G.E.M. Anscombe. Oxford: Blackwell.

Wynd, Oswald (1988). *The Ginger Tree*. London: Eland.

Yamaguchi, Masao (1977). Kingship, Theatricality, and Marginal Reality in Japan. In *Text and Context*, ed. Ravindra K. Jain, pp. 151–79, Philadelphia: Institute for the Study of Human Issues.

—— (1987). The Dual Structure of Japanese Emperorship. *Current Anthropology* 28/4, Supplement 5–10.

Yoshida, Atsuhiko (n.d.). Summary of "Japanese Mythology and the Indo-European Trifunctional System." Paper to be read at the Cosmos Project conference on Triality being held at Edinburgh University in August 1991.

Yoshida, Teigo (1989). The Feminine in Japanese Folk Religion: Polluted or Divine? In *Unwrapping Japan*, eds E. Ben-Ari and others, pp. 58–77. Manchester: Manchester University Press.

—— and Andrew Duff-Cooper (1989). A Comparison of Aspects of Two Polytheistic Forms of Life: Okinawa and Balinese Lombok. *Cosmos* 5, 212–42.

Zurbuchen, Mary S. (1987). *The Language of Balinese Shadow Theater*. Princeton: Princeton University Press.

Notes on Contributors

SUSANNA ÅKERMAN is a research fellow at the Department of the History of Ideas and Learning, Uppsala University, Sweden. She has recently published *Queen Christina and her Circle: The Transformation of a Seventeenth-Century Philosophical Libertine* (Brill, 1991). She is now working on a book entitled *Swedish-Baltic Immaterialism 1621–1688*.

SHARON ARNOULT is completing her dissertation on worship and religious identity in early modern England at the University of Texas-Austin, Department of History. She is also a part-time faculty member of the Department of History at Southwest Texas State University.

ANDREW DUFF-COOPER studied Sociology and Philosophy at the University of Kent, and Social Anthropology at the University of Oxford. Under the guidance of Rodney Needham, he did fieldwork in Balinese communities on the island of Lombok, and later moved to Japan where, at the time of his death in 1991, he taught anthropology at Seitoku University, Tokyo. He published numerous articles on Balinese culture and Forms of Life on Lombok, and had embarked on a study of contemporary Japanese culture. In both ethnographic fields his interests concentrated on the social principles underlying cognitive classification and ritual symbolization. His study of these combined a holistic ethnographic approach with an analytic interest in their genesis and functioning as ideologies. Andrew Duff-Cooper died, aged forty-three, during the publication of this book.

LOUISE OLGA FRADENBURG is Associate Professor of English at the University of California, Santa Barbara. She is the author of a number of essays on Chaucer and on Middle Scots poetry, and of *City, Marriage, Tournament: Arts of Rule in Late Medieval Scotland* (University of Wisconsin, 1991). She is now at work on a study of *Chaucer's Voice Memorial*.

CARLA FRECCERO is Associate Professor in the Board of Studies in Literature at the University of California, Santa Cruz. She has published in a number of fields including medieval and early modern French literature, feminist theory, and popular culture. Her study of Rabelais, *Father Figures*, recently appeared from Cornell University Press, and she is currently writing a book on Marguerite de Navarre.

DIANA HENDERSON is Assistant Professor of English and currently Co-Chair of Women's Studies of Middlebury College. She has published articles on Thomas Heywood and James Joyce, and has contributed essays on early modern women lyricists and on Spenser for forthcoming collections from Cornell University Press and Publications of the Modern Language Society. She is completing a study of love lyric, gender and dramatic performance in Elizabethan England, provisionally entitled *Passion Made Public*.

MÁIRE HERBERT, Lecturer in the Department of Early and Medieval Irish, University College, Cork, has co-edited the *Catalogue of Irish Manuscripts in Cambridge Libraries* (with P. De Brun; Cambridge, 1986) and *Irish Biblical Apocrypha: Selected Texts in Translation* (with M. McNamara; T. and T. Clark, 1989). She is the author of numerous articles on medieval Irish literature and culture, and of *Iona, Kells and Derry: The History and Hagiography of the Monastic Familia of Columba* (Oxford, 1988).

CHARLES JEDREJ is a lecturer in the Department of Social Anthropology, University of Edinburgh. He has conducted several years of ethnographic research in West Africa and the Sudan, and has published numerous articles on the anthropology of ritual symbolism. He is a co-editor of *Dreaming, Religion and Society in Africa*, forthcoming from Brill.

EMILY LYLE, General Editor of *Cosmos*, is a research fellow at the School of Scottish Studies, University of Edinburgh, and is currently President of the Traditional Cosmology Society. Her many publications in the fields of literature, folklore, and comparative religion and mythology include *Archaic Cosmos: Polarity, Space and Time* (Polygon, 1990).

DEAN A. MILLER is Professor of History at the University of Rochester, New York. His published work includes *The Byzantine Tradition, Imperial Constantinople*, and numerous articles in *Byzantion, Journal of Indo-European Studies, History of Religions* and other periodicals. He is co-editor and now managing editor *pro tem* of *Incognita*, and is completing work on *The Book of the Hero*.

JOHN CARMI PARSONS is presently a Senior Fellow of the Centre for Reformation and Renaissance Studies at Victoria University in the University of Toronto, and is a former Junior Fellow of the Pontifical Institute of Mediaeval Studies in Toronto. He has published a monograph, *The Court and Household of Eleanor of Castile in 1290* (Pontifical Institute, Toronto, 1977) and several articles on medieval queenship. His biography of Queen Eleanor is now in preparation, as is an edition and study (with Rev. Ambrose Raftis) of fourteenth- and fifteenth-century borough court rolls. Dr. Parsons is now editing an anthology on medieval queenship for St. Martin's Press.

JOCELYN WOGAN-BROWNE lectures in the English Department of Liverpool University and publishes principally on women and literature in early Britain. Recent work includes (with Bella Millett) an edition and translation of *Medieval English Prose for Women: Selections from the Katherine Group and Ancrene Wisse* (Oxford, 1990) and articles on early English and Anglo-Norman hagiography. She is currently working on a book called *Authorized Virgins: The Literature of Female Celibacy in Medieval England* (forthcoming from Oxford University Press).

CHARLES T. WOOD, Daniel Webster Professor of History and Comparative Literature at Dartmouth College, has written widely on the importance of gender to the study of medieval history. His recent work includes "The Thrice Unburied Guinevere," "Shakespeare and the Drama of History," and *Joan of Arc and Richard III: Sex, Saints, and Government in the Middle Ages* (Oxford, 1988).

ROSEMARY MUIR WRIGHT has been a lecturer in the Department of Art History at the University of St. Andrews since 1987. In 1972 she took up an appointment at the University of Stirling to set up the new subject of Art History. She is engaged in research on medieval and Renaissance iconography; her work on

"The Iconography of the Coronation of the Virgin" appeared in *Cosmos* 2 (1986). Two articles are forthcoming: "Sound in Pictured Silence: The Significance of Writing in the Illustration of the Douce Apocalypse" (*Word and Image*) and "An Image Fit for a King: The Glazier Psalter Re-considered" (*Journal of Medieval History*).

ABBY ZANGER is Assistant Professor of French at Harvard University. She has published a number of essays on issues of representation in classical French theater. She is currently re-editing a selection of those essays for publication, and is also completing a study of the portrayal of the Queen in the marriage of Louis XIV.

ELIZABETH KRISTOFOVICH ZELENSKY is completing her dissertation in the Department of History at Georgetown University on monarchic imagery in late seventeenth-century Muscovy; she is also a lecturer in the Department of History at Goucher College. She has translated a number of works, including S. Mstislavskii's *Five Days Which Transformed Russia* (Indiana University Press).

MELINDA ZOOK has taught history at the University of Dayton, George Washington University and Georgetown University. She is completing a dissertation at Georgetown University on radical politics and ideology in Restoration England.